Caribbean Irish Connections

Caribbean Irish Connections
Interdisciplinary Perspectives

EDITED BY

Alison Donnell

Maria McGarrity

Evelyn O'Callaghan

THE UNIVERSITY OF THE WEST INDIES PRESS
Jamaica • Barbados • Trinidad and Tobago

The University of the West Indies Press
7A Gibraltar Hall Road, Mona
Kingston 7, Jamaica
www.uwipress.com

A catalogue record of this book is available
from the National Library of Jamaica.

ISBN: 978-976-640-504-5
978-976-640-516-8 (Kindle)
978-976-640-527-4 (ePub)

Cover illustration: Derek Walcott, *Seascape with Figures,* 2002. Courtesy of the artist
and the June Kelly Gallery, New York.
Cover and book design by Robert Harris
Set in Minion Pro 10.5/14.2 x 27
Printed in the United States of America

Contents

Foreword
Irish Routes

HILARY McD. BECKLES
Vice-Chancellor, University of the West Indies

ACCORDING TO THE RECEIVED NARRATIVE, THE IRISH were systemically stereotyped within the English imperial imagination and were handed notoriously damaging roles as participants in "New World" colonialism. In social and political commentaries, the Irish were constructed as one-dimensional colonial characters who showed the effects of consistently being battered and bruised by a triumphant imperial Englishness that viewed them as "baggage" along the route from Cork and Limerick through Bristol to Boston and Barbados. Excluded from the spoils of African enslavement and slave trading on account of their ethnicity, they were rarely represented with the admiration reserved for early colonial aristocrats of the sugar estates or of the cotton kingdoms along the Mississippi delta. Their "whiteness" questioned, qualified and sometimes denied, the Irish found English-ruled colonial societies arduous, disempowering places. Dichotomized as outsiders within the metropolitan centres of empire, they were socially represented in demeaning ways within English narratives. To some who shaped British colonial discourse, the Irish were undesirable, subversive or at best suspicious.

It is critical, then, and especially timely given the widening remit of Caribbean studies, that the limited and limiting literature in which these perspectives are enshrined now be confronted and in some instances reconstructed. For too long, the Irish have been entrapped and indentured within colonial accounts that speak to their victimhood within worlds forged by the political expressions of militant nationalist Englishness. The proposition that the English and Irish represented conflicting cultures and polarized political perspectives which traversed the Atlantic, there to find further fertile fields for ferocity, is here interrogated and reimagined with a nuance that was previously not widely available to scholars. There was undoubtedly importation into the Caribbean "sugar colonies" of bitter Anglo-Irish relations, and this indeed framed critical aspects of discourses of the Irish Caribbean route. But as a hegemonic history this static model is inadequate. Instead, the Caribbean is presented as a salient stage on which the drama of ethnic conflict and cohesion, nationalist tensions and contentions, and sideshows of religious and cultural abrasions and attachments are played out before a majority audience of enslaved Africans and dispossessed natives – the most excluded of subjects within the Atlantic world and radical outsiders to the colonial savagery of Englishness and whiteness.

The Irish navigated the tense routes of this colonial stage with extraordinary skill. No doubt English investors and colonial administrators would have them enslaved as culturally inferior Catholic infidels, were it not for the primacy they had come to place on whiteness as a hallmark of wealth and wisdom. In this regard some good fortune did follow the Irish poor and powerless to the killing fields of slavery. But even when as indentured servants they were described as "white niggers" and "white slaves", the power of the prefix presupposed a privilege that could not be denied. From this vantage point the Irish had grounds on which to refuse, as best they could, the diminished status assigned to them, and they fought back with dexterity and tenacity. Typically, early Irish indentured servants stepped away from the stigmatized spaces allotted them by their English overlords and rejected the concept that they should be obedient to their employers in the interest of building successful colonial projects.

This simmering ethnic revolt and labour rebellion emphasized the spectre of ideologies that terrorized the English, who dug daily to find damaging evidence that would prove Irish collaboration with insurgent Africans, whose loss of freedom they understood, and with dispossessed natives, whose circumstances mirrored their own. But living as they did on the oppressed labour margins of an emerging "Britishness", their meagre benefits lured them towards the possibility of profit from the culture-crossing. They cursed the English but remained reluctant to cross swords with them when it mattered most. They spied on them for the French and claimed that they received direction from the Pope, in whose name they blasphemed. But ultimately for many, the fear of blackness was there to bind them to their oppressors on the estates and in the towns.

Irish towns did emerge and flourish on the frontiers where English armies met with African maroons and persistent native militants. Promised free and cheap land in return for military service, some Irish militiamen retrieved runaways and infiltrated Indian territory to expose the weaknesses of the insurgents. Such were the ultimate ironies of loyalty to an England that had ravished their homeland and scattered them as near-slaves to sugar and cotton. Montserrat, the only majority Irish community in the seventeenth and early eighteenth centuries, could have been a metaphor that signalled ultimate capitulation against the background of a prior passion for political independence and cultural credibility. In the end it was a place that told the master narrative: it is better to live in peace and poverty on the periphery than with the daily pain of persistent persecution on English plantations. After living on this most Irish island of the Caribbean, the Irish and their progeny – sometimes no longer overtly or discernibly Irish, using conventional racial and ethnic markers – moved into the more complicated and dynamic race, class and status systems of the archipelago.

The complications and contradictions that followed the Irish from Belfast to Barbados are brilliantly captured in these essays, which address their adventures and misadventures, their achievements, their historical disappearances and traces, and, above all, the ongoing ambivalent status of Irish Caribbean connections. Crisscrossing the Americas and connecting the Caribbean, these Irish routes have now been charted and mapped as monuments to a "nation" that made its way to the centres of colonialism. The text of each chapter represents intriguing and innovative research, and the collection as a whole casts light for the first time on the mindsets of the menial and the consciousness of the courageous, revealing how the Irish in the Caribbean were much more than a "riotous and unruly lot". These essays, from a range of disciplinary perspectives, endeavour to close windows on tired old views and open panoramic new perspectives for future researchers.

Acknowledgements

THE EDITORS WISH TO THANK DEREK WALCOTT for his generous permission to use his painting *Seascape with Figures* for the book cover, and Hilary McD. Beckles, vice chancellor of the University of the West Indies, who challenged us to put together this collection. We are grateful to him and to the Cave Hill campus for a publication subvention and their gracious support as part of the campus's fiftieth anniversary celebrations. We must also thank Gale Stevens Haynes and the Office of Campus Operations at Long Island University for their support of the original conference out of which this collection grew. Additionally, we want to thank Caryn Rae Adams, whose energetic yet patient manner made the Barbados conference such a successful foundation for this work, and Miles Guilford, whose attention to detail and equal patience helped to ready the final collection for publication. We also extend our thanks to Bianca Dorsey and the June Kelly Gallery, Julie Zeftel and the Metropolitan Museum of Art, Kay Menick and Art Resource, as well as Glenn Dunne, Keith Murphy and Berni Metcalfe at the National Photographic Archive at the National Library of Ireland for making images of works available to include in this collection. The Craftsman photograph appears courtesy of the University of Wisconsin Digital Collections and the image from *Chim-Chim Stories* courtesy of the Schomburg Collection of the New York Public Library. Their generosity is noted and much appreciated.

Caribbean Irish Connections

Creolizing Histories, Historicizing Imaginings

ALISON DONNELL, MARIA McGARRITY
AND EVELYN O'CALLAGHAN

THIS COLLECTION IS IN PART A RESPONSE to a direct challenge from a Caribbean writer. In the middle of a story about a Jamaican woman named Miss Manda, whose speech-acts reveal her as both multiply situated and "out of place", the renowned Jamaican novelist Erna Brodber issues a surprising provocation to scholars of Caribbean studies: "I want to know what the Irish, the Scottish, the Welsh gave to the Creole mix as much as I want to know . . . what particular part of Africa is my heritage. . . . I will solve the African riddle but who will tell me about the others?"[1] In her expression of desire for a fuller Caribbean history and self-knowledge, Brodber identifies some of the key issues that have also motivated the critical interventions of this volume, the works that are analysed within it and the modes of scholarship that comprise it.

Within Caribbean studies there has been a necessary focus on seeking to recover and re-evaluate the historical origins and links to an African ancestral world violently denied and ruptured by enslavement and colonial plantation culture, and more recently on tracing South Asian and Chinese histories lost to their Caribbean descendants through the brutal conditions of indenture-ship and other forms of early migration. The defining lines of racial power between white and non-white in the Caribbean have made the study of white ethnic minorities a less compelling field within the general push to decolonize historiography. Very recently, works on Jewish populations in the Caribbean and other white minorities such as the Portuguese have begun to emerge.[2] Yet the broad divide in historiographical interest between those who were the victims of colonialism in the Caribbean and those who benefited from it does not easily accommodate a study of the Irish. The particular and stubborn riddle of the Irish is that they fell on both sides of this divide, identified by an ethnic label – *Irish* – that was itself radically unstable and constantly called upon to do the work of paradox.

Even the most basic account of the Irish in the Caribbean needs to accommodate a disparate cast of characters: from Lady Nugent, wife of the colonial governor of Jamaica in the early nineteenth century and a mistress of slaves, to the unnamed thousands of indentured servants who were transported to Barbados in the seventeenth century to labour alongside enslaved Africans on the plantations. Historical evidence, though often fragmented and uncertain, points to the fact that the Irish were part of the creole mix and shared the cruel consequences of colonial rule with other ethnic groups that we now identify as unproblematically Caribbean in identity, but it also shows that their whiteness afforded possibilities for mobility and empowerment not available to Africans and Indians. Given the emergent pigmentocracies at work in the Caribbean over many centuries, the privilege of white skin should not be minimized; it conferred status not only for the original migrants but also for their progeny, even the products of mixed couplings who might not have been easily recognizable as Irish in Ireland. It is this shifting dynamic of entanglement and separation among these peoples, ethnicities and identities that marks the troubled and troubling tensions facing both the subjects themselves, such as Brodber's Miss Manda, and scholars seeking to explore the connections.

Orlando Patterson's 1985 field-defining exploration of enslavement and race in the Caribbean, *Slavery and Social Death*, articulates the shifting power dynamics that altered over time, island, class and race to make and remake distinctions between groups and individuals, such as Irish and African, masters and enslaved. While the difference between indenture and an inherited condition of enslavement by birth cannot be overstated, structures of relations between people(s) remained in flux. For Patterson, as for many observers of the seventeenth- and eighteenth-century West Indies, the Irish represent a distinct social group that contributed to the complex formations of peoples in syncretic slave societies. He notes that in all slave societies of the Americas, there were numbers of slaves who were in fact lighter than many European masters: the probability that the mulatto slave offspring of an African mother and a very blond Cornish or Irish father was lighter than the average dark Welsh overseer was significantly above zero. Within a couple of generations the symbolic role of color as a distinctive badge of slavery had been greatly muted – though, of course, not eliminated.[3]

Crucially, Patterson acknowledges the defining import of race while simultaneously revealing its inherent instability as a cultural and ethnic marker.

Over time it would seem that either the Irish became so much part of a densely overlapping cultural and ethnic Caribbean population that their Irishness was no longer available for extraction in any overt way, or they were able to pass into the white ascendant class of the Caribbean world that required them to set themselves apart from their ethnic origins and Catholic religion, and thereby also set aside the significance of their Irishness. As a consequence, the possibilities for theorizing and imagining historical alignment between the Irish and non-white Caribbean subjects, as well as for recognizing the Irish as Caribbean subjects, need to be informed by awareness of the differentiated structures of racial power and their force and consequences at all levels of social relation.

The question of how then to trace, articulate and make meaning from such connections runs throughout this collection. Some of the interdisciplinary essays here grapple with the problems of ethnic visibility and its legacies today, as well as with significant individuals and events positioned along a fluid continuum of Irish Caribbean identities. Some examine the Caribbean as an important location for challenging the more commoditized histories of Irishness that function within the contexts of US or Australian migration, as narratives attempting to locate ideas of ethnic authenticity. Many other writers, like Brodber, turn to the imagination to place the Irish – an often unexpected Caribbean identity – within the fluid boundaries of the archipelago.

A striking kinship between Irish and Caribbean peoples is a constant, if modest, feature of many Caribbean literary works. Eric Walrond, an early twentieth-century Guyanese-Barbadian writer, reimagined James Joyce's "The Boarding House" from *Dubliners* in his "The Palm Porch" in the 1926 collection *Tropic Death,* turning Joyce's sublimated tale of selling flesh and the daughter of the house into an overt critique of prostitution in a colonial contact zone.[4] In the 1960s, Garth St Omer's influential novel *Shades of Grey* compared the Irish and Caribbean colonial experiences through the character of an Irish priest.[5] Recent prose and poetry by Curdella Forbes and Roger Robinson call upon an

Irish ancestor whose life is part of a Caribbean family's narration of itself.[6] In many other literary works too, the Irish and Ireland function as almost spectral presences haunting Caribbean literature, and the collective significance of this deserves recognition beyond the naming of lost family members. In his collection *Letters from Ulster and the Hugo Poems*, the Montserratian poet E.A. Markham highlights the connection across the Atlantic between the islands of the Caribbean archipelago and those Irish isles perched on the edge of Europe.[7]

For the St Lucian poet and playwright Derek Walcott – probably the most notable Caribbean writer to date – the link between the Irish and the Caribbean references the possibility of a deep collective bond of cultural subalternity beyond shared history and geography. Walcott sees the Caribbean and the Irish as analogous populations: both are diasporic peoples who share the historical experiences of dislocation, rupture and colonization, as well as an extraordinarily rich tradition of cultural expression:

> I've always felt some kind of intimacy with the Irish poets because one realized that they were also colonials with the same kind of problems that existed in the Caribbean. They were the niggers of Britain. Now, with all that, to have those outstanding achievements of genius whether by Joyce or Beckett or Yeats illustrated that one could come out of a depressed, depraved, oppressed situation and be defiant and creative at the same time.[8]

Despite the relatively privileged class of the writers Walcott cites, in this articulation of shared historical and cultural sensibility he positions the Irish within the vibrant ethnic and cultural pulse of the Caribbean, as he also does within his own creative work.

This linking of historical interest in the Irish with the imagination of Caribbean lives, which has been so productive in generating literary works within the anglophone Caribbean tradition, has a parallel creative impetus within Irish studies. The post-revisionist turn in Irish historiography has seen increasing attention being paid to the impact of English colonialism and the beginning of public interest in the Irish in the Caribbean. This is in some measure due to the publication of works such as journalist Sean O'Callaghan's *To Hell or Barbados: The Ethnic Cleansing of Ireland* and Kate McCafferty's novel *Testimony of an Irish Slave Girl*.[9] Music by Irish and Irish-American artists has also drawn inspiration from the suffering of Cromwellian exiles sent to Barbados; examples include Damien Dempsey's eponymous track on the album *To Hell or Barbados* and Flogging Molly's anti-Cromwell anthem "Tobacco Island".[10]

The focus within popular history on the Irish in Barbados in the mid-seventeenth century and on their capture and transplantation to the island, where they worked as "slaves" in the sugar fields, has a particular ideological purchase. However, the thicker history of the Irish in the Caribbean is a much more complicated and still unfolding story. What is known is that, despite the distinctive presence of Irish people on other islands, Barbados was the epicentre of both sugar cultivation and an indentured Irish diaspora during the seventeenth and eighteenth centuries. The historical timeline provided in this volume sketches the bare bones of Irish settlement in the region, beginning in the Amazon in 1612, then consolidated in Barbados and extending across the Leeward Islands. Cromwell's campaign in Ireland in 1649 was followed by nearly two decades of forced transportation of dispossessed Irish to the New World. The sugar revolution and the invasion of Jamaica in 1655 – part of Cromwell's "Western Design" – vastly expanded the market for Irish indentured labour across the broader Caribbean archipelago and eventually led to profitable Irish investments, especially in the Leeward Islands. By the end of the seventeenth century, the reputation of Irish servants as a troublesome lot with a suspect faith had resulted in a preference for African slaves; in the period that followed, the Irish presence appeared to be much more diffuse and was less remarked upon in sources. In 1715 officials in Barbados compiled a census of all the white inhabitants of its eleven parishes. The count totalled 16,888, but the list contains no information as to ethnic origins or socioeconomic status. However, given the limited number of property owners on the island, it is evident that the majority of the white inhabitants were small farmers and/or poor. Irish names appear throughout the census, in all the parishes.

While the overwhelming majority of Irish immigration to the Caribbean region occurred more than three centuries ago, the notion of Irish heritage is still remarked on, particularly in Montserrat, Barbados and parts of Jamaica. The persistence of Irish surnames speaks to an Irish presence, and the growth of the genealogy industry has inspired some Caribbean residents to claim partial Irish heritage. Irish place names also crop up throughout the Caribbean. In Barbados these are typically associated with smaller Irish settlements which likely date back to the seventeenth century. For example, Glendalough Road can be found in a small village in the rural northern parish of St Lucy, outside the boundaries of any plantation, and is no doubt a tribute to the early monastic site in County Wicklow, Ireland. In Montserrat the village of Kinsale (inaccessible after the volcanic eruption), was established in the seventeenth century and named after a major port of emigration in County Cork, Ireland (its name is hardly surprising, since the island's population was largely Irish throughout that period). In Jamaica, Sligoville, the first free village on the island, was named after Howe Peter Browne, second Marquess of Sligo, who was governor of Jamaica in 1834, the time of emancipation.

A more comfortable axis of political alignment can be identified in the shared histories of colonialism that bolster connections between Ireland and the Caribbean region, particularly the anglophone Caribbean islands. Just as Marcus Garvey and the Universal Negro Improvement Association (UNIA) drew upon the example of the Irish Republican Brotherhood for its model of political liberation in the early decades of the twentieth century, so too other abolitionists, nationalists and Pan-Africanists found commonalities between the plight of the Irish and enslaved Africans under English rule. The parallel importance of the Caribbean in the Irish political imaginary is also significant to note; the Irish historians D.B. Quinn and Nicholas Canny have long argued that strong ties exist between British ideologies and practices of colonialism in Ireland and the New World.[11] In the contemporary period, researcher Matthew C. Reilly notes a conversation with the Barbadian George Medford, who has led hikes for the Barbados National Trust for well over a decade. Aware that his surname, like many other Barbadian names, is English in origin, he nonetheless insists that an Irish heritage is to be found in Barbados and sympathizes with Irish struggles for liberation from English rule. In fact his son bears the middle name O'Neal, in tribute to the Barbadian national hero Charles Duncan O'Neal and to signal a link with Ireland. While remaining well aware of the reality of racial and cultural differences that often retain their historically determined purchase within today's postcolonial Caribbean, such dialogues shed light on the nuances of Atlantic interactions and refocus attention on the complex relationships fostered among those caught in the "web of empire".[12]

Perhaps the most obvious site for the investigation of Caribbean–Irish cultural exchanges is the island of Montserrat, which is unique in Caribbean history as Ireland's only "colony". Donald Harman Akenson's *If the Irish Ran the World: Montserrat, 1630–1730*, explores the early decades of settlement and focuses on the Irish presence on the island, both documenting the indentured labourers, small farmers and merchants and acknowledging the plantation owners and officials.[13] As emerges from this complex pattern of powerlessness and privilege, Montserrat's history is a prime resource for dissecting the unstable meaning of *Irish*, as the island was home to native Irish Catholics; "New Irish" (or Anglo-

Irish), from families that had migrated from England to Ireland in the sixteenth and seventeenth centuries; and "Old English", who were descended from English immigrants to Ireland during the Anglo-Norman invasion of the twelfth century. Montserrat's Irish past now figures strongly in its tourist marketing. Branding itself the "Emerald Isle of the Caribbean", and with its national flag depicting Erin, the female symbol of Ireland, holding a harp alongside the Union Jack, Montserrat is the only country outside Ireland to celebrate St Patrick's Day as a national holiday. But even this declarative performance of ethnic solidarity is not as resolved as may initially appear. As Krysta Ryzewski and Laura McAtackney note in their essay in this collection, 17 March also commemorates an aborted slave rebellion in Montserrat in 1768; its significance to the island's history and its ongoing status as a national holiday are likely to be inadequately explained by the Irish connection alone.

More recently, scholarly attention has sought to contextualize and illuminate the complexities and tensions in the Irish experience in the Caribbean and ongoing Caribbean Irish connections. The contradictory historical status of the Irish – as exploited bond labourers but also as owners of large-scale plantations, their service in island militias and imperial armies, and their occupying of positions of political power – clearly underpins the diversity of this experience, as well as the difficulties and risks of investing in ethnic categorization. Not only does dominance of any one narrative of the Irish in the Caribbean inevitably deny complicated local histories and contingencies, but identity-based politics are also increasingly inadequate for meaningful analysis of such ethnic performances and cultural constructions. Accordingly, intellectual interest in this field is informed by resistance to facile or essentialist projects of cultural extraction.

Given the unevenness surrounding the historical experiences of the Irish in the Caribbean, this collection aims to open a dialogue on Caribbean Irish connections as an inclusive rubric, exploring how it might pertain to history, politics, language, geography, expressive cultural forms, and everyday practices (such as the shamrock passport stamp of Montserrat). While there is much work still to be done, particularly in the fields of musicology, linguistics and art history, the essays assembled in this collection bring together and reflect the multiple interests and approaches of scholars working within this highly focused yet potentially broad field to help shape the emerging critical discourse.

The first section, "Histories of Encounter and Exchange", presents a historical grounding beginning in the seventeenth century and moving forward chronologically. These essays flesh out the historical scaffolding of our timeline, focusing on different groups of Irish immigrants, servants and settlers in different parts of the Caribbean. Their historical accounts are necessarily complicated as the place of the Irish emerges and is continually modified over time. What becomes evident is that, even from their earliest arrival, there is no stable or generalized frame within which to fix the Irish presence in the Caribbean archipelago. In the first essay, "A Changing Presence", Nini Rodgers shifts the delicate balance of historical accounts to examine the Irish as a would-be colonizing force with varied interests and opportunistic agendas. She asserts that the Irish immigrants who struggled and suffered in the seventeenth-century Caribbean had moved into positions of greater prominence and significant material comfort by the eighteenth century. Jerome S. Handler and Matthew C. Reilly's account of Father Antoine Biet's narrative offers an in-depth examination of the difficult circumstances of immigrant life on Barbados in 1654 and how Irish religious identity functioned as a social marker of both inclusion and exclusion. Matthew C. Reilly's discussion of Irish settlement in early Barbados, described as an "archaeological story", provides an intricate record of the early material culture of Barbados and Irish settlements there to show that while the foundations of Irish life in the Caribbean may be elusive, they can also be revealing. In the essay that follows, Kevin Whelan's "Liberty, Freedom and the Green Atlantic" establishes the Irish presence in the Caribbean during the critical Age of Revolution and examines how the United Irishmen, an eighteenth-century Irish republican revolutionary organization, functioned in the transatlantic nexus amid the shifting allegiances and perspectives of the New World. He forcefully argues that the rhetoric of slavery is fundamental to understanding the Irish position in the Caribbean. Karina Williamson's contribution moves the discussion to nineteenth-century Jamaica, where she analyses the role of specific Irishmen who, contrary to expectation, were not outsiders in the plantation system but sophisticated participants in its fraught social and political economies. Collectively, this section demonstrates how positioning of the Irish is realigned according to time, island, class and religion so as to resist easy categorization.

The second broad movement, "Cultural Performance and Exchange", negotiates history, literature, ethnic performance and visual culture in order to explore the kinds of cultural labour and identities that were set in motion within the vibrant transatlantic nexus between Ireland and the Caribbean. This section is interested in identifying and exploring how these two cultures, identities and histories call upon each other in particular ways and for particular ends.

Alison Donnell's essay opens this section with a challenge to conventional understandings of cultural encounter and performance. The piece argues that thinking through Caribbean Irish connections also requires us to think through how Irishness and Caribbeanness are so differently constituted and valued as identity-giving ethnicities. Drawing on the methodologies of queer commentary, Donnell offers a way of understanding the riddle of the Irish in the Caribbean by releasing the pressures of a dominant politics of originary identity within Irish studies to conceive of Irish ethnicity in the Caribbean not as a deterministic signature but as an expression of co-belonging in the "creole mix", with its multiple possibilities for affiliation and historical direction. Krysta Ryzewski and Laura McAtackney discuss historical and contemporary Irish identity on Montserrat, the "Emerald Isle of the Caribbean", focusing on the now most visibly Irish island in the Caribbean. The essay charts early Irish settlements and social claims before moving into a discussion of the twentieth-century Montserratian performance of Irish identity, particularly noting the transformation of St Patrick's Day celebrations from commemoration of an eighteenth-century slave revolt to a postmodern performance of cultural syncretism. Maria McGarrity uncovers Derek Walcott's use of early twentieth-century Dublin museum culture to frame his portraits of the Irish in *Omeros* as subtle homage to James Joyce's depiction of a museum director named Plunkett, connecting St Lucia and Ireland through the lens of Walcott's inclusive vision. Elizabeth O'Connor's study examines the curious primitivist performances of Jamaican folklore by Pamela Colman Smith, a renowned illustrator who was a member of W.B. Yeats's circle. Both Colman Smith's illustrations and her personal embodied practice intensify the otherwise often nuanced engagement of modern writers and artists with Caribbean Irish primitive rhetorics at home and abroad. Finally, Harvey O'Brien analyses the television documentary *The Redlegs*, which provides an overview of the seventeenth-century human traffic between Ireland and Barbados and the supposedly Irish-descended contemporary community known as Redlegs. O'Brien points out the ambiguous construction of "otherness" and national identities in the film's somewhat distanced gaze.

The final section of the collection, "Comparative Readings and Critical Encounters", builds on the possibilities for cultural comparison and cross-fertilization within the context of comparative readings of Caribbean and Irish writers across literary genres. In answer to Brodber's question "What did the Irish contribute to the Caribbean creole literary mix?", the essays in this section amply demonstrate how Caribbean writers have connected with and been profoundly influenced by aspects of the writings of Joyce, Yeats, Heaney, Synge and Beckett, among others. Even where explicit intertextuality is not apparent, writers across the two postcolonial spaces share mutual concerns: the haunt-ing of history; a deep attachment to land denied them for centuries; the pres-ence of the sea; the importance of orality and storytelling; experiments with non-English linguistic registers; and the need to constantly break and reinvent language and form.

Such commonalities lend unexpected richness to comparative readings. This final movement engages a full range of creative practices, appropriations and correspondences between Irish and Caribbean writers. It seems that fiction writers, playwrights and poets seek to represent in and through the imagina-tion what often eludes contemporary scholars and escapes the historical record.

Lee M. Jenkins's essay analyses the repeating signifier of W.B. Yeats's famed sonnet "The Lake Isle of Innisfree" as radically reimagined by three Jamaican poets. Jenkins suggests that this distinctively Irish poem operates as a reiterated yet fluid marker of the island imaginary of the Caribbean. Leif Schenstead-Harris examines the creative referencing of Synge's *Riders to the Sea* in Walcott's *The Sea at Dauphin*, with a particular focus on how the sea functions as a repository of memory and a marker of transformation between critical and cultural realms in both works. K. Brisley Brennan uses the shibboleth as an analytic construct by which to compare relations between Haiti and the Dominican Republic with those between Ireland and Northern Ireland. Her study scrutinizes the intimate and troubling relationships of language, community and terror through the shared demarcation of identity in linguistic performance as a marker of exclusion in both Ireland and the Caribbean. Elaine Savory reads Medbh McGuckian and Dionne Brand in tandem, discussing these two challenging poets of contem-porary letters by framing their practices within transnational environmental engagement to reveal their distinct but politically analogous elegiac projects that mourn ecological and human catastrophes. Richard McGuire's discussion of confluent Irish and Caribbean settler-colonist worlds charts correspondences between the Irish Big House novel (Elizabeth Bowen's *The Last September,* 1929) and Caribbean plantation fiction (Jean Rhys's *Voyage in the Dark*, 1934), genres characterized by fiery ends and traumatic renderings of failing empire. Jean Antoine-Dunne notes the import of language and space in signifying parallel modes of imaginative worlding across Ireland and the Caribbean. She traces how the paring down of language and ritual to a minimal degree – a Beckettian technique observable in the Irish writer's renowned plays – manifests in the works of Walcott and Brathwaite, two Caribbean poets with distinctly different styles but an equal gift for crafting cultural self-knowledge. Finally, Emily Taylor reaches back to the famed nineteenth-century novel *Wuthering Heights*, and to Terry Eagleton's modern depiction of Heathcliff as an Irish famine migrant, to reveal Maryse Condé's conception of her Caribbean figure with a surprising and unique Irish provenance. As this section shows, the "defiant and creative" wealth that Walcott attributes to the Irish has flourished in the Caribbean too; the number of links between the two literatures ingeniously teased out in this section is clear testament.

This provocative and valuable collection of new essays demonstrates both the range and the richness of Caribbean Irish historical relations and cultural entanglements, and the possibility for a distinctive critical discourse that will enable productive engagement with these often complicated relations. We see the collection as helping to transform the current parameters of both Caribbean and Irish studies and to lay the groundwork for a new field of research and publication. Attention to the Caribbean context makes an important intellectual contribution to Irish studies, by challenging the dominance of a US diasporic history and a disciplinary preference that privileges displacement and immigration to the United States rather than to the wider Americas. Likewise, within Caribbean studies, the Irish presence troubles the orthodox historical models for understanding race and the plantation and the raced nature of class structures, as well as questions about ethnic and religious minorities and how to think about diaspora in new and engaging ways. While much work within ethnic studies traditionally relies on an investment in cultural authenticity and continuity, the gradual softening of the edges between *Caribbean* and *Irish* that inevitably results from this kind of multiply focused exploration of connections tends to result in a useful complication of identitarian politics, such that it might be possible, for example, to cite a text or to claim a cultural identity that is neither Caribbean nor Irish but both. Clearly this is not unproblematic, for while the practice of genealogical history-making has always been quite fluid in the Caribbean, and ideas of creolized ethnicities are increasingly relevant in globalized post–Celtic Tiger Ireland, the attachment to ideas of origins, norms and stable ethnicities remains strong.[14]

A telling and perhaps even unwitting example of this attachment is a pair of television documentaries – *Barbado'ed: Scotland's Sugar Slaves* and *The Redlegs: Ireland's Sugar Slaves* – both produced in 2009 by Moondance Productions for BBC Scotland and Ireland's TG4, respectively.[15] Both of these short films engage with the same "poor white" community on Barbados's eastern coast, tracing their origins via a chronicle of the experiences of Irish and Scottish indentured servants. The presenter in both cases is Chris Dolan, some of the same experts and informants are interviewed, and shared footage is used to suggest that a clear line exists between these Barbadians and their European forebears. But in each case leading questions are designed to lend credence to the fact of either Irish *or* Scottish ancestry, depending on which national audience is being targeted by the documentary. In this transferrable gesture, twenty-first-century Barbadian subjects are repackaged for Scottish and Irish audiences as their lost relatives. Paradoxically, the films exploit the Caribbean's creolized mix, in which individual parts are no longer distinguishable from the whole, in order to spin fictions that serve two ethnic identities, both of which have concerns about their own stability and singularity. A more interesting area of enquiry presented by these Barbadian subjects is surely how their ethnicity – both multiply marked and unmarked – is surplus to the grammars we possess for understanding white identities in the Atlantic world.

Since Hilary Beckles's ground-breaking *White Servitude and Black Slavery in Barbados, 1627–1715,* was published in 1989, there have been a handful of book-length studies on the connections between Ireland and the Caribbean. These include *The Black and Green Atlantic: Cross-Currents of the African and Irish Diasporas,* edited by Peter O'Neill and David Lloyd; *Ireland: Slavery and Anti-slavery,* by Nini Rodgers; *Transatlantic Solidarities,* by Michael Malouf; and *Washed by the Gulf Stream: The Historic and Geographic Relation of Irish and Caribbean Literature,* by Maria McGarrity.[16] Most recently, Michael Monahan's *The Creolizing Subject: Race, Reason, and the Politics of Purity* deals with the Irish as both colonized and colonizer in Caribbean contexts, and Jenny Shaw's *Everyday Life in the Early English Caribbean: Irish, Africans and the Construction of Difference* provides another take on the story of the Irish in the early modern Caribbean.[17] Yet there still remains too little conversation between scholars based in Caribbean studies and those in Irish studies.

This collection highlights the work that remains to be done across and between the different fields, disciplines and islands. While the essays in this volume offer multiple perspectives in response to Brodber's challenge to solve the riddle of what the Irish "gave to the Creole mix", they only begin to explore what the Caribbean might mean in Ireland, and this remains a significant part of the dynamic relationship that merits further enquiry. The volume concludes with a list of archival and other research resources in Ireland, North America and the Caribbean, as well as selected primary and secondary readings. The aim is to map the territory of this new interdisciplinary domain for those who will follow and to encourage and facilitate future research in this fascinating field of cross-cultural and intercultural studies.

Notes

1. Erna Brodber, "Where Are All the Others?", in *Caribbean Creolization: Reflections on the Cultural Dynamics of Language, Literature and Identity*, ed. Kathleen Balutansky and Marie-Agnes Sourieau, 68–75 (Gainesville and Kingston: University Press of Florida and University of the West Indies Press, 1998), 75.

2. See Jane S. Gerber, ed., *The Jews in the Caribbean* (New York: Littman Library of Jewish Studies, 2014); Mordechai Arbell, *The Portuguese Jews of Jamaica* (Mona, Jamaica: University of the West Indies Press, 2002); and Sarah Casteel, "Port and Plantation Jews in Contemporary Slavery Fiction of the Americas", *Callaloo: A Journal of African Diaspora Arts and Letters* 37, no. 1 (forthcoming).

3. Orlando Patterson, *Slavery and Social Death* (Cambridge, MA: Harvard University Press, 1985), 61.

4. See Louis J. Parascandola and Maria McGarrity, "'I'm a Naughty Girl': Prostitution and Outsider Women in James Joyce's 'The Boarding House' and Eric Walrond's 'The Palm Porch'", *CLA Journal* 50 (2006): 141–61.

5. Garth St Omer, *Shades of Grey* (London: Faber, 1968).

6. Curdella Forbes, *Ghosts* (Leeds: Peepal Tree, 2012); Roger Robinson, *The Butterfly Hotel* (Leeds: Peepal Tree, 2013).

7. E.A. Markham, *Letters from Ulster and the Hugo Poems* (Todmorden, UK: Littlewood Arc, 1993).

8. Edward Hirsch, "An Interview with Derek Walcott conducted by Edward Hirsch", *Contemporary Literature* 20, no. 3 (Summer 1979): 288.

9. Sean O'Callaghan, *To Hell or Barbados: The Ethnic Cleansing of Ireland* (Dublin: Brandon, 2001); Kate McCafferty, *Testimony of an Irish Slave Girl* (New York: Viking Penguin, 2002).

10. Damien Dempsey, *To Hell or Barbados* (United for Opportunity Records, 2006); Flogging Molly, "Tobacco Island", on *Within a Mile of Home* (Side One Dummy Records, 2004).

11. David B. Quinn, *Ireland and America: Their Early Associations, 1500–1640* (Liverpool: Liverpool University Press, 1991); Nicholas Canny and Anthony Pagden, eds., *Colonial Identity in the Atlantic World, 1500–1800* (Princeton, NJ: Princeton University Press, 1987).

12.   Alison Games, *Web of Empire: English Cosmopolitanism in an Age of Expansion, 1560–1660* (New York: Oxford University Press, 2008).

13.   Donald Harman Akenson, *If the Irish Ran the World: Montserrat, 1630–1730* (Montreal: McGill-Queen's University Press, 1997).

14.   David Conrad, "Some Irish Need Not Apply", *New York Times*, 15 October 2013 http://p.nytimes.ation=InCMR7g4BCKC2wiZPkcVUjFLGL9WAoD4&user_id=4d51e d7a475028e24f659b8b44a7c899&email_type=eta&task_id=1381934852552545&regi _id=0.

15.   *Barbado'ed: Scotland's Sugar Slaves*, directed by Paul Arnott (Dublin: Moondance Productions, 2009), broadcast by BBC 2 (Scotland), 26 April 2009; *The Redlegs: Ireland's Sugar Slaves / Na Redlegs: Sclábhaithe Siúcra na hÉireann*, directed by Shane Brennan and Paul Arnott (Dublin: Moondance Productions, 2009), broadcast by TG4 (Ireland), 28 December 2009.

16.   Hilary Beckles, *White Servitude and Black Slavery in Barbados, 1627–1715* (Knoxville: University of Tennessee Press, 1989); Peter O'Neill and David Lloyd, eds., *The Black and Green Atlantic: Cross-Currents of the African and Irish Diasporas* (New York: Palgrave Macmillan, 2009); Nini Rodgers, *Ireland: Slavery and Anti-Slavery* (New York: Palgrave Macmillan, 2007); Michael G. Malouf, *Transatlantic Solidarities: Irish Nationalism and Caribbean Poetics* (Charlottesville: University of Virginia Press, 2009); Maria McGarrity, *Washed by the Gulf Stream: The Historic and Geographic Relation of Irish and Caribbean Literature* (Newark: University of Delaware Press, 2008).

17.   Michael Monahan, *The Creolizing Subject: Race, Reason, and the Politics of Purity* (New York: Fordham University Press, 2011); Jenny Shaw, *Everyday Life in the Early English Caribbean: Irish, Africans and the Construction of Difference* (Athens: University of Georgia Press, 2013).

Part 1

Histories of Encounter and Exchange

Chapter 1

A Changing Presence

*The Irish in the Caribbean in the
Seventeenth and Eighteenth Centuries*

NINI RODGERS

THE IRISH HAVE BEEN A PRESENCE IN the Caribbean since the seventeenth century. The terms *Irish*, *Irish nation* and *Irish Catholics*, scattered and synonymous, appear in both the English and Spanish archives, the main historical sources for this period.[1] Irish Protestants are of course mentioned, but as individuals rather than a general category or community. The main focus in this essay is the fortunes of the Irish Catholics over two centuries. In the seventeenth century they were demographically and politically important but their experiences were disillusioning. This became the age of the Irish servant, in which the indentured, the free and the transported merge in popular memory as "white slaves". Suspected by the authorities of making common cause with the growing workforce of enslaved Africans, the Irish struggled to benefit from their whiteness in a colonial society based on colour.

In the eighteenth century, shrunken in number, they moved into a more prosperous era, achieving in some cases a startling degree of wealth and power. As settlers on the British islands, they participated in the commercial expansion of the slave and sugar economy. To a more limited extent they followed a similar trajectory in French Martinique and Saint-Domingue, while increasingly the Spanish Caribbean offered advancement to the career soldier. This chapter seeks to explain the strategies Irish Catholics employed to found their own colony in the New World, the failure of this project, and their eventual assimilation into a Caribbean dominated by the great European powers: Britain, France and Spain.

The Seventeenth Century: Pioneer Days and Political Presence

In the sixteenth century it was the needy nobles of Portugal and Spain who built Europe's first overseas empires. By the seventeenth century Tudor and Stuart plantations in Ireland had produced an impoverished Catholic gentry eager to recompense themselves in the Americas. An early pioneering venture to the Amazon (1612–29), bartering for tobacco with the Tupi Indians, proved lucrative though short-lived. It did, however, convince leading Catholics in Munster and Connacht of the desirability of an Irish colony in the New World.

The creation of an overseas colony required the support of a powerful sovereign. Here the Irish had to make a choice between their official rulers, the Protestant Stuarts, and their Catholic patron, the Habsburg king of Spain.[2] It was a difficult position, forcing them to stress different aspects of their identity – acceptance of the state or dedication to religion – in order to survive and pursue profit. The Irish were welcomed in Spain as soldiers and exiles for the Catholic faith, but the Spanish crown, valuing and fearing for its riches in Mexico and Peru, was very strict about who entered its empire; it was closed to Jews, religious dissidents and foreigners. Its special relationship with the Catholics of Ireland did not persuade Spain to lift this ban. In matters of commerce it was felt that wherever the Irish went, they brought in the English.[3]

Access to England's empire was quite another matter, based as it was on a policy of "shovelling out dissidents", whether these were English Puritans, vagrants or Irish Catholics. By the late 1620s the Stuarts were attempting to establish tobacco colonies in the Caribbean, on islands claimed but unoccupied by the Spanish. The preferred destination for the Irish was the island of St Christopher, whose founder and governor, the Englishman Sir Thomas Warner, was himself a disillusioned adventurer from the Amazon. From St Christopher the Irish found their way to nearby islands being settled by the Stuarts: Nevis, Antigua and particularly small, volcanic Montserrat. In 1634 Montserrat was described by an English priest as "a noble plantation of Irish Catholics" and in 1668 by an English governor as "almost an Irish colony".[4]

The 1630s marked a build up of Irish people in the Caribbean. Catholic sources reveal that Captain Peter Sweetman brought "many farmers and soldiers to settle and break up the land" on St Christopher.[5] From Galway, the bishop of Tuam, Malachy O'Queely, recorded the departure of six hundred emigrants, including two priests.[6] The Stuart colonies needed labour, for unlike the Tupi Indians of the Amazon, the Carib of the Leeward Islands were not an amenable native workforce. Munster ports became exit points for the servant trade to the Caribbean; Dutch and English captains offered to convey emigrants across the Atlantic in exchange for signing an indenture which committed them to unremunerated labour for anything from three to seven years. Young men were preferred, but it is estimated that women made up about a third of the number. Servants were recruited with the promise of a freedom bounty, a sum with which to buy cheap land when their bond expired; women were to receive a sum which would make them more marriageable. St Christopher was the most popular destination for the early Irish servants, but Barbados, another developing tobacco island further south, was also attractive. Chain migration developed as people left because they had heard of others (Irish-speaking Catholic neighbours and relatives) who had done so, all hoping to escape poverty and political disturbance at home.

In the 1620s the French, like the English, sought to establish tobacco colonies on islands officially claimed by Spain. In the case of St Christopher, the two groups arrived simultaneously; Sir Thomas Warner occupied the centre of the island and the French the eastern and western ends. From an Irish point of view the proximity of the French added to the advantages of St Christopher, as in those frontier days the borders were decidedly porous. The practice of Catholicism was forbidden within the English colony, but the French area was served by the Capuchin order.

An Irish Jesuit, Father Stritch from Limerick, arrived in 1650 and built a chapel in French territory. He circulated throughout the Leewards, crossing to Montserrat to celebrate Mass in the forest, disguised as a woodcutter.[7] Religion as a political reality was a force to be reckoned with in the seventeenth-century Caribbean, but as an ecclesiastical institution it was weak in the Stuart colonies. The islands were regarded as an extension of the see of the bishop of London; in 1671 there were forty parishes in the Leewards but only two Anglican clerics.[8] As with all colonies, land and trade were the original spurs, so in frontier conditions a degree of religious diversity might exist in practice if not in principle.

It has been estimated that by 1639 three thousand Irish Catholics were living in the Leewards.[9] News of the 1641 rebellion in Ireland (a rising of natives against the new Protestant settlers) reverberated across the West Indies. Quarrels broke out between the English and the Irish on St Christopher, and the Stuart governor sought to ease tensions by removing more of the Irish to Montserrat. Some Irish settlers sought to escape rising anti-Catholic feeling by seeking asylum in Spanish territory. The largest group was led by Richard Hackett, sailing from Barbados, where he had lived as a substantial planter and a Protestant. At Montserrat he expanded his little expedition by chartering a Dutch vessel, in all landing more than three hundred men and a considerable number of women and children on Hispaniola.[10] The authorities, suspicious that Hackett actually intended to take over their island, dispatched him to Spain, where his hopes of heading an Irish settlement in the Caribbean were dismissed. He was given low-status employment in the Spanish military, a career trajectory which the rest of his group was supposed to follow.[11] To what extent they did is hard to tell. Even the leaders' names surface only briefly and occasionally in the official record, and except when they proved troublesome, the rank and file rarely received mention: their history is often unrecoverable. Richard Hackett's male followers appear to have been thrust into the role of soldier or labourer as the colonial situation demanded.

The Spanish rules were strict but enforcement was not always easy; Hispaniola was large and patchily inhabited, with much of it beyond the control of government. In the following years talk circulated about the Irish there, often in connection with the successful John Murphy Fitzgerald Burke, or Don Juan Morfo Geraldino y Burco, a soldier of fortune who described himself as a noble from Galway. After deserting the French and English buccaneers of Tortuga and using his Irishness as a passport to Spanish employ, he guided his new patrons in a successful raid on that island stronghold. Though he was forced for a time to serve the Spanish in continental Europe, most of his life was spent on Hispaniola, where he prospered. In 1655, when Cromwell launched his Western Design, focused on conquest of Columbus's first settler colony, it was Don Juan Morfo who led the local Spanish force to victory – another visible example of the Irish political presence.[12]

As France replaced Spain as the greatest Catholic power, relations between the French and English deteriorated. War on the islands increased the political importance of the Irish. In 1666 they sided with the French, helping to deliver Montserrat and the central section of St Christopher into their control, though later negotiations in Europe (resulting in the Treaty of Breda) returned the territory to the English. Lord Willoughby arrived, dismissed the Irish Protestant

Governor Briskett for colluding with the French, and appointed William Stapleton, an Irish Catholic, in his place, because he would "understand how to govern his countrymen". In the next decade Stapleton rose to be governor of the English Leewards: Antigua, Nevis, Montserrat and the relevant section of St Christopher. Describing himself as a soldier of fortune, he based his career on his military effectiveness and unswerving loyalty to the crown.[13] In matters of religion he pursued a middle route. He built two parish churches, acquired the island's first resident Anglican clergyman, and married a Protestant heiress from the ruling English elite on the island of Nevis. He held office without taking the required oaths of supremacy and allegiance that recognized the king as head of the church, defending himself by pointing to his record of unimpeachable support for Charles II. Stapleton encouraged the others to follow his example, and Catholics on Montserrat were elected as assemblymen and took on other official positions, including that of census taker.[14]

Census material was demanded by the Board of Trade in London to enable them to make informed policy decisions. Security and economic growth were their two main concerns, and both were inextricably involved with the production of sugar – by now recognized as the most valuable commodity a tropical colony could produce. Unlike tobacco, which could be grown by smallholders, sugar was both labour- and capital-intensive, requiring investment in crushing mills, boiling houses and substantial land acreage, as well as an extensive workforce. By mid-century the sugar planters were showing a preference for African slaves as more cost-effective than indentured servants.

The exact information recorded in West Indian censuses varied according to place and time, but everywhere the population was ascribed racial categories of black or white. Only in the Leewards were nationalities also recorded. Stapleton's 1678 census for Montserrat proved that the island was indeed "almost an Irish colony"; 69 per cent of whites belonged to that group, the rest being English, plus a few Dutch and Scots. But in status the English always dominated: the richest planter, Wyke, was English, and the town of Portsmouth was bigger than Kinsale.[15] In many ways Montserrat was a microcosm of Ireland with its English overlords and Protestant Irish ("New English") families such as the Parsons and Fryes. Successful Catholics, mostly from the dispossessed gentry of Munster and Connacht, formed a planter/trader elite above the smallholders and servants. Below the latter, because it was the Caribbean, lay another stratum: the African slaves.

On Barbados – "the English island" – the number of Irish exceeded that on

Montserrat. In 1668 Lord Willoughby was worried because the four-thousand-strong militia contained two thousand Irish Catholics. Given the location of the island, he was concerned less about the French threat and more with keeping the slaves in subjection.[16] Well supplied with indentured servants, Barbados had developed more quickly as a tobacco colony than divided St Christopher, and the shift to sugar and slaves was also swifter. In 1655 the black population was estimated at twenty thousand and the whites at twenty-three thousand (more than thirteen thousand of them servants, bonded and free).[17] How many of these servants were Irish it is impossible to say, but Cromwellian transportation had raised their numbers, as well as resultant antipathy, to the point where Irish servants were accused of hiding in the woods and making common cause with runaway slaves. Anti-Irish regulations were issued, banning their right to purchase arms and demanding that all Irish servants absent from their master's plantation carry written permission. In the turmoil of Cromwellian Barbados, where the planters claimed that twelve thousand military deportees (English, Scots and Irish) had arrived by 1655, these regulations proved impossible to police; in the 1660s they were withdrawn.[18]

Throughout the seventeenth century, political crises in Europe reverberated in the Caribbean and continued to fuel suspicions about Irish Catholics. The accession of the Catholic James II and then the triumph of the Protestant William III provoked rumours that on Barbados Irishmen had agreed to supply weapons to slaves plotting an uprising.[19] On St Christopher the Irish had declared for King James and joined with the French to drive the English settlers off to Nevis. By July 1690 King William's authority had been reasserted, but Governor Christopher Codrington feared that another such crisis might occur, and he wondered if in such an event he should arm the slaves.[20] As on Barbados, fear of the Irish caused the colour line to waver.

In the seventeenth century the Irish in the Caribbean were demographically and politically important but had failed to acquire their own colony, whether through rebellion, petitioning or manoeuvring between one side and another. Intermingling, however, had proved more rewarding, and intermingling led to assimilation. The descendants of successful soldiers such as Stapleton and Don Juan Morpho were absorbed into English or Spanish society. From the Leewards and Barbados, Irish smallholders and servants, unable to afford rising land prices, moved on to newly developing areas such as Jamaica, where, again in frontier conditions, they found some degree of economic improvement and political agency. They acquired smallholdings and supported the Catholic James

II (1685–88), who cultivated them as voters and assemblymen. But this rise in their fortunes was soon reversed with the triumph of the Protestant William III.[21]

In the colonial world of the Americas, those who left Europe with advantages were most likely to succeed. Throughout the English Caribbean, very few wealthy sugar planters emerged from the servant class. How often members of this class managed to obtain land remains obscure, particularly in the case of the Irish.[22] Irish servants who remained on Barbados mixed with English people of similar social status, lost their distinctive language, accent and Catholicism, and became "poor whites". As long as slavery lasted they enjoyed certain privileges as "military tenants", supplied with small plots of land to enable them to man the militia. But neither they nor visiting nineteenth-century commentators, who noted their poverty, were conscious of this group's Irish roots.

The Eighteenth Century: Penal Era and Golden Age[23]

By the eighteenth century, Jamaica, developing as a slave and sugar economy, had replaced Barbados as Britain's most valuable Caribbean colony. In 1731 Governor Robert Hunter complained that Irish Catholics constituted the greater part of the lower ranks on the island and were still arriving "in sholes", a situation which he considered dangerous. At a higher level, he was suspicious that closet Catholics were infiltrating Jamaica's government. The British West Indies had always suffered from a shortage of legal personnel, and in Jamaica this want was increasingly met by gentry families from Munster and Connacht. When Governor Hunter launched an attack on suspect Irishmen holding office, Catholic sympathizers were sufficiently strong to use the Assembly to repel his assertions.[24]

Time proved that Hunter was quite wrong to fear that the presence of Irish Catholics threatened the development and loyalty of this valuable colony, for success in Jamaica turned Catholics into Protestants. For example, the founders of this judicial tradition were the Kellys of Lisaduff, County Galway. In the 1720s Edmond Kelly became attorney general of Jamaica, and in the 1740s Denis was appointed its chief justice. By then Kelly property dominated the island's centre from south to north. Denis, who inherited the Lisaduff estate, was known in Ireland as "Jamaica Kelly". His daughter and heiress, Elizabeth, married into the Browne family of Westport, County Mayo, in 1752. Like the Kellys, the Brownes had retained and added to their property by changing their religion in penal times. Already powerful in the Dublin parliament, Elizabeth

Kelly's wealth now made the Brownes Ireland's premier absentee plantation owners in the British Caribbean.[25]

Hunter was equally mistaken about the threat offered by the arrival of Irish Catholics from a lower social background. At a time when Jamaica's white population numbered some seven thousand and its black population fifty-five thousand, all newcomers were eager to benefit from their whiteness in an expanding economy. Jamaica became known as a forcing house for the adoption of British West Indian standards, including acceptance of an established Protestant church which made minimal spiritual demands upon its parishioners.

In Montserrat, with its long-established Catholic community, things developed rather differently. Penal laws preventing Catholics from holding office were now strictly enforced. Public practice of their religion was still outlawed; a Dominican priest, Father Lynch, lived on Montserrat, but he celebrated Mass in private houses, being forbidden to build a church. However, unlike Ireland under the penal laws, in the New World colonies there was no restriction on Catholics owning and purchasing land. Trade between the Caribbean and Britain was growing and Montserrat was in a good geographical position to take advantage of this. Its increasingly creditworthy Catholic community, possessing land and slaves and producing sugar, tobacco and cattle, extended their plantations and mercantile ventures.[26]

Britain had become the Atlantic's biggest slave trader, which gave its colonies access to bargain-price slaves. On the western end of Hispaniola, France was developing Saint-Domingue, the greatest sugar producer and the most successful tropical colony in the world. The economic orthodoxy that colonies existed for the benefit of the metropole caused states to surround their possessions with protective tariffs. Under trade regulations constructed in London, Ireland's role was to supply provisions (heavily salted and pickled butter and beef, packed tightly in firkins and barrels – convenience food for a hot climate) to the West Indies. Increasingly the French islands became dependent on Irish "cow beef" – the carcasses of elderly dairy animals and rejected cuts from other cattle – as the staple protein for their slaves' diet. In peacetime the British permitted this trade but during war it became illegal, leading to an increase in smuggling, with more risk and more profit for those concerned.

An important player in this development was the Dutch colony of St Eustatius, whose volcanic peak was visible from St Christopher. St Eustatius was nicknamed "the Golden Rock" because of its commercial success, partly as a smugglers' haven but also as a result of its neutral status in the Anglo-French wars of the eighteenth century. Montserratians traded eagerly with St Eustatius, but by the 1740s they were developing a special relationship with another neutral island. The Danish king, like all monarchs with a maritime economy, was eager to acquire his own sugar colony. In 1733 he purchased Saint-Croix from the French, only to find that his subjects had no interest in settling and developing the island. The vacuum was filled by Montserratian plantation owners and traders: Tuites, Farrells, Ryans, Kirwans, Skerrets, Husseys, Bodkins, Blakes and Bourkes. Using St Croix as a base, they smuggled slaves to Saint-Domingue and then loaded up with bargain sugar there to sell in Europe.[27]

The leading figure in all this activity was Nicholas Tuite (1705–72), eventually the owner of seven plantations and part-owner of seven others. Born on Montserrat, he left in his thirties to live on St Croix; twenty years later he had settled in London, acting as an agent for those who remained in the Caribbean and as an advisor to the Danes on their mercantile interests. In 1760 he travelled to Copenhagen, where the king welcomed him as the founder of St Croix and made him a chancellor, granting him Danish citizenship.[28] The Danish envoy in London referred to Tuite as Irish, but the island's governor described him as "an English planter and the true ruler of the St Croix", a reflection of the instability of his identity.[29] In the Caribbean and in London he was at the centre of an elite merchant network, the Montserratian Irish, whose wealth was based not only on sugar production but on knowing how to circumvent, manipulate and negotiate the complex trade regulations of this age of mercantilism.

Economic historians see such behaviour as having created a new Atlantic world of continuously expanding trade, arguing that the voluminous state regulations were of interest only to those who wrote them. Kin and ethnicity determined these merchant groupings, rather than attachment to a particular state; such men were "citizens of the world".[30] Tuite was just such a figure. He and his Montserratian circle were Irish by descent, not by birth, yet they maintained direct links with their original homeland. During their lives and in their wills they remembered poor relations back in Ireland, offering them West Indian opportunities as overseers, bookkeepers and clergy, thus securing a flow of new arrivals. Among these were legatees, who often found it difficult to collect their inheritances unless they were prepared to leave for the Caribbean to contest legal disputes, sort out debts and mortgages and run the businesses they had suddenly acquired.[31]

Religion forged another Caribbean Irish connection. Once again Tuite's activities throw light on both his personal position and the nature of the colonial society in which he lived. He persuaded Frederick V of Denmark to grant freedom of religion on St Croix and negotiated with Rome for permission to supply Irish clergy. Full toleration on St Croix enabled Nicholas Tuite to build a Catholic church in the capital, Christiansted. This was first served by Father Dominic Allen, while a second Dominican, Hyacinth Kennedy, was sent to live on a Tuite plantation, where he baptized 150 slaves.[32] The founders of this Dominican mission – two of whom died within three years of their arrival – wrote letters vividly recording their encounter with St Croix. They were men of very different character.

Dominic Allen was reclusive and Irish-speaking. Hyacinth Kennedy was a worrier, uneasy lest the demands of his African converts draw him into flouting Catholic orthodoxy. He feared that runaway slaves from nearby Puerto Rico, who were seeking Catholic baptism, had already received it in Spanish territory. Agonizing about breaking the rule that an individual should not be baptized twice, he was also suspicious that recently converted slaves now seeking marriage were using the opportunity to discard former partners and take on new ones. In contrast, Thomas Devenish was witty, worldly and optimistic, while the practical Terence MacDonnell was harassed by the collapse of Devenish's scheme to fund the mission by buying a £3,000 plantation.[33] Though they disagreed on many issues, they were united in their reaction to the Irish community to which they ministered: "The white people are totally engaged in their worldly cares to the neglect of . . . the salvations of their souls" (Allen); "they who are good Christians in Europe are reprobates here. . . . They are all judges and divines" (Kennedy); "a well united clan . . . presbyterian-like if a clergyman don't do what any or all of them would have, they set him adrift" (Devenish); "obstinate and self sufficient. No restraint can be put upon their pleasures and liberties" (MacDonnell).[34] They describe in detail a commercial community scrambling for profit; ignoring fast days; turning to the Danes' Lutheran clergy if their demands for marriage within the bounds of consanguinity were not quickly accepted; and arguing confidently and loudly on theological matters, uninhibited by lack of knowledge. Irish ethnicity, based upon shared faith and historical experience, had evolved into a West Indian colonial identity.

The Dominicans' letters also hint incisively at another West Indian characteristic prevalent among their flock: sexual relations between whites and blacks. Whether or not the sugar islands' reputation for sexual excess was deserved or apocryphal, spiritual reinvigoration often played a part in the colonists' European experience. The Tuites and other Montserratians had felt their religious life revived in London as they enjoyed attendance at the Catholic chapel of the Sardinian embassy. A wealthy Anglican planter from Antigua, Samuel Martin, back in England in the 1770s, encountered the evangelical revival and returned to his plantation intent on introducing his slaves to the Christian message.[35] All rich West Indians in the British colonies felt the financial pull of London and the social attraction of Bath, and many settled permanently in England. The Irish Montserratians found themselves well received by the recusant community – English Catholics delighted to welcome Caribbean heirs and heiresses. Intermarriage among succeeding generations meant that Catholicism was maintained but Irish identity eliminated.[36]

Across the channel in France a very similar pattern gradually emerged. At the beginning of the eighteenth century the Irish mercantile community there possessed a strong sense of ethnicity and an interest in the growing Caribbean economy. Based on the Atlantic coast, its numbers had expanded with the arrival of James II's defeated army and its wealth through activities in the slave and sugar ports of Nantes and Bordeaux. Over the years these families became French nationals. Profits made in the French slave trade were used to buy chateaux, equip their owners with French titles, and build up coffee and sugar plantations in the booming colony of Saint-Domingue. Military service for the king of France could also lead to colonial reward and political assimilation.[37]

Like clerical training, soldiering on the Continent was a well-established professional path for Ireland's Catholic gentry, who were propelled by Jacobite loyalty and their inability to take the oaths of supremacy and allegiance to the British Crown. In the eighteenth century, Irishmen in the Spanish army increasingly saw service in the Caribbean as a promotional step in their military careers. Alexander O'Reilly (born 1722, Baltrasna, County Meath) was the most successful; he helped build defences in Havana and Puerto Rico and managed to promote the fortunes of a number of his fellow soldiers and countrymen there. In the 1780s, when Britain negotiated favourable access to the Spanish colonies, the Irish were attracted by economic opportunities in Catholic societies, moving from St Croix to Puerto Rico and from Liverpool and the Leewards to Trinidad.[38] Only by going to the Spanish or French colonies or by remaining on Montserrat did the Irish in the Caribbean retain their Catholicism throughout the eighteenth century.

The Irish appeared early in the Caribbean, but their failure to found a colony meant that their history was rarely considered part of the official account. Working within the empires of others, they left behind no distinctive state structure, language or architectural style, as the Spanish, British, French and Dutch had done. Because they were largely shut out by the Spanish, used by the French as allies when convenient, and treated as second-class subjects by the British, assimilation into these dominant groups increasingly became the only strategic possibility. However, they played an important part in turning the Leewards and Barbados into tobacco colonies, helped to prevent the Cromwellian conquest of Hispaniola, and applied their expertise to the development of Jamaica as a sugar island.

A distinctive Irish Catholic identity, seeping away in the eighteenth century, was reinvigorated in the nineteenth. This age of emancipation allowed a new generation to arrive as soldiers, policemen, priests and nuns, while the twentieth century would see Ireland itself emerge as an icon of anti-colonialism, attracting Caribbean interest and empathy. These later perceptions have obscured earlier Irish activities: breaking the ground in St Christopher; hiding out in St Philip parish (Barbados) with runaway slaves; ministering to Catholics on Danish St Croix; selling Africans and buying sugar on Saint-Domingue. Arriving, disappearing and re-emerging in different forms, the Irish have been a changing but constant presence in the history of the Caribbean.

Notes

1. Hilary McD. Beckles, "A 'Riotous and Unruly Lot': Irish Indentured Servants and Freemen in the English West Indies, 1644–1713", *William and Mary Quarterly* 47, no. 4 (October 1990): 516, 517, 519; Joyce Lorimer, ed., *English and Irish Settlement on the River Amazon, 1550–1646* (London: Hakluyt Society, 1989), 399, 401, 448, 459.

2. The individuals involved came in the main from two groups that had long been at loggerheads: the "Old English" (Anglo-Norman conquerors present in Ireland from the twelfth century onwards) and the native Gaelic lords. In the first half of the seventeenth century they banded together in the face of Protestant plantations and land confiscations.

3. Lorimer, *English and Irish Settlement*, 401–6.

4. Kirsten Block and Jenny Shaw, "Subjects Without an Empire: The Irish in the Early Modern Caribbean", *Past and Present* 210 (February 2011): 35n7, 68.

5. Lorimer, *English and Irish Settlement*, 452. Sweetman was an "Old English" name associated particularly with Tipperary.

6. Aubrey Gwynn, "The First Irish Priests in the New World", *Studies: An Irish Quarterly Review* 21 (June 1932): 223.

7. Natalie A. Zacek, *Settler Society in the English Leeward Islands, 1670–1776* (Cambridge:

Cambridge University Press, 2010), 43; Donald Harman Akenson, *If the Irish Ran the World* (Liverpool: Liverpool University Press, 1997), 44; Gwynn, "First Irish Priests", 226–27.

8.   Akenson *If the Irish*, 43; Zacek, *Settler Society*, 124.

9.   Akenson, *If the Irish*, 35; Gwynn, "First Irish Priests", 224. In the "English century", when the mother country supplied the majority of emigrants to its colonies in the New World, the Irish may have comprised half of the settler population in the Caribbean. This suggestion is put forward by Carl and Roberta Bridenbaugh in *No Peace Beyond the Line: The English in the Caribbean, 1624–1690* (Oxford: Oxford University Press, 1972) and endorsed by Akenson as "speculative but well informed" (*If the Irish*, 26).

10.   Block and Shaw, "Subjects", 40, 42.

11.   Ibid., 43.

12.   Ibid., 44–47; Karst de Jong, "The Irish in Jamaica During the Seventeenth Century, 1655–1693" (MA thesis, Queen's University of Belfast, 2010), 11.

13.   Alan Burns, *History of the British West Indies* (New York: Barnes and Noble, 1965), 342. Like so many others prepared to adventure in the Caribbean, William was a younger son from an Old English background – the Stapletons of Tipperary, who had lost land under Cromwell.

14.   Akenson, *If the Irish*, 78, 101–2, 124–25.

15.   On the other English Leewards the Irish comprised a quarter of the white population (Akenson, *If the Irish*, 107).

16.   Beckles, "Riotous and Unruly", 503.

17.   Hilary McD. Beckles, "Blackmen in White Skins: The Formation of a White Proletariat in West Indian Slave Society", *Journal of Imperial and Commonwealth History* 15 (1986): 6.

18.   Richard B. Sheridan, *Sugar and Slavery: An Economic History of the British West Indies, 1623–1775* (Kingston: University of the West Indies Press, 1974), 236. Patrick Corish says that the heaviest years of transportation were 1652–55. His figures, covering soldiers, political undesirables, vagrants, women and children, "indicate" eight thousand to Barbados and four thousand to the other islands; Patrick J. Corish, "The Cromwellian Regime, 1650–60", in *A New History of Ireland*, Vol. 3, *Early Modern Ireland, 1534–1691*, ed. T.W. Moody, F.X. Martin and F.J. Byrne, 353–86 (Oxford: Clarendon Press, 1976), 363–64. Akenson, stressing that all estimates are speculative, prefers ten thousand (*If the Irish*, 63).

19.   Beckles, "Riotous and Unruly", 518.

20.   Block and Shaw, "Subjects", 56.

21.   Sheridan, *Sugar and Slavery*, 160–61.

22.   Nothing has so far been discovered in Montserrat's scanty records. In Barbados, with its more extensive archive, two cases have been unearthed by historians. In

1656 Cornelius Bryan was sentenced to be publicly whipped and deported for using mutinous language. Some thirty years later he made a will leaving a "mansion house", twenty-two acres and eleven "Negroes with their increase" to his wife, Margaret, and their six children (Block and Shaw, "Subjects", 33–34). Edward Bourke, who was favoured by his master, acquired a lease on a substantial plantation and became an officer in the militia. However, his religion prevented him from becoming a member of the council and in the 1690s his economic success declined (Colonial State Papers 1693–96, 647; 1696–97, 52; 1697–98, 296–98). The most neglected group of all – poor white women – furnishes an example which is more typical of the Irish experience. In 1679 Elizabeth Connell was paid by St John's vestry to care for the indigent Dormand Kelly and an illegitimate child fathered by the brother of the parish clerk. This entry shows the Irish drawing upon poor relief and in doing so moving closer to the Anglican establishment. See Cecily Jones, *Engendering Whiteness: White Women and Colonialism in Barbados and North Carolina, 1627–1865* (Manchester: Manchester University Press, 2007), 35.

23.   T. Bartlett and D.W. Hayton, *Penal Era and Golden Age: Essays in Irish History, 1690–1800* (Belfast: W. and G. Baird, 1979).

24.   Joseph J. Williams, *Whence the "Black Irish" of Jamaica?* (New York: L. MacVeagh, Dial Press, 1932), 66; Lewis Namier and John Brooke, eds., *The History of Parliament: The House of Commons, 1754–1790* (London: Oxford University Press for the History of Parliament Trust, 1964), xl, 26; Vere Langford Oliver, *Caribbeana* (London, 1909–19), v, 260–61.

25.   Jackie Ranston, *Belisario: Sketches of Character* (Kingston, Jamaica: Mill Press, 2008), 189–91. In 1833, when Britain abolished slavery within its empire, Elizabeth Kelly Browne's grandson, the second Marquess of Sligo (governor of Jamaica, 1834–36), owned 286 slaves. The largest claim for compensation was made by James Blair, for his 1,598 slaves. He was the absentee heir of two Presbyterian brothers from Newry, County Down, who had built up a number of plantations in Demerara (British Parliamentary Sessional Papers, 15 November–16 August 1837–38, xlviii, British Guiana; ibid., Jamaica. Now online at the Legacies of British Slave-Ownership database, http://www.ucl.ac.uk/lbs). See also Nicholas Draper, "'Dependent on Precarious Subsistences': Ireland's Slave-Owners at the Time of Emancipation", *Britain and the World* 6, no. 2 (2013): 220–42, doi:10.3366/brw.2013.0097.

26.   In 1720 there were only ninety-five white servants, bonded and free, on the island; Howard Fergus, *Montserrat: History of a Caribbean Colony* (London: Macmillan, 1994), 53. By 1729 there were only 641 persons of Irish ethnicity on the island (Akenson, *If the Irish*, 117).

27.   Orla Power, "Irish Planters, Atlantic Merchants: The Development of St Croix, Danish West Indies, 1750 to 1766" (PhD thesis, National University of Ireland, Galway, 2011), 134, 143–51.

28. Philip C. Yorke, ed., *The Diary of John Baker, Barrister of the Middle Temple and Solicitor-General of the Leeward Islands* (London: Hutchinson, 1931), 62.

29. Power, "Irish Planters", 117, 114.

30. David Hancock, *Citizens of the World: London Merchants and the Integration of the British Atlantic Community, 1735–1785* (Cambridge: Cambridge University Press, 1995), 14 (quoted in Power, "Irish Planters", 5). Hancock deals with a group of London Scots; Power's detailed researches in the Danish archives reveal that the London Montserratians played a similar role in Atlantic commerce.

31. Power, "Irish Planters", will of Nicholas Tuite, 5 February 1772, image reference 64. Power accessed Irish wills in both London and Denmark. She also examined the wills of poorer members of the Irish community on St Croix itself, and the nature of their bequests to relatives and the church (188–90). See also National Library of Ireland, Dublin, MS D16, 326–45, Gaynor Papers. This collection is a mine of information on the complexity of Irish kin and Caribbean connections. Peter Gaynor died a very wealthy planter in 1737 on Antigua. His papers, which indicate that Gaynor had properties in various unspecified parts of the world, concern Irish legacies. One thousand pounds in English money was to be distributed among his relatives in Ireland: his six sisters and their progeny and members of his mother's family, the Dowdalls. The main legatees were his sister Elizabeth Pethony's children in County Kildare. Henry Pippard, a wealthy Catholic merchant in Drogheda, was appointed to distribute the Irish legacies, which he managed to do by 1743. In 1745 James Penthony, Elizabeth's eldest son, reached Antigua.

32. Hugh Fenning, ed., "The Mission to St Croix in the West Indies, 1750–1769", documents from San Clemente, Rome, in *Archivium Hibernicum* 25 (1962): 85, 87.

33. Since the seventeenth century the Catholic Church had seen English, French and Irish as the combination of languages most suited to those serving Irish communities in the Caribbean (Gwynn, "First Irish Priests", 225). Nicholas Tuite's request for priests for St Croix reiterated the need for an Irish-speaker, but Hyacinth Kennedy complained that Allen was ill-suited for ministering there because he was not "voluble in the English tongue". English, the language of commerce, was at a premium in the Caribbean (Fenning, "Mission", 110, 89). Once the servant class disappeared, the largest number of Irish-speakers was to be found among the sailors. The pressure to acquire a linguistic dual identity is encapsulated in the life of the Kerry poet Eoghan Rua Ó Súilleabháin (1748–84), master of the Jacobite aisling genre. Forced by poverty to join the British navy, he was present at the Battle of the Saints, after which he produced a poem in English titled "Ode to Rodney's Glory". See James McGuire and James Quinn, eds., *Dictionary of Irish Biography* (Cambridge: Cambridge University Press, 2009), 7:955–57.

34. Fenning, "Mission", 86, 92, 98, 120.

35. Caribbean wills occasionally reveal the existence of interracial relationships. Cited

here is a very rare Irish example. National Library of Ireland, Dublin, MS 10, 422, O'Sullivan Papers contains the will of Eugene Mahony, a planter of St John's parish, Jamaica, who died on the island in 1813. He possessed slaves valued at £6,260 and currency totalling some £7,256. From the currency he left his mother £2,000 and his four sisters £5,000, to be divided between them, and to Johanna Lee, a free Lumba woman, £200. Everything else went to his brother. Johanna's second name is an Irish name quite frequently found in the Caribbean. Mahony put his mark, not his signature, on the will, which means that either he was too ill to write his name or, against the statistical odds, he began life as poor and illiterate and had risen to become a rich planter.

36.   Yorke, *Diary of John Baker*, 152; Fenning, "Mission", 84n4; Sheridan, *Sugar and Slavery*, 485.

37.   Nini Rodgers, *Ireland, Slavery and Anti-Slavery, 1612–1865* (London: Palgrave Macmillan, 2007), 105–12; Rena Holohan, *The Irish Chateaux: In Search of Descendants of the Wild Geese* (Dublin: Lilliput, 1999), 29, 97–100; F.W. Van Brock, "The Defeat at Les Plantons", *The Irish Sword* 13 (1977–79): 89–104. See also the entry for Martin Victor O'Gorman (born 1746, County Clare) in Richard Hayes, *Dictionary of Irishmen in France* (Dublin: H.M. Gill and Son, 1949), 232.

38.   Oscar Rico Morales, *Ireland and the Spanish Empire, 1600–1825* (Dublin: Four Courts, 2011), 244; Jorge L. Chinea, "Irish Indentured Servants, Papists and Colonists in Spanish Colonial Puerto Rico, ca. 1650–1800", *Irish Migration Studies in Latin America* 5, no. 3 (November 2007): ii–iii, http:www.irlandeses.org./0711chineab3.htm.

Chapter 2

Father Antoine Biet's Account Revisited
Irish Catholics in Mid-Seventeenth-Century Barbados

JEROME S. HANDLER AND MATTHEW C. REILLY

IN 1654 ANTOINE BIET, A FRENCH CATHOLIC priest, travelled to Cayenne, in South America, but unforeseen circumstances led him to a short stay in Barbados; ten years later he published an account of his experiences in the New World, including his visit to the island. In 1967 Jerome Handler published a translation of the two chapters of Biet's volume that describe his three-month Barbados sojourn.[1] Since this publication, historians and other writers have found the translation useful in their discussions of Barbadian society in the middle of the seventeenth century.[2] Biet's account offers a unique first-hand glimpse into life in Barbados during a period when the so-called sugar revolution was well underway and the island was generating an enormous amount of wealth from sugar produced on large-scale plantations worked largely by enslaved Africans. Although, as we discuss below, writers have used Biet's account to illustrate a number of features of Barbadian society, little attention has been paid to his interactions with Irish nationals on the island, and how such interactions reflect broader issues concerning the lives of Irish Catholics in a Protestant-dominated English colony. We contend that colonial antecedents in Ireland informed perceptions of Irish Catholics in Barbados, conflating Catholicism and socioeconomic status while fostering an environment of anti-Irish discrimination.

Antoine Biet's New World journey began in mid-1652, when, at the age of thirty-one, he left his congregation near Paris to join a group of priests accompanying a several-hundred-member expedition intending to re-establish a colony in Cayenne. The earlier French colony had collapsed about a decade before; the new one would suffer a similar fate within a year because of internal personal and political conflicts, attacks from indigenous populations, and problems of basic sustenance. A particularly decimating epidemic forced the remaining settlers to leave Cayenne, and they, Biet included, made their way to the English colony in Surinam.[3] There they found a ship bound for Barbados, and in February 1654 the French party of about sixty persons arrived at the island. Biet remained in Barbados for about three months before returning to France, via Martinique and Guadeloupe, in August 1654 – a little over two years since his voyage had begun.[4]

Two short chapters of Biet's account, which was based on his recall and notes he had made earlier, are devoted to Barbados. Chapter 31 is primarily a chronological narrative relating various incidents that befell him and his party during their stay on the island. He briefly records, for example, his arrival, his attempts to pray, the celebration of Catholic services, the French party's accommodations in Bridgetown and their purchase of a plantation, interactions with neighbouring planters and their feasting and drinking, and the party's eventual departure from Barbados. Chapter 32 provides a more systematic view of the "situation, climate and wealth of the island of Barbados and the customs, morals, and religion of its inhabitants".[5] Here Biet offers brief descriptive passages on Barbados's geography, ports, towns and architecture, shops, taverns and climate, but most of the chapter treats socioeconomic conditions, including the relationship between planter wealth, sugar, and slavery; the lives and treatment of enslaved Africans and indentured servants; the status of various religious denominations; and finally, festivities honouring James Drax, the island's wealthiest and most important planter, who was about to embark on a trip to England.

Richard Ligon's well-known and classic account *A True and Exact History of the Island of Barbados*, first published in London in 1657, was based on his stay in 1647–50.[6] It provides a wealth of materials on early Barbadian life which has been mined by scholars and other writers for generations. Although Biet does not come close in richness of detail and subject matter, in a primary-source literature that is generally devoid of first-hand accounts of Barbados during a crucial period in its history, his account has proved useful to researchers, primarily to complement other contemporary accounts on a variety of topics.[7] For example, writers have used and often quoted from Biet to illustrate and comment on the lavish lifestyle and opulence of the new sugar planters, including their elaborate meals and abundant consumption of alcohol as well as their ostentatious display of wealth and concerns about social status. Biet's observations on the enslaved population, particularly their fundamental role in the sugar industry and in generating wealth for the planter class, have also been noted, as well as his comments on the harsh treatment and disciplinary measures meted out to enslaved Africans and the severity of their working and living conditions.

Given Biet's occupation and his purpose for being in the New World, it is not surprising that he devoted a relatively substantial amount of his book to commenting on the state of European religious denominations and what he perceived to be the state of religion in Barbados in general. As a Catholic priest, Biet was critical of what he considered to be a lack of – or only superficial engagement with – religious practices, the English planters' preoccupation with pecuniary matters, and their disinterest in and antipathy towards extending Christianity to the enslaved population. His observation that "Calvinism is the only [religion] that is professed in public", but that nonetheless "one is free to do what one wants in his house",[8] has been cited by scholars to illustrate the relatively tolerant religious environment of Barbados, despite the colony's control by English Protestants. While he was initially anxious about how Catholicism was perceived in Barbados, Biet was to discover that his apprehension was unfounded; he would come to experience the official legislative and governmental stance of religious tolerance.

The principle of tolerance was encoded in the Barbados Charter and subsequent legislation. When the forces of the Commonwealth of England ("the Roundheads") took control over Barbados from the Royalists ("the Cavaliers") in late 1651, as a consequence of the English Civil War and the Battle of Worcester, "articles of agreement" – commonly known as the Charter of Barbados – were signed between representatives of both political interests in January 1652. The first article of the Charter, which is reproduced in the earliest published compilation of Barbados's laws, specified "that a libertie of conscience in matters of religion be allowed to all". Echoing this article, the first law, enacted in October 1652 and published in the same collection, states that "all the Acts which are now of force within the Common-Wealth of England, concerning free enjoyment of Religion, be published within this Island; And that the same be duely observed by all the Inhabitants of the same, in such manner . . . as in, and by the said Statutes of the Parliament of England".[9] On the island there was a general acceptance of Jews and Protestant dissenters, including Quakers, until the Quakers started being persecuted around 1660. However, despite the "strain of anti-Catholicism on the island", as Peter Campbell, a historian of Barbados, has observed, "Roman Catholics for the most part escaped persecution so long as they conducted their religious exercises privately and unobtrusively".[10]

Father Andrew White, an English Jesuit en route from England to Maryland, spent three weeks in Barbados in January 1634. He reported that on the island "some few Catholiques there be both English and Irish", clearly establishing the presence of Catholics from both national groups at this early date.[11] By the time Biet arrived in Barbados in 1654, some twenty years later, the white population – augmented by prisoners taken in military campaigns in England, Ireland and Scotland and transported to the West Indies – may have been around twenty-five thousand persons, approximately 56 per cent of the total population, which included enslaved Africans.[12]

The white population, reported Henry Whistler, an English visitor in early 1655, included "English, French, Dutch, Scots, Irish, and Spaniards". While there are no contemporary figures or estimates of the size of each group, Pedro Welch has argued that "for Barbados, there are some detailed lists of the early migrants, along with statements about their origins, to suggest that while there was a sizable Irish component, the bulk of the servant population was probably of multi-ethnic origin". Of this heterogeneous white population, Biet claims that "more than two thousand Catholics" lived on the island, likely repeating a conventional figure given to him by local residents. In any event, despite the presence of English Catholics (as noted by Andrew White), we assume that most of the Catholics were Irish, since the Irish population was sizable at the time of Biet's visit, and according to Richard Dunn, Irish Catholics "constituted the largest block of servants on the island, and they were cordially loathed by their English masters".[13] However, it bears emphasis that not all Irish in the English Caribbean were Catholic, nor were all of them impoverished. In Montserrat, for example, although 40 per cent of its population was Irish in 1678, this demographic consisted of native Irish (who were overwhelmingly Catholic and a clear majority); "Old English", who had arrived during the Anglo-Norman invasion of Ireland in the twelfth century; and "New English", mainly Protestants who settled in Ireland during the late 1500s and 1600s.[14]

However, unlike Montserrat, which received a large number of New English planters, most of the Irish who came to Barbados were native Irish Catholics, including priests exiled to the West Indies. In addition, although Ireland in the seventeenth century contained individuals of various socioeconomic classes, as well as people who had come largely from England and Scotland, explicit discrimination against native Irish Catholics was an essential component of England's colonizing ideology, and such prejudices were transferred to the Americas, including Barbados. In Barbados, most of the island's Irish were servants and poor; their arrival was a major aspect of the new Cromwellian colonizing schemes, in which migration played a major role.[15] Following such migrations, the servant population of Barbados in 1667–68 was described by an anonymous writer as "being poor men that are just permitted to live, and a very great part Irish, derided by the Negroes and branded with the epithet of white slaves".[16]

Biet arrived in Barbados at a time of heightened tension between English colonists and Irish exiles, given the recent influx of immigrants and threats of rebellion (both in Ireland and in Barbados). Specific incidents involving Biet reveal the fragile social position of Irish Catholics in Barbados and suggest Biet's preconceived notions of how English Protestants would treat Catholic priests. When he first arrived at Barbados, a member of the French party who held a grudge against him – because Biet had "always been critical of his dissolute life" – was waiting on the wharf. As soon as Biet landed the Frenchman cried out, "'A priest, a priest,' by his shouts wanting to excite the English, who abhor priests. . . . I do not know what would have happened if most of the people on the roadstead had been able to understand French." The tension was relieved with the assistance of one Donat O'Shea, who came to Biet's defence.

Years earlier, O'Shea had gone to France from Ireland to study for the priesthood; he recognized Biet as a French priest from his past. In describing their reunion on the dock, Biet writes, "neither of us could refrain from shedding tears of joy". O'Shea explained that he had arrived in Barbados as servant to a "gentleman whose name was Major Bayanne"; this was Major William Byam, a prominent Royalist who had been forced to leave Barbados in 1652 for the English colony in Surinam. O'Shea, more familiar with the social climate of the island, was quick to jump to Biet's defence, assuring those within earshot that Biet was not a Catholic priest but rather "a gentleman who he had served in France". O'Shea purposely concealed Biet's religious identity in favour of proclaiming his socioeconomic position.[17]

Days later, while still in the Bridgetown area, Biet walked to a secluded spot in order to say his prayers. Another man of the "Irish nation" soon approached him, speaking a "corrupt language intermixed with Italian, Portuguese, and

Provençal . . . which those who sail on the Mediterranean understand very well". Biet, by his own admission, did not speak or understand English well, if at all. The man addressed Biet as "*Seignor Padre*", identifying himself as "a servant of your Lady". Biet "gave him an angry look", replying in the same language that he was "not a priest"; he explains this denial by noting that he "feared that [the man] was someone who came to expose me and reveal me as a priest". But the man persisted, bowing deferentially to Biet, making the sign of the cross and reciting various Catholic prayers – all to affirm his strong Catholic identity and assure Biet that the priest had nothing to fear from him. Biet was moved and finally revealed his true identity, confessing, "I considered myself happy to be able to serve him and all good Catholics . . . who were in great distress without any spiritual comfort."[18]

During Holy Week, Biet visited Bridgetown and was led by a "Captain Halay" (or Hallett, a family name found in Barbados at this period) into a "large dwelling" containing a "very large room which was decorated with a great number of palm leaves; which led me to believe that this was the house of some Catholics who were observing the solemnity of Easter as much as they could". Men and women, Biet writes, "kissed my hands and threw themselves at my feet, crying with joy to find themselves so close to a priest". Humbled by the experience, he notes that he was "unable to console them" because of the language barrier, but the encounter that he describes is a powerful scene despite the lack of direct dialogue.[19] Biet does not mention the nationality of those observing the Easter holiday during this encounter, but we can infer from the previous two interactions with Irishmen that some, if not many, in the room were Irish.

When Biet arrives in Barbados, as described above, an Irishman quickly conceals his identity by announcing that Biet is a gentleman rather than a priest. Later, a different Irishman bemoans the lack of spiritual comfort and guidance facing the island's Catholics. During Holy Week, several Catholics are overjoyed to be in the company of a priest, possibly illustrating the delicate position on the island of such individuals. These incidents, we believe, suggest that the social precariousness felt by Irish Catholics derived not from explicitly anti-Catholic sentiment but rather from anti-Irish feelings that reflected tensions along class and ethnic lines, materializing in practices of religious discrimination. Additional clues pertaining to the discrimination faced by Irish Catholics in Barbados can be gleaned from a broader look at Irish Catholics within the English Atlantic world and from contemporaneous records and legislation of Barbados.

Throughout the English West Indies in the seventeenth century, the large majority of Irish inhabitants fell into the category of labouring Irish Catholics, who were perceived by colonial authorities to be rebellious and undesirable for the purposes of establishing a civilized and successful colony. English–Irish relations in Barbados were fuelled by tensions that had begun centuries earlier in Ireland; the attitudes of early English planters in Barbados seem to have been heavily influenced by these earlier prejudices, as were, undoubtedly, the sentiments of the Irish who laboured for them.[20] These prior prejudices were surely exacerbated by labour conditions in Barbados, the treatment that indentured servants experienced, and their reactions to this treatment.

As early as 1631, Henry Colt, an English visitor, reported that about forty servants had escaped from the island. Father White learned that not long before his arrival in Barbados, on 3 January 1634, "the servants of the iland had conspired to kill their masters and make themselves free. . . . The ringleaders were 2 brothers named Westons"; the plot was discovered before it could be put into effect.[21] In neither case are Irish servants specifically mentioned, but the colonial authorities and the Barbadian plantocracy viewed them as particularly rebellious and associated them with various plots throughout the seventeenth century.[22] Other "rebellious" incidents in Barbados and sea escapes from the island were major problems for masters throughout the period; occasionally servants and slaves helped each other escape, and a number of early laws dealing with fugitives – an omnipresent problem for planters during the seventeenth century – dealt with servants as well as slaves. Such incidents were compounded by English antipathy towards the Irish and mistrust of Irish servants. These sentiments seem to have been reflected in a 1644 act "for the prohibition of landing Irish persons" aimed at limiting the size of the Irish population. However, as Gragg has observed, this act became "meaningless" because of the island's labour demands.[23]

Servants in Barbados received harsh treatment in general and were restricted in their actions and movements. Many of Barbados's early laws passed in the 1650s were intended to circumscribe the daily lives of servants and control the conditions of their servitude. As for their actual treatment, Richard Ligon, while living in Barbados in the late 1640s, observed:

> as for the usage of the servants, it is much as the master is, merciful or cruel; those that are merciful, treat their servants well. . . . But if the masters be cruel, the servants have very wearisome and miserable lives . . . some cruel masters will provoke their servants so, by extreme ill usage, and often and cruel beating them, as they grow desperate, and so join together to revenge themselves upon them.

A few years later Biet made similar observations:

> All are very badly treated. When they work, the overseers . . . are always close by with
> a stick with which they often prod them when they do not work as fast as is desired.
> I found it strange that they sent from England those persons who were suspected of
> being Royalists, and who had been taken prisoner [at the Battle of Worcester]. . . . They
> were sold, especially when it was discovered that they were Catholics, the husband in
> one place, the wife in another, and the children in another place so as not to receive
> any solace from each other.[24]

The treatment received by Irish indentured servants, undoubtedly fuelled by long-standing antipathies of the English, caused the former to react violently to their situation. For example, although Ligon does not specifically mention either Catholics or Irish, he does report on a large plotted revolt by servants which was discovered in 1649 before it could be put into effect; given the number of Irish among the island's servants, it is hard to believe that they were not involved. In the 1650s tensions continued between the English settlers and planters and the Irish, whether free or indentured. In July and November 1655, about one year after Biet's visit, the Barbados Council learned "there are several Irish Servants and Negroes out in Rebellion".[25] During this period, Larry Gragg reports (using Barbados Council minutes), an Irish servant received a severe whipping for uttering a curse against the English and was forced to leave the island, and several others "were flogged and put in a pillory for slander and mutiny"; two others "so frightened their master" that he had them arrested, and for behaving "rebelliously and mutinously" they also received a severe whipping. Events such as these apparently caused the passage in November 1655 of an act aimed to "restrain the wandering of servants, and to suppress the insolencies of the Scotch and Irish servants".

Irish servants later joined with enslaved Africans in several plots of revolt. In fact, the large presence of both Irish servants and enslaved Africans caused alarm in Barbados, and Governor William Willoughby, presumably reflecting the sentiments of the plantocracy, lamented to his superiors in London that Barbados was "in an ill condition, in regard of the multitude of negroes and Irish".[26] The friction between Irish servants and English masters continued through the seventeenth century. It was, for example, reflected in false rumours that spread in late 1685 or early 1686, concerning a "rising designed by the Negroes . . . in combination with the Irish servants . . . to destroy all masters and mistresses". In general, as Hilary Beckles has argued, "It was the Irish who were perceived by English masters as a principal internal enemy – at times more dangerous and feared than the blacks", and it was Irish servants who were viewed "as belonging to a backward culture, unfit to contribute anything beyond their labor to colonial development". This view of the Irish poor was strongly expressed in 1697 by Christopher Codrington, the governor of the Leeward Islands. In his opinion, Zacek summarizes, "Irishmen were lower than many animal species; they were automaton-like 'brutes' whose only skill lay in warfare."[27]

The Irish population in the West Indies was not socioeconomically homogeneous. However, the Irish whom English planters regarded as security threats and disparaged ethnocentrically were not the Protestant "New English" Irish settlers who became large landowners and sometimes held high administrative positions. Although we cannot be certain of the religious affiliations and class backgrounds of the Irish in Barbados, the evidence indicates that the majority were Catholic and from the labouring class.[28]

Following the Irish rebellion of 1641, a strong English anti–Irish Catholicism existed, before and during Cromwellian times. The prejudice against Irish Catholics as Catholics, exacerbated by Cromwell's conquest of Ireland from 1649 to 1652, is reflected in an incident that occurred two years after Biet's stay in Barbados. Four Irish Catholic priests arrived at the island, probably as "political" exiles of Cromwell's campaign in Ireland, which resulted in the transportation of many other Irish to Barbados as servants.[29] In May 1656 the Barbados Council gave the priests "15 days liberty to seeke passage for their departure", prohibiting their settling on the island.[30] Politics certainly played a heavy role in the religious environment of Barbados, since the perception of Irish Catholic priests as possibly catering to an already rebellious and dangerous population made them a potential threat to the social order. Additionally, socioeconomic class was a significant variable of identity; Biet, perceived by Barbadians as a French "gentleman", experienced a religious freedom that was afforded only to residents and visitors who belonged to social categories acceptable to the governing authorities and the plantocracy.

The combination of characteristics that defined an "Irish identity" has led the historians Kristen Block and Jenny Shaw to argue that, "In the English colonies, servants of all nationalities were subject to harsh working conditions, but Irish Catholic subjugation was magnified by English Protestants' sense of cultural and religious superiority." In the eyes of colonial authorities and the Barbadian plantocracy, the Irish were comprised of distinct strata and were not characterized solely by adherence to Catholicism. Rather, Catholicism was one element of an Irish identity that marked the Irish as having, Beckles notes, the "lowest socioeconomic status within the West Indies' Anglican-dominated communities". What Biet initially perceived as anti-Catholicism in Barbados, we believe, was largely anti-Irish sentiments fuelled by the political and rebellious character of Irish Catholics and those who were perceived to be leaders, particularly Irish Catholic priests. Such an interpretation explains why Biet's experience on the island as a Catholic differed greatly from that of Irish Catholics. As a French "gentleman", Biet's presence did little to threaten colonial and plantocratic authority. For the Irish, their Catholicism signalled political and socioeconomic elements of their identity and therefore helped perpetrate their rebellious reputation. "At the most basic level", Zacek has written, "Irishness denoted Catholicism, and Catholicism Irishness, and both were connected in the public consciousness with rebellion and treachery".[31]

Father Antoine Biet's account of his stay in Barbados has proven useful as an eyewitness record of Barbadian life in the middle of the seventeenth century. However, although Biet in fact says very little about the Irish in Barbados, his report is to our knowledge the only seventeenth-century account which describes actual encounters with the island's Irish Catholics and expresses their voices, however indirectly through the passage of time and his recollections. Gragg has argued that Barbados was a colony of "growing religious pluralism and toleration" in the mid-seventeenth century, an argument supported by the early Barbados charter and established laws. However, a broader analysis of the Irish in Barbadian society at the time of Biet's visit presents the possibility that English discourse concerning the Irish "presented them as a monolithic group".[32] Class, religious, ethnic and political identities were conflated to portray the Irish as an inferior yet dangerous group. At a pivotal period in the development of Barbadian society, Biet's account suggests the prejudices against Irish Catholics, as their identities were judged based on colonial antecedents and produced and reproduced in the New World by Anglican society.

Acknowledgements

This article was written while Matthew Reilly held a Fulbright Institute of International Education grant. We thank Monsignor Vincent Harcourt Blackett for his help in investigating Irish Catholicism in Barbados. Larry Gragg and Katharine Gerbner were kind enough to comment on an earlier draft of this chapter.

Notes

1.   Antoine Biet, *Voyage de la France équinoxiale en l'Isle de Cayenne, entrepris par les François en l'année MCDLII* (Paris, 1664), 268–95; Jerome S. Handler, "Father Antoine Biet's Visit to Barbados in 1654", *Journal of the Barbados Museum and Historical Society* 32 (1967): 56–76.

2.   For example, in one form or another, the translation of Biet's account has been cited by Susan Dwyer Amussen, *Caribbean Exchanges: Slavery and the Transformation of English Society, 1640–1700* (Chapel Hill: University of North Carolina Press, 2007), 31; Hilary McD. Beckles, "Plantation Production and White 'Proto-Slavery': White Indentured Servants and the Colonisation of the English West Indies, 1624–1645", *Americas* 41, no. 3 (1985): 21–45; Carl Bridenbaugh and Roberta Bridenbaugh, *No Peace Beyond the Line: The English in the Caribbean, 1624–90*, vol. 2 of *The Beginnings of the American People* (Oxford: Oxford University Press, 1972), 119, 120, 139, 142, 145; Richard S. Dunn, *Sugar and Slaves: The Rise of the Planter Class in the English West Indies, 1624–1713* (1972; reprint, Chapel Hill: University of North Carolina Press, 2000), 69, 240–41; Larry Gragg, "A Vagabond in Paradise: Thomas Verney in Barbados", *History Today* 45, no. 8 (1995): 40–46; Larry Gragg, "The Pious and the Profane: The Religious Life of Early Barbados Planters", *Historian* 62, no. 2 (2000): 265–83; Larry Gragg, *Englishmen Transplanted: The English Colonization of Barbados, 1627–1660* (New York: Oxford University Press, 2003); Derek Hughes, *Versions of Blackness: Key Texts on Slavery from the Seventeenth Century* (Cambridge: Cambridge University Press, 2007), 313–17; Frederick C. Knight, *Working the Diaspora: The Impact of African Labor on the Anglo-American World, 1650–1850* (New York: New York University Press, 2010), 54, 68, 77; Karen Kupperman, introduction to Richard Ligon, *A True and Exact History of the Island of Barbados* (Indianapolis: Hackett, 2011), 1–36; Matthew Parker, *The Sugar Barons: Family, Corruption, Empire, and War in the West Indies* (New York: Walker, 2011), 80, 83–84, 151, 155; Peter Thompson, "Henry Drax's Instructions on the Management of a Seventeenth-Century Barbadian Sugar Plantation", *William and Mary Quarterly* 66, no. 3 (2009): 565–605; John K. Thornton and Linda M. Heywood, *Central Africans, Atlantic Creoles, and the Foundation of the Americas, 1585–1660* (New York: Cambridge University Press, 2007), 274, 329; Katharine Graebner, "The Ultimate Sin: Christianising Slaves in Barbados in the Seventeenth Century", *Slavery and Abolition* 31 (2010): 60.

3.   This colony had been founded in 1650 with settlers from Barbados. When a group of prominent Royalists was forced to leave Barbados in 1652, they joined the Surinam settlement. The new settlers included Major William Byam, who was very hospitable to Biet's group when it arrived.

4.   Handler, "Father Antoine Biet's Visit", 50–51.

5.   Ibid., 64. All quotations in English are from the Handler translation.

6. The second edition, with the same contents as the first, was published in London in 1673; it was reprinted by Frank Cass (London, 1970) and we cite the reprint here.

7. Ligon is the most outstanding of these accounts. For others around the same period, see Jerome S. Handler, *Guide to Source Materials for the Study of Barbados History, 1627-1834* (Carbondale: Southern Illinois University Press, 1971), 2, 136, 163.

8. Handler, "Father Antoine Biet's Visit", 69.

9. John Jennings, comp., *Acts and Statutes of the Island of Barbados* (London, 1654), 1, 12–13.

10. P.F. Campbell, *The Church in Barbados in the Seventeenth Century* (Bridgetown: Barbados Museum and Historical Society, 1982), 64. See also Gragg, *Englishmen Transplanted*, 74-77, 182; and Gary A. Puckrein, *Little England: Plantation Society and Anglo-Barbadian Politics, 1627-1700* (New York: New York University Press, 1987), 98.

11. Father Andrew White, "A Briefe Relation of the Voyage unto Maryland", in *Narratives of Early Maryland, 1633-1684*, ed. Clayton Colman Hall (New York: Barnes and Noble, 1910), 37. There are two versions of the original White manuscript, one in English and the other in Latin, and several translations. For background, see C.C. Hall, ed., *Narratives of Early Maryland*, 27– 28; and cf. Handler, *Guide to Source Materials*, 98. The sentence we quote appears only in the Hall volume.

12. For example, in England prisoners were taken following the Battle of Worcester, while a number of prisoners were taken during Cromwell's invasion of Ireland in 1649–50, most notably during his raid on Drogheda. There was no systematic census of the Barbados population before 1679–80, and population estimates are not available for many earlier years. Citing early manuscripts in the British Library, Harlow estimates a white population of twenty-three thousand in 1655. Of these the majority were labourers, and Richard Dunn has argued that the Irish made up the largest portion of servants on the island in the mid-seventeenth century; V.T. Harlow, *A History of Barbados, 1625-1685* (Oxford: Clarendon Press, 1926), 338; Dunn, *Sugar and Slaves*, 69; cf. Puckrein, *Little England*, 131.

13. The journal of Henry Whistler, in Frank W. Pitman, *The Development of the British West Indies* (New Haven, CT: Yale University Press, 1917), 5–7; Pedro L.V. Welch, "Poor Whites in Barbadian History", in *Narratives of the Occluded Irish Diaspora*, ed. Mícheál Ó hAodha and John O'Callaghan (Oxford: Peter Lang, 2012), 125–48; Handler, "Father Antoine Biet's Visit", 61; Dunn, *Sugar and Slaves*, 69; cf. Hilary McD. Beckles, "A 'Riotous and Unruly Lot': Irish Indentured Servants and Freemen in the English West Indies, 1644–1713", *William and Mary Quarterly* 47, no. 4 (October 1990): 506.

14. Natalie Zacek, *Settler Society in the English Leeward Islands, 1670-1776* (New York: Cambridge University Press), 85; Donald Harmon Akenson, *If the Irish Ran the World: Montserrat, 1630-1730* (Belfast: McGill-Queen's University Press, 1997), 16–17.

15.   For transportation in general, see John P. Prendergast, *The Cromwellian Settlement of Ireland* (University of California Libraries Press, 1868), and specific to the West Indies, see Aubrey Gwynn, "Documents Relating to the Irish in the West Indies", *Analecta Hibernica* 4 (1932): 139–286. Also see Nicholas Canny, "The Ideology of English Colonization: From Ireland to America", *William and Mary Quarterly* 30 (1973): 575–98. Cf. Alison Games, *The Web of Empire: English Cosmopolitans in an Age of Expansion, 1560–1660* (New York: Oxford University Press, 2008), 256.

16.   Jerome S. Handler and Lon Shelby, "A Seventeenth Century Commentary on Labour and Military Problems in Barbados", *Journal of the Barbados Museum and Historical Society* 34 (1973): 118.

17.   Handler, "Father Antoine Biet's Visit", 58, 59.

18.   Ibid., 60–61.

19.   Ibid., 63.

20.   Beckles, "Riotous and Unruly", 503–22; Akenson, *If the Irish*; Nicholas Canny, *Making Ireland British, 1580–1650* (Oxford: Oxford University Press, 2001).

21.   Henry Colt, "The Voyage of Sr. Henrye Colte", in *Colonizing Expeditions to the West Indies and Guiana, 1623–1667*, ed. V.T. Harlow (London: Hakluyt Society, 1925), 74; White, "A Briefe Relation", 34.

22.   See Beckles, "Riotous and Unruly"; Jill Sheppard, *The Redlegs of Barbados: Their Origins and History* (Millwood, NY: KTO Press, 1977), 23–24, 125n22.

23.   Beckles, "Plantation Production"; Jerome Handler, "Escaping Slavery in a Caribbean Plantation Society: Marronage in Barbados, 1650s–1830s", *New West Indian Guide* 71 (1997): 183–225; Richard Hall, *Acts, Passed in the Island of Barbados* (London, 1764), 450; Gragg, *Englishmen Transplanted*, 158. The full text of the 1644 act is unknown, so we cannot establish the precise reasons that led to its passage or for how long it was in effect. The act is listed as "obsolete" and is known by its title only in Hall, *Acts*, 450.

24.   See, for example, Jennings, *Acts and Statutes*, passim; Hall, *Acts*, 449–71; Ligon, *True and Exact History*, 44–45; Handler, "Father Antoine Biet's Visit", 66. See also Amussen, *Caribbean Exchanges*, 123–29. For examples of punishment of Irish servants under the laws, see Gragg, *Englishmen Transplanted*, 129; and Beckles, "Riotous and Unruly", 513–15.

25.   Ligon, *True and Exact History*, 45–46; Gragg, *Englishmen Transplanted*, 159; Barbados Council, quoted in Jerome Handler, "Slave Revolts and Conspiracies in Seventeenth Century Barbados", *New West Indian Guide* 56 (1982): 9.

26.   Gragg, *Englishmen Transplanted*, 158; Hall, *Acts*, 467. Cromwell had sent many Scots to the West Indies after the Battle of Worcester in 1651, and there was no love lost between the Scots and the English. Writing of the Leewards but in a comment that could also be applied to Barbados, Zacek observes: "The Scots carried their own burden of prejudice, but outside of certain exceptional circumstances 'Scot' gener-

ally did not function, as 'Irish' usually did, as a term of opprobrium denoting an individual's poverty, criminality, or disloyalty" (*Settler Society*, 99). On Willoughby's comments, see "Report of the Committee for Foreign Plantations", 12 March 1668, in Noel Sainsbury, ed., *Calendar of State Papers, Colonial Series, America and West Indies, 1661–1668* (London, 1880), 553.

27.   Handler, "Slave Revolts", 20–21; Beckles, "Riotous and Unruly", 504, 510–11; Zacek, *Settler Society*, 98. Cf. Gragg, *Englishmen Transplanted*, 158.

28.   Beckles, "Riotous and Unruly"; Campbell, *Church in Barbados*, 80; Handler and Shelby, "Seventeenth Century Commentary", 118; Games, *Web of Empire*, 255–88.

29.   Gragg, *Englishmen Transplanted*, 142; for the transportation of Irish priests, see Prendergast, *Cromwellian Settlement*. Between 1646 and 1668, the laws of Montserrat prohibited Catholic priests "from residing on the island, of even visiting it to celebrate Mass or to dispense any of the other sacraments" (Zacek, *Settler Society*, 75).

30.   Quoted in Campbell, *Church in Barbados*, 65.

31.   Kristen Block and Jenny Shaw, "Subjects Without an Empire: The Irish in the Early Modern Caribbean", *Past and Present* 210 (2011): 35; Beckles, "Riotous and Unruly", 506; Zacek, *Settler Society*, 98.

32.   Gragg, "Pious and Profane", 267; Block and Shaw, "Subjects Without an Empire", 57.

Chapter 3

The Irish in Barbados

Labour, Landscape and Legacy

MATTHEW C. REILLY

THE STORY OF THE IRISH WHO ARRIVED in Barbados in the seventeenth century is an episode in Caribbean history that seems at odds with the often normalized notion of white ownership and power and black enslavement and labour that has justifiably dominated the plantation narrative. However, closer attention to Barbados as a socioeconomic experimentation ground, one that eventually spawned a plantation system which disseminated throughout the New World,[1] reveals a history of those who lived and worked on this island that is as nuanced and complex as the Caribbean region itself. The Irish men, women and children who arrived in Barbados, and their descendants after them, were an integral part of the historical processes that altered the trajectory of Barbadian society. Their story speaks to the Atlantic interconnectedness that defined the New World.

While reliable figures are lacking, by the mid-1650s thousands of Irish men, women and children had arrived in Barbados.[2] Many would have arrived as indentured servants along with other European migrants such as the English, Scottish and Welsh. During the first half-century of English colonial rule in Barbados (beginning in 1627), these individuals came to constitute a substantial labour force on the island before planters began favouring the labour of enslaved Africans.[3] Following their replacement on the plantations, the large majority of this white underclass, including the Irish, faded into the background of Barbadian society and history. However, glimpses of Irish presence on the island exist within the historical record and on the Barbadian landscape. Tracing these clues in order to understand the Irish legacy more comprehensively is the major concern of this chapter. Additionally, I attempt to take this narrative into the present, indicating what the Irish-Barbadian connection entails today in terms of memory and identity.

Interestingly, most historical analyses of the Irish in Barbados begin in the second quarter of the seventeenth century and then halt abruptly around the turn of the eighteenth century.[4] There are a number of explanations. By 1715 Barbados's white population had diminished from more than thirty thousand in the early 1650s to less than seventeen thousand, whereas the population of enslaved Africans had exploded from about twenty thousand in 1655 to nearly forty-two thousand by 1712.[5] While this does not render insignificant the story of the white underclass in Barbados, it illustrates one reason why Barbadian historiography has traditionally focused on African enslavement and the social and economic contours of the plantation. Second, once the Irish (and other European) labourers made their exit from the plantations, they occupied spaces outside the realm of the colonial planters and authorities and therefore seldom appeared in official documents and records. Finally, an investigation into the "Irish" population of Barbados in and after the eighteenth century remains problematic. Generations of Barbadians of Irish descent grew up knowing very little, if anything, of their "homeland" beyond what had been passed down from older generations; they became further and further removed from any Irish origins. Additionally, as with most Caribbean peoples, the processes of creolization, beginning in the seventeenth century, eventually led to hetero-geneous bloodlines and lineages and to mixed, rather than specifically Irish, communities.

The investigative difficulties discussed above explain why historical analyses of the Irish in Barbados have traditionally been restricted to the seventeenth century. Nonetheless, the limitations can be addressed by modes of analyses that focus on the Barbadian landscape as a location of evidence, even though little has been written to date concerning the tangible physical manifestations of an Irish presence on the island. It is my contention that an interdisciplinary approach, using historical, geographic and archaeological methodologies, can shed some light on the footprints left on the island by its former Irish inhabitants.

Roots and Routes: From Ireland to Barbados

When English colonists first officially settled Barbados in 1627, England was simultaneously grappling with its colonial enterprise in Ireland. Since the mid- to late sixteenth century there had been heightened English involvement in Irish affairs, to the point of explicit plantation projects, specifically in Ulster and Munster. While the full extent of these colonial interactions is far beyond the scope of this chapter, it is significant to note that Ireland was experiencing processes of modernization, with various degrees of success in the eyes of the English colonial authorities and settlers.[6] Agricultural and mercantile forms of proto-capitalism were established throughout Ireland, which created the condi- tions that gave rise to a propertyless rural poor population. As the Barbadian colonial engine picked up steam, the Irish were considered to be a useful source of labour, through a number of avenues.

Contrary to notions presented in various popular fiction and nonfiction pub- lications, Irish emigrants to Barbados cannot simply be reduced to Cromwellian "slaves".[7] In fact, prior to the late 1640s, many of the Irish who sailed for Barbados along with their English, Scottish and Welsh counterparts did so willingly, in search of a better life. It is evident that such individuals were left with few options, but their circumstances of emigration were dramatically different from those of political prisoners or enslaved Africans. Many poor Irish would have signed contracts of indentured servitude for their passage across the Atlantic. Though the terms varied across space and time, these individuals contracted to work for their master for an agreed-upon period (usually between three and seven years) in exchange for the cost of their passage, clothing and provisions while in service, and the promise of between two and ten acres of land upon completion of their term of indenture.[8]

However, some early migrants were not so willing. The practice of kidnapping (the term being said to have originated in this context) took place in England and, particularly, in Ireland: children were taken from their homes, "spirited away" during the night.[9] Throughout Ireland (as well as in England) vagrants and criminals were commonly exiled to Barbados. Authorities were thus able to kill two birds with one stone, relieving themselves of redundant and trou- blesome populations while supplying the sugar fields in the Caribbean with labourers.[10] A final route of arrival to Barbados was by way of transplantation as a result of military campaigns. Tensions mounted between the Irish and English following the 1641 rebellion and the rise of Oliver Cromwell and the

Parliamentarians. When Ireland was invaded with the intention of punishing the rebels and Royalist supporters,[11] several thousand Irish were "Barbadosed" for their roles in the rebellion, their Royalist sympathies, their religious beliefs or, indeed, their low socioeconomic status.[12]

While the Cromwellian invasion of 1649 certainly led to a large number of Irish deportees, the realities of emigration were far more complex than mass enslavement of Irish Catholics at the hands of the English colonizer. Scholars have recently begun to shed light on the role of select Irish individuals and families in financing, establishing and managing plantations (including ownership of slaves) throughout the Caribbean region.[13] It is necessary to keep this in mind as we more closely analyse the realities faced by the Irish in Barbados. As will become evident in the discussion that follows, the Irish occupied a particularly low position in colonial Barbados but they were not enslaved; further, their situation does not necessarily represent the experiences of other Irish individuals in other New World contexts who invested in, owned and operated plantations.

The Irish in Seventeenth-Century Barbados: On and Off the Plantation

The Irish arrived in Barbados during a critical time in the island's early history. From the late 1620s to the mid-1640s, Barbadian planters experimented with various cash crops and met with differing levels of success. During these early years, small farms of less than fifty acres were common, producing crops for profit such as tobacco, cotton, indigo and ginger and provisions that included yam, cassava, potato and pineapple.[14] These plots were worked by smaller labour pools, initially made up of predominantly European indentured servants who often worked alongside enslaved Africans. Some small planters were fortunate enough to generate profits sufficient to invest in the burgeoning sugar market, but many were unable to prosper from the cultivation of tobacco, cotton or indigo.[15]

The lived reality for indentured servants in early Barbados has been most thoroughly described in Richard Ligon's *True and Exact History of Barbados*. Commenting on his stay in Barbados from 1647 to 1650, Ligon describes in detail the journey across the Atlantic of indentured servants, their arrival in Barbados, attempts to construct shelter, daily work schedules and the general treatment they received from their masters. In terms of daily living there seems to have been little difference in the experiences of white indentured servants and enslaved Africans.[16] As Ligon describes, "if the masters be cruel, the servants have very wearisome and miserable lives. . . . I have seen such cruelty there done to Servants, as I did not think one Christian could have done to another."[17] While there were fundamental differences between contracts of indenture and the institution of slavery, Ligon's account illustrates stark similarities in terms of daily life.[18]

Sugar was brought to Barbados in the 1630s but was not a major staple crop until it began to be grown at a large scale, beginning in 1643. The 1640s were a watershed decade in Barbadian history in terms of the monumental social, economic, political and geographical transformations sparked by the shift to sugar production. As planters began to favour the labour of enslaved Africans for social and economic reasons, white labourers found little opportunity within the sugar plantation scheme and had too little money to establish farms on an island being taken over by large-scale plantations (estates of three hundred acres or more).[19] Indeed, as plantations underwent the process of consolidation to make way for sugar cultivation, the prospects of being "ten-acre men" became severely limited for former indentured servants because of the lack of available and affordable land.[20]

These transformations affected the entirety of the white labouring class on the island: English, Scottish, Welsh and Irish alike. However, there was a particular stigma against Irish inhabitants of the island that affected their experiences and limited their opportunities. As early as 1644, An Act for the Prohibition of Landing Irish Persons was put into effect. Although the act and its execution were short-lived, it is evident that Barbadian planters had an aversion to Irish nationals.[21] Contributing to the distrust and dislike of Irish people was their reputation for revolt. Following the rebellion in Ireland in 1641 and a proposed 1649 uprising in Barbados, the Irish were proclaimed a "riotous and unruly lot".[22] Aside from their perceived rebellious nature, they were characterized by their state of poverty. In 1667, an anonymous author described indentured servants as "being poor men that are just permitted to live, and a very great part Irish, derided by the Negroes and branded with the epithet of white slaves".[23]

Following the decline in the use of indentured servants with the growth of large sugar plantations, many white labourers were rendered unemployed and landless, forcing several Irish to wander the countryside in search of charity. In 1657 Governor Daniel Searle noted

> it hath been taken notice that several of the Irish Nation, free men and women, who have no certain place of residence, and others of them do wander up and down from Plantation to Plantation, as vagabonds, refusing to labour, or to put themselves into

any service but continuing in a dissolute, lewd, and slothful kind of life, put them-selves on evil practices, as pilfering, theft, robberies, and other felonious acts, for their subsistency.[24]

Clearly, many Irish in Barbados were at odds with the English colonial author-ities, and recent unemployment had contributed to the planters' perceptions of Irish idleness and criminality.

While poverty may have been common among the Irish in Barbados fol-lowing the shift to sugar cultivation, there is evidence to indicate that certain individuals were able to amass enough wealth to leave money to friends and family upon their deaths. In his 1668 will, Teige Connell left between three and ten pounds sterling to four individuals: Honora Sullivan (the wife of a John S[h]ea), his cousin Daniel Connell, Honora Connell and Thomas O'Hally. He also mentioned that his cousin Daniel was still serving his time as an indentured servant.[25] This short will is particularly revealing of the socioeconomic position of the Irish in Barbadian society when sugar dominated the island. First, we see that Connell has left his modest holdings to close friends and family, all with Irish surnames, which may be indicative of a broader kinship pattern among Irish communities on the island; further evidence of this phenomenon will be discussed below. Additionally, the position of his cousin as a servant reveals that servitude among the white population was still a common practice, even though planters were primarily using the labour of enslaved Africans at the time the will was written.[26] Finally, Connell bequeathed pounds sterling to his friends and family, whereas other wills of the era bequeath pounds of musco-vado sugar, a common form of currency in Barbados. Therefore we can deduce that he was not in the business of producing sugar but had acquired his money through wage employment or small-scale farming.

Teige Connell's will is a unique indication of the position of the Irish within broader Barbadian society. The development of the sugar industry in Barbados brought about tremendous wealth for the plantocracy but had tragic conse-quences, particularly for the hundreds of thousands of enslaved Africans who would work the sugar fields for centuries to come. The sugar revolution would therefore provide conditions that spawned a burgeoning white proletariat.[27] This white underclass, including the Irish, found itself unneeded and unwanted on the island but lacking the means to emigrate. As a particularly detested pop-ulation, the Irish had restricted opportunities for social mobility and would become a demographic central to the engenderment of the "poor whites" or "Redlegs" of Barbados.

"Poor Whites" and Creolization

Following the mass exodus of white labourers from Barbadian sugar plantations, this newly created un(der)employed, poor and propertyless population sought refuge in the less inhabited regions of the island. In tandem with their physical departure as labourers from the plantation landscape, this newly minted poor white, or Redleg,[28] demographic became largely invisible in the historical record. Not only were they unnecessary to the functioning of the sugar-and-slave economy (except when their services in the militia were needed), their very existence as a white-skinned pauper class directly contested the development of normative notions of white supremacy and black inferiority within plantation society. It is therefore at this juncture that the narrative of the white underclass in Barbados becomes difficult to trace. Clues have been unearthed through detailed historical and ethnographic case studies, but to this date comprehensive historiographies of the Redlegs or poor whites are generally lacking.[29]

My shift here to the terminology *Redlegs or poor whites* is intentional, and more fitting to this period's demographic. While discussions of the Irish in seventeenth-century Barbados benefit from a historical record that explicitly details the immigration of Irish nationals to Barbados, following the sugar revolution and the eventual departure of the white labourer from the plantations, it becomes problematic (particularly after 1700) to trace tangible instantiations of an Irish identity on the island. Additionally, unlike the African and Afro-Barbadian population, which continuously received new arrivals from Africa through to 1807 (when the English abolished the African slave trade), few Irish nationals came to Barbados in the eighteenth century.[30] These circumstances necessitate moving from referencing a distinctly Irish population to the more ambiguous and inclusive category "poor whites or Redlegs". These pejoratives, along with others such as "ecky-becky" and "backra", came to identify the white underclass of Barbados. While many among these groups likely had Irish ancestry, cases can equally be made for English, Scottish, Welsh and even African ancestry in the family lineages. Rather than hindering historical research or calling into question the veracity of empirical data, these circumstances speak meaningfully to the processes of creolization that affected the earliest Irish arrivals to Barbados and their descendants.

I use the term *creolization* carefully; it often serves as a literary, historical and sociological *deus ex machina*, an ambiguous catch-all that often essentializes the creation of "mixed" or "hybrid" cultural characteristics which emerge in

zones of cultural contact.[31] Approached more pragmatically, a dialectical understanding of the phenomenon explores the lived dialogue between structural
circumstances and localized responses and reactions that often result in the (re)
construction of creolized ways of life. Understood in this way, creolization may
be viewed as "a historicized process of selective creation and cultural struggle".[32]
This approach is useful in analysing the processes that led to engendering of
the poor white communities of Barbados.

From indentured servants to poor whites or Redlegs, this population established communities on the fringes of the plantation landscape. In what follows,
data from the historical record and the Barbadian landscape will illustrate the
processes of creolization as they acted upon the Irish and shaped their communities. Over time, the lines and boundaries defining nationality, ethnicity
and race became empirically blurred as interaction between poor whites (of
all ethnic categories) and people of colour (whether enslaved or free) led to
miscegenation.[33] Historical circumstances and contingencies, coupled with
colonial control and plantocratic rule, provided the impetus for establishment
of communities that became creolized over time as their residents adapted to
living away from the plantation, though still connected with its economy and
society through wage employment and their interactions with enslaved labourers.

Constructing "Irishness" in Barbados

Time spent in Barbados or a quick survey of its phone book reveals an abundance of Irish surnames on the island: Farrell, Murphy, Downey (Downie),
Moore, Collins, Roach, Riley, O'Neal and Sullivan are all common entries.
Although seventeenth-century documents that record the names of Irish arrivals are rare, evidence suggests that these surnames were present on the island
in the seventeenth century. The Barbados census of 1715 is a useful source of
information on the Irish population and their geographical concentrations.[34]
In total, nearly seventeen thousand white inhabitants were recorded for all of
the parishes (St Philip is a unique case in that some individuals were listed as
"mulatto" or of "Negro extract").

Of interest for the purposes of this analysis are surnames of Irish origin and
the places where those individuals lived. The use of surnames for genealogical studies is obvious and essential, but it is important to acknowledge that
the association of surnames with places of origin is far more dubious when
considering sixteenth- and seventeenth-century Ireland. This period of early

colonization by England in Ireland was a catalyst for heightened mobility of individuals throughout England, Ireland, Scotland and Wales.[35] With families migrating in all directions within this broader area before and during the initial settlement of Barbados in 1627, it becomes increasingly difficult to establish the place where an individual holding a particular surname would have been migrating from. In short, we cannot rule out the possibility that an individual with a traditionally Irish surname may have been born in England as a result of familial migration in the sixteenth century, and eventually arrived in Barbados in the seventeenth century having never set foot in Ireland.

In spite of these potential difficulties it is still possible to garner a semblance of Irish community living in early Barbados. All of the traditionally Irish surnames listed above can be found in the 1715 census. Additionally, because of the substantial drop in the number of labourers coming to Barbados from Europe in the final decades of the seventeenth century, despite efforts to increase the European population at this time, we can assume that many of these individuals were second-, third- or even fourth-generation Barbadians of Irish ancestry. Furthermore, we can provisionally construct local communities. In the parish of St Philip, for example, in twenty-five sequential household listings the following families were found: Doughty, Flanagan, Boyce, Murphy, Farrell, Lanahan, Hallegan, Clarke and Vaughan. This is but one example of a broader pattern of Irish communities found throughout the eastern parishes of the island.

The geographical positioning of these communities with Irish inhabitants also bears witness to an earlier history of discrimination against the Irish on the island. Many of the traditional Irish names found in Barbados in the 1715 census are recorded in parishes along the island's east coast, which is home to the Scotland District, rugged terrain named for its resemblance to the Scottish Highlands. These areas were settled by former indentured servants in search of inexpensive land following the conclusion of their term of indenture. Although located south of the Scotland District, the communities found in St Philip are of specific significance, given the area's association with the rebellious reputation of the Irish in seventeenth-century Barbados. In the minutes of the Barbados Council from 1655 it is reported that there were "several Irish servants and negroes out in rebellion in the Thicketts and thereabout"[36] – "the Thicketts" was a heavily wooded region near the northern boundary of St Philip. Based on census data, it seems likely that several Irish servants remained in St Philip following their indenture and established communities among other Irish individuals and people of Irish descent.

The contemporary Barbadian landscape also bears the imprint of an Irish presence on the island through road names. For example, among the back roads in the parish of St Lucy is found Glendalough Road. Glendalough, a sixth-century monastic site, is in County Wicklow, Ireland. It is unknown how or when this road in a small Barbadian village got its name, but it suggests a significant knowledge of Irish history or a familiarity with Irish geography. Oral tradition on the island indicates that roads bearing family surnames were often named after the first household found on the road. Therefore it is fairly common to find streets bearing Irish surnames throughout the parishes of the Scotland District. For instance, one can find Hurley Road in St Lucy and Farrell and Redman Roads in St Andrew. These districts in particular are known to have been inhabited by numerous poor white families bearing such surnames. While the dates of origin of the street names are unknown, names appearing in the 1715 census correspond to road signs bearing the same names in given parishes.

A more explicit link to the Irish presence on the island is suggested by the former village of Irish Town, located in St Thomas near its border with St Andrew and surrounded by the largest hills on the island (including Mounts Hillaby and Misery). Now thick forest, this village was home to the second largest population in St Thomas in 1851: 227 inhabitants.[37] What is known about Irish Town comes from its few brief appearances in nineteenth-century records, including police magistrate reports, election reports, parish vestry minutes, landowner records, voter lists and burial records.[38] Of these, the burial records provide several entries that list Irish Town as the place of residence of the deceased. The earliest year that such information was recorded was 1825, so we can be certain that the village was established before emancipation in 1834.[39]

While limited nineteenth-century data provide clues as to the social make-up of Irish Town, little is known of its origins. It would seem that it was established by a small group of Irish or Irish-descended individuals who had either finished their period of indenture or were unable to find employment or housing on the plantations. This would imply a seventeenth-century date of establishment. After the place of residence of deceased individuals began to be recorded in 1825, an interesting picture of Irish Town begins to emerge. From 1825 to 1848, eighty-six individuals were buried listed with Irish Town as their place of residence. The most striking figure from these entries is that forty-one of them, or 47.7 per cent of the individuals buried, were five years of age or younger, and many of them infants.[40] This may be an indication that freehold villages such as Irish Town suffered a severe lack of access to adequate medical care, chronic disease, unsanitary conditions or chronic malnourishment, and that the consequences were high mortality rates for children and infants.[41]

Among these eighty-six individuals are several repeated surnames that indicate larger families in the village, such as Taylor, Ford, Small, Clarke and Woodroffe. Explicitly Irish surnames are lacking within this dataset, which may be an indication of transformation of the village over time. It can be hypothesized that the establishment of Irish Town was a response to rapid changes on the island in the wake of the sugar revolution, when the Irish labourers who were no longer needed or wanted on plantations had to find alternative ways of life within such communities. As time went on and the processes of creolization became more apparent, the Irish identity of the community would have given way to that of a distinctively Barbadian village, home to individuals and families of plural genealogies.

Villages such as Irish Town are not uncommon. The poor white community known as Below Cliff was established as a tenantry of the Clifton Hall plantation as early as the 1650s; it was located below Hackleton's Cliff, in the parish of St John.[42] Formally abandoned in the early 1960s following land slippages (to which the region is prone), a hurricane and new availability of affordable land nearby, the area, like Irish Town, became overgrown by forest. The stone foundations of former chattel houses are scattered throughout the forest, testimony to the historical circumstances that led several impoverished families to settle in the area centuries ago.[43] Archaeological excavations have been undertaken in the tenantry, and the material culture collected from sampled households provides insight into the daily lives of Redlegs of years past.[44] The surnames of former residents of Below Cliff include Downie, Mayers and Croney, supporting the claim for a partial Irish heritage of the village. Their neighbours included the Gibsons, Goddards, Fentys and Kings. While the majority of the families of this village and their descendants are phenotypically light-skinned, complexions and family genealogies suggest that African ancestry is also a common feature among the former residents.

Conclusion

The evidence illustrates what led to Irish immigration to Barbados and the circumstances experienced upon arrival. In the Barbadian context the Irish were identified as having white skins but occupied a marginal position within English colonial society; hence they complicated the establishment of a race-based social hierarchy central to a slave plantation economy. As such, Irish people found themselves relegated to less desirable regions of the island, in some cases living in close quarters with other Irish families. Such communities would inevitably become creolized, transforming what may have been the distinctive Irishness of particular communities into Barbadian villages.

Historiography of the Irish in Barbados has traditionally concentrated on the seventeenth century, when an Irish population on the island was explicitly defined as such, either self-defined as in the villages discussed above or by colonial authorities or planters, as seen in seventeenth-century documents. Evidence demonstrates a general disdain among planters and colonial authorities alike towards the Irish demographic on the island – a discrimination no doubt fuelled by prior colonial tensions between Ireland and England. The Irish adapted to the transition from indentured servants to unnecessary or un(der)employed resources on sugar plantations, by establishing communities on plantation tenantries or in neighbouring freeholds.

Attempts to connect present-day descendant communities (the so-called Redlegs of today) to the Irish in seventeenth-century Barbados (and the larger Anglo-Caribbean) have seemingly glossed over centuries of significant local history, often succumbing to derisive stereotypes that reinforce racial essentialisms.[45] In this chapter I have attempted to overcome these pitfalls by considering the Irish experience and heritage in Barbados in terms of the *longue durée*, unravelling the historical trajectory of the Irish on the island, however faded or attenuated it may be. My essay contributes to historical investigations of the Irish in seventeenth-century Barbados by complementing this research with an analysis of the Barbadian landscape from the seventeenth century to the present. While this volume privileges the connections between Ireland and the Caribbean, it should not distract from the reality that this is but one of many relationships in the web of entanglements that defines the Caribbean region. To illustrate, conversations with Barbadians, immigrants and visitors to the island on the topic of local accent and dialect usually lead to claims of a wide assortment of influences. Informal cases are made that the accent and dialect echo those of County Cork, of Somerset, and of parts of West Africa. Each is correct.[46]

Acknowledgements

Many thanks to the editors of this volume for their comments on earlier versions of this chapter. I also thank Monsignor Vincent Harcourt Blackett, Newlands Greenidge and Woodville Marshall for their generous assistance in providing some of the information used in this chapter.

Notes

1.   For a recent analysis of the spread of the plantation system see Simon P. Newman, *A New World of Labor: The Development of Plantation Slavery in the British Atlantic* (Philadelphia: University of Pennsylvania Press, 2013).

2.   For materials illustrating the degree and nature of transplantation, see Aubrey Gwynn, "Documents Relating to the Irish in the West Indies", *Analecta Hibernica* 4 (1932): 139–286; Joseph J. Williams, *Whence the "Black Irish" of Jamaica?* (New York: Lincoln Mac Veagh, Dial Press, 1932). Welch has warned of the dangers of overestimation and emphasizes the multi-ethnic make-up of the servant demographic; Pedro Welch, "Poor Whites in Barbadian History", in *Narratives of the Occluded Irish Diaspora*, ed. Míchaél Ó hAodha and John O'Callaghan (Oxford: Peter Lang, 2012), 125–48.

3.   Hilary McD. Beckles, "Plantation Production and White 'Proto-Slavery': White Indentured Servants and the Colonisation of the English West Indies, 1624–1645", *Americas* 41, no. 3 (1985): 21–45. Dunn has argued that during this period the Irish made up the most substantial block of indentured servants; Richard Dunn, *Sugar and Slaves: The Rise of the Planter Class in the English West Indies, 1624–1713* (1972; reprint, Chapel Hill: University of North Carolina Press, 2000), 69.

4.   Hilary McD. Beckles, "A 'Riotous and Unruly Lot': Irish Indentured Servants and Freemen in the English West Indies, 1644–1713", *William and Mary Quarterly* 47, no. 4 (October1990): 503–22; Kristen Block and Jenny Shaw, "Subjects Without an Empire: The Irish in the Early Modern Caribbean", *Past and Present* 210 (2011): 33–60; Welch, "Poor Whites".

5.   Barbados Department of Archives (hereafter BDA), *A Census of the Island of Barbados, West Indies: With the names and ages of all the white inhabitants of the island arranged under their several parishes* (1715). For population figures for 1712, see Richard Dunn, "The Barbados Census of 1680: Profile of the Richest Colony in English America", *William and Mary Quarterly* 26, no. 1 (1969): 7.

6.   For Ireland during this period see Nicholas Canny, *Making Ireland British, 1580–1650* (New York: Oxford University Press, 2001).

7.   For examples of this recent trend see Rhetta Akamatsu, *The Irish Slaves: Slavery,*

Indenture and Contract Labor among Irish Immigrants (CreateSpace Independent Publishing, 2010); Kate McCafferty, *Testimony of an Irish Slave Girl* (New York: Viking Penguin, 2002); Sean O'Callaghan, *To Hell or Barbados: The Ethnic Cleansing of Ireland* (Dublin: Brandon, 2001); Maggie Plumber, *Spirited Away: A Novel of the Stolen Irish* (CreateSpace Independent Publishing, 2012).

8. No reliable figures serve to differentiate between voluntary and coerced forms of indenture, but for specifics on early indentureship in Barbados, see Hilary McD. Beckles, *White Servitude and Black Slavery in Barbados, 1627–1715* (Knoxville: University of Tennessee Press, 1989).

9. Matthew Parker, *The Sugar Barons: Family, Corruption, Empire, and War in the West Indies* (New York: Walker, 2011), 47–49.

10. See John Prendergast, *The Cromwellian Settlement of Ireland* (1865; reprint, London: Trafalgar Square, 1996), Appendix XI; Williams, *Whence the "Black Irish"*, 10–11.

11. For the politics and practice of transplantation, see John Cunningham, *Conquest and Land in Ireland: The Transplantation to Connacht, 1649–1680* (London: Royal Historical Society, 2012).

12. Aubrey Gwynn, "Cromwell's Policy of Transplantation, Part I", *Studies: An Irish Quarterly Review* 19, no. 76 (1930): 607–23; Aubrey Gwynn, "Cromwell's Policy of Transplantation, Part II", *Studies: An Irish Quarterly Review* 20, no. 78 (1931): 291–305.

13. For Montserrat in particular, see Donald Harman Akenson, *If the Irish Ran the World: Montserrat, 1630–1730* (Montreal: McGill-Queen's University Press, 1997) and Natalie A. Zacek, *Settler Society in the English Leeward Islands, 1670–1776* (Cambridge: Cambridge University Press, 2010). For St Croix, see Orla Power, "Beyond Kinship: A Study of the Eighteenth-Century Irish Community at St Croix, Danish West Indies", *Irish Migration Studies in Latin America* 5, no. 3 (2007): 207–14. Jenny Shaw discusses the successes of the Irish Rice brothers in seventeenth-century Barbados in *Everyday Life in the Early English Caribbean: Irish, Africans, and the Construction of Difference* (Athens: University of Georgia Press, 2013). See also Nini Rodgers, *Ireland, Slavery and Anti-Slavery: 1612–1865* (New York: Palgrave Macmillan, 2007).

14. See Henry Colt's 1631 account, found in Vincent T. Harlow, ed., *Colonising Expeditions to the West Indies and Guiana, 1623–1667*, Hakluyt Society Series 2, vol. 36 (London: Hakluyt Society, 1925).

15. The social and economic landscape that seventeenth-century Irish labourers likely encountered is discussed in more detail in Douglas V. Armstrong and Matthew C. Reilly, "The Archaeology of Settler Farms and Early Plantation Life in Seventeenth-Century Barbados", *Slavery and Abolition* 35, no. 3 (2014): 399–417. For more on the early successes and failures of pre-sugar planters and their role in the sugar boom, see Russell R. Menard, *Sweet Negotiations: Sugar, Slavery, and Plantation Agriculture in Early Barbados* (Charlottesville: University of Virginia Press, 2006).

16.   Similarities in daily life led to significant degrees of social interaction, which is explored in Shaw, *Everyday Life*.

17.   Richard Ligon, *A True and Exact History of the Island of Barbados* (1657; reprint, Bridgetown: Barbados National Trust, 2000), 64–65.

18.   See Hilary McD. Beckles, "The Concept of 'White Slavery' in the English Caribbean During the Early Seventeenth Century", in *Early Modern Conceptions of Property*, ed. John Brewer and Susan Staves (New York: Routledge, 1995), 572–84.

19.   Beckles, *White Servitude*; Dunn, *Sugar and Slaves*.

20.   "Ten-acre men" refers to indentured servants who were granted ten acres of land following completion of their term of indenture.

21.   Robert Hermann Schomburgk, *A History of Barbados: A Geographical and Statistical Description of the Island* (1848; reprint, London: Frank Cass, 1971), 84.

22.   Beckles, "Riotous and Unruly". This particular proclamation relates to larger rebellious acts in the parish of St Philip, which will be discussed in more detail below. The Irish would again be involved with rebellion conspiracy in 1692; see Jerome S. Handler, "The Barbados Slave Conspiracies of 1675 and 1692", *Journal of the Barbados Museum and Historical Society* 36, no. 4 (1982): 326.

23.   Jerome S. Handler and Lon Shelby, "A Seventeenth Century Commentary on Labour and Military Problems in Barbados", *Journal of the Barbados Museum and Historical Society* 34 (1973): 118.

24.   Gywnn, "Documents Relating to the Irish", 236.

25.   BDA RB6/10, 126.

26.   Pedro Welch has provided specific evidence detailing the use of Irish indentured servants on selected plantations in Christ Church parish ("Poor Whites").

27.   Hilary McD. Beckles, "Land Distribution and Class Formation in Barbados, 1630–1700: The Rise of a Wage Proletariat", *Journal of the Barbados Museum and Historical Society* 36, no. 2 (1980): 136–43.

28.   The term *Redleg* is said to originate in the seventeenth century from the sunburns suffered by white labourers unaccustomed to working in a tropical environment. However, it may also be related to the term *Redshanks*, which relates to Scottish mercenaries in Ireland in the early seventeenth century.

29.   Local histories and ethnographies include Karen Francis Davis, "The Position of Poor Whites in a Color-Class Hierarchy: A Diachronic Study of Ethnic Boundaries in Barbados" (PhD diss., Wayne State University, 1978); Harry Rosenberg, "Social Mobility among the Rural White Population of Barbados (MA thesis, Brandeis University, 1962); Peter Simmonds, "'Red Legs': Class and Color Contradictions in Barbados", *Studies in Comparative International Development* 11, no. 1 (1976): 3–24; Karl S. Watson, "The Redlegs of Barbados" (MA thesis, University of Florida, 1970); and "'Walk and Nyam Buckras': Poor-White Emigration from Barbados, 1834–1900", *Journal of Caribbean History* 34, no. 1 (2000): 130–56. For the most comprehensive

history of the Redlegs to date, see Jill Sheppard, *The Redlegs of Barbados: Their Origins and History* (Millwood, NY: KTO Press, 1977).

30.   It has been argued that Barbados was home to the most creolized enslaved population in the Caribbean region, a result of reproduction of the black population rather than reliance on the importation of enslaved Africans. However, substantial numbers of Africans were still being sent to Barbados throughout the period of slavery. See Hilary McD. Beckles, "Creolisation in Action: The Slave Labour Elite and Anti-slavery in Barbados", in *Questioning Creole: Creolisation Discourses in Caribbean Culture*, ed. Verene A. Shepherd and Glen L. Richards (Kingston: Ian Randle, 2002), 181–201.

31.   For a more thorough critique of the unreflexive use of creolization, see Stephan Palmié, "Creolization and Its Discontents", *Annual Review of Anthropology* 35 (2006): 433–56.

32.   The dialectical approach to creolization is proposed by O. Nigel Bolland, "Creolisation and Creole Societies: A Cultural Nationalist View of Caribbean Social History", in *Questioning Creole: Creolisation Discourses in Caribbean Culture*, ed. Verene A. Shepherd and Glen L. Richards (Kingston: Ian Randle, 2002), 15–47. This definition of creolization is borrowed from Michaeline Crichlow, *Globalization and the Post-Creole Imagination: Notes on Fleeing the Plantation* (Durham, NC: Duke University Press, 2009), 1.

33.   For the instability of racial categories in Barbados see Cecily Jones, *Engendering Whiteness: White Women and Colonialism in Barbados and North Carolina, 1627–1865* (Manchester: Manchester University Press, 2007).

34.   BDA, *Census of the Island of Barbados.*

35.   Alison Games has thoroughly described the significance of mobility and migration within the British Isles during this period; Alison Games, *The Web of Empire: English Cosmopolitans in the Age of Expansion, 1560–1660* (New York: Oxford University Press, 2008).

36.   Beckles, "Riotous and Unruly", 515.

37.   BDA, *Police Magistrates' Half-Yearly Reports*, 1851.

38.   I thank Newlands Greenidge for bringing Irish Town to my attention and Woodville Marshall for sharing some of his data on the village.

39.   Many poor white villages developed as a result of the militia disbandment that followed emancipation. Irish Town was likely a poor white village, given that surnames were provided for buried and baptized individuals, a practice not undertaken for the enslaved population, who were infrequently baptized or buried in the church grounds.

40.   BDA, RL1/50 and 51.

41.   Infant mortality was a significant concern on the island, and its occurrence among the enslaved in the early nineteenth century was often associated with weaning and

dietary practices; see Jerome S. Handler and Robert S. Corruccini, "Weaning among West Indian Slaves: Historical and Bioanthropological Evidence from Barbados", *William and Mary Quarterly* 43, no. 1 (1986): 111–17.

42.   A 1653 deed of sale for the Clifton Hall plantation describes forty acres of land below the cliff as leased land; BDA, RB3/3, 11.

43.   Chattel houses are boarded structures that sit atop piled stone foundations. Argued to have been a post-emancipation development of former enslaved Africans, the houses were constructed by tenants of all ethnicities in order to easily move a home to a new location in the event of eviction or voluntary movement; see Henry Fraser and Bob Kiss, *Barbados Chattel Houses* (Port of Spain: Toute Bagai, 2011).

44.   Matthew C. Reilly, "Archaeological Approaches to the 'Poor Whites' of Barbados: Tired Stereotypes and New Directions", *Journal of the Barbados Museum and Historical Society* 59 (2013): 1–32; Matthew C. Reilly, "At the Margins of the Plantation: Alternative Modernities and an Archaeology of the 'Poor Whites' of Barbados" (PhD diss., Syracuse University, 2014).

45.   In particular See O'Callaghan, *To Hell or Barbados*.

46.   For a linguistic case study, see John R. Rickford, "Social Contact and Linguistic Diffusion: Hiberno-English and New World Black English", *Language* 62, no. 2 (1986): 245–89.

Chapter 4

Liberty, Freedom and the Green Atlantic

KEVIN WHELAN

Liberty, Freedom and Slavery

THE PLIGHTS OF THE IRISH CATHOLIC POOR and African slaves in the West Indies were frequently linked in eighteenth-century discourse. The rhetoric surrounding Irish dispossession and African enslavement becomes striking when seen through a Caribbean lens. Analysis of diaspora is critical when considering Atlantic history, and Caribbean models of syncretic cultural norms are particularly valuable in enriching discussion of the Irish experience. No binary was more embedded in Irish political discourse during the "long" eighteenth century (1690–1829) than that of freedom and slavery. Ultimately rooted in classical republican discourse, this binary enjoyed fresh currency in the eighteenth century and formed a central trope of both the American and French Revolutions. In thinking about the imaginative connections relating Ireland to the West Indies, it is instructive to trace the genealogy of these ideas in both Irish and diasporic contexts, exploring the contrasting resonance of *freedom* and *liberty* in Catholic and Protestant circles. Particular attention will be paid to the Irish radical republicans of the 1790s – the United Irishmen – and their efforts to rethink these concepts. Consideration will also be given to how they were deployed in the O'Connellite project; these contexts informed Daniel O'Connell's deeply personal crusade against slavery and framed discussion of the fraught relationship between class and race as it emerged in the Atlantic world at this time.

One should note here the historic distinction between *freedom* and *liberty* in an anglophone context. The concept of liberty (Latin *libertas,* meaning "unbounded" or "unrestricted") centred on the individual and his independence and autonomy – the ability to follow "the life of one's choosing". Liberty required vigilance against the tyranny of government and its infringements on personal autonomy. In a British context, it also became entangled in Protestant resistance to popery, generating the arrogant notion that only an exclusively Protestant polity could grant and sustain "civil and religious liberties". This Protestant version of liberty was counterpointed by authoritarian or despotic systems, notably French and Spanish, that were seen as dictated by their Catholic culture. A late eighteenth-century pamphlet decried French contempt for liberty and their bogus desire to help Ireland with their "black rye-bread, the chesnuts [*sic*], the garlick, the onions, the wooden shoes of the French, who, they are told, are to come and better their condition".[1]

The Protestant concept of liberty did not necessarily consort well with democracy, and it was this version of liberty without democracy that buttressed the British imperial system. The peculiarly English variant of liberty offered a passive right – a negative, the absence of coercion – granted arbitrarily from on high to subjects. The monarch and the state protected the individual from the interference of others, a protection enforced by a strong Hobbesian state – what Bentham called security.[2] Liberty's primary concern was with how an individual was permitted to act within the polity; by contrast, freedom was concerned with membership in that polity. Freedom emphasized exclusion from the polity, promoting the right of all groups within a state to full citizenship and equality of esteem. Liberty stressed separation, while freedom stressed connectedness.

In Ireland, the word *freedom* became widely current only after the French Revolution, when *liberté* was read as equating to freedom rather than liberty. French *liberté* was assumed to have a universal abstract appeal (human liberty or freedom), while the English word *liberty* was restricted to a more specific English or British provenance, confined to particular liberties obtained in a precise historical context (such as the Glorious Revolution). Liberty was limited in extent, associated with the individual as part of a select community freed from general tyranny and despotism. It was constitutional and had ascertainable legal structures. In the nineteenth century, liberty metastasized into liberalism. By contrast, freedom was a positive right wrested by active citizens from a reluctant or coercive state. Freedom was often accompanied by a sense of "freedom from"; it flourished with the collapse of the first British Empire, the rise of Romanticism and the formation of new nation-states. Liberty was bounded, whereas freedom was universal. Liberty was associated with the state and freedom with the nation; the shift in emphasis from liberty to freedom marked the transition from patriot to nationalist. Liberty invoked civil liberties, whereas freedom involved human rights. In late eighteenth-century Ireland, liberty was a Protestant concept and freedom a Catholic one.

Quentin Skinner and Philip Pettit have drawn our attention to the equal prevalence of the concept of "negative liberty", theorized as the absence of constraint, domination or interference.[3] Negative liberty concerns not merely whether this actuality is present in lived experience but also whether the mere potential for it to exist (for example, under a monarchy) equally constitutes a form of servitude. Drawing on an analysis of freedom and slavery in Roman law, this approach focused on the issue of dominion: if rights are capable of being taken away, they are not rights at all but rather licences or privileges (liberties) that are held at discretion. The absence of dependence constitutes the proper mark of the republican citizen. Constraint of liberty does not necessarily require jackboot oppression. True liberty depends on being a citizen of a self-governing republic, while subjects of a monarch are by definition slaves.

A corollary of this central republican argument is that those who acquiesce in slavery deserve to be enslaved. The Irish republican tradition constantly used the rhetoric of "freeman" (the *Freeman's Journal*, for example) and reprobated "slavish" tendencies. For some Irish republicans such as John Binns and John Mitchel, the passivity of enslaved subjects – "happy slaves" – demonstrated their unfitness for democratic freedom, and that explains the paradoxical willingness of these Irish republicans to accept and even defend slavery in America.[4] The same argument had been applied to Catholics under the penal laws. Gustave de Beaumont commented in 1839 on the mistaken acquiescence of Catholics to the penal laws: "The man who goes to sleep, trusting his freedom to the faith of another man, deserves to awake a slave."[5] It was irrelevant whether the laws were executed harshly or not; their very existence on the statute books was an unequivocal demonstration of a society of masters and slaves – Pettit's central observation.[6]

Significantly, the language of slavery was repeatedly applied in eighteenth-century Ireland to link the common experience of the Irish Catholic poor and the Atlantic slave. In 1721 the Irish poor were described as "poor wretches who think themselves blessed if they can obtain a hut worse than the squire's dog kennel, and an acre of ground for potato planting, on condition of being as very slaves as any in America".[7] In the same year, Tadhg Ó Neachtain, a Dublin scholar and scribe, described his fellow Catholics as *schlabhaithe* (slaves).[8] In 1735 the well-known philosopher Bishop George Berkeley quoted a plantation proverb: "If negro was not negro, Irishman would be negro."[9] Lord Chesterfield commented in 1746 that "the poor people of Ireland are used worse than negroes by their lords and masters".[10] By the 1790s this trope had become commonplace, as when Tone described Catholics as political slaves.[11] Edward Wakefield made a revealing comparison in 1812: "The situation of these people [Ulster Catholics] often reminded me of the natives of Jamaica, who were driven to the northern and eastern mountains of that island, when it was taken from the Spaniards in 1655."[12]

Most tellingly of all, the Irish cottiers (agricultural labourers who were paid in kind rather than in cash) used the word *sclábhái* (slave) to describe themselves and their labours. Ó Duinnín's dictionary translates *sclábhaidhe* as "a serf or slave, a workman, a day labourer, an agricultural drudge"; *sclábhaidheacht* means "slavery, servitude, manual labour, spade work".[13] A Munster labourer in 1745 "hoped soon to see the day that he would not be obliged to slave for 5d a day".[14] In 1801 the Cork poet and United Irishman Mícheál Óg Ó Longáin, temporarily reduced to day labouring, described himself as *im dhubh-sclábhaí bheag bhocht* ("a poor little black slave").[15] James McMahon, a Clare labourer, observed in 1834:

> We are worked harder and worse treated than the slaves in the colonies; I understand they are taken care of by their masters when they are sick or old. When we are sick, we must die on the road, if the neighbours do not help us. When we are old, we must go out to beg, if the young ones cannot help us, and that will soon happen with us all; we are getting worse and worse every day, and the landlords are kicking us out of every little holding we have. This last May 28 families were put out, and next May I am sure there will be as many again within five miles of Kilkee; and if something is not done for those who are turned out upon the world without a rag on their backs, God knows what will happen this country! When we suffer all these hardships, is it wonderful our spirits should be broken down; that we should grow grey, and give up the spark at 58 or 60?[16]

McMahon thus overtly compares his condition as a labourer to that of an enslaved subject as he condemns landlords' dislodgments of his fellow workers.

The 1844 evidence of Father Michael Fitzgerald to the Devon Commission, which was exploring the Irish land situation, assailed the evicting landlord: "If he possessed honest feelings, he ought to be ashamed of his Durhams and his South Downs and his interminable fields of corn, tilled by miserable serfs (more miserable than the fellahs of Egypt or the blacks of Cuba), and occupy the place from which human happiness and human enjoyment were rooted out and exterminated."[17] In this appeal, Irish workers are again compared to forced labourers, and the Cuban/Caribbean context is striking here.

This awareness of denial of liberty to Irish Catholics was embedded at elite as well as popular levels. William of Orange, following the Treaty of Limerick, believed that "a number of slaves, too large for the rule of their masters, are at all times a dangerous object in a state".[18] The Williamite tradition had a profoundly anti-democratic effect in Ireland. For Catholics, the Glorious Revolution was one "which, under Providence, preserved us from wooden shoes, and left us free to go barefoot".[19] The jailed Franciscan Séamus Carthún, in his seventeenth-century poem "Deor-chaoineadh na hÉirinn", emphasized the bonding impact on the dispossessed:

> *D'imigh an ainnis oruin i n-énfheacht,*
> *An bocht 's an saibhir, an fann 's an tréinfhear,*
> *An tigherna lear ghaoththuigheadh na céata*
> *An calma neartfur 's fear a' cheachta*
> *Tá tuadh is eaglais faoi éan-ghoin*
> *'s an chroich ar ghualainn gach ein fhir.*
> This disaster has affected us all,
> rich and poor, weak and strong,
> the chief who scattered hundreds,
> the valiant warrior and the ploughman,
> lay and clergy under the same oppression,
> and the cross on every man's shoulder.[20]

The inclusivity of the named social classes and professions underscores the broad effect of such dispossession(s). In 1795 Count Daniel O'Connell of the Derrynane family recalled "the situation of men working as hedgers and ditchers on the estates their ancestors possessed".[21]

Identification between the Irish poor and the slave was argued by the United Irishman Thomas Russell in 1796:

> Are the Irish nation aware that this contest [between republicanism and monarchy] involves the question of the slave trade, the one now of the greatest consequence on the face of the earth? Are they willing to employ their treasure and their blood in support of that system, because England has 70 or 7,000 millions engaged in it, the

only argument that can be adduced in its favour, monstrous as it may appear? Do they know that that horrid traffic spreads its influence over the globe; that it creates and perpetuates barbarism and misery, and prevents the spreading of civilization and religion, in which we profess to believe? Do they know that by it thousands and hundreds of thousands of these miserable Africans are dragged from their innocent families like the miserable Defenders [a secret society that asserted the rights of the Irish poor], transported to various places, and there treated with such a system of cruelty, torment, wickedness and infamy, that it is impossible for language adequately to express its horror and guilt, and which would appear rather to be the work of wicked demons than of men. If this trade is wrong, is it right for the Irish nation to endeavour to continue it? And does not every man who contributes to the war contribute to its support? After this statement of the immediate and remote consequences of war, after its appearing that every man who pays taxes contributes to it and to every act of the government of his country, is it not evident that it is not only the right but the essential duty of every man to interest himself in the conduct of the government.[22]

The rhetoric in this call to action for the Irish to work against the slave trade relies on a comparison between the Defenders and enslaved African subjects. In this pamphlet, Russell courageously (if foolhardily) publicly proclaimed himself a member of the radical republican United Irishmen, by then a banned organization, and committed to supporting a French invasion. Its publication immediately precipitated a warrant for his arrest.

Russell was an outspoken advocate of enslaved peoples throughout his political career. His 1792 treatise translated his critique of English justice to the exploitation and violence of plantation slavery:

> How much selfishness and ostentation must we suspect in the boasts of the English, that their laws are thus free, and declarative of the natural rights of mankind, while the same laws hold thousands of our fellow creatures in a bondage worse than that of Pharaoh. There is perhaps no part of the earth where beasts of burden are so much oppressed as the negroes are in the sugar plantations. They are sixteen hours in the service of cruel masters; and the shouts of their drivers, and the cracks of the whip on their naked bodies, which cuts out small pieces of flesh at almost every stroke, are heard all day in the fields.[23]

Russell's comparison of the lives of the Irish poor to those of Atlantic slaves infused many other writings and speeches through this closing decade of the eighteenth century. The Presbyterian minister T.L. Birch assailed Henry Grattan, the leading Irish reform politician, in 1792 for encouraging slavery by "wishing to send away to the West Indies [Irish] beef, pork, linen cloth and even herrings" and importing "a liquid poison called rum".[24] Theobald Wolfe Tone, another United Irishman, observed in 1794 that the slaves in the West Indies were better treated than the Irish poor.[25] In 1796 the *Northern Star* compared Ireland to the West Indies: "Ireland exhibits a specimen of close colonial government. One of the settlements in India or one of the sugar islands could not be less trusted to either natives or settlers."[26] The United Irishman John Sweeney reiterated the same point in his 1798 address to the citizens of Cork city: "The poor wretches of this country are reduced to a state of degradation below that of the negroes of the West Indies."[27] At the close of the eighteenth century, an English Whig visitor, George Cooper, repeated the comparison to draw attention to the extreme wretchedness of the poor Irish: "The condition of the West Indian negro is a paradise to it. The slave in our colonies has meat to eat and distilled spirits to drink, whilst the life of the Irish peasant is that of a savage who feeds upon milk and roots [potatoes]."[28]

The English radical John Thelwall had made the same comparison on 18 September 1795, using his meditation on the extension of human sympathies across the Atlantic to give force to his argument for Ireland's independence.

> But it is impossible this system should succeed. The light of reason has gone abroad, humanity has warmed the breast of man; and we have found (strange indeed that we should have been so long in making the discovery!) that even the sooty *African* is our brother: that even the poor "whip-galled slave", in the *West Indies*, deserves our commiseration: and, this being the case, do you suppose we can be blind to this still more evident truth, that the *English, Scotch and Irish*, are one and all the same – that they are united and bound together in the chains of inseparable interest – and that to attempt to employ one of them, as an instrument of coercion against the other, is an attempt to make men the assassins of each other ... *think not to make us brutes and savages, to tear each other's breasts, we are all men,* WE ARE ALL BRETHREN, *and will not shed the blood of those whose manly hearts are warmed with affection for us, and whose generous virtues call for our admiration and esteem!* ... For can we be extravagant enough to suppose, that, by mere military force, we can retain *Ireland* as a dependant colony? No – She has a right to be considered as an equal part; possessing all the immunities that we ought to possess; and, therefore, in subjection she never will be held.[29]

The ancillary point could be made that the Irish gentry were just a pack of slave-owners. The radical Catholic priest Father James Coigly pointedly challenged them: "Why have you rejected the glorious title of United Irishmen to accept that of West Indian bloodhounds?"[30] Lord Charlemont reported that he had personally heard the Earl of Carrick declare, after he had first employed his very young son (Lord Ikerrin) in hunting down Whiteboys (Irish agrarian protesters) in Kilkenny, "I have blooded my young dog. I have fleshed my bloodhound."[31]

The native Irish were routinely compared to Negroes – "inferior, semi-brutal people, incapable of managing the affairs of their country".[32] A 1799 pamphlet, reprising Swift's *Modest Proposal*, made the point satirically:

> As the lower classes of Irish women are remarkable for being excellent breeders, we shall certainly have a great number of young people, more than can find employment at home; and shall we not be grateful to the English if merely to accommodate you, they take these off to recruit their troops and shipping, to fill their seraglios, to fight the battles of their honourable merchants in the East or to replace the waste of their Negroes in the West India islands, or in their newly founded empires of Sierra Leona and around Botany Bay?[33]

Once this eighteenth-century context of comparing the Irish Catholic poor with Atlantic slaves is established, we can more readily understand the striking success of Olaudah Equiano's Irish visit. Equiano, an Igbo-born African enslaved in the Atlantic world and later prominent in the abolition movement, was promoting his highly influential autobiographical work *The Interesting Narrative of the Life of Olaudah Equiano*, whose ninth edition was published in Dublin in 1790. He brought with him letters of introduction from the American confidential agent, novelist and adventurer Thomas Attwood Digges, a friend of Tone and Russell in Belfast. Equiano spent nine months in Ireland, hosted by the Quakers and the United Irishmen, especially James Napper Tandy in Dublin and Samuel Neilson in Belfast, who can be considered the leading republicans in their respective communities at that time. Equiano sold nineteen hundred copies of his *Narrative* in Ireland and was particularly welcomed in Belfast, then a significant port.

In the eighteenth century the constant shuttling of ships tied and untied connections across and between disparate worlds. A commonality emerged in Atlantic port cities, on every shore of that great ocean, where emerged the most complex blending of peoples and cultures.[34] Late eighteenth-century Belfast prided itself on its cosmopolitanism. In the Belfast Academy were "to be seen young lads of colour, sent by their fathers for education, both from the East and the West Indies, intermingled with the sons of the proudest gentry and nobility in the land".[35] At the Belfast Bastille Day procession in 1790, two Volunteers carried a portrait of Mirabeau with the motto drawn from his oration on the rights of man: "Can the African slave trade, though morally wrong, be politically right?"[36] That same year, in a procession in favour of the popular candidates in the Dublin election, one of the participants was "a Negro boy well dressed and holding on high the cap of liberty"[37]; this was Tony Small, the confidant and servant of Lord Edward FitzGerald. These encounters stimulated Irish engagement with anti-slavery and the centrality of its vocabulary to the radical movement.

A half-century later, Frederick Douglass demonstrated a remarkable exercise in empathy during his Irish visit of 1845: "I see much here to remind me of my former condition, and I confess I should be ashamed to lift my voice against American slavery, but that I know the cause of humanity is one the world over. He who really and truly feels for the American slave cannot steel his heart to the woes of others."[38] In an astonishing gesture of solidarity, the "Negroes of Antigua, Tobago and British Guiana" subsequently contributed to Irish famine relief.[39] Another well-informed American visitor, Asenath Nicholson, compared the position of American slaves and the Irish lower classes on the eve of the famine: "Never had I seen slaves so degraded. These poor creatures are in as virtual bondage to their landlords and superiors as is possible for the mind and body to be."[40] In Harriet Beecher Stowe's *Uncle Tom's Cabin* (1852), a quotation from the Irish radical lawyer John Philpott Curran begins chapter 37 (titled "Liberty"), in reference to the celebrated case of the Jamaican slave James Somerset.[41] A reference to Thomas Moore's "Weep Not for Those" opens chapter 26, a further striking example of how the rhetorics of Irish radicalism and abolitionism intersected.[42]

British trade brought Ireland into closer contact with slavery in another way: the country imported slave products – sugar, rum, tobacco and cotton. This brought up the problem of taste. Tea, tobacco, coffee, chocolate and sugar were all tied up with slavery and were its embedded, if invisible, products in the freshly integrated Atlantic world of the eighteenth century. Seventy per cent of slaves worked in sugar plantations, and apparently innocent domestic consumption was accordingly tainted – ladies sipping sweetened tea were literally tasting slavery. There is a match between this shift in sensibility, the rise of abolitionism and the popularity of anti-consumption campaigns, especially among women.[43] In 1792 the Quaker merchants the Grubbs of Clonmel announced that they "respectfully inform their customers that they will discontinue the sale of West India sugar when present stocks are exhausted, until it ceases to be the cause of the slavery and death of such a number of their fellow creatures".[44]

The United Irishmen, America and the West Indies

Ideas about slavery circulated across and among the Caribbean, America and Ireland, creating a vigorous circuit of intellectual and political exchanges. Plantation slavery and consciousness of the West Indies was cited widely in Irish discourse at home and in the diaspora. America occupied an evocative if ambiguous rhetorical space as the "land of liberty", a phrase widely used for advertising emigrant ships from 1783 onwards. The Irish insistence on rejecting "slave status" fostered the construction of America as the land of liberty after its revolution, but this rested on a paradox, given the failure of the Americans to end slavery.

As repression of radicals mounted in the 1790s, the attraction of America intensified. In the 1790s alone, sixty thousand Irish entered the United States, the bulk of them political rather than economic migrants. It was only in 1803 that the British Navigation Acts restricted the number of passengers and tripled the cost of the Atlantic voyage; throughout the United Irish period, emigration remained cheap and accessible. Between 1776 and 1809 an astonishingly high proportion of immigrants to America – more than half – were Irish (150,000 out of 273,000). This gives an upper limit for the removal from Ireland of those with radical and United Irish sympathies within what was still a heavily northern and Dissenter emigrant stream. Two-thirds of these predominantly Presbyterian emigrants were drawn from Ulster, most leaving from the heavily politicized and dominantly Dissenter hinterlands of Derry and Belfast. Nearly 100,000 radical Presbyterians may have emigrated from Ireland during the revolutionary period, facilitating a decisive transformation of the political dynamic of Ulster. The cumulative effect was to dismantle the United Irish leadership there after 1798. By 1803 they were reduced to "a rope of sand . . . here and there a particle but without power".[45] Another commentator noted that their "masses of men [were] almost pulverised into banditti" by the end of the summer of 1798.[46]

After 1798 the United Irishmen were scattered to America, to Napoleon's Irish Legion, to Botany Bay, to the Silesian coalmines, to the fleets and, importantly, to the West Indies. Reconstruction of the shattered debris of this radical diaspora is still in its early stages.[47] In the United States, United Irish societies are known to have existed in the 1790s in Pennsylvania (Philadelphia, Wilmington and Montgomery County), Delaware, Maryland (Baltimore), South Carolina (Charleston), New York (Albany) and Ohio. The Philadelphia society was by far the most celebrated and attracted the ire of the federalists. Some alleged it to harbour an assassination committee and categorized the United Irishmen as the "dagger men of Philadelphia". William Cobbett assailed them as "a reckless and rebellious tribe of Jacobins . . . factious villains which Great Britain and Ireland have vomited from their shores". He also claimed that in Virginia and the Carolinas "free Negroes have already been admitted into the conspiracy of the United Irishmen". Others claimed that "the negroes of St Domingo and Guadaloupe" had been infected by the United Irishmen and were "sufficiently numerous to raise collections and transmit them to the insurgents in Ireland".

On 5 July 1803, some hard-line magistrates in North Wexford received an anonymous warning about the likelihood of their cruelties provoking a second rebellion:

> It is horrid to think of joining a second rebellion whilst it can be prevented with ease by the gentlemen. Let them not think that we will stand to be cut like dogs while others are slurping and feasting on the industry of the poor. . . . We were destroyed these five years past by tyranny and they want to send away the industrious people of the country to the field of slaughter whilst their fellows will remain persecuting the remainder at home. If they want good men, let them go and bring them back from Botany Bay, from the East Indies and all other parts of the world they were dispersed to.

New Geneva barracks and the adjacent Duncannon Fort in Waterford Harbour acted as a "slave market" where convicts deemed capable of military service were unceremoniously conscripted. At least fifteen hundred were drafted into the "condemned regiments" and dispatched to the West Indies – effectively a death sentence, given their susceptibility to diseases such as yellow fever and malaria. Nine hundred more "volunteered" to serve in other regiments of the British army. In 1793 the British invaded Saint-Dominigue (renamed Haiti after its revolution) in support of French slavers, essentially to prevent a spillover to Jamaica. They were forced out by 1798; more than half of the British troops who embarked on this campaign – "condemned regiments" with massive numbers of Irish recruits – died, usually of disease.[48] Four hundred were legally banished, scattering mainly to France and America. Thousands more, drawn mainly from Ulster, were forced out or left under more anonymous circumstances. In 1810, when County Down vernacular poet Andrew M'Kenzie published his *Poems and Songs on Different Subjects* in Belfast, no fewer than forty-five of his subscribers were from Jamaica.

These reciprocities and fluxes[49] across the Green Atlantic were also evident in the Irish reaction to Toussaint L'Ouverture.[50] Many exiled United Irishmen had joined maroon colonies in Jamaica in 1799:

> A vast number of United Irishmen, transported from this kingdom, have been landed there [Jamaica] and incautiously drafted into the regiments. As soon as they got arms into their hands, they deserted, and fled into the mountains, where they have been joined by large bodies of the natives and such of the French as were in the island. There have already been some engagements between this party and the King's troops; several have been killed and wounded on both sides.[51]

An example was Hugh Boyd McGuckian, a veteran of 1798 and former law agent of the celebrated radical Arthur O'Connor, who returned to Ireland to partic-ipate in planning the 1803 Emmet insurrection. McGuckian subsequently fled to Jamaica, where he joined the French army, conspired with the local slaves and devised a thwarted plan to seize the island from the British.[52] Another County Antrim United Irishman, McClelland, who had sought refuge in the West Indies engineered the blackballing and shunning of a British regiment's officers in Jamaica for their harsh treatment of Belfast women in 1798.[53]

The veteran United Irishman James Napper Tandy, although based in France, disapproved of the ruthless French suppression of the Toussaint insurrection: "We are all of the same family, black and white, the work of the same creator."[54] In 1808 John Sweeney named one of his sons Toussaint. The black revolutionary's struggle also engaged the attention of the Irish "rhyming weaver" and United Irishman James Orr, of Ballycarry, County Antrim. His "Toussaint's Farewell to St Domingo" (originally published in September 1805) is full of Irish resonance:

> Can ye look, without grief, on your land's devastation?
> Can ye think, without rage, on your foe's usurpation?
> Are ye men? Are ye soldiers? and shall the great nation
> Enslave this, our small one? – No! curs'd be her chain![55]

The apostasy of the English radical generation led to their being at once fasci-nated, repelled and tortured by L'Ouverture, Despard and Emmet – emblems of a fate they had personally shrunk from, and therefore accusing ghosts for the failure of political nerve of the English Romantics of the 1790s.

A further way of exploring reciprocities across the "Black" and "Green" Atlantics of the eighteenth century is to envisage gains to the New World system as being balanced by losses to the Irish one. An entire generation of rad-ical leadership was removed from Ireland in the 1790s, by exile, transportation or hanging. The effect was the dismantling of the United Irish leadership in Ulster after 1798. The upshot was a profound change in the political character of the province. In Ireland this cull led to the retrenchment of radicalism for a generation. Given the lack of an available public sphere, politics relapsed into sectarian backwaters, as seen in the brutal Orange–Ribbon disputes of the 1810s. The cull of United Irish activists had precipitated a lull in radical politics.

Daniel O'Connell

We can understand Daniel O'Connell's sustained and principled involvement in anti-slavery only against the long-standing context of Irish interest in slavery and the widespread appropriation of its metaphors and tropes to describe Irish conditions. O'Connell, the undisputed leader of Irish Catholics in the first half of the nineteenth century, constantly used Byron's "Hereditary Bondsman" image to describe and inspire Irish Catholics. In 1814 he reached for the analogy when confronted by the continued refusal of Catholic emancipation: "I did imagine we had ceased to be whitewashed negroes, and had thrown off for them [the Whigs] all traces of the colour of servitude."[56] At the Clare election in 1828, O'Connell asked rhetorically whether Irish Catholics were "like negroes to be lashed by their drivers to the slave market and sold to the highest bidder".[57] He called the Irish people "crawling slaves" in 1839.[58]

In 1845 O'Connell reviewed an ambitious float in a Cork parade, presented by the local coopers. Two youths stood beneath a tree. One, representing Africa, held the label "Free" and displayed broken chains. The other, portraying Ireland, was tightly bound, with the inscription "A slave still" around his neck. The float stopped before O'Connell and "Africa" praised the liberator for advancing his freedom; he then pointed to his fettered companion and declaimed Thomas Moore's lines:

> Oh, where's the slave so lowly,
> Condemned to chains unholy,
> Who, could he burst
> His bonds accursed,
> Would pine beneath them slowly?

"Ireland" then knelt before O'Connell, who broke his chains. As the float moved off through the city, "Ireland" brandished his freed arms to the multitude lining the streets.[59]

In 1831 O'Connell called for "speedy, immediate abolition"[60] of slavery throughout the world. He remained consistent and principled on this issue even when it hurt him with certain constituencies. His vehemence – "we do not want blood-stained money"[61] – split New World Repeal societies.[62] In his opinion, shared oppression should have nurtured a political affinity between Irish Catholics and enslaved Africans, a principled internationalism, and he rebuked Irish "cruelty" in supporting the slavery cause in the West Indies and America.[63] O'Connell personally declined to set foot in the United States while it remained a slave society. He refused to set limits to his principles and would not allow his ethical vision to be constrained by Irish concerns. In 1830 he observed: "Ireland and Irishmen should be foremost in seeking to effect the emancipation of mankind."[64] In 1845 he stressed: "My sympathy with distress is not confined within the narrow bounds of my own green island – it extends itself to every corner of the earth."[65] His efforts were recognized within America and the Caribbean. In 1833 the African American church in New York held a meeting honouring O'Connell, "the uncompromising advocate of universal emancipation, the friend of oppressed Africans and their descendants and the unadulterated rights of man".[66] O'Connell's son John pointedly stated in his *Repealer's Dictionary* (Dublin, 1845) that, because of slavery, liberty did not exist in America.

Conclusion

This essay has tracked the rhetoric of Irish slavery as well as the cultural and political reciprocities among Ireland, the Caribbean and America in the late eighteenth century, at both the elite and popular levels. It also seeks to broaden the insular horizons of Irish historiography. It reflects the Irish experience of the Enlightenment and its representative others at home and abroad, viewed through the optic of its diasporic relationship with the Atlantic world across the long eighteenth century. Used carefully, the concept of diaspora can transcend national histories, generating the space for a transnational approach especially appropriate to the study of migration and globalization. A history of Ireland that is only about Ireland is too rigid; the Irish experience as a historically rooted concept transcends the island.

This approach also has repercussions for how we conceive of the Irish abroad. The standard treatment revolves around the concept of assimilation – slow absorption of the Irish into their host countries. This is usually understood as occurring in stages: a national identity (Irish) gives way to an ethnic identity (Irish-American, for example) that finally evolves in its mature phase into a fully fledged immigrant identity (American, for example). Migration is generally regarded as voluntary and assimilation as normative. This model is challenged by the concept of diaspora, with its more troubled emphasis on uprooting, coerced migration, retention of interest in the homeland, and an enduringly partial absorption. The idea of diaspora retains catastrophic dispersal and estrangement as a continuous historical phenomenon, not just as an originating moment. Culturally conceived, the concept of diaspora involves processes of unsettling, recombination and hybridization. Diaspora is in this sense a process, not a product, a historical formation in constant flux.

The Caribbean model of cultural hybridity and creolization is useful in broadening excessively rigid views of Irish society in the eighteenth and nineteenth centuries. In Barbados, assimilation had occurred by the late eighteenth century, with the absorption of the Irish Catholic poor – former indentured servants – into the creolized poor white underclass. It is intriguing to find the Callan (County Kilkenny) shopkeeper Amhlaoibh Ó Súilleabháin strongly suggesting an affinity between Ireland and Montserrat in 1831:

> Is clos dom gur ab í an teanga Gaodhalach ur teanga mathara a Montsearrat san India shiar ó aimsir Oilebher Cromuil, noch do dhíbir cuid de clan Gaodhal ó Éirinn gus an oileán sin Montsearrat. Labartar an Gaoidhilge ann le daoine dubha agus bána. Muise mo ghrádh croíd na díbearthaigh bochta Gaodlacha; cia dubh bán iad, is ionmhuin liomsa clanna Gaodhal. [I hear that Irish is the mother tongue in Montserrat in the West Indies, since the time of Oliver Cromwell, who banished some of the Irish to that island. Now Irish is spoken there by both black and white people. Well, the unfortunate Irish exiles are the love of my heart: whether black or white, all the children of the Gael are well regarded by me.][67]

In 1926 W.B. Yeats produced his profound meditation on Irish history "The Tower". In it he praised the autonomous individual who can resist the gravity of history:

> The pride of people that were
> Bound neither to Cause nor to State,
> Neither to **slaves** that were spat on,
> Nor to the **tyrants** that spat.

This vocabulary, as we have seen, has itself a long genealogy in Irish history.

Notes

1. *Reform or Ruin: Take Your Choice!* (Dublin, 1798), 27.
2. Thomas Hobbes (1588–1679) provided the classic defence of the strong state in his *Leviathan* (1651), while Jeremy Bentham (1748–1832) was the great protagonist of utilitarianism in the late eighteenth century.
3. Martin van Gelderen and Quentin Skinner, eds., *Republicanism*, vol. 1, *Republicanism and Constitutionalism in Early Modern Europe* (Cambridge: Cambridge University Press, 2002); Martin van Gelderen and Quentin Skinner, eds., *Republicanism*, vol. 2, *The Values of Republicanism in Early Modern Europe* (Cambridge: Cambridge University Press, 2002); Philip Pettit, "Republicanism American, French, and Irish: The Tree of Liberty", *Field Day Review* 1 (2005): 29–43.
4. John Binns, *Recollections of the Life of John Binns* (Philadelphia: Parry and M'Millan, 1854); James Quinn, *John Mitchel* (Dublin: University College Dublin Press, 2008); Thomas Kennealy, *The Great Shame and the Triumph of the Irish in the English-Speaking World* (London: Chatto and Windus, 1999), 308–12.
5. Gustave de Beaumont, *Ireland* (Cambridge, MA: Harvard University Press, 2006), 72.
6. Philip Pettit, *Republicanism: A Theory of Freedom and Government* (New York: Oxford University Press, 1997).
7. *Mist's Weekly Journal*, 30 September 1721.
8. M. Ní Chléirigh, ed., *Eolas ar an domhan* (Baile Átha Cliath: Oifig an tSolathair, 1944), 9.
9. George Berkeley, *A Word to the Wise: Address by the Bishop of Cloyne to the Roman Catholics of Ireland* (Dublin: M. Rhames, 1735).
10. Chesterfield to Bishop of Waterford, 1 October 1746, in Philip Mahon, *History of England from the Peace of Utrecht to the Peace of Versailles* (London: John Murray, 1858), 5:123.
11. Theobald Wolfe Tone, *The Writings of Theobald Wolfe Tone: 1763–1798* (New York: Oxford University Press, 1998–2007), 1:296–97.
12. Edward Wakefield, *An Account of Ireland, Statistical and Political* (London: Longman, 1814), 730.
13. The word *schlabaí* appeared in Hiberno-English as *slavey*, a word used to describe hired help such as Nora Barnacle in Finn's Hotel. Joyce's stated aim was to refract Irish society through "the cracked looking-glass of a servant".
14. Cited in David Dickson, "Jacobitism in Eighteenth-Century Ireland: A Munster Perspective", *Eighteenth-Century Ireland* 19, no. 3/4 (2004): 50.
15. Cited in B. Ó Conchúir, *Scríobhaithe Chorcaí, 1700–1850* (Baile Átha Cliath: Clóchomhar, 1982), 107.

16. Evidence of James MacMahon, a labourer of Kilfearagh parish, Kilkee, cited in Noel Crowley, ed., *Poverty before the Famine: County Clare, 1835* (Ennis: Clasp, 1996), 91–92.

17. Evidence of Father Michael Fitzgerald, Devon Commission Report on the Occupation of Land in Ireland, vol. 2, British Parliamentary Papers, 1845 (Dublin, Ireland: A. Thom, 1848), 790–92.

18. *All's Well: A Reply to the Author of The Alarm, by a Protestant of the Church of Ireland* (Dublin: Bernard Dornin, 1783), 13–14.

19. William Sampson and Thomas Russell, *Review of the Lion of Old England; or The Democracy Confounded* (Belfast, Northern Star, 1794), 47.

20. Séamus Carthún, "Deorchaoineadh na hÉireann" [Ireland's tearful lament], in *Dánta na mBráthar Mionúr*, ed. Cuthbert Mhág Craith (Baile Átha Cliath: Institiúid Árd-Léinn Bhaile Átha Cliath, 1967), 1:251–55. My thanks to my colleague Peter MacQuillan for this reference.

21. Jean Agnew, ed., *The Drennan–McTier Letters, 1776–1819* (Dublin: Irish Manuscripts Commission, 1998), 2:146–47.

22. Thomas Russell, *A Letter to the People of Ireland, on the Present Situation of the Country* (Belfast: Northern Star, 1796), 22–23.

23. Thomas Russell, "Enslavement of Africans", 11 February 1792 (Dublin, Ireland: National Archives), Rebellion Papers 620/19/56.

24. T.L. Birch, letter to the *Northern Star*, 6 February 1792 (Dublin, Ireland: National Archives), Rebellion Papers 620/19/53.

25. Tone, *Collected Writings*, 3:44.

26. *Northern Star*, 17–20 June 1796.

27. [John Sweeney], *Address to the Patriots of Imokilly* (reprint: Dublin, 1978).

28. George Cooper, *Letters on the Irish Nation Written During a Visit to That Kingdom in the Autumn of the Year 1799* (London: J. Davis, 1800), 72–73.

29. Gregory Claeys, ed., *The Politics of English Jacobinism: Writings of John Thelwall* (Philadelphia: Pennsylvania State University, 1995), 242–43.

30. Daire Keogh, ed., *A Patriot Priest: The Life of Fr James Coigly, 1761–1798* (Cork: Cork University Press, 1998), 68.

31. Cited in W.H.P. Lecky, *A History of Ireland in the Eighteenth Century* (London: Longmans, Green, 1898), 2:40. The original is in the Royal Irish Academy (hereafter RIA), Ms. 12/R/7, f. 50.

32. [W.J. MacNevin], *Pieces of Irish History* (New York: Bernard Dornin, 1807).

33. *A Sketch of the Most Obvious Causes of the Poverty, Ignorance and General Want of Civilisation amongst the Peasantry of Ireland* (Dublin: J. Milliken, 1799), 32.

34. Peter Linebaugh and Marcus Rediker, *The Many-Headed Hydra: Sailors, Slaves, Commoners and the Hidden History of the Revolutionary Atlantic* (Boston: Beacon, 2000).

35. William Grimshaw, *Incidents Recalled* (Philadelphia: G.B. Zieber, 1848), 17.

36. John Lawless, *The Belfast Politics Enlarged* (Belfast: D. Lyons, 1818), 532.

37. William Drennan to Samuel McTier, 3 May 1790, in Agnew, *Drennan–McTier Letters*, 1:349.

38. Frederick Douglass, *Narrative of the Life of Frederick Douglass, an American Slave, Written by Himself* (Dublin: Webb and Chapman, 1846), 1:140–41.

39. Christine Kinealy, "Potatoes, Providence and Philanthropy: The Role of Private Charity during the Irish Famine", in *The Irish World Wide: History, Heritage, Identity*, ed. Patrick O'Sullivan, vol. 6, *The Meaning of the Famine* (Leicester: Leicester University Press, 1997), 164.

40. Cited in Maureen Murphy, "Asenath Nicholson and the Famine in Ireland", in *Women in Irish History*, ed. Maryann Valiulis and Mary O'Dowd (Dublin: Wolfhound Press, 1997), 112.

41. James Somerset was carried from Jamaica to London in 1769 by his owner, Charles Stewart of Boston. In 1771 he escaped but was recaptured and placed on a ship bound for Jamaica. The judge, Lord Mansfield, ruled that Somerset should be freed, as "the claim of slavery can never be supported". This set a crucial precedent in English Common Law, establishing that a slave who set foot on English soil became free.

42. George Bornstein, *The Colors of Zion: Blacks, Jews and Irish from 1845 to 1945* (Cambridge, MA: Harvard University Press, 2011), 87–88.

43. Charlotte Sussmann, *Consuming Anxieties: Consumer Protest, Gender and British Slavery, 1713–1833* (Stanford, CA: Stanford University Press, 2000).

44. *Clonmel Gazette*, 13 February 1792.

45. Cited in Thomas Bartlett, "Dublin Castle and Robert Emmet", in *Reinterpreting Emmet*, ed. A. Dolan, P. Geoghegan and D. Jones (Dublin: Irish Academic Press, 2007), 13.

46. Henry Alexander to Thomas Pelham, 4 September 1798, Add. Ms. 33, 106, British Library, London.

47. For a beginning, see Kevin Whelan, "The Green Atlantic in the Eighteenth Century", in *A New Imperial History: Culture, Identity and Modernity in Britain and the Empire, 1660–1840*, ed. Kathleen Wilson (Cambridge: Cambridge University Press, 2004), 216–38.

48. Saint-Dominigue/Haiti was the first non-European state to detach itself successfully from empire. The French under Napoleon sought again to impose slavery in 1802 and lost fifty thousand soldiers in two years. The Republic of Haiti was declared in 1804. Franklin Knight, "The Haitian Revolution and the Notion of Human Rights", *Journal of the Historical Society* 5, no. 3 (2005): 391–416.

49. While this chapter focuses on radicals, black men also served in the British army in Ireland; John Ellis, "The Black, the Red and the Green: Black Redcoats and Ireland During the Eighteenth and Nineteenth Centuries", *Iron Sword* 23, no. 94 (2003):

409–24 (the appendix lists fifty known soldiers). See also W. Hart, "Africans in Eighteenth-Century Ireland", *Irish Historical Studies* 23, no. 129 (2002): 19–32.

50.   *Bonaparte in the West Indies; or, the History of Toussaint Louverture, the African Hero* (Dublin, 1804) ran through at least four editions.

51.   Alexander Marsden to Lord Castlereagh, 10 October 1799, in Charles Vane, ed., *Memoirs and Correspondence of Viscount Castlereagh* (London, 1850), 2:417. See also Michael Duffy, *Soldiers, Sugar and Sea Power: The British Expeditions to the West Indies and the Wars against Revolutionary France* (Oxford: Oxford University Press, 1987).

52.   Paris, France, Archives Nationales, A.N.P., F7 6338, dos. 7, 123: Geoghegan, *Emmet*, 129, 188.

53.   Robert Magill Young, ed., *Historical notices of old Belfast and its vicinity; a selection from the mss. collected by William P* (Belfast: M. Ward and Co., 1896), 85.

54.   James Napper Tandy to James Tandy, Dublin, 1 Prairial, Year 10 [17 June 1802] (Dublin, Ireland: National Archives), Rebellion Papers 620/12.

55.   James Orr, *The Posthumous Works of James Orr of Ballycarry, with a Sketch of His Life* (Belfast, 1817), 31–33.

56.   *Select Speeches of Daniel O'Connell, M.P.*, ed. J. O'Connell (Dublin: James Duffy, 1865), 1:408.

57.   Cited in Fergus O'Ferrall, *Catholic Emancipation: Daniel O'Connell and the Birth of Irish Democracy, 1820–30* (Dublin: Gill and Macmillan, 1985), 196.

58.   Cited in Séan Ó Faoláin, *King of the Beggars: A Life of Daniel O'Connell* (London: Thomas Nelson and Sons, 1938), ix.

59.   Gary Owens, "Nationalism Without Words: Symbolism and Ritual Behaviour at Repeal Monster Meetings of 1843–5", in *Irish Popular Culture, 1650–1850*, ed. J.S. Donnelly and Kerby Miller (Dublin: Irish Academic Press, 1998), 250–51.

60.   "Daniel O'Connell upon American Slavery", *Liberator*, 9 June 1843, 8.

61.   Ibid., 31.

62.   Douglas Riach, "Daniel O'Connell and American Anti-slavery", *Irish Historical Studies* 20 (1976): 3–25; Douglas Riach, "O'Connell and Slavery", in *The World of Daniel O'Connell*, ed. Donal McCartney (Dublin: Mercier, 1980), 175–85; Maurice Bric, "Daniel O'Connell and the Debate on Anti-slavery, 1820–50", in *History and the Public Sphere: Essays in Honour of John A. Murphy*, ed. Tom Dunne and Laurence Geary (Cork: Cork University Press, 2005): 69–82; Angela Murphy, *American Slavery, Irish Freedom: Abolition, Immigrant Citizenship and the Transatlantic Movement for Irish Repeal* (Baton Rouge: Louisiana State University Press, 2010).

63.   Cited in Bruce Nelson, *Irish Nationalists and the Making of the Irish Race* (Princeton, NJ: Princeton University Press, 2012).

64.   "Daniel O'Connell upon American Slavery", 7.

65.   Ibid., 33.

66. Cited in Gilbert Osofsky, "Abolitionists, Irish Immigrants and the Dilemmas of Romantic Nationalism", *American Historical Review* 80 (October 1975), 892.

67. Amhlaoibh Ó Súilleabháin, *Cinnlae Amhlaoibh Ui Shúileabháin/The Diary of Humphrey O'Sullivan*, ed. Michael McGrath (London: Irish Texts Society, 1930–36), 3:32.

Chapter 5

Irish Encounters with the Jamaican Plantocracy, 1814–1838

KARINA WILLIAMSON

THIS ESSAY ADDS TO NINI RODGERS'S GROUND-BREAKING history *Ireland, Slavery and Anti-slavery, 1612–1865* by providing case studies of five Irishmen who lived in Jamaica in the period leading up to the end of slavery. The source is a cluster of works, written by four of the men themselves, which were all published in the space of five years, from 1835 to 1839. The general scarcity of printed works by Irish residents of the British West Indies (in contrast to the abundance by English and Scottish authors) gives these texts special value as relatively rare first-hand accounts of Irish experiences in the Caribbean. On this evidence, the Irish in Jamaica found themselves out of step with the attitudes of the planters and merchants who formed the ruling class of the island. All but one of the Irishmen in this study came into conflict with the plantocracy over issues of the treatment of slaves or former slaves (apprentices) in the years between 1834 and 1838.

The first and most eminent of these men was Howe Peter Browne, second Marquess of Sligo (1788–1845), who was governor of Jamaica from 1834 to 1836. The others were Dowell O'Reilly (1795–1855), attorney general of Jamaica from 1831 to 1855; Richard Robert Madden (1798–1886), who recorded his experiences as a special magistrate in Jamaica in *A Twelvemonth's Residence in the West Indies, During the Transition from Slavery to Apprenticeship* (1835) in 1833–34;

James Kelly, author of *Jamaica in 1831: Being a Narrative of Seventeen Years' Residence in That Island* (1838); and Benjamin McMahon, author of *Jamaica Plantership: Eighteen Years Employed in the Planting Line in That Island* (1839).

The Marquess of Sligo

In 1835 a free settlement was established in the hills above Spanish Town, Jamaica, and named Sligoville in honour of Lord Sligo – not because he was a colonial figurehead but in gratitude for his sympathy with the slaves during the troubled period of transition from slavery to apprenticeship, following the Slavery Abolition Act of August 1833. However, his efforts to ensure that the new system functioned with justice and humanity earned him the bitter enmity of the ruling class of the island; even after his departure, "violent attacks" on him, describing him as "the calamity of Jamaica", were still being made in the House of Assembly.[1] In 1838 Sligo published an anonymous account of his travails as governor in a book titled *Jamaica under the Apprenticeship System*; writing in the third person, he said that "the line of conduct which he adopted towards the negroes certainly gained him their confidence; but at the same time it placed an invincible barrier between him and the planters".[2]

The Slavery Abolition Act provided the broad framework for emancipation throughout the colonies, leaving the detailed terms of regulation of the apprenticeship system to be laid down by individual colonial legislatures. The main provisions of the parliamentary act were that from 1 August 1834 the ex-slaves had to serve as apprentices for a limited period (four years for domestic and non-praedial workers, six for field labourers), during which they would be required to work forty-five hours a week for their former owners. They would receive no wages but would be supplied with food, clothing, medical attention and such other allowances as had been required under slave laws. Special (stipendiary) magistrates, appointed and paid by the British government, were to act as protectors of the apprentices and arbitrators in disputes between them and their employers. Finally, the colossal sum of twenty million pounds was allocated for compensation of owners for the loss of their slaves, to be paid once local legislation had been passed putting the abolition programme into effect.

The Jamaican Abolition Act was passed by the House of Assembly in December 1833 and quickly confirmed by the secretary of state, overriding criticisms by the Colonial Office's legal adviser, James Stephen (1789–1859, son of the famous abolitionist), that it showed bias in certain respects towards the masters and against the apprentices, failed to define terms and was imprecise in its use of language.[3] The vagueness of both this act and the subsequent Act in Aid of the Abolition Act (July 1834) left opportunities for obstructing the governor and his officers which the planters were not slow to exploit. Sligo's own verdict after four years' struggle was that "much abuse of the intentions of the Abolition Act has taken place – and that every species of evasion within the letter of the law – certainly far beyond its spirit – has prevailed".[4]

During this period, appointment to the governorship of Jamaica was a poisoned chalice. It entailed mediation between various warring parties: the Assembly versus the Colonial Office; plantation owners versus their former slaves; planters versus missionaries. Sligo was not alone in finding the colony almost ungovernable under such conditions; in 1838 his successor, Sir Lionel Smith, protested privately to the secretary of state that it was "impossible for anyone to answer for the conduct of the House of Assembly. Many are there in the island who would be delighted to get up an insurrection for the pleasure of destroying the negroes and missionaries. They are, in fact, mad."[5]

Sligo recounted in detail the stratagems employed by the House of Assembly to frustrate his efforts to implement the British abolition act, but he explained their venomous hostility towards him charitably: "the planters thought that the new system was effecting their ruin; and not being able to separate the man from the measures which it was his duty to pursue, they visited him with their most angry feelings". He observed also that his "unpopularity in the colony" was increased by his sympathy with the missionaries, who were regarded by the planters as "fomenters of rebellion, and promoters of discontent and disobedience on the part of the negroes".[6] But it was not the intransigence of the planters that ended his career; he resigned as a matter of principle because he was overruled by the Colonial Office when he suspended a notoriously insubordinate magistrate who, ironically, had accused him of "gross partiality to the planters".[7]

A further irony is that Sligo was himself a slave owner: in 1834 he was paid £5,526 compensation in respect of 286 slaves employed on the Kelly's and Cocoa Walk estates.[8] This fact worked against him on Emancipation Day, as he himself relates. Despite forecasts by the planters that the freed slaves would refuse to work as apprentices, there was no trouble except on one estate in St Ann, where they "threw down their hoes, and other agricultural implements, declaring that King William had 'given them free,' and that they would not work any more without payment", and saying, "Gubernor Mulgrave gave we free, but Gubernor Sligo keep we slaves because him hab slaves of him own."[9]

Sligo was Anglo-Irish by descent, Church of Ireland by persuasion, and educated at Eton and Cambridge, but the Brownes had married into Irish families from the seventeenth century onwards and Sligo himself voted for Catholic emancipation.[10] Moreover, his Jamaican estates came down to him through Irish forbears: Mary Daly, who had married his great-grandfather, and Elizabeth Kelly (daughter of Denis Kelly, a former chief justice of Jamaica), who had married his grandfather.[11]

Dowell O'Reilly

Dowell O'Reilly, the attorney general, was the fourth son of Matthew O'Reilly of Knock Abbey Castle, County Louth. He graduated from Trinity College, Dublin, in 1816 and was called to the Irish Bar. He died in Jamaica and was buried in the Roman Catholic cemetery in Kingston.[12] Richard Madden, who served under him, paid warm tribute to O'Reilly's "fearless advocacy of the negroes' rights" under the apprenticeship system, and to his "earnest support of its remedial character".[13] Madden's opinion was confirmed and enlarged by two American anti-slavery campaigners, James Thome and Horace Kimball, who met O'Reilly in Jamaica in 1837. The attorney general, they reported, was "one of the ablest men in the island", having formerly been "a prominent politician, and a bold advocate of Catholic Emancipation" in Ireland. They were struck by his entire freedom from prejudice: "with all his family rank and official standing, he identifies himself with the colored people as far as his extensive professional engagements will allow". They were consequently surprised to find him "highly respected by the whites". O'Reilly freely aired his criticism of the way the apprenticeship system was functioning, telling them that it was "in no manner preparing the negroes for freedom, but was operating in a contrary way; especially in Jamaica, where it had been made the instrument of greater cruelties, in some cases, than slavery itself". Thome and Kimball point out that his criticism could not be construed as "mere partizan feeling assumed in order to be in keeping with the government under which he holds his office", for apprenticeship was "the favorite offspring of British legislation".[14]

Despite the respect which O'Reilly apparently enjoyed among the whites in 1837, he too came into conflict with the planters. Madden describes a dispute over apprentices' entitlement to allowances of food which, under previous laws, slave-owners had been obliged to provide for their workers. Their first action after Emancipation Day in 1834 was to take away all the allowances "which were not literally specified in the new law".[15] When the apprentices complained, the special magistrates appealed to the attorney general for an opinion as to the legality of the planters' action. O'Reilly decided in favour of the apprentices, basing his judgment on broad general principles:

> The Slavery Abolition [Act] is a remedial Act, and to be construed liberally in order to effectuate the benevolent intentions of the Legislature. The slaves now Apprentices are not to be placed in a worse condition than they heretofore were: their allowances some of them were by custom, but so too was Slavery; for it never at any time had any support save from custom, which when universal, as it was in Jamaica, is law. Slavery is and was, however, contrary to common law; and as it invoked the aid of custom in making it valid, so I conceive may the Apprentices invoke custom in the support of their usual allowances, even whilst they are in the intermediate state of Apprentices.[16]

The planters, however, appealed to the former attorney general, Mr Batty (a plantation owner himself), whose opinion was that the apprentices were *not* entitled to the allowances in question. Wasting no time on broad principles or humanitarian arguments, he astutely exploited the slippage between various acts relating to the obligations of slave-owners. That strategy enabled him to argue that since the Jamaican act of 1833 contained "no clause respecting allowances to the apprentice", it followed that "an owner is *not obliged to give any of the above allowances*".[17] Batty's opinion prevailed, and Lord Sligo, caught between a rock and a hard place, was compelled to overrule his own legal adviser.

Richard Madden

Richard Robert Madden is best known as the first historian of the United Irishmen. A Catholic from a prosperous Dublin family, he travelled widely in Europe and the Levant, had published two books and was practising as a qualified surgeon in London before he went to the West Indies. When the Slavery Abolition Act was passed in 1833, he decided to abandon his profession in order to help in "that great work of humanity".[18] With the help of Sir Thomas Fowell Buxton and others in the Anti-Slavery Society, he secured an appointment as special magistrate and arrived in Jamaica in November 1833. He was posted to Kingston by Lord Mulgrave, Sligo's liberal predecessor as governor, but he found the antagonism of the white populace towards his attempts to protect the rights of the apprentices so obstructive that he resigned his appointment after a year, considering it impossible "to discharge my duties with honesty to the measures under which I acted".[19] The Corporation of Kingston, he said, was composed of "infuriated planters" whose complete control over the local militia and police force enabled them to prevent the "decrees of the Special Magistrates" from being enforced.[20]

Madden's alienation from the whites in Jamaica was virtually inevitable, however. A man who had declared that "an interest in the Irish Insurrectionary movement of 1798" was his "ruling passion"[21] was never likely to feel at home in a British colony in which effective power was in the hands of an overwhelmingly English and Scottish plantocracy. But a peculiarity of his situation was that both by family connection and by marriage he belonged to the Jamaican plantation-owning class himself. Through a great-uncle, Dr Lyons of Roscommon, he had claims to the Marley estate in St Mary, while his wife's father, John Elmslie, owned Serge Island and other estates on the island.[22] Madden's involvement with slave-owners was brought home to him uncomfortably during a visit to Marley, as he self-mockingly relates. At the plantation he met "an old African negro" who had been Dr Lyons's "favourite waiting-boy" forty years earlier. The old man showed none of the joy or gratitude towards a descendant of "his revered master" that Madden had anticipated, responding contemptuously to his friendly overtures. Enquiring afterwards into the history of the plantation under his great-uncle, Madden learned that the benevolent regimen he had imagined was pure fantasy: the old man "had no benefits to be grateful for – but great neglect, and many hardships, and, eventually, cruelty, to turn the milk of kindly feelings towards his master or his family to gall and bitterness".[23]

Madden's Irish compatriots in Jamaica rallied to his support after his resignation. Among tributes to his energy and integrity quoted in *A Twelvemonth's Residence* are warm letters from Lord Sligo and Dowell O'Reilly; another was from Lord Mulgrave, who by then had been appointed lord lieutenant of Ireland, where he was welcomed by the Catholics and won the friendship of Daniel O'Connell.[24] The striking concurrence of all four men in their views on the rights of both Catholics in Britain and slaves in Jamaica was not fortuitous; as Nini Rodgers shows, "the issues of Catholic emancipation and African slavery were closely linked".[25]

James Kelly

Unlike the representatives of colonial authority discussed so far, James Kelly and Benjamin McMahon worked in the lower ranks of plantation society throughout their time in Jamaica. Nothing is known of either except through their books. Kelly, on the evidence of *Jamaica in 1831* (renamed *Voyage to Jamaica* in the second edition, the text used here), was probably an Ulster Presbyterian. Both editions of his book were published in Belfast by subscription; his religious leanings are suggested by the list of 101 subscribers, eight of whom are identified as churchmen by title or suffix (*Rev.* or *DD*). These could be either Presbyterian or Church of Ireland ministers, but a disparaging reference in the text to "the supineness of the Established Church"[26] makes it unlikely that Kelly himself was a member. Another subscriber is listed as "Alex S. Mayne, Editor of [the] *Ulster Missionary*" – a periodical also known as the *Temperance and Sabbath School Journal*. The remaining subscribers, where identified, were mostly doctors or lawyers from Belfast and neighbouring towns or villages.[27]

Kelly's text indicates that he was one of the Irish "sojourners" described by Nini Rodgers. Typically Ulster Presbyterians, they established themselves mainly in the ports as agents who dealt in linen and Irish provisions.[28] His narrative begins: "In the month of March, 1814, having consulted neither friends nor friendly advisers, but my wayward disposition, I paid twenty guineas for a passage in the ship *Hugh Crawford* – took my portmanteaux on board in Belfast Lough, and a week after, was at anchor in the Cove of Cork, in the midst of upwards of one hundred sail of merchantmen, assembled to join convoy, it being war-time."[29] Kelly spent his seventeen years in Jamaica trying without much success to work his way up the ladder of plantation society, first as a bookkeeper, then as a merchant, until finally, "having experienced a share of afflictions, and much mercantile disappointment, I bade adieu to Jamaica, recrossed the Atlantic, and arrived in Liverpool in 1831".[30]

Voyage to Jamaica is a reprint of the first edition enlarged by the addition of several new pages. Even so, it remains a very short and oddly constructed work: fully a third of its seventy-two pages are taken up by an appendix which consists mainly of extracts from a report on the apprenticeship system by two Quakers, Joseph Sturge and Thomas Harvey, published early in 1838 under the title *The West Indies in 1837*. Kelly claims that when he began writing his "little book" in 1832 he had no intention of publishing, "but, having been advised by friends, with due deference I offer it to the public".[31] The advice was probably that the narrative was too short for publication on its own but the addition of the extracts from Sturge and Harvey would both bulk it out and give it topical appeal. *The West Indies in 1837* caused a considerable stir in Britain and supplied powerful ammunition for abolitionists in the parliamentary debates of 1838.

On arrival in Jamaica, Kelly stayed with a merchant in Kingston to whom he had letters of introduction. He thought Kingston "a fine city" and was particularly struck by the "Negro market" (noting with sabbatarian disapproval that until the arrival of the first bishop of Jamaica it "was held on Sunday!").[32] After a month he secured a job as bookkeeper on the Industry coffee plantation, where, under "a humane and intelligent" overseer, he spent his "happiest year" in Jamaica.[33] He then set up in partnership as a storekeeper in Hope Bay, dealing in "Irish provisions".[34] In 1815 his business partner died and Kelly moved to Buff Bay, extended his business and took charge of the public wharf. His activities made him familiar with plantation life; the overseers of the nearby estates used to assemble at his store and he would sometimes ride out to dine with them and stay overnight. On such occasions, "I generally rode with the overseer in his morning round, or visited the works with him; and, being a coffee-planter, I easily became a sugar-planter by observation."[35] Despite his friendly relations with employees on the plantations, Kelly was shocked by their sexual habits, declaring that the depravity of Jamaican society was a greater danger to an incomer even than tropical fevers. "A young man arrives – is sent as book-keeper to an estate – he sees the temptation of many young Creoles, black or brown, all essaying to win 'new book-keeper.' Alas! he falls prey to the demoralizing, customary, licentious libertinism of the country – not to its epidemics."[36]

Kelly's views on slavery are hard to gauge. He seems to disapprove of it in principle, but his allusions to the subject are evasive and inconsistent.[37] His first encounter with slaves was on the voyage out, when the ship called at Barbados and he disembarked for a few hours in Bridgetown. There he was "disgusted with the appearance of the white Creoles", especially in contrast with "the shining faces of the Negroes":

> I was astonished to learn that they were the slaves of the same haggard-looking Creoles I had been so shocked with. There is a lesson in this, I thought, and I resolved *that I would be no slave-owner*. I remembered how the Israelites of old, under the most cruel oppression, flourished in bodily health and fruitfulness; and here I beheld the yet more debased Negro slave sustained by a merciful adaptation to his condition; and I began to moralize about oppressions and analogies – but I put my hand on my mouth.[38]

The "lesson" – that Providence rewards the oppressed, Israelites and Africans alike, with good health while punishing their oppressors – is either ironic or a cynical argument against slavery on the grounds of self-interest; it is impossible to tell which. Elsewhere, although disapproving in principle (with comments

such as "the odious name of slavery" *et simile*), Kelly raises no moral objection
to the use of slave labour in practice. He represents the slave laws as just and
humane but recognizes (without citing examples) that they are liable to abuse
by brutal overseers or excessively punitive magistrates.

On one issue, however, Kelly is firm: that consciousness of their loss of freedom
must always be a source of anguish to the enslaved, no matter how humanely
they are treated. He makes the point most forcibly in an interesting passage
(based on his experience as a wharfinger) about the friendships between sailors
and slaves. "Sailors and Negroes", he observes, "are ever on the most amicable
terms". He attributes their "mutual confidence and familiarity" to "a feeling of
independence" in the slaves' relationships with sailors, as contrasted with "the
consciousness of a bitter restraint" in their dealings with the resident whites,
who "very generally affect a supercilious superiority over them": "In the presence of the sailor, the Negro feels as a man; – in that of the [white] man who
lives in the continual view of his degradation, he feels as a slave. – Alas! all the
meliorations or petty advantages they may possess, are not to be named as the
smallest equivalent to the misery of this consciousness."[39]

Kelly's perception that the assumption of superiority by the white residents
was the alienating factor is particularly shrewd. He seems to have arrived intui-
tively at Linebaugh and Rediker's theory that fellow-feeling between sailors and
slaves was a manifestation of class solidarity, based on common experiences of
hard labour, savage discipline and exile.[40] Kelly later put his empathy with the
enslaved into practice. Finding it useful to possess a slave himself, he bought a
man named John Brown, whom he had previously hired to work his wharf. After
six months of good service he devised an ingenious scheme to enable Brown
to earn his manumission. The success of the scheme convinced him that "the
Negroes would work the estates well, as hired labourers".[41] This was a standard
line of argument in the 1830s for the abolition of slavery, and although Kelly
does not make that point, he appears to imply it.

The missionaries in Jamaica emerge from this narrative with untarnished
credit. Kelly admired them for their energy in attracting worshippers and spreading the Christian message, and especially for their beneficial influence on the
"moral character" of the "Negroes, and free people of colour".[42] He strenuously
defends them from accusations that were made after an attempted insurrection in 1824 that they had incited the slaves to rebel. The charge arose from the
fact that plans for a general uprising "were formed, and nearly matured" at
clandestine meetings on the plantations, which were "cloaked under the name

of religious meetings". But these meetings, Kelly insists, were "of an opposite nature" to the teachings of the missionaries. "I am safe in saying, that there never was one solitary instance of collusion with the Negroes."[43] Indeed, the very failure of the insurrection could be attributed to divine intervention: the conspiracy was betrayed by "a Negro, – who had been mysteriously ordered, no doubt, by an overruling Providence, to divulge the whole plan".[44]

Benjamin McMahon

Benjamin McMahon, author of *Jamaica Plantership* (London, 1839), reveals nothing about his background except that he was a native of Ireland and young, poor and "friendless, in a strange country" on arrival in Jamaica.[45] He was clearly not a typical "sojourner", for his adventures started in Venezuela. "On the 28th of July in the year 1818 I left my native country, Ireland, as a volunteer in the patriot service of the Colombian army, for the purpose of assisting in the liberation of the South Americans from the Spanish yoke."[46] The ship arrived in "the harbour of Juan Grego, in the island of Margueritta, on the 28th of September", having narrowly escaped capture en route by the Spanish, "although we had been entered at the Custom-house in Dublin, as passengers bound to Trinidad".[47]

It is clear from McMahon's tantalizingly brief account of his military service that he sailed with the first contingent of recruits of the Irish Legion, which left Dublin in 1819 to support Bolívar's campaign (*1818* must be either a misprint or the result of a lapse of memory; 1819 fits with other dates in the text). The legionaries were victims of shameless exploitation by their commander, the self-styled "Major-General" John Devereux. They endured terrible hardships in Venezuela, with grossly inadequate clothing, food and medical supplies and no pay, while Devereux remained in Ireland, "living handsomely off the fees he charged officers for their commissions in the Legion".[48] Large numbers of the recruits deserted and hundreds of them went to Jamaica. McMahon was one of those; sometime after "the flag of liberty was hoisted in every part of Venezuela", he and his comrades became "so dissatisfied with our treatment by the commanders, that many of us threw up our engagements, and became scattered about. I, together with about 200 others, determined to go to the West Indies; and we sailed for Jamaica in the beginning of June [1820]."[49]

Jamaica Plantership opens with a passionate manifesto declaring the author's hatred of slavery in every form. His determination was "to expose the treachery, the torture, and the tyranny, practised by the overseers and attorneys of Jamaica, towards the slaves . . . the opposition made to ministers of the Gospel": in short, to demonstrate "the total unfitness of the old Planters to manage the estates in the Colonies under their present altered circumstances" (meaning the apprenticeship system).[50] McMahon's book is, however, not merely (or even mainly) a polemic but also an eventful, highly readable narrative and a useful source of plantation history. It includes, for example, a first-hand account of the brutal military campaign which followed the slave rebellion of 1831–32. McMahon worked on twenty-four different estates and carefully recorded the names of all the people he encountered, from proprietors and attorneys to bookkeepers, overseers, doctors, surveyors, shopkeepers, missionaries and slaves.

On arrival in Jamaica, "a gentleman named Burke who kept a druggist's shop in Kingston, got me a berth in the planting line".[51] If this gentleman was Irish, as his name suggests, we might infer that there was an Irish network operating in Jamaica, like the well-documented network which Scottish newcomers could rely upon. But there is no other evidence of one; on the contrary, McMahon feared at one point that his Irish identity would be an impediment. He discharged himself "foolishly" from a good job at the Cherry Garden estate, St Dorothy, "because I was told by a brother book-keeper that Mr. McCook [attorney for the estate] had cast reflections on my country men, from which I supposed I should stand no chance of promotion".[52]

McMahon learned about the adversities of his fellow countrymen when he moved on to the Exeter estate, where his overseer was "an old Irishman, named Kelly" who had made a fortune in Jamaica but had "entirely lost it in speculations" after leaving the island. Seventeen years later he had returned to work again as an overseer. One of the ways in which he had previously grown rich was by acting as an executor on a large scale. He had "imported twenty-one poor Irishmen, to act as book-keepers and tradesmen on estates", eighteen of whom died at various points after their arrival, leaving him as their executor. "Kelly told me he was confident that there were not three of these poor fellows, who had been book-keepers, who had not met their deaths from the tyranny and oppression of the overseers they were under."[53]

McMahon himself suffered the tyranny of overseers on several occasions. At the Osborne estate in St George, for example, he was "keeping spell in the boiling-house" and, "as everything was going well, I was walking up and down, whistling". The overseer came in and said, "'Mr. McMahon, is this the way you are doing your duty? You are whistling for the amusement of the negroes' – and he forthwith discharged me for whistling."[54] However, a more frequent reason for McMahon's lack of success in the planting line, according to his version of events, was his failure or refusal to accept standard attitudes. A telling incident occurred while he was working as a bookkeeper on the Manchester estate, Trelawny, and conversation with fellow employees turned to the spread of religion among the slaves. The others described "the different sorts of punishment they inflicted on the '*black rascals*'" for praying and going to chapel, but their worst abuse fell on the Baptist missionaries. McMahon – "my feelings getting the better of my prudence" – defended them, saying that "they were doing a great deal of good in the country, and ought to be encouraged by every one". When, in spite of "loud cursing and swearing", he persevered with his argument, the rest "one by one rose from the table and went away"; his remarks were soon reported to his employer "and had the effect of stopping my promotion".[55] McMahon's conduct made him popular with the slaves, however. He was asked by one of them if he knew "Mr. Wilberforce, Mr. Macaulay, and Buxton, who, they were told, were their friends", and as "they never saw me drinking, with the others, telling lies upon and abusing the negroes, or cursing the parsons, they supposed I must be a friend also".[56]

Shortly after this, the 1831–32 rebellion broke out. As a member of the Trelawny militia McMahon was obliged to serve in the campaign of suppression, during which he observed many arbitrary killings and brutalities committed by the militia. The only action of his own that he reports was during a search for rebels in a cane field:

> while I was engaged in this duty, I found a stout able negro, with a cutlass in his hand, crouching down among the canes. No one being near, I said to him in a low tone, "lie down where you are, and do not move, I won't touch you, but if you attempt to come near me with your cutlass, I'll shoot you." The poor man expressed his gratitude in dumb show with his hands; immediately afterwards several others of the militia passed close to where the man lay, but did not see him. I pretended that I heard a noise in the other direction, so as to draw them off, and thus the poor fellow escaped.[57]

He was happy to reflect that "throughout the rebellion, although I was in the midst of such scenes of carnage, I never once pointed a gun at a negro, nor ever hurt a hair of one of their heads. All my inclinations, in fact, were to have joined with the unfortunate people, had I seen the smallest chance of success."[58] This bold claim, however, should be taken as merely rhetorical; it is clear from the rest of his Jamaican narrative that McMahon was a revolutionary in language only.

Should McMahon's anti-slavery protestations then be distrusted? That is Matthew Brown's view; he argues that McMahon's main motive throughout was not sympathy for the enslaved but ambition to succeed as a planter. The fact that he "even served in the militia against slave rebels" shows that "for all his shared humanity with blacks and slaves . . . M'Mahon's loyalty to other whites came before any supposed solidarity with the unfree".[59] But McMahon did not join the militia out of loyalty to whites; under Jamaican law he was compelled to do so. Moreover, it is misleading to equate racial attitudes with views on slavery. It is true but irrelevant that McMahon "did not advocate racial equality".[60] In fact he never discusses the issue at all; as he announces at the outset, his abhorrence of slavery was based firmly on *ius civis* (civil law). "As a friend of civil and religious liberty, I abhor slavery in my very soul: knowing as I do, that no man has a just right to deprive his fellow-man of his property, of his limbs, or of his life except for some crime against society."[61] The facts that he did not choose to face the penalties for refusing to join the militia and that he continued to work on plantations afterwards does not show that he was hypocritical in his professed hatred of slavery, but only that he was not prepared to sacrifice his livelihood for his principles. Like a much better-known anti-slavery campaigner, Zachary Macaulay, he doubtless reconciled himself to his situation by reflecting that "there was no medium between doing so and starving".[62]

In 1832 McMahon became "so disgusted with the planting line" that he left and started up a small business of his own, "but, as I had only a small capital, it was soon sunk in speculations, and as the planters in the neighbourhood were entirely against me, I was unable to succeed".[63] He returned to planting in 1836 but, finding conditions no better under the apprenticeship system, he resolved to act on a long-laid plan "of coming to England, to lay before the public, and particularly absentee proprietors, what I knew of the proceedings of the Jamaican planters".[64] Presumably he chose England rather than Ireland as his destination in order to make his views heard in the seat of power.

Conclusion

No general conclusions about Irish views on slavery can safely be drawn from this set of case studies. But Kelly's failure as a merchant and McMahon's incessant changes of employment prompt a different kind of speculation: was it peculiarly hard for Irish incomers who lacked wealth, influence or professional qualifications to succeed in Jamaican society in this period? A quick search for Irish names among holders of public office listed in the *Jamaica Almanack for 1822* suggests that it may have been. Even allowing for the probability that a few owners of seemingly English names were actually Irish and some with Scottish-sounding names were Ulster Scots, the scarcity of common Irish names is striking. Out of fifty members of the Council and House of Assembly, only one name – Henry Burke, member of the Assembly for Portland – looks Irish. There is only one Irish name (Thomas Murphy) among eighteen command-ing officers in the militia, and none at all in the long list of "Public Officers" of various kinds. Such a rough-and-ready test proves nothing, of course, but it is suggestive. Perhaps McMahon was not altogether foolish to fear that his Irish identity might get in the way of his advancement.

Notes

1.   Joseph Sturge and Thomas Harvey, *The West Indies in 1837* (1838; reprint, London: Dawsons, 1968), 188.

2.   [Howe Peter Browne, Marquess of Sligo], *Jamaica under the Apprenticeship System, by a Proprietor* (London: J. Andrews, 1838), 106. Sligo's "meticulous efforts to enforce the rule of law" with strict impartiality are documented by Diana Paton in *No Bond but the Law: Punishment, Race, and Gender in Jamaican State Formation, 1780–1870* (Durham, NC: Duke University Press, 2004), 67–69.

3.   See William A. Green, *British Slave Emancipation: The Sugar Colonies and the Great Experiment, 1830–1865* (Oxford: Clarendon, 1976), 122–23.

4.   *Jamaica under the Apprenticeship System*, i.

5.   Private letter to Lord Glenelg, 17 May 1838, C.O. 137/228.

6.   *Jamaica under the Apprenticeship System*, xviii–xix.

7.   Sligo Personal Papers, National Library of Jamaica, quoted in Tim Barringer, Gillian Forrester and Barbaro Martinez-Ruiz, eds., *Art and Emancipation in Jamaica: Isaac Mendes Belisario and His Worlds* (New Haven, CT: Yale Center for British Art, 2007), 370.

8.   University College London, Legacies of British Slave-Ownership, accessed 6 June 2013, www.ucl.ac.uk/lbs/person/view/20713.

9.   *Jamaica under the Apprenticeship System*, v–vi.

10.   See Denis Edward Browne, Marquess of Sligo, *Westport House and the Brownes* (Ashbourne: Moorland, 1981), 33–37.

11.   See Barringer et al., *Art and Emancipation*, 390–93. Cocoa Walk had formerly belonged to Denis Daly of Carrownakilly, County Clare, Mary Daly's first husband (393n9). Sligo's secretary, Lieutenant-Colonel Doyle, was probably Irish also.

12.   *Alumni Dublinenses*; Frederic Boase, *Modern English Biography* (Truro, 1892–1908), 2:1253–54.

13.   Richard Robert Madden, *A Twelvemonth's Residence in the West Indies, During the Transition from Slavery to Apprenticeship* (London: James Cochrane, 1835), 2:254.

14.   James A. Thome and J. Horace Kimball, *Emancipation in the West Indies: A Six Months' Tour in Antigua, Barbadoes, and Jamaica, in the Year 1837* (New York: American Anti-Slavery Society, 1838), 344–45.

15.   R.R. Madden, *Twelvemonth's Residence*, 2:267.

16.   Ibid., 268–69.

17.   Ibid., 272–73 (emphasis added).

18.   Thomas More Madden, ed., *The Memoirs Chiefly Autobiographical from 1798 to 1886 of Richard Robert Madden* (London: Ward and Downey, 1891), 1.

19.   R.R. Madden, *Twelvemonth's Residence*, 2:321.

20.   T.M. Madden, *Memoirs*, 71.

21.   Ibid., 1.

22.   Ibid., 60. See also Nini Rodgers, "Richard Robert Madden: An Irish Anti-slavery Activist in the Americas", in *Ireland Abroad: Politics and Professions in the Nineteenth Century*, ed. Oonagh Walsh (Dublin: Four Courts, 2003), 119–31.

23.   R.R. Madden, *Twelvemonth's Residence*, 1:221–23. The episode is reprinted in *Contrary Voices: Representations of West Indian Slavery, 1657-1834*, ed. Karina Williamson (Kingston: University of the West Indies Press, 2008), 299–301.

24.   R.R. Madden, *Twelvemonth's Residence*, 2:325–26. For Mulgrave, see Richard Davenport-Hines, "Phipps, Constantine Henry, First Marquess of Normanby (1797–1863)", *Oxford Dictionary of National Biography*, 44:176–77. As the second Earl of Mulgrave he was governor of Jamaica in 1832–34 and lord lieutenant of Ireland in 1835–39; he was created Marquess of Normanby in 1838.

25.   Nini Rodgers, *Ireland, Slavery and Anti-Slavery, 1612-1865* (London: Palgrave Macmillan, 2007), 259–68.

26.   James Kelly, *Voyage to Jamaica, and Seventeen Years' Residence in That Island: Chiefly Written with a View to Exhibit Negro Life and Habits; with Extracts from Sturge and Harvey's "West Indies in 1837"*, 2nd ed. (Belfast: J. Wilson, 1838), 44.

27.   Ibid., iii–iv.

28.   Rodgers, *Ireland, Slavery and Anti-Slavery*, 82.

29.   Kelly, *Voyage to Jamaica*, 9.

30.   Ibid., 45.

31.   Ibid., v.

32.   Ibid., 16–17.

33.   Ibid., 18.

34.   Ibid., 21–23. "Irish provisions" meant salted beef, herrings and butter, which along with linen were the staples of Irish trade with the New World colonies; see Rodgers, *Ireland, Slavery and Anti-Slavery*, 120–28.

35.   Kelly, *Voyage to Jamaica*, 30–31.

36.   Ibid., 32.

37. This inconsistency is exacerbated by the addition of a preface and an appendix written in 1838 to a narrative written before the 1833 Abolition Act.
38. Ibid., 11 (emphasis in original).
39. Ibid., 29–30.
40. Peter Linebaugh and Marcus Rediker, *The Many-Headed Hydra: Sailors, Slaves, Commoners, and the Hidden History of the Revolutionary Atlantic* (London: Verso, 2000).
41. Kelly, *Voyage to Jamaica*, 41–42.
42. Ibid., 44–45.
43. Ibid., 35. For the uprising, see Mary Turner, *Slaves and Missionaries: The Disintegration of Jamaican Slave Society, 1787–1834* (Kingston: University of the West Indies Press, 1998), 110–11.
44. Kelly, *Voyage to Jamaica*, 36.
45. Benjamin McMahon, *Jamaica Plantership, by Benjamin McMahon, Eighteen Years Employed in the Planting Line in That Island* (London: Effingham Wilson, 1839), 19, 22.
46. Ibid., 11.
47. Ibid., 12.
48. Brian McGinn, "Venezuela's Irish Legacy", *Irish America Magazine* 7, no. 11 (1991): 34–37, http://www.illyria.com/irish/irishven.html, accessed 6 November 2012.
49. McMahon, *Jamaica Plantership*, 13–14.
50. Ibid., i–iii, v–vi.
51. Ibid., 17.
52. Ibid., 68–69.
53. Ibid., 71–72.
54. Ibid., 74–75.
55. Ibid., 83–84.
56. Ibid., 84–85.
57. Ibid., 94.
58. Ibid., 106–7.
59. Matthew Brown, *Adventuring through Spanish Colonies: Simon Bolívar, Foreign Mercenaries and the Birth of New Nations* (Liverpool: Liverpool University Press, 2006), 144.
60. Ibid.
61. McMahon, *Jamaica Plantership*, i–ii.
62. Iain Whyte, *Zachary Macaulay, 1768–1838* (Liverpool: Liverpool University Press, 2011), 13. See Diana McCaulay's novel *Huracan* (Leeds: Peepal Tree, 2012) for a fictional treatment of Macaulay's dilemma.
63. McMahon, *Jamaica Plantership*, 109.
64. Ibid., 127.

Part 2

Cultural Performance and Exchange

Chapter 6

Entanglements of Root and Branch

The Queer Relations of the Caribbean Irish

ALISON DONNELL

ALTHOUGH TRACES AND SIGNS OF IRISH LIVES in the Caribbean are now scant and proofs of cultural encounter and exchange among different ethnic groups are principally momentary, fragmented and incomplete, there is still enough to suggest an intriguing and complicated history of lived experience in intimacy with one another, if never quite in equivalence. It is likely that Irish and Caribbean peoples of African descent came to know and understand each other in conditions of proximity, facing corresponding oppression and discrimination most consistently when they shared boarding houses and worked alongside each other in hospitals or on building sites in London or other cities in 1950s and 1960s England, where many landlords posted signs announcing "No Blacks, No Irish". The Caribbean locations that are the subject of enquiry in this collection reveal a much more uneven and uncertain pattern of relations between these two groups since their arrival in the region in the seventeenth century. In particular, historically unresolved questions around enslavement, race and the resulting power relationships remain justifiably controversial and vexed. All the same, the compelling residual evidence of Irish place names and family names and the repeated references to Irish and Caribbean peoples as aligned in their experience of British colonial injury (which finds expression in different cultural forms), as well as the lively scholarly interest in marking

Irish ethnicity within the Caribbean crucible, does suggest the value of a project exploring Caribbean Irish connections, however inadequately such connections map onto a contingent geography of historical belonging, continuous ancestry or claims to authentic ethnic markers.

While the relations between Ireland and the Caribbean yield inconsistently but nevertheless productively to archaeological, historiographic and comparative cultural modes of enquiry, my own interest lies with the limit points of conventional scholarly and disciplinary enquiry. Indeed, I want to suggest that we might conceive of the Caribbean experience as a highly specific knowledge horizon for thinking about Irishness that affords a politically significant opportunity for rethinking what happens when identities travel and come into contact with a whole range of different economic, cultural, linguistic and value systems which they must negotiate. Rather than seeking to identify, uphold or substantiate claims of authentic Irishness marked through origin or residual ethnic traits such as religion, language and domestic habits (as in the hyphenated affirmations of Irish-American and Irish-Australian identities), I am interested in how "Irish Caribbean" and "Caribbean Irish" operate somewhat differently as identity categories. Specifically I am motivated to consider how these diasporic creolized subjectivities not only disallow but also disparage a calling on ethnic authenticity or originary prerogatives for an explanation of being and belonging.

In order to attend purposefully to the transformation that occurs when the substance of this seemingly known and stable diasporic ethnicity – Irishness – is dissolved within the cultural solution of Caribbeanness, I propose to draw on the practice of queer commentary. This approach is inspired by Eve Kosofsky Sedgwick's observation that "a lot of the most exciting recent work around 'queer' spins the term outward along dimensions that can't be subsumed under gender and sexuality at all: the ways that race, ethnicity, postcolonial nationality criss-cross with these".[1] The particular methodological value of queer commentary, therefore, lies in its working at the seams of this entropic encounter, consciously mindful of the productive critical return for both Caribbean studies and Irish studies in reading the Irish as queer figures, whose ethnic attributes and attachments could not be guaranteed in the black Atlantic world. The radically unstable performativity of Caribbean Irishnesses audibly rattles established and guarded models of dominant diasporic Irishness, and it also helps to make visible the strange grammar of identities that express national affiliation with a homeland that is itself often dependent on diasporic fictions of national legitimacy for global authentication of its ethnic characteristics.

The theoretical bearings of my enquiry are informed by my more general interest in reading the (notoriously homophobic) Caribbean as a culturally "queer" place, through the deliberately expansive rubric of queer commentary that places value on "a more thorough resistance to regimes of the normal".[2] Certainly, in as much as it is marked by a proliferation of cultural overlappings and ethnic heterogeneities that not only undo the possibility for singular normativities or deterministic signatures of being, but also diminish the epistemological moorings that uphold such regimes of the normal, the Caribbean can be understood as a queer place. The region is widely acknowledged globally as a place that has made possible new ways of experiencing culture and new ways of theorizing identities as syncretic, hyphenated and hybrid – creole. It is distinguished as a region and a travelling culture that models fluid identities as they form in and through cultural encounter, transformation and openness, and by identities that come into being through discontinuities, fissures and improvisations, to assemble a broad continuum of possibilities not organized around a prior norm.

Importantly, in contradistinction, Irishness has often been celebrated and purposed – especially in the diaspora – in such a way as to sustain identities that are based on claims of ethnic stability, continuity and solidarity with specific places and with historical traumas from long ago and far away. Such ideological investments in the integrity and relevance of the original nation transparently call upon heteronormative indexes such as those of genealogy, generation and family in order to style transnational fastenings, as I will go on to discuss. However, in his essay "Self-Queering Ireland?", Joseph Valente turns his attention to the internal turbulence of Irish national identities to argue against this grain: to propose that Ireland too is an inherently queer place, with a "felt correlation . . . between the programmatic contestations of all homogeneous identity forms under the sign of queer and the imposed division and hybridity of the Irish subject under colonialism, metrocolonialism, partition, postcolonialism, etc.".[3] Citing the work of Louise Ryan on how "Irishness can function discursively to queer British identity", Valente articulates the disruptive and deconstructive vocation of "Irish" as an identity, in relation to Britishness, that makes it a "self-queering proposition".[4] His encouragement to read Irish as a denormativizing identity is a highly effective strategy for raising awareness of the cultural and historical imperatives through which Ireland's conflicted identifications have been stage-managed and produced at home. The internal disorder of "Irishness", and particularly how it primed Ireland's diasporic subjects for such radically different possible futures, is certainly relevant to my own thoughts here. Primarily, though, my interest is in how the normalization and replication of a stable Irish identity that has been successfully sustained within the diaspora meets with failure in the Caribbean, and in what it may be about the Caribbean context that unmasks the already queer character of the decentred Irish identity.

In her article " 'Everyone Can Be Irish for the Day': Towards a Theory of Diasporic Performance in the St Patrick's Day Parade", Aoife Monks explores the intricate, theatrical parade performances of Irishness in both Ireland and New York, in order to think through the complicated multiple and intersecting identities they reveal, despite their attempts to conceal "the fault lines of conflict and dissent within its imagined community".[5] Monks reads these parades as non-identical performances that simultaneously style and authorize an " 'Irish-effect' which has material and political consequences".[6] While this fashioning of ethnic and national attachment is revealed in seemingly benign investments such as the Irish pub and the St Patrick's Day parade, which give sustenance to the hyphenated Irish-American identity of second and third generations, a conservative gender and sexual politics is often imbricated in these nostalgically nationalist performances that is far from innocent. *Rock the Sham*, Anna Maguire's book on Irish gays and lesbians and the New York Fifth Avenue St Patrick's Day parade, takes up this very issue. Maguire analyses the way that preserving and performing a diasporic fiction of Irish identity as heteronormative is integral to holding on to a conservative Catholic identity long outdated in Ireland itself, especially in the wake of the clerical abuse scandals. The declared incompatibility between Irishness and non-heteronormativity is highly suggestive of the imagined possibility of an uncorrupted ethnic line: "They were shouting, 'Faggots. Queers. You're not Irish. Your parents must be English.'"[7]

The pertinence of Monks's line of enquiry for my own consideration of queer diasporic Irishness lies in her articulation of the double movement of identitarian performativity, through which "the myth of an original or essential national identity is debunked by the performative circumstances of the parades, while simultaneously being the foundation upon which the parades rely for their logic and coherence".[8] This same paradoxical move may also be read in Valente's reasoning as a self-queering of Irishness, though it often appears as a gesture of identification that is determinedly unambiguous in its own terms.

The question, then, is what such a reliance on the stylization of an authentic identity signifies and how it feeds into cultures of encounter and exchange. Within the global diaspora, where Irishness functions as an identity that can claim both the privileges of whiteness and the rewards of ethnic distinctiveness, the Caribbean may be seen as an exceptional location. In an environment where, as the Cuban theorist and writer Benítez-Rojo argues, "the spectrum of Caribbean codes is so varied and dense that it holds the region suspended in a soup of signs", the markers of Irish ethnicity, continuity and origin cannot be tasked to perform, parade and commodify themselves in the same way as they do in the settler colonies (predominantly America and Australia).[9] While this relates partly to the different configuration of settler colonies, where Europeans remain the dominant group, compared to postcolonial societies, where the descendants of enslaved Africans and Indians remain the majority group, I want to highlight how the clashing epistemologies of Irishness and Caribbeanness as identity classifications bring into intensified focus the use and the value of origins within subjectivity stories. My particular interest here is in thinking about how the plasticity and contingency of Caribbeanness rub up against the kind of performative diasporic Irishness which is commercially packaged and performed – if not uniformly experienced – as undiminished yet displaced, genuine yet dispersed.

In his landmark 1982 study *Slavery and Social Death*, the Jamaican historical and cultural sociologist Orlando Patterson speaks about the enslaved: "alienated from all 'rights' or claims of birth, he ceased to belong in his own right to any legitimate social order".[10] The effects of this alienation are not only of serious consequence to the slaves' capacity for community but are also central to the question of ancestral belonging and the impossible futurity of self-knowledge and identification. As Patterson describes, "the heart of what is critical in the slave's forced alienation [is] the loss of ties of birth in both ascending and descending generations. It also has the important nuance of a loss of native status, of deracination."[11]

Even for those Caribbean population groups that were not enslaved, in particular the Indians who arrived post-emancipation on indentured contracts and were entitled to their religions and languages, the devastating conditions and brutal practices of the plantation made their ability to return practically impossible; they received a double blow by being effectively brushed aside by their mother country during India's independence period. The complicated range of agency and powerlessness which African, Indian, Chinese and Irish populations variously faced when they arrived in the Caribbean will long remain a subject of historical enquiry and debate. However, it is evident that the extent of human diversity and the subsequent mixing and combining among these groups and others over time made the possibility of restoring natal identity not only increasingly difficult for those who did not have established sources to turn to but also, and crucially, increasingly irrelevant. While certain recitals of and claims to ethnic clarity – such as the Afrocentric Rastafari movement – have a durable presence in the Caribbean, they are demonstrably performative gestures of an inherited belonging; they must creatively style the signatures of ancestral cohesion within the wider context of a creolized cultural maelstrom such as Benítez-Rojo describes.

Somewhat remarkably, but also inevitably, from the historical experience of loss, trauma and injury a different politics of identity emerges in the Caribbean, in which the rights and claims of birth and ethnic distinctiveness do not figure as signatures or explanations of co-belonging. The imagining of Caribbean people as culturally pluralistic and ethnically supple can be seen aphoristically in virtually all of the region's national mottos – Trinidad's "Together We Aspire, Together We Achieve"; Jamaica's "Out of Many, One People"; Guyana's "One Nation, One People, One Destiny" – and even in the virtual community, in WestIndian.com's banner "All ah we is one family!" In the postcolonial period the nation- and community-making practices of the Caribbean have been, partly from necessity and partly from political determination, structured around the possibilities presented by horizontal relations – those of proximity and collectivity – rather than the vertical lines of genealogy.

The blending of utopian and everyday social description that this Caribbean situation authorizes is captured beautifully in St Lucian Derek Walcott's Nobel Prize acceptance speech, "The Antilles: Fragments of Epic Memory", and his subjunctive rendering of the Trinidadian capital city, Port of Spain: "it would be so racially various that the cultures of the world – the Asiatic, the Mediterranean, the European, the African – would be represented in it, its humane variety more exciting than Joyce's Dublin. Its citizens would intermarry as they chose, from instinct, not tradition, until their children find it increasingly futile to trace their genealogy."[12] What Walcott catches (with an expedient aside to Dublin) is how the Caribbean is a cultural location that incarnates the possibility of a future in which ancestral and ethnic motivations are no longer in play, and in which the possibilities for lateral solidarity in the absence of common origins emerge from the freedom of human desires, unregulated by the regimes of the normal which genealogical traditions seek to impose.

However, if the practices of co-belonging and community have been released from the conventions of genealogy and the norms of ancestral claims to historical belonging in the Caribbean – though not free of ongoing divisions based on ideas of race and ethnic difference – this offers an interesting opposition to the framing of Irishness as an identity that is inextricably, even if invisibly, linked to the missing ancestor. While the Caribbean's structure of co-belonging through proximity and collectivity suggests the horizontality of branches, popular and commercial Irish identifications retain an obsession with genealogy and roots. This attachment could be read as refusal to assimilate into the dominant culture – something akin to the deracination that Patterson argues is a primary injury of the unfree – that diaspora threatens, or as resistance to the surface performativity of an Irishness that is freely available and paraded on St Patrick's Day, which diaspora also occasions.

In either case, the story of the Irish in the Caribbean does not fit with and is not accommodated by the main narrative of an Irish diaspora, which was at a peak from the 1840s and the Great Famine period through to the 1950s and post–Second World War labour demands, even though the migrations of the nineteenth century can barely be conceived of as voluntary or economically driven. The historical memory of the main Irish diasporic era is exhibited by monuments in cities as geographically dispersed as Liverpool, New York, Sydney, Toronto and Boston, and its scholarly afterlife thrives in Irish studies centres. In these locations, many resources and records seek to locate, enumerate and connect Irish diasporic populations – to one another and to their ancestral homeland – and thereby to imply a knowledge tradition in which natal identity can and should be preserved. The claims of a historical archive are complemented by the generous Irish national right of return, which extends citizenship even to second-generation immigrants. As a consequence, many Irish diasporic subjects have remained part of the history of Ireland, both in political status and in a more imaginary, mythic sense of belonging. These possibilities were never manifest for enslaved Africans, and they were seriously eroded for indentured Indians and migrant Chinese, who did not retain their place within continental or national narratives.

Indeed, for those identifying as Irish, or part Irish, there is a continued investment in knowledge of the specifics of place, family, kinship and community as a form of continuity of being. The plethora of books on the subject of tracing Irish ancestors and the popularity of magazines such as *Irish Lives Remembered* and *Irish Roots* suggest a strong cultural inclination for tracing and restoring ancestral links that were seemingly severed by migration. A whole grammar of reconnection via symbols of natal belonging offers an entry point to a historical substitutability that feeds into the imagination of Irishness as a global identity. Such identification in action was evident in US president Obama's visit to Ireland in May 2011. The president told the Dublin crowd gathered to welcome him, "My name is Barack Obama, of the Moneygall Obamas, and I've come home to find the apostrophe we lost somewhere along the way."[13] Sure enough, Obama did visit his ancestral home in Moneygall, County Offaly, from where his great-great-great-grandfather on his mother's side, Falmouth Kearney, emigrated in 1850 at the age of nineteen. The president was also photographed drinking Guinness, holding a hurley and in Templeharry Church consulting parish records where the birthdates of his ancestors could be read.

Although Obama's visit was documented in ways that most acts of reconnection are not, for those who identify as Irish and want to know "where they come from", there is a confidence in both the historical record and the value invested in ancestry as an index of identity that is not replicated for Caribbean subjects. In his book *A Guide to Tracing Your Kerry Ancestors*, one of a series promising the rewards of genealogy in different Irish counties, Michael O'Connor advises those in search of their Irish "family" to "(a) Set a Goal: Decide which branch of the family you wish to trace and in which direction . . . (b) Work from the known to the unknown: Use the details of those ancestors you have the most amount of information about to locate other ancestors . . . (c) Work from the most recent to the most distant."[14] O'Connor also lists sources that can usefully be consulted: administrative divisions; censuses; church records; civil registrations of births, marriages and deaths; commercial and social directories; wills and administrations; memorial inscriptions; land tenure and ownership deeds; newspapers; national and local government records; military records; educational records; and family histories.

Despite the gaps in the genealogical record subsequent to destruction of the Irish Custom House in 1921 during the War of Independence, this archive of historical certainty presents a grave comparison to that available for African Caribbean people before 1838. The usual sources such as church registers, employment records, Poor Law records and wills cannot be mined as, under slavery, Africans had no status as human subjects, and thus no such records. Importantly though when trying to position the Irish who migrated or were transported to the Caribbean before and even during the 1840s, their disappearance from the record seems not to be unusual either; a book called *Tracing*

Your Caribbean Ancestors would struggle to commence in the same buoyant register as the O'Connor guide.

Nevertheless, the cultural fascination with identifying and restoring Irishness to those disconnected from their roots by the Caribbean experience has not been deterred by the obstacle of insufficient historical records. In March 2013 the genealogical project of tracing Irish ancestors in the Caribbean took on a new form with the launch of Maurice Gleeson's Irish Caribbean Ancestry – Reconnecting through DNA (iCARA). The stated aim of the project is to "help people with Irish Caribbean ancestry to reconnect with both their ancestral Irish homeland and with their distant cousins living in Ireland today".[15] Gleeson's project is open to anyone with an Irish surname who lives in the Caribbean, or who can trace their ancestry back to the Caribbean, and can provide an attempt at family history on the Irish line. Its foundational vision is of a unified Irish community of "cousins" whose shared genetic ancestry functions as a presumed reason for global community. In this way iCARA reproduces an otherwise invisible and unknowable identity under the rubric of historical retrieval and validation: "in the absence of documentation to the contrary, the location of the Clan Homeland may be as close as we can get to defining the Ancestral Homeland of the Caribbean & Irish cousins".[16]

Brushing against the grain of this mode of hereditary reconnection and the restoration of diasporic Irishness to the places and kinship networks of Ireland, I am interested here to gesture towards what else happens to Irishness when it encounters the Caribbean and how it is transformed into and by zones of association and unexpected substitutability. Invoking Judith Halberstam's call in *In a Queer Time and Place* for "other logics of location, movement and identification" beyond the heteronormative, I shift attention and value away from modes of identification that rely on establishing originary kinship and biological source.[17] While this is a theoretical and political gesture, it is also shaped by the limit points and failures of seemingly "straight" modes of scholarship and recovery research that seek to articulate, locate and recover the subject of the Irish in the Caribbean. Significantly, it seems that the historical record of the Irish in the Caribbean is already primed for this entropic encounter, and for the production of queer identities that eschew organization and categorization based on established norms.

At the most basic level, accounts of the numbers of Irish sent to the West Indies in the 1650s seem to vary from twelve thousand to sixty thousand. Equally, Caribbean Irish historical narratives appear extraordinarily susceptible to complication and ambiguity. The story of the 1779 Irish Brigade, under the command of Count Arthur Dillon and his brother Edward – who arrived in Grenada with d'Estaing as part of the French army, formed a Catholic alliance and successfully retook control of the island from the British – is somewhat knotted by its mixing of French and Irish, as well as by the fact that the British garrison in Grenada was commanded by Lord George Macartney, a Scotsman who traced his roots back to an ancient Irish family. Yet another incongruity comes in the reporting of the *Robert Kerr*, one of the last ships to carry Irish migrants to Jamaica; it left in 1841 despite significant local agitation, led by Tom Steel, against this "most atrocious and damnable scheme to entrap unwary Irishmen".[18] Printed in London, the *Patriot* newspaper of 4 January 1841 reported from Limerick that "[t]he vessel left our quay this morning with about twenty on board, the majority of whom, it is said, were unfortunate women of the town, although the numbers engaged amounted to over 300".[19] Meanwhile, J.J. Williams, drawing on William James Gardner's 1873 *History of Jamaica* as his source, reports that "in February, 1841, one hundred and twenty-seven [Irish] arrived from Limerick".[20]

Amid such conflicting accounts of migrant populations and confusions caused by the variety and instability internal to Irish identity, the ethnic traits and belongings that feed into historical definitions of Irishness and of the Irish in the Caribbean seem impossible (and possibly senseless) to preserve as reliable indices of cultural or historical knowledge. The complicated layering that is concealed beneath assumptions regarding ethnic ascriptions and the illusion of stylized ethnic substance that Monks identifies continues even today. Fascinatingly, the iCARA DNA project cites the St Patrick's Day celebrations in Montserrat in its background notes to suggest evidence of an unbroken line of blood ancestry: "the descendants of these Irish exiles are very much alive today, and this is reflected by the plethora of Irish Surnames in the Caribbean, as well as the celebration of Irish culture in places like Monserrat [*sic*], the only country outside of Ireland to celebrate St Patrick's Day as a National Holiday".[21] In fact, as the evidence presented by Krysta Ryzewski and Laura McAtackney in this book suggests, the link between this celebration and "the descendants of Irish exiles" is altogether more tenuous.

The queering of St Patrick's Day as an Irish event in Montserrat can be observed in two facts: that 17 March was a significant date in the island's calendar on account of an attempted slave rebellion in 1768 as well as St Patrick's Day, and that the revival – or possibly even the inauguration – of an island-wide co-ordinated celebration in the late 1990s coincided historically with a need to offer a rallying point for Montserratians in the diaspora (predominantly African descended) and also an opportunity to market the island as a tourist destination within the Irish diaspora. With costumes and the people wearing them demonstrably announcing a crossing of Caribbean and Irish peoples and cultures, St Patrick's Day in Montserrat is a distinctly non-normalizing celebration of Irishness; it makes visible the styling and performing of identities that have little to do with genealogically established or deterministic ancestry.

The cut and fabric weight of Montserrat's St Patrick's Day costumes are noticeably Caribbean in style, whereas the colours of the plaid design are interestingly inclusive of multiple markers of Irish identity – Protestant orange and Catholic green alongside the francophone islands' madras checks. What interpretive weight such cultural queering may carry is less relevant here than the deliberate de-investment in ethnic authenticity via distinctiveness. For the community, the rewards of the parade appear to be experienced through shared – rather than separated – historical experience and belonging. Gleeson's faith in scientific tools to identify grounds for genetic Irish kinship and his expression of the Caribbean as simply another historical context for Irish exile are clearly flawed in terms of understanding the history of Caribbean Irish connections. And his approach is perhaps more fundamentally flawed in its refusal to confront and embrace what the Caribbean offers as a location for rethinking how diasporic and multiple identities come into being, and what functions they may serve beyond reassertion of reimagined appropriations of ancestral histories based elsewhere.

Interestingly, the way in which the creolized Caribbean queers disciplinary sincerity and clarity has its own history in other attempts to offer an authoritative and reliable account of Caribbean Irish connections. This dates back to the first book-length study on this subject, *Whence the "Black Irish" of Jamaica?*, written by the Jesuit priest Joseph J. Williams and published in 1932. Although the title seems to promise an answer to a historical question, the account given is intriguingly inflected in both its methodology and deductions by the volatility of the designation "Irish" and the instability inherent in the sources themselves. Although Williams is keen and earnest in his attempts to discriminate historical fact from the competing narratives of events that his sources appear to present, he too inevitably becomes entangled in a matrix of possibility that exceeds any reliable accounting of actuality. Read in its entirety, Williams's study becomes a patchwork of quotations that spins more chaos than order. His

Figure 6.1. "Typical of the 'Black Irish' in Jamaica". Joseph J. Williams, *Whence the "Black Irish" of Jamaica?* (New York: Lincoln Mac Veagh, Dial Press, 1932).

reading of Oliver Cromwell's letters is followed by confrontation with the denial of Cromwell's figures for Irish transportation by the English historian Samuel Rawson Gardiner. Moreover, he openly cites sources within which his core findings are already dubiously framed: "Robert Dunlop, in his Preface to *Ireland under the Commonwealth*, tells us: ... At the time I was of the opinion that the view taken by Prendergast in his well-known book – *The Cromwellian Settlement in Ireland* – was not an entirely impartial one."[22]

While Williams's fourteen-page bibliography evidences his commitment to recovering this history in detail and exactness, he continually implies the difficulty of overcoming national, faith and class bias in his sources, as well as the exaggerations of hearsay. Significantly, Williams concludes his study with an important shift in perspective that acknowledges the incompleteness and uncertainty of knowledge around these origins and lines of ancestry:

> whatever, then, may be the final conclusion about the fate of the Irish "wenches" and boys who were ordered by Cromwell to be shipped to Jamaica, a question which, for the present at least, must be left as an open one, this much is certain, that from the earliest days of the English occupation of the Island, there was a large proportion of Irish, both Catholic and non-Catholic, in the make-up of the population, and that not only Irish names but Irish blood as well is widely diffused throughout the island today.[23]

Finally, then, he offers an alternative to a history of the Irish in the Caribbean by moving closer to a Caribbean-style history of the Irish, in which the markers of distinctiveness are eroded by the accelerated cultural and ethnic mixing and intermixing that characterizes this region. Williams may even be seen here to offer a backward glance at his own history that is not out of keeping with the lens of queer commentary and its emphasis on maintaining an awareness of and alertness to diverse and often contradictory calls upon meaning.

What makes Williams's understanding of the history of the Irish in the Caribbean so demonstrably one of queer relations are the images that accompany his text. The book opens with the title page, framed on the left-hand side by a remarkable figure. For Williams, having worked through the fragments of the historical record and all its twists and contradictions, such "typical" black Irish are unproblematic and unremarkable – a consequence of a characteristically Caribbean history, in which phenotype no longer functions as a guarantee or even a sign of origin. While normative cultural frameworks in Ireland, and its conventional confines amid the diaspora, that summon hegemonic indices of Irishness would be perplexed by this seemingly conventional studio portrait of a man of African descent, the culture-queerness of the Caribbean – where seeming and being do not answer to the calls of origin and ethnicity in any straightforward way – creates a context in which such queer belonging is entirely typical. I use *culture-queerness* here to identify a mode of being and knowing in the Caribbean that enables plural overlapping, creolized and contingent cultural belongings which are not authenticated by reference to normalizing of a singular origin or biological essentialism.

In his poem "Lines Composed to Test the Idea of Montserrat", published ninety years after Williams's study, the Montserratian poet E.A. (Archie) Markham – who looked much like one of Williams's typical "Black Irish" – similarly refuses a linear organization of space, time and ethnic markers as a way to know his Caribbean self. The poem states:

> I'm writing an autobiography,
> was born there, grew up here, etc.
> Somewhere I'll lay claim to heritage, why not Irish;
> so, to get there I won't start from here, sort of thing.
> Here, you see, is the wrong place.[24]

The framing of Markham's interrogative "why not Irish" is of particular significance here. His orientation to ethnicity – genetic or ancestral – is not straight but rather an expression of the possibility of multiple directions that exceed geographical belonging (though Markham did reside in Northern Ireland while writer-in-residence at the University of Ulster, Coleraine between 1988 and 1991). The poem situates heritage not as the predetermined compulsion of bloodline but as a product of choice, of assent, of craft. In this way he situates Montserrat within the logics of "queer time and place" – a Caribbeanized version of Judith Halberstam's alternative to heteronormative time, which is traditionally based around successive generations. What Halberstam argues as the particular liberation offered by this remodelling of temporality can also be argued of Caribbeanness in its parallel release from the bearings of hereditary structures: "what has made queerness compelling as a form of self-description in the past decade or so has to do with the way it has potential to open up new life narratives and alternative relations to time and space".[25] Markham's temporal and spatial grammar of an autobiography is consciously skewed by the imprecision of a creolized inheritance and a diasporic life, here made into a virtue and a subject-making practice by the will to allow imagination to act as memory and the present to own its own history-making.

Rather than being a process that sheds new light on how Ireland and the Caribbean have come together, I want to suggest that thinking through Caribbean Irish connections compels us to think through how Irishness and Caribbeanness are so differently constituted and valued as identity-giving ethnicities. The Caribbean is a place that queers the bearings of Irishness in "its fragmentation; its instability; its reciprocal isolation; its uprootedness; its cultural heterogeneity; its lack of historiography and historical continuity; its contingency and impermanence; its syncretism, etc." as defined by Benítez-Rojo.[26] On the other hand, it is within the Caribbean that the Irish can emerge most visibly as queer figures who embody the disruption of seemingly clean and known edges between white and black, powerful and powerless, victim and criminal.

What happens at these horizons where the known changes shape remains an absorbing line of enquiry, and one that may help us work with, rather than against, the possibilities for accommodation and co-belonging that culture-queer identities present. For Irishness, it may be that the queerness of the Irish Caribbean presents a more open formation of identity that makes visible the possibilities for living together in the much more ethnically mixed post–Celtic Tiger Ireland, as well as in creolized diasporas. For Caribbeanness, it may be that acknowledging plasticity and contingency as the region's distinctive basis for individual and collective identity formations will provide a powerful position from which to critique the anomalous attachment to an idea of normative or deviant identities with regards to sexuality that remains an urgent task in most of the anglophone Caribbean.

Notes

1. Eve Kosofsky Sedgwick, *Tendencies* (Durham, NC: Duke University Press, 1993), 8–9.

2. Michael Warner, "Introduction", in *Fear of a Queer Planet: Queer Politics and Social Theory*, ed. Michael Warner, vii–xxxi (Minneapolis: University of Minnesota Press, 1993), xxvi.

3. Joseph Valente, "Self-Queering Ireland?", *Canadian Journal of Irish Studies* 36, no. 3 (2010): 27.

4. Ibid., 28. Quotation from Louise Ryan, *Gender Identity and the Irish Press, 1922–1937: Embodying the Nation* (Lewiston, NY: E. Mellon, 2002), 259.

5. Aoife Monks, "'Everyone Can Be Irish for the Day': Towards a Theory of Diasporic Performance in the St Patrick's Day Parade", *New England Theatre Journal* 16 (2005): 124.

6. Ibid., 128.

7. Anna Maguire, *Rock the Sham* (New York: Street Level, 2006), 17. The homophobic attitudes of the Ancient Order of Hibernians that Maguire refers to are, importantly, contested by the Queer Irish parade in the Bronx.

8. Monks, "Everyone Can Be Irish", 128–29.

9. Antonio Benítez-Rojo, *The Repeating Island: The Caribbean and the Postmodern Perspective* (Durham, NC: Duke University Press, 1992), 2.

10. Orlando Patterson, *Slavery and Social Death: A Comparative Study* (Cambridge, MA: Harvard University Press, 1982), 5.

11. Ibid., 7.

12. Derek Walcott, *What the Twilight Says* (New York: Farrar, Straus and Giroux, 1999), 74. For a reading of Walcott's subjunctive mood see Shalini Puri, *The Caribbean Postcolonial: Social Equality, Post/nationalism, and Cultural Hybridity* (New York: Palgrave Macmillan, 2004), 88.

13. "Obama in Ireland: President Searches for 'Missing Apostrophe'", *Daily Telegraph*, 24 May 2011, http://www.telegraph.co.uk/news/worldnews/europe/ireland/8532091/Obama-in-Ireland-president-searches-for-missing-apostrophe.html.

14. Michael H. O'Connor, *A Guide to Tracing Your Kerry Ancestors* (Dublin: Flyleaf, 1990), 11.

15. http://www.icara.ie.

16. Ibid.

17. Judith Halberstam, *In a Queer Time and Place: Transgender Bodies, Subcultural Lives* (New York: New York University Press, 2005), 1.

18. *Patriot*, 4 January 1841, 2.

19. Ibid.

20. William James Gardner, *History of Jamaica* (London: Oxford University Press,

1873), 411; cited in Joseph J. Williams, *Whence the "Black Irish" of Jamaica?* (New York: Lincoln Mac Veagh, Dial Press, 1932), 73.

21. http://www.icara.ie.

22. Williams, *Whence the "Black Irish"*, 21.

23. Ibid., 75.

24. E.A. Markham, "Lines Composed to Test the Idea of Montserrat", in *A Rough Climate* (London: Anvil, 2002), 34.

25. Halberstam, *Queer Time and Place*, 1–2.

26. Benítez-Rojo, *Repeating Island*, 2.

Chapter 7

Historic and Contemporary Irish Identity on Montserrat

The "Emerald Isle of the Caribbean"

KRYSTA RYZEWSKI AND LAURA McATACKNEY

CONTEMPORARY MONTSERRAT IS MARKETED GLOBALLY AS THE "Emerald Isle of the Caribbean". This tagline inspires tourists and scholars to visualize a verdant, fertile paradise bolstered by genuine and lasting historic links to Ireland. Both conceptions are only partial truths. This chapter enlists historical and archaeological sources to explore the nature and changing forms of Irishness on Montserrat. Documentary sources confirm significant Irish connections to the island from the seventeenth to the early nineteenth centuries. These sources reveal that Montserrat's historic Irish settlers were as divided by class and religion as they were united by a common nationality; furthermore, archaeological findings add further complexity to the island's cultural narrative. A unique material culture of Irishness is not readily apparent in any of the extant domestic or industrial artefact assemblages that span the first two centuries of European settlement. Indeed, recognizable motifs of Irishness – many of which are still prevalent today – emerged in the form of mass-produced material culture only relatively recently, after the Famine-era mass migrations of the 1840s. Building upon these ambiguities, we argue that there is a need for historians and

Figure 7.1. Map of Montserrat in the Caribbean (modified by K. Ryzewski, 2012).

archaeologists alike to re-examine the material culture and circumstances of the Irish diaspora in the centuries predating mid-nineteenth-century migrations. In this context we will explore the extent to which present-day conceptions of Irishness, such as the recent adoption of St Patrick's Day as a national holiday, are mapped onto historical realities.

Over the past two decades the island of Montserrat and its inhabitants have experienced total upheaval in all aspects of daily life. This small (102 square kilometres) British Overseas Territory in the Leeward Islands of the Lesser Antilles has been physically and socially transformed by natural disasters, beginning with the widespread damage caused by Hurricane Hugo in 1989 and followed by ongoing eruptions of the Soufrière Hills volcano beginning in 1995. The long process of coping and recovery associated with these disasters has been punctuated by major population loss, economic instability and variable success in redevelopment efforts. As volcanic activity gradually buried the former capital city of Plymouth and its surrounding villages in the late 1990s and early 2000s, the entire southern half of the island was designated an uninhabitable (exclusion) zone; Montserrat's pre-volcano population of twelve thousand has reduced to four thousand. Those who remain on the island inhabit the non-exclusion

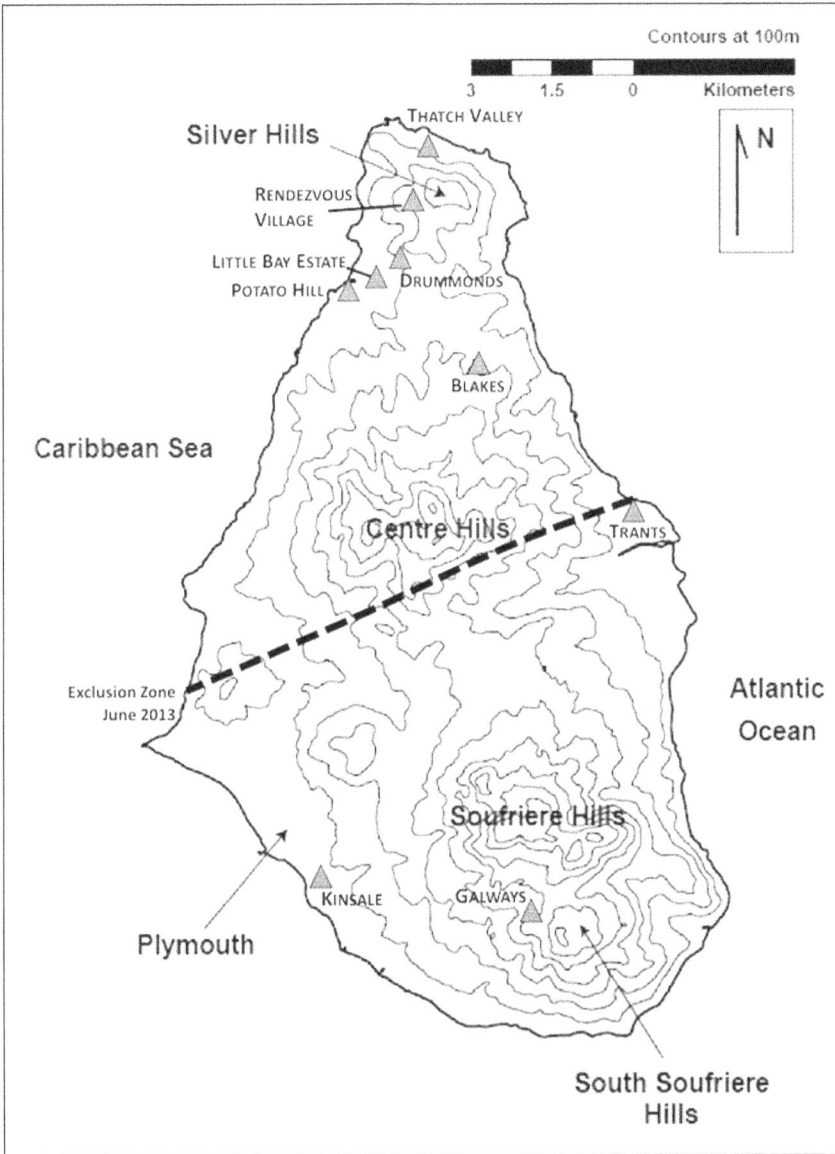

Figure 7.2. Map of Montserrat with location of sites and places discussed in text and volcanic exclusion zone boundary as of June 2013 (T. Leppard, 2012, modified by K. Ryzewski, 2013).

zone, in the previously marginal northern region. Major changes to the regional landscape include newly constructed infrastructure, resettlement villages and relocation of government headquarters and the capital city to Little Bay.

These disasters have devastated the island's tangible cultural heritage, including monuments, historic villages, homes, fortifications, plantation estates, prehistoric settlements and well-known landscape features. In their evaluation of damages to the island's known historic landmarks, archaeologists David Watters and Gillian Norton determined that thirty-five of the fifty plantation-era estates on Montserrat had been either completely destroyed or severely damaged.[1] Countless other previously unstudied archaeological sites of varying age and composition have also been affected, but the extent of the damage is unknown in the absence of a complete inventory of the island's historical and archaeological resources. A comprehensive inventory of cultural resources in the island's non-exclusion zone is underway in the midst of ongoing resettlement and development efforts. Since 2010 the Survey and Landscape Archaeology on Montserrat project, jointly directed by Krysta Ryzewski (Wayne State University) and John F. Cherry (Brown University), has worked with the Montserrat National Trust to conduct a survey of the north. The survey team has recorded more than fifty archaeological sites, from all time periods, and recovered more than fifteen thousand artefacts that shed light on the everyday lives and cultural identities of Montserrat's past inhabitants.[2]

A visible part of the disaster recovery process has been Montserrat's official rebranding as the "Emerald Isle of the Caribbean". Though the island's Irish connections have long been a source of interest for local residents and tourists alike, over the past two decades government agencies, the tourism industry and local communities have made concerted efforts to craft Montserrat's image in ways that foreground and bolster its Irish legacy. These efforts build upon perceived connections between present-day Montserrat and historic Irish communities, through formalization and promotion of interconnected cultural heritage such as iconography, material culture and cultural events. By foregrounding both traditional Irish and creolized Afro-Irish identities in a promotional narrative, Montserratians are establishing the island's "authorised heritage discourse" and orienting its reception to a global audience.[3]

The most prominent example of these efforts is St Patrick's Day, a national holiday that simultaneously commemorates the island's Irish heritage and a failed uprising by Afro-Caribbean slaves and members of the island's free black community on the same day in 1768.[4] In the wake of volcanic devastation, the St Patrick's holiday has grown into a week-long festival that attracts international tourists and acts as a major homecoming event for Montserrat's diaspora community. The following discussion addresses why, in the absence of accessible physical and historical traces of a distinctly Irish presence, Montserrat's Irish identity remains so strong. We first evaluate the evidence for historical antecedents of the Irish legacy on Montserrat and then critically examine the ways in which the foregrounding of Irish heritage discourse during contemporary recovery and revitalization efforts intersects or diverges from such accounts.

The Historical Irish Presence and Its Legacy

Montserrat's Irish legacy is rooted in the demographics and social dynamics of the late seventeenth and early eighteenth centuries. The island's first generations of European settlers were mostly of Gaelic Irish or recently planted British ancestry, broadly defined as either native Irish and predominantly Roman Catholic or of English/Scottish planter origins and predominantly Protestant. Distinctions between these two broad ethnic categories were, however, blurred by the presence of a smaller population of long-standing Anglo-Irish Roman Catholics who were connected to the earliest plantation in Ireland from the twelfth century.

Some of the upper echelons of Montserrat's society were Roman Catholics, and they found themselves affected at different times by anti-Catholic legislation in Great Britain and Ireland. Such legislation built on previous legal precedents to impose restrictions barring Irish Catholics from owning land, holding political office and occupying other positions of influence.[5] Although this legislation varied in its reach and impact outside Ireland, there is evidence of Irish landowners changing religious affiliation because of political expediency, and of finding their interests in other areas of the British Empire forfeited, including their rights to make financial claims, maintain political positions and hold land, although this varied across time and space.

Beginning in 1632, European settlers arrived in Montserrat from the neighbouring islands of St Kitts and Nevis, as well as from other Caribbean islands, Ireland and England.[6] The Irish arrivals in Montserrat were part of a widespread population movement to the Caribbean during the seventeenth century, which had multiple causal factors. The upper echelons of both Gaelic and Anglo-Irish society were driven to the Caribbean by a desire to exploit and benefit from the profitable industrial, mercantile and maritime enterprises associated with the islands' plantation economies. The demand for labour was met in part by less fortunate Gaelic Irish who, in the wake of the Cromwellian wars and displacements, were either seeking economic opportunities in the Caribbean as indentured servants or had been involuntarily transported from Irish and English institutions.

The first Leeward Islands census, collected in 1678 by Governor William Stapleton (himself described as Irish), indicates that Montserrat had by far the largest concentration of Irish inhabitants in the Lesser Antilles. Seventy per cent of Montserrat's white population self-identified as Irish, in comparison to much lower percentages of the populations on nearby St Kitts (10 per cent), Nevis (23 per cent) and Antigua (26 per cent).[7] Of the island's white population, at least two-thirds of those who identified as Irish were poor farmers, labourers or indentured servants who lived in close proximity to one another in St Patrick's parish, located in the southwest part of the island.[8] By 1678 the island was also home to Anglo-Irish and English settlers, a small number of other Europeans linked to trade interests, and African slaves.

Despite sharing a country of birth and broad cultural practices, Montserrat's Irish were not a homogeneous or cohesive group during the plantation era. During the late seventeenth and early eighteenth centuries, while the majority of Montserrat's Irish settlers struggled to live on small plots in the harsh environmental conditions of St Patrick's parish, a small elite class of planters established sugar estates across the island. The planters had emerged from among the island's Irish residents, from settlers with Anglo-Irish or Gaelic Irish roots, and to a lesser degree from English and other European colonists. With the introduction of the sugar industry came the importation of African slaves, tremendous wealth from sugar profits and escalating socioeconomic, racial and ethnic inequalities. Generally among the Irish planters, concerns about the profitability of sugar production took priority over other allegiances.[9] David Galway exhibited such political expediency when he signed a petition of loyalty to the British Crown in 1669, an act through which he officially distanced himself from his Irish political and Roman Catholic religious background in order to secure and expand business interests.[10]

Among the Irish planters there is little to suggest that they asserted Irish ideological or cultural connections in order to achieve positions of power in the island's plantation economy. But there is more subtle evidence that Irish planters, including the Blakes, Lynches and Trants, moved to secure their wealth, elite status and personal legacies through strategic marriages between their families during the late seventeenth and early eighteenth centuries.[11] Some Irish planter families also married within the wider circles of elite British military and administrative figures established in neighbouring islands. For example,

William Stapleton secured his position as governor of the Leeward Islands within months of his marriage to the daughter of the governor of Nevis, Lieutenant-Colonel Russell.[12] Such inter-island and local marriage patterns indicate mixed and overlapping motivations among the planters, who were simultaneously concerned with expanding their influence and wealth as regionally powerful planters and with maintaining their Irish connections among their peers within Montserrat's plantation economy.

Through the growth and profitability of the sugar industry during the eighteenth century, Montserrat's plantation owners accumulated sufficient wealth to relocate to preferred residences off the island, either on nearby islands or back in Ireland or England. A significant decrease in the island's white population during the peak of eighteenth-century sugar production reflects in large part the increase of imported enslaved labour and accompanying absenteeism among the planter elite.[13] Whereas in 1678 Montserrat's population of 3,775 was 74 per cent white, by the time of the 1729 census the island's population of 6,998 was 16 per cent white. Forty-six years later, in 1775, the population had nearly doubled in size to 11,148 and was 12 per cent white.[14] However, though Irish planters and labourers were among those who left the island in large numbers, their departure was not as rapid as the census statistics might suggest. On the contrary, as historian Frank Pitman observes, in comparison to the other Leeward Islands, Montserrat's white population declined more gradually during the first two decades of the eighteenth century. Pitman argues that this decline was due to a dual process in which Irish settlers continued to arrive at the island in significant numbers at the same time as long-term Irish inhabitants of Montserrat were leaving, as was the case with their counterparts on neighbouring islands.

The vast majority of unflattering references by the British Crown to Montserrat's Irish were directed towards the lower-class communities of St Patrick's parish. Though the government's actions were intended to marginalize the region's Irish residents, the effectiveness of its restrictions and commentaries is questionable. The frequency with which the government's denigrating comments appear in historical records, and their content, suggests the continuity and persistence of Irish self-identification and affiliation in St Patrick's throughout the seventeenth and eighteenth centuries. While the maintenance of Irish identity among Montserrat's lower classes served to preserve and reinforce links to fellow countrymen, it was also a reaction by Irish settlers to the prevalent anti-Irish (and anti-Catholic) feeling widespread throughout British society in the wake of the Cromwellian conquest of Ireland (1649–53).[15]

The Irish from St Patrick's and its neighbouring villages responded as a community to such sentiments by staging numerous overt acts of rebellion and resistance against the British authorities. In groups as large as two thousand they routinely assisted invading forces, fighting against the island's English government and planter elite during the many minor foreign raids on the island that occurred before 1800.[16] In one account, following the French invasion of 1667, the English commander-in-chief, William Willoughby, detailed how Montserrat had been robbed and plundered by "a party of rebellious and wicked people of the Irish nation".[17] Such incidents among a sizeable proportion of lower-class Gaelic Irish settlers suggest that these residents – who were not the primary economic beneficiaries of the island's colonial experience – were perhaps differently tied to and invested in their Irish connections than their predominantly loyal planter counterparts, who occupied the other extreme of Montserrat's socioeconomic spectrum.

Despite the local differences among the island's Irish residents, contemporary British officials commonly depicted all the Montserratian Irish as a cohesive group united by what was presumed to be a shared Roman Catholic faith. This act of collective identification by the colonial authorities served to identify and isolate the perceived threat that Catholics posed to the (Protestant) British Crown, without taking into account the Irish communities' different social connections, economic interests or religious affiliations.[18] Suspicion of the Irish during the plantation era was a Caribbean-wide sentiment that the British could direct towards all ranks of Irish society, if one is to heed Sir Charles Wheler's warning to the British administration: "[H]is majesty would take speciall Care, y't after Colonel Stapleton's time (whose fidelity he is sure of) that not onely an English Governour be always instituted, but that there be some Cittadell and small Garrison of English in pay."[19] Such advice states unambiguously that not only should an Englishman govern the island but also that a permanently stationed force of English soldiers was necessary to ensure the loyalty of the masses of Irish settlers. As with all historical sources there is a need to question the motivation of the informants, who may display varying degrees of personal bias and exaggerate circumstances in order to bargain for greater political control and military resources.

In summary, a somewhat duplicitous climate of disenfranchisement frames the history of the Montserratian Irish, resulting in a complicated and tangled account of the island's Irish legacy, with no overarching thread of perspective or experience. The Irish, viewed by the British government as a collective group, were subjected to numerous restrictions during the seventeenth and eighteenth centuries. Nevertheless, during the same period the Irish provided many of the governors of the island and were among the most profitable planters. At least in the higher ranks of society, and perhaps on a case-by-case basis, economic influence and political acumen temporarily assuaged pervasive ethnic prejudice and legislative barriers. Given the competing biases and contradictory narratives framing Montserrat's Irish history, attempts to understand the Irish settler reality may benefit from integrating other sources of evidence beyond the colonial documents – most notably, material culture and archaeological evidence.

Archaeological Traces and Irish Connections

Abundant archaeological remains survive on Montserrat that date to the period of historic Irish residency on the island. Standing ruins of plantations, footprints of residential structures, landscapes modified for agricultural activities, faint trackways connecting villages, and extensive collections of artefacts are tucked away in what were historically the most remote northern and eastern margins of the island. These sources of material culture comprise a repertoire of the material world and the everyday lives of the island's earliest European inhabitants; they offer alternative lenses through which we can interpret the unwritten history of the majority Irish experience on Montserrat. Ongoing archaeological research, focused on the island's non-exclusion zone and conducted by Ryzewski and Cherry, has identified fifty-one known and previously

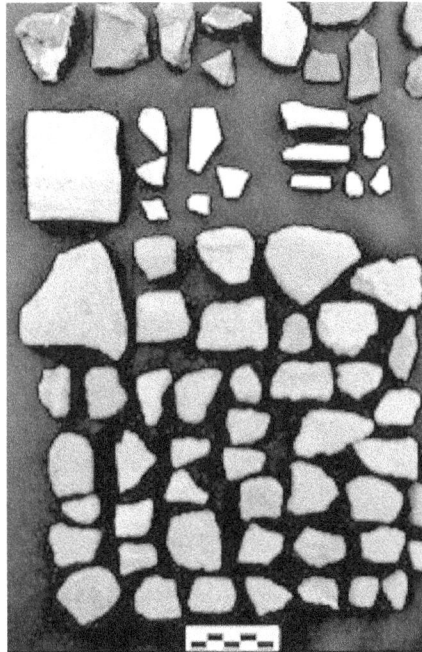

Figure 7.3. Artefact assemblage collected by archaeological survey of the residential area of the Thatch Valley site (Area B) includes predominately coarseware pottery with lesser quantities of seventeenth- and eighteenth-century and English-made stoneware and refined earthenware, tobacco pipes, glass bottle fragments and iron. © K. Ryzewski, 2013.

unknown plantation, residential and other properties that date between 1632 and 1900.

Several of the properties studied archaeologically once belonged to families of Irish ancestry. The largest property, Blake's Estate, includes a sugar process-ing complex and an adjacent uphill agricultural area, known locally as Upper Blakes.[20] Archaeologists have located several additional sites in the region whose original names and owners no longer survive in folk memory but which may yet be identified through archival research. Three of these sites – the contem-porary Thatch Valley, Potato Hill and Rendezvous Village – have connections to the island's older non-elite populations, potentially including the Irish.[21] The findings from these plantation-era archaeological sites present subtle and nuanced clues about past resident communities. All three sites are located in what were remote or isolated areas, with limited access to fresh water and other resources. Fieldwork and excavations at the sites have revealed an abundance of coarse earthenware pottery and the presence of more than a dozen objects refashioned and repurposed from broken glass bottles and pottery vessels to serve utilitarian, decorative or symbolic purposes.[22]

From the abundance of plantation-era sites examined, archaeologists have recovered no artefacts with distinctively Irish origins or decorations. This absence hints at a salient difference between more modern nineteenth- and twentieth-

Figure 7.4. Montserrat flag hanging in a roadside bar. © L. McAtackney, 2011.

century conceptions of Irish diasporic identity and its historical antecedents among Montserrat's early-period Irish communities. A straightforward explanation for the absence of Irish-affiliated symbols or objects in Montserrat's seventeenth- and eighteenth-century assemblages can be found in archaeological investigations of the Irish diaspora elsewhere. Archaeologists Stephen Brighton and Charles Orser have argued that assemblages of Irish artefacts recovered from mid-nineteenth-century sites in New York "provide unique insights into the *beginnings* of the commodification of an Irish and/or Irish-American identity".[23] Their statement highlights the fact that such identifiably Irish motifs and symbolism – such as harps, shamrocks and common political motifs such as "Home Rule" – are not likely to be present in earlier assemblages connected to the Irish diaspora. Similarly, in the Australian context James Symonds has connected the appearance of "Irish" decorated artefacts with the politicization of Irish nationalism – in both Ireland and the diaspora – in the same period.[24] In both the Australian and New York case studies, the Irish diaspora materializes its identity in a form that is easily deciphered archaeologically, but at a point in time that considerably postdates the main period of Irish settlement on Montserrat. The material culture recovered from sites on Montserrat suggests how the lower classes, including the Irish, would have lived with and used standard wares and utilitarian objects at multiple sites across the island well before modern-day material articulations of Irish nationalism.[25]

Archaeological evidence on Montserrat does not reveal a distinctly identifiable or homogeneous Irish population whose material expressions of Irish ethnicity and identity were in line with familiar modern symbolisms. This discrepancy serves as a poignant reminder that there exist two centuries' worth of social and material dynamics that remain poorly understood by historians and archaeologists alike. Nevertheless, the absence of identifiably "Irish" material connections should not be taken to suggest that the island's Irish inhabitants did not, for example, possess shared tastes for certain culinary styles or attach symbolic value to particular ceramic vessel types. Such Irish connections may have existed and may be decipherable in material culture assemblages, but understandings of their significance will remain obscured until research in Montserrat and elsewhere in the Caribbean focuses more extensively on the material world of the Irish diaspora in the centuries prior to the Famine-era migrations.

Irish Identity on Contemporary Montserrat

An expectation that archaeological evidence of Irishness from the seventeenth and eighteenth centuries will mirror the types of Irish imagery and symbolism used in the nineteenth century oversimplifies historical circumstances. Such a belief shares similar tendencies with the present-day reappropriation of Irish identity in Montserrat's post-disaster heritage discourse. Presently the contemporary material culture of Montserrat displays "Irish" motifs and identifiers in abundance. The first symbol that visitors arriving in Montserrat encounter is the official passport stamp: a large shamrock printed in green ink. Shamrocks also proliferate on tourist information notices, shop signage, luggage tags and roadside bars.

Likewise, Montserrat's national flag, based on the British Blue Ensign, has a Union flag in the top left corner and the national coat of arms – a harp-playing white colleen ("The Lady with the Harp") – as its main feature. Her physical resemblance to the Irish personification of Erin is unmistakable. With iconography dating from at least 1909, the flag is one of the island's most long-standing examples of material culture that displays Irish connections. Though the general

Figure 7.5. "Emerald Shamrock" dancers, St Patrick's Day, Festival Village. © K. Ryzewski, 2007.

symbolism has remained consistent over the past century, it is only in the past two decades that the flag's use has become widespread and its design standard-ized (for example, the colour of the colleen's hair and skin and the shape and size of the components).

Academic interest in Irish connections in Montserrat dates at least to the early decades of the twentieth century; it has sought to reveal an Irish legacy and to question or supplement what might constitute the true nature of the Irish facet of contemporary Montserratian identity. Father Aubrey Gywnn, an Irish Jesuit, was one of the earliest and most influential historians of the Irish on Montserrat and elsewhere in the Caribbean. Also working during the 1920s and 1930s was the civil servant T. Savage English, who transcribed many (now lost) government documents from Montserrat while working for the British government.[26] Gwynn's working papers, held in the Jesuit Archive in Dublin, include short items of correspondence between the two men, indicating that they were aware of each other's work.

Since the 1960s, two Montserratian academics, Sir Howard Fergus and J.A. George Irish, have questioned the positive interpretation of the Irish presence in Montserrat created by Gywnn and Savage English by drawing attention to relationships between the Irish and black slave populations on the island, and in particular the Irish's role as slave-owners. The rise of the US civil rights move-ment and postcolonial movements on neighbouring islands evidently shaped their discursive orientations. This critical engagement with Irish relationships on Montserrat can also be seen in more recent work by historians such as Donald Akenson and the current Irish president, academic Michael D. Higgins. The treatment of Montserrat's Irish history and the shaping of contemporary heritage discourse over the course of the twentieth century and into the twenty-first is divided between accounts that promote, on one end of the spectrum, a unique shared history and, on the other, narratives that associate the Irish (as a whole) with brutal oppression. We have already illustrated in this discussion how a combination of historical and archaeological evidence might nuance these polarized historical interpretations of the Montserratian Irish.

Other disciplinary researchers, especially anthropologist John Messenger, have moved beyond the document to theorize from cultural practices the last-ing traces of Irish culture and socialization on the island. Messenger cites as evidence of ongoing Irish influence such apparent commonalities as speech pat-terns (a southwestern Irish "brogue" is said to be identifiable), the eating of goat water (supposedly similar to Irish stew), musical instruments (a bodhrán-like drum) and even a predilection for hospitality.[27] While local historian Howard Fergus has critiqued many of these claims as fanciful, it is undeniable that Irish resonances do continue, particularly in names that recur geographically in landscape features, towns and estates. The Montserrat phonebook testifies to the enduring existence of Irish surnames, as well as the names *Ireland* and *Irish*, which indicates at the very least a lack of active expunging of historical, colonial names, as occurred on other Caribbean islands. Rather, this enduring connection to Irish nomenclature reveals the complicated relationship that Montserrat maintains with a conception of Ireland that is ambiguously post-colonial but also connected to the colonial project. The degree of maintenance of what could be considered an authentic Irish identity is less clear.

St Patrick's Day, Montserrat Style

The case study of St Patrick's Day serves to question the longevity, connectivity and continuity of Irish identity into the present. The Montserrat Public Library's newspaper archive provides a chronicle of the recent mass adoption and formalization of St Patrick's Day on the island, transforming it from an occasionally mentioned religious celebration to a national holiday and festival. St Patrick's Day became an officially designated national holiday in 1985, and since 1995 it has become a week-long festival that includes a parade in national dress, a road race called "the slave run", dinners, dancing, pub crawls and public talks.

Before the early 1980s, St Patrick's Day was observed primarily in St Patrick's parish, an area in the southwest of the island where early historic-period Irish settlements were numerous and where continued connection to Irish facets of identity seemed to be most intensely felt. Traditionally the celebration was organized by and centred on the local Roman Catholic church. Articles and editorials in the *Montserrat Reporter* during the 1980s and early 1990s champion the push towards nationalization of the holiday. A 1995 editorial included a complaint that the "national affair" of St Patrick's Day needed to be better centrally organized and controlled.[28] Presently the island is one of the few places outside Ireland where the date is officially marked as a national holiday. The short length of time during which this holiday acquired national status provokes questions as to how "traditional" it actually is and to what extent it has been repackaged for economic and cultural purposes in the wake of Hurricane Hugo in 1989 and the volcanic devastation which began in 1995.

The earliest newspapers archived on Montserrat date from the early 1950s.

They make no mention of St Patrick's Day until 1958, when the parish bulletin for St Patrick's Church in the *Observer* notes, "Monday 17th St Patrick's Day".[29] In the early 1960s St Patrick's Day is infrequently mentioned in newspapers and again is restricted to church bulletins. A newspaper report from 1966 states: "During the Royal visit of Feb. 19 references were made to the Irish connection of Montserrat, and is understood that several correspondents on the Royal Tour were seeking information on the matter."[30] The newspaper uses this opportunity to note that St Patrick's Day – "the national day of Ireland" – would occur the following week. Although the article acknowledges a historical Irish connection, there is no mention of formalized celebrations taking place on Montserrat.

By the mid-1970s, clear attempts to reinvigorate Montserrat's link with Ireland, and thus St Patrick's Day, appear in a variety of sources. The newspapers at the time reveal strong left-wing, anti-colonial politics among the public intellectuals on the island. The desire for self-government is articulated, along with reluctant acceptance that the size and limited resources of the island would make such independence unlikely on an economic basis. The impact of contemporary politics on the publicly articulated Irish history of the island was multifaceted. The Irish links were highlighted to emphasize a historic connection that differed from the contemporary British rule but was forthright in its negative assessment of historical Irish treatment of the slave ancestors.

In the late 1970s to mid-1980s, the newspapers question accepted discourses of Irish history on the island and the role of the Irish as slave-owners, painting them as vicious and cruel as their British counterparts. The *Montserrat Mirror* commended the attempts at "ideological re-orientations" led by Fergus and Irish.[31] Public discussions questioned whether the celebration should be called "St Patrick's Day" or "Heroes' Day", and these continued throughout the early 1980s. Such ambivalent messages resulted in calls for the celebration of a national holiday on St Patrick's Day being accompanied by anti-Irish and anti-British rhetoric, focusing less on the day as a connection with Irish culture and more on the remembrance of the failed slave revolt on that date in 1768. These debates about the adoption of St Patrick's Day at the very least highlight a public move towards formalizing celebration of the Irish presence on the island as a facet of contemporary Montserratian identity, even in cases when the Irish connection is portrayed in negative terms.

Alongside the growing anti-colonial and civil rights political rhetoric evident in Montserratian newspapers, the 1970s also witnessed a move towards engaging with the historic Irish nature of Montserrat as part of locally based tourism strategies. The main headline in the *Montserrat Mirror* on 18 March 1961, from "Our US Correspondent", notes a need to develop air travel to the island to allow tourists to avail of its many attributes: "the scenery, it has comparable beaches and it has picturesque villages".[32] At this point there is no mention of the historic Irish links as a selling point. However, by 1979 a tourist policy document in the Montserrat Library collection lists, as its point 12, "building up the 'Irish Connection' more".[33] Being relegated to point 12 suggests little urgency about emphasizing the historical connection, but it is under formal consideration to be promoted as a unique selling point of the island. Seven years later, in a less than subtle 1986 newspaper headline, the *Montserrat Times* exclaims: "Irish Connection Pays Off". The associated report links increasing tourist revenues from the Irish-American (rather than Irish) market to the recent adoption of St Patrick's Day as a national holiday in 1985.[34] Newspaper promotion of St Patrick's Day as a tourist event is notable from the early 1980s onwards. Reports from this time increasingly advertise the events and report on the scale and attendance of celebrations.

Perhaps the most visible invention of the present-day St Patrick's Day festivities is the national dress, which is ubiquitous during contemporary celebrations. Despite its centrality to the festivities, this national costume is of even more recent vintage than the national holiday of St Patrick's Day. Announcement of a competition to design a national dress first appears in the island's newspapers in 1987. The creation and adoption of the national dress over the next decade followed a specific agenda to promote the multi-ethnic origins of the island, referred to in 1988 as "roots awareness".[35] The rules for the competition emphasized that the "African–Irish/European–Arawak" origins of the population should be included. The design, now hugely popular, was formalized in 2002: a green, white and orange tartan (a design that has Scottish, Welsh and Irish historic precedents). The pattern is promoted as symbolizing all of the island's cultural roots, and the overall costume design aims to connect the island's contemporary Caribbean identities. For example, its components – a tartan skirt and white blouse for women – are similar in form to national costumes worn on other Caribbean islands. The green in Montserrat's plaid is meant to symbolize African heritage, while its combination of green, white and orange clearly references the Irish tricolour.

With the depopulation and economic collapse of the island as a result of Hurricane Hugo and the Soufrière Hills volcano, the meaning of St Patrick's Day has once more noticeably changed. Post eruption, it has become a national

Figure 7.6. Sign welcoming visitors to Montserrat posted outside of the airport arrivals hall. Note the strip of Montserratian tartan tied to the four corners of the sign. © K Ryzewski, 2014.

event to which the Montserratian diaspora returns annually. During the disaster recovery process, the holiday has been the backbone that supports the struggling tourism industry. Impassioned debates about the meaning and the real nature of the Irish presence on the island have become less contested. Nevertheless, an emphasis on the slave background of the holiday is clearly an ongoing feature of the celebrations. In recent years the Alliouagana Festival of the Word – *Alliouagana* is the Carib Amerindian name for the island – the fourth of which was held in December 2012, was established to celebrate Montserrat's local literature, theatre and culture. The festival takes place in either summer or late fall and is not in direct competition with the more established St Patrick's Day festival. However, the use of the pre-colonial native name of the island and the lack of reference to Irish connections could suggest a desire to establish a cultural event that does not rely on an Irish historical connection.

The evidence in newspapers from the 1950s onwards indicates that knowledge of the island's Irish past has existed for some time. An enduring folk knowledge of and interest in the Irish connection has resulted in a complicated response to that connection. One example is the appropriation of the Irish patron saint's day conflated with celebration of African resistance to slavery – important for both tourism and the black majority in Montserrat. Likewise the national dress suggests that the visibility of Irishness is not so much linked to recognition of a historic shared diasporic space as it signifies a sense of ethnic pride that links to colonial rule and postcolonial aspirations. The ways in which historical sensitivities about continued British dependency seem to intensify a national interest in Irishness indicate a complex sociopolitical matrix in which cultural expressions and celebrations of non-British – even anti-British – identities create an alternative historical narrative that is both inclusive and non-racialized.

This essay emphasizes the need for acknowledgement of historical and archaeological evidence of the "Irish" presence in Montserrat's history and in contemporary Montserratian identity discourse. To an extent, this discourse is based on a shared historic, diasporic Caribbean Irish connection, with historical records emphasizing the "Irish" nature of the island's early colonial period that was eventually supplanted by African slaves during the sugar plantation era. However, the material culture from the seventeenth and eighteenth centuries recovered from archaeological investigations of the island does not present clear indicators of the sort of Irish associations that are found among the later, better-known, post–Great Famine diasporas of the mid-nineteenth century. Indeed, since groups with a clearly Irish origin had disappeared by the mid-nineteenth century, trajectories of historical authenticity, connectivity or continuity do not offer adequate courses for explaining either the social dynamics of Montserrat's early historic-period Irish population or the twentieth- and twenty-first-century formalization and incorporation of various Irish symbols into the island's national image and heritage discourse.

Notes

1.   David R. Watters and Gillian E. Norton, "Volcanically Induced Loss of Archaeological Sites in Montserrat", in *Proceedings of the 21st Congress of the International Association for Caribbean Archaeology*, ed. B. Reid, Roget H. Petitjean and L.A. Curet, 48–55 (St Augustine, Trinidad: University of the West Indies, 2007).

2.   John F. Cherry, Krysta Ryzewski and Thomas P. Leppard, "Multi-period Landscape Survey and Site Risk Assessment on Montserrat, West Indies", *Journal of Island and Coastal Archaeology* 7, no. 2 (2012): 282-302.

3.   Laurajane Smith, *Uses of Heritage* (London: Routledge, 2006); Laura McAtackney, Krysta Ryzewski and John F. Cherry, "Emerald Isle of the Caribbean? Insights into the Historic Irish Presence on Montserrat" (paper presented at the Contemporary

Historical Archaeology in Theory Conference, University of York, UK, 16 November 2012).

4. John C. Messenger, "St Patrick's Day in 'the Other Emerald Isle'", *Éire-Ireland* 29, no. 1 (1994): 12–23; Jonathan Skinner, *Before the Volcano: Reverberations of Identity on Montserrat* (Kingston, Jamaica: Arawak, 2004), 141–70.

5. Charles I. McGrath, "Securing the Protestant Interest: The Origins and Purpose of the Penal Laws of 1695", *Irish Historical Studies* 30, no. 117 (May 1996): 25–46.

6. Richard S. Dunn, *Sugar and Slaves: The Rise of the Planter Class in the English West Indies, 1624–1713* (Chapel Hill: University of North Carolina Press, 1972), 124.

7. Dunn, *Sugar and Slaves*, 127; Hilary McD. Beckles, "A 'Riotous and Unruly Lot': Irish Indentured Servants and Freemen in the English West Indies, 1644–1713", *William and Mary Quarterly* 47, no. 4 (October 1990): 508. While Barbados's Irish connections may appear to provide a suitable comparison to Montserrat, in this case we do not consider the figures from Barbados, as the island is both geographically and demographically outside the regional scope of our discussion in the Lesser Antilles.

8. Vere Langford Oliver, ed., "Mounserrat, 1677–78: A Census", in *Caribbeana: Being Miscellaneous Papers Relating to the History, Genealogy, Topography, and Antiquities of the British West Indies* (London: Mitchell, Hughes and Clarke, 1910), 2:316–20, 342–47; Donald Harman Akenson, *If the Irish Ran the World: Montserrat, 1630–1730* (Montreal: McGill-Queen's University Press, 1997), 171–87; Howard Fergus, *Montserrat: History of a Caribbean Colony* (London: Macmillan, 1994), 73–76, 266; Lydia M. Pulsipher, "Resource Management Strategies on an Eighteenth Century Caribbean Sugar Plantation: Interpreting the Archaeological and Archival Records", *Florida Anthropologist* 35, no. 4 (1982): 243–50; Dunn, *Sugar and Slaves*. Pulsipher, "Resource Management Strategies", 246 and Map 4, refers to the St Patrick's area as "the Irish ghetto" and an area where the Irish (mainly freed indentures) "produced a cultural landscape that varied drastically from that controlled by the English planters" (246).

9. Natalie A. Zacek, *Settler Society in the English Leeward Islands, 1670–1776* (Cambridge: Cambridge University Press, 2010), 66–120.

10. Pulsipher, "Resource Management Strategies", 247.

11. H. Blake, *Blake Family Records, 1600–1700* (London: Blake, 1905).

12. Letter from Sir Thomas Lynch to Arlington, 15 June 1671, Colonial Office CO1/38, no. 65, National Archives, London, 226, cited in working papers of Aubrey Gwynn, Jesuit Archive, Dublin (consulted June 2013).

13. Keith Mason, "The World an Absentee Planter and His Slaves Made: Sir William Stapleton and His Nevis Sugar Estate, 1722–1740", *Bulletin of the John Rylands University Library* 75 (1993): 103–31; J.R.V. Johnston, "The Stapleton Sugar Plantations in the Leeward Islands", *Bulletin of the John Rylands Library* 48 (1965): 175–206; T. Savage English, *Ireland's Only Colony: Records of Montserrat, 1632 to the End of*

the Nineteenth Century (London: West India Committee, 1930), 226. Despite the increasing erosion of connections between Montserrat and its early Irish settlers during the eighteenth and nineteenth centuries, some planters with Irish ancestry maintained connections to the island by amassing property and wealth from their holdings until well after emancipation in 1834. Most notable among these families were the Blakes, who in 1850 remained Montserrat's largest landowners; see English, *Ireland's Only Colony.*

14. Oliver, "Mounserrat, 1677–78", 316–20, 342–47; Vere Langford Oliver, ed., "Mounserrat, 1729: A Census", in *Caribbeana: Miscellaneous Papers Relating to the History, Genealogy, Topography, and Antiquities of the British West Indies* (London: Mitchell, Hughes and Clarke, 1916), 4:302–11.

15. See Diane Purkiss, *The English Civil War: Papists, Gentlewomen, Soldiers and Witchfinders in the Birth of Modern Britain* (Cambridge: HarperCollins, 2006), 507.

16. Donald R. Crandall, *A Military History of Montserrat, W.I.: Attacks, Fortifications, Cannons, Defenders, 1632–1815* (Montserrat, 2000), 3; Lydia M. Pulsipher, *Seventeenth Century Montserrat: An Environmental Impact Statement*, Historical Geography Research Series 17 (Norwich: Geo Books, 1986), 23.

17. William Willoughby, "Report of William Willoughby on Montserrat", February 1668, Colonial Office CO1/24, no. 71, National Archives, London, cited in Beckles, "Riotous and Unruly", 519.

18. This includes the "Report of Sir Charles Wheler", 9 December 1671, Colonial Office CO1/27, no 52, National Archives, London, cited in working papers of Aubrey Gwynn, Jesuit Archive, Dublin (consulted June 2013).

19. Ibid.

20. Krysta Ryzewski and John F. Cherry, *Survey and Landscape Archaeology on Montserrat: Narrative Report on the Third Field Season, May–June 2012* (report submitted to Montserrat National Trust, Olveston, Montserrat, 2013).

21. Ibid.; John F. Cherry and Krysta Ryzewski, *Archaeological Activities on Potato Hill, Montserrat, 2010–2013* (report submitted to Montserrat National Trust, 2013).

22. Ibid. Coarse earthenware pottery comprised 47 per cent of total artefact assemblage at Thatch Valley (N=147), 13 per cent of the total at Potato Hill (N=4,360) and 10 per cent of the total at Rendezvous Village (N=330).

23. Stephen Brighton and Charles Orser, "Irish Images on English Goods in the American Market", in *Images, Representations and Heritage: Moving Beyond Modern Approaches to Archaeology*, ed. Ian Russell, 61–88 (New York: Springer, 2006), 63–64 (emphasis added).

24. James Symonds, "Historical Archaeology and the Recent Urban Past", *International Journal of Heritage Studies* 10, no. 1 (2004): 33–48.

25. Ibid., 40.

26. English, *Ireland's Only Colony.*

27. Messenger, "St Patrick's Day".

28. "St Patrick's Day Celebrations Flop", *Montserrat Reporter*, 24 March 1995, 1–2.

29. "Parish Bulletins", *Observer*, 15 March 1958.

30. "St Patrick's Day", *Montserrat Mirror*, 12 March 1966, 1.

31. "March 17th! / Montserrat's National Day?", *Montserrat Mirror*, 17 March 1979, 1.

32. "The Time for Tourism in Montserrat Is Now: Montserrat Is Right on the Beaten Track", *Montserrat Mirror*, 18 March 1961, 1.

33. "Preliminary Report: Visitor Expenditure and Motivational Survey, Montserrat, February–March 1979" (n.p.), 47.

34. "Irish Connection Pays Off", *Montserrat Times*, 27 March 1986, 3.

35. "National Dress Competition", *Montserrat Times*, 11 March 1988, 6

Chapter 8

Cataloguing Ireland

Exile and Indigeneity in Derek Walcott's Omeros

MARIA McGARRITY

DEREK WALCOTT'S LIFELONG INTEREST IN AND FACILITY with painting is well documented. His study of painting while a young student, his friendship with Dunstan St Omer, and his use of his own paintings to illustrate his poems, not to mention his shows and representation by the June Kelly Gallery in New York, clearly evince a lifelong commitment to that art.[1] In an early manuscript for his autobiographical poem *Another Life*, Walcott explains a striking union of the textual and architectural when referencing a painting as "one of the many haunting portraits in a book that I used as my imaginary museum. There I had learnt all that I knew about the old masters."[2] Walcott reveals a critical practice in his conceptualization of books as museums; what intrigues me here is not so much his love of painting as his connection of the book with what he calls his "imaginary museum".[3]

Walcott's way of representing the world frequently enacts a fusion of visual art and his poetic medium. In this early work *Another Life*, written from 1965 to 1972, he is responding to the urging of his artistic mentor, Harry Simmons, towards models of indigeneity – cultural forms characteristic of life in St Lucia. Simmons also advocated for the creation of "little galleries", analogous to the "little magazines" of the early twentieth century that were articulating so much localized cultural expression that mainstream publications overlooked.

According to Didacus Jules,

> Harry Simmons's influence on his students and on *Another Life* is most profound where he strongly advocates St. Lucian models rather than European. In a 1948 article about the importance of "Little Galleries" as opposed to large national museums, Simmons advocated that little galleries be organized in towns and villages throughout the island so that "the worker, the shopper would unconsciously understand that art was not a luxury, something extra, but part of everyday life and a social responsibility".[4]

Simmons proclaims "that if a strong art is to flourish in the West Indies, it must not be rooted in European art, not blossom into forms that bloomed and served its purpose fifty years ago or more. New wine must not be placed in old bottles."[5] Thus the question of indigeneity was at the centre of Walcott's coming of age as an artist and as a poet. Throughout his works, as his artistic methods develop, Walcott asks his readers to consider what it means to belong to a place, whether it is a location of origin or of exile. He engages with complex issues: how to represent and imagine the local at home and, when abroad, how to represent and imagine home from an increasingly distant perspective. These questions of indigeneity, displacement and imaginary museums in books become reflected in a more complex form in Walcott's *Omeros,* published in 1990: a modern, Caribbean-centred but broadly Atlantic poetic journey of wandering and return, exile and homecoming.

While a discussion of the perspectives and identities of *Omeros*'s Achille, Hector and Helen as indigenous St Lucians is worthwhile, this essay will focus on Walcott's cataloguing of Irishness as a contrasting yet equally complex network of identity in St Lucia. Attention to Walcott's catalogue of Irish characters – a highly organized and sometimes illustrated collection – reveals how he negotiates a salient yet subtle reticulation amid multiple categories of Irish identity, all of which negotiate the question of place: of what it means to live in exile from or to belong to a certain location. In *Omeros* his Irish references predominantly surround a particular set of characters, Major Plunkett, Maud Plunkett and Lawrence, all of whom have cultural associations not simply with Ireland but also with a specific collection of historical figures who helped shape Dublin museum culture of the late nineteenth and early twentieth centuries. What seems most striking is the degree to which this network of allusion becomes reframed and reimagined on St Lucia in the mid-twentieth century. In short, Walcott's imaginary museum of the book includes several dominant cultural and political figures from Ireland, from radically different social registers and affiliations, and relocates them to the West Indies.

Ireland in *Omeros* operates as a location of longing, melancholy and exile. In an interview in 1977, Walcott explained: "The whole Irish influence was for me a very intimate one."[6] Irish Presentation Brothers taught at St Mary's College, Walcott's secondary school in Castries, and featured Irish writers such as Joyce in their curriculum. Walcott's intimacy with Ireland is manifested throughout his writing career. In *Another Life* he alludes to his experience of Irish instruction in Castries: "'. . . Santaaa Lucheeeea.' / Steered now by Irish hands to their new epoch."[7] The new epoch of coming of age and independence in *Another Life* becomes a modern epic of ultimate homecoming in *Omeros*. In this later work, which celebrates a return to the Caribbean, Walcott uses his intimate knowledge of Irish culture to critique the hierarchies of cultures and peoples that colonialism enacts. From Sergeant Major Plunkett to Colonel Plunkett, Count Plunkett and Joseph Mary Plunkett; from Maud Plunkett to Maud Gonne; from Lawrence the waiter to T.E. Lawrence and William Lawrence, Walcott's depiction of Irishness is created through textual portraits that link icons of Irish history at home to the practices of imperialism abroad. In such depictions Walcott asserts a radical redefinition of identity that becomes predicated on his juxtaposition of the extraordinary and heroic with the everyday and common. What finally emerges in his catalogue of Ireland is not simply a questioning of what it means to be Irish but ultimately how these figures become intimately drawn in exile, the nature of which questions conceptions of cultural and national belonging and of indigeneity itself.

Walcott explains in an essay "Reflection on *Omeros*" that "the book is really not about a model of another poem; it is really about associations, or references, because that is what we are in the Americas: we are a culture of references, not certainties".[8] Unlike many European cultures that often operate with singular notions of ethnic, racial and religious identities aligned with a single nation-state, ethnic, racial and religious histories in the Caribbean have created a conception of identity that is more fluid; it need not be aligned along a single route but can recognize, if not embrace, an identity that multiplies across various cultural markers. In Walcott's culture of references and space-clearing gestures, these expansive myths of the New World become dramatically reimagined. *Omeros* becomes a work that is itself a collection of images, references and narratives that serve as a cultural repository: a collection of artefacts in a dramatically challenging textual exhibit. His curatorial style destabilizes any facile notion of centredness or a single cultural particularity while at the same time playing with multiple routes of meaning. His galleries are connected by passageways that create an elaborate network within which Irishness operates as a nuanced yet clear route throughout his broad Atlantic journey.

Readers are accustomed to imagining the Plunketts (the Major and Maud) in the mid-twentieth century. However, what becomes evident through an analysis of the allusive matrix surrounding them is that, in fact, they are products of an enduring Victorian-era vision of the British Empire and the complex Irish position within it. If we imagine their pig farm not as an "institution of confinement but of exhibition", to borrow a phrase from Tony Bennett's well-known essay "The Exhibitionary Complex", then we can examine their inclusion in the spectacle of settler/colonial society as a representation of cultural power.[9] This famed complex developed in the late eighteenth and nineteenth centuries during the rise and height of British global power. According to Bennett,

> Museums, galleries, and, more intermittently, exhibitions played a pivotal role in the formation of the modern state and are fundamental to its conception as, among other things, a set of educative and civilizing agencies. Since the late nineteenth century, they have been ranked highly in the funding priorities of all developed nation-states and have proved remarkably influential cultural technologies in the degree to which they have recruited the interest and participation of their citizenries.[10]

Museum culture in Britain and Ireland developed in the nineteenth century out of a series of spectacles and exhibitions: "the Museum Bill of 1845 . . . empowered local authorities to establish museums and art galleries: the number of public museums in Britain increased from 50 in 1860 to 200 in 1900".[11] At the apex of empire, Britain needed a way to represent its conquests and celebrate them in a manner for mass consumption under the guise of educating its public at home. In the development of "exhibitionary culture" there frequently existed a duality of representation: official displays that were remarkably serious catalogues of peoples, provinces and material products which often contrasted with unabashedly popular entertainments such as freak shows, mechanical rides and burlesque shows. The latter often included even prostitution. The resulting pressured affiliation between the two, notes Burton Benedict, "led to exposition organizers frequently attempting to turn the amusement zone into an educational enterprise or at least to regulate the type of exhibit shown".[12] The juxtaposition of official "high" culture with casual "low" amusement seems a remarkably apt metaphor for considering the scope of Walcott's references and naming techniques – his common method of joining the mythic and quotidian. Within these connections between the mythic hero and regular folk there rests a stunning network of allusion. In a recent article that examines more contemporary refractions of this most nineteenth century of phenomena, part of a larger cultural movement towards classification of peoples, geographies and objects, Laura Kriegel remarks, "the exhibitionary complex resembles its historical analogue. . . . Like the Victoria & Albert Museum, with its labyrinthine halls, the exhibitionary complex turns out to be something of a maze."[13]

Walcott engages overtly with a complexity of representation amid the power and knowledge of the maze-like museumizing tendency that he encounters both at home and abroad. In St Lucia "the islet's museum" is the Pigeon Island Museum, located in a colonial British mess hall built in 1803, which focuses on colonial history and the Battle of the Saints.[14] The museums abroad invoked by Walcott range from the Rijksmuseum in Amsterdam to Madame Tussaud's and the National Gallery in London and ultimately to the Metropolitan in New York.[15] Walcott includes references to museums throughout *Omeros*. In this work there appears a productive tension in what he casually observes: "Museums endure; but *sic transit gloria* [all the glory of the world fades]" and "Art has surrendered / to History with its whiff of formaldehyde".[16]

Walcott acknowledges the battle between preservation and decay intrinsic to any act of collecting, while he also includes remarkable depictions of individual works. For example, he describes Achille's journey to Africa partly with a description of a painting in the Metropolitan Museum of Art:

> [Achille] turned his head towards Africa in *The Gulf Stream*,
> which luffed him there, forever, between our island
> and the coast of Guinea, fixed in the tribal dream,
> in the light that entered another Homer's hand,
> its breeze lifting the canvas from the museum.[17]

Winslow Homer's *The Gulf Stream* defies the boundaries seemingly placed on it in its sanctioned and curated metropolitan space.[18] For Walcott, Homer's work symbolically transports Achille to Africa. Walcott's use of art and museums in *Omeros* endures throughout the remainder of his subsequent oeuvre.

In *Omeros*, references to museums seem to be drawn predominantly in terms of the Plunketts, though the allusions range geographically from Europe to St Lucia and North America. Walcott inaugurates his museum references with an allusion to British heroism embalmed in a museum, the Victoria and Albert:

Figure 8.1. Winslow Homer, *The Gulf Stream*, Metropolitan Museum of Art, 1899. © Metropolitan Museum of Art.

"the war in the desert under Montgomery, / and the lilac flowers under the crosses were / preserved by being pickled at the Victoria".[19] The Victoria and Albert collection originated in the Great Exhibition of 1851 at the Crystal Palace. It underwent various reconceptualizations and in 1857 opened formally as the South Kensington Museum; it was renamed the Victoria and Albert Museum in 1899. Walcott's marker of heroism in the war becomes merely another object for display in the Victoria and Albert. The second invocation also concerns the art of British martial history; the "islet's museum" is invoked subsequently in reference to the Battle of the Saints.[20] In this museum – the only one noted on the island of St Lucia itself – Walcott undercuts attempts to write British history and concludes merely that "the myth widened its rings every century".[21]

The growth of the historical record as it is displayed in museums is akin to an emerging sapling myth. When Walcott ventures towards Major Plunkett's very personal search for history, the poet undercuts the quest entirely: " 'No heir,' he told the mummy from Madame Tussaud." [22] Not only is Walcott explicitly refuting the possibility of finding an heir, he also makes the assertion part of a dialogue with a figure (the mummy) that is both embalmed and made of a substance that captures not actual history but representations of it that may potentially melt away despite all preservation efforts. Walcott undercuts the representation of history in multiple museums. When in London, the narra-

Figure 8.2. Joseph Mary Plunkett. © National Photographic Archive at the National Museum of Ireland.

tor notes, "Where is the light of the world? In the National Gallery. In Palladian Wren. In the City that can buy and sell us / the packets of tea stirred with our crystals of sweat."[23] The museum is highlighted not for its collection but for the exploitation that underlies its very existence.

Major Plunkett has been identified in several articles and books about *Omeros* as an Englishman with a complicated Irish resonance. According to Paula Burnett, "Dennis's historical namesake, the Irishman Joseph Mary Plunkett, not only took part in the 1916 Rising but was a key figure in it. He was a signatory to the Proclamation of the Irish Republic and carried Robert Emmet's sword into the General Post Office, where he fought until capture. He was executed at Kilmainham Gaol on 4 May 1916."[24] Joseph Mary Plunkett has been memorialized in a museum at the gaol. Burnett further explains:

> The role of Ireland . . . is in a parallel position to St. Lucia. It . . . shares . . . the historical role as victim of English colonialism. Walcott . . . show[s] the imperialist side of the historical story as morally complex. The Plunketts are central in this. In fact, the apparently even-handed English/Irish binarism of their national identities emerges differently when seen against the symbolism of the Plunkett name, for it is not only an Irish name and an unusual one, it is famous as the surname of a hero and martyr of the 1916 Easter Rising against British colonialism. By giving such a name to the poem's white Englishman, Walcott is implicitly staging him as "Irish", and moving him from a potentially negative position in the political map of the poem toward one with highly positive connotations.[25]

Burnett calls attention to the Plunkett name and its resonance in an Irish context. The interesting question then becomes why he appears in this poem and what historical basis Walcott might have used to chart such a nuanced vision of Irish cultural identity drawn in such remarkably intimate terms.

Walcott's Major Dennis Plunkett is primarily a representation of the settler or British colonial class on St Lucia. Yet although he was formerly in British service, many of his associations are in fact more specifically Irish. Aspects of a possible Plunkett connection beyond Joseph Mary Plunkett remain unexamined in studies of *Omeros*. In 1895 a Colonel G.T. Plunkett was appointed head of the Dublin Museum (known today as the National Museum of Ireland). Fintan Cullen notes that Colonel Plunkett was

> zealous in producing booklets, organizing lecture series and, in 1903, publishing an elaborate schema for the display of artefacts in a museum. The eclectic nature of the display at the Science and Art Museum is graphically depicted in the numerous Lawrence photographs dating from Plunkett's period in office [and continues]. . . . According to the *Freeman's Journal* of 1899, Col. Plunkett supplemented the display in Dublin of Birch's group [a statue of Walter Hamilton, a hero of the Second Afghan War who was born in County Kilkenny, standing over a fallen enemy] of this Irish-born soldier and the vanquished Afghani tribesman with an equally victorious exhibition of "trophies, armour, swords . . . from Omdurman" presented by no less a personage than his son, Lt. Plunkett.[26]

The mention of Lieutenant Plunkett will conjure up a striking spectre to readers of *Omeros*. Walcott's Plunkett wishes for progeny and creates one in a historical analogue: a drowned sailor, a Lieutenant Plunkett. Both Plunketts, real and fictional, privilege their sons as they endeavour to shape history, and in shaping history they create a new form of progeny – a display of the textual and architectural at once. What seems intriguing in Walcott's portrait is his use of such a military man, whose progeny actively engaged in military action against the British Empire.

The name Plunkett likely came to Walcott's attention not just from the historical record but also through the literary legacy of James Joyce's *Ulysses*. Critics have detailed the manifest links between *Omeros* and *Ulysses* in broad studies of influence such as Michael Malouf's *Transatlantic Solidarities* and my own *Washed by the Gulf Stream*, but there remain smaller and subtler echoes between these works.[27] In the "Circe" chapter of *Ulysses*, Colonel Plunkett is mocked; "the keeper of the Kildare street museum appears, dragging a lorry on which are the shaking statues of several naked goddesses".[28] Cullen explains: "The appointment of an ex-army man such as Colonel Plunkett as Director in 1895 (until 1907) was . . . a well-worn Department of Science and Art tradition for the employment of military men. . . . Indeed, a future director of the Dublin Museum,

Figure 8.3. Count George Noble Plunkett.
© National Photographic Archive at the
National Museum of Ireland.

Adolf Mahr, described the London
Department of Science and Art that
ran the Museum in its early years, as
a 'dumping ground for gentlemen
from . . . the Army'."[29]

Colonel Plunkett was replaced at
the museum by Count Plunkett. As
Kathleen St Peters Lancia has noted,
"in an increasingly nationalist
Ireland, efforts were made to trans-
fer the museum's administration
from the Department of Science and
Art in South Kensington to a new
Dublin-based unit, the Department
of Agriculture and Technical
Instruction".[30] She continues:

the separation from South Kensington
occurred in spite of what the museum
director, Colonel G.T. Plunkett, considered to be in the best interest of the institution.
When in 1907 "another Plunkett", Count George Noble Plunkett, a nationalist and
supporter of Home Rule, became museum director, the museum officially became the
"National Museum". . . . . Fierce disagreement about the role of cultural institutions in
modern Ireland . . . exists even within one family of museum administrators. . . . the
unionist Colonel Plunkett [gives way to] the nationalist Count Plunkett.[31]

Count Plunkett was forced out as director when his son, Joseph Mary Plunkett,
was executed for his participation in the 1916 Rising. After his son's execution
he became a Sinn Féin member of parliament and eventually served in the Irish
Dáil (Parliament).[32] What seems striking in this movement of power, historical
catalogues of Irish art and profound personal loss is the implicit acknowledgement, crafted by Walcott's use of these men in a matrix of historical allusion,
that – in one name and its invocation of cultural inheritance – the writer shows
the importance of a search for home and belonging even as he acknowledges
the Plunketts' multiple forms of exile and shifting allegiances.

Walcott strikingly appropriates *Plunkett*, a name associated first with an
English museum director – Colonel G.T. Plunkett – who heads an Irish museum.
This first Plunkett is replaced as museum director by a man also named Plunkett

– Count George Noble Plunkett – an
Irish leader who then has a revolutionary son, Joseph Mary Plunkett.
Walcott joins and transforms these
three men into a decidedly lower-
class settler figure, a Sergeant Major
Plunkett. As he does with the naming of Achille and Hector and Helen,
Walcott undercuts the heroic and
mythic with his Plunkett, as well as
with Maud and Lawrence, replacing
all with decidedly ordinary characters. He uses the eternal and historical to celebrate the regular and mun-
dane; thus he elevates the lives of
regular folk into a highly egalitarian
twentieth-century mythic system.

While the complexity of
Plunkett's individual and collective

Figure 8.4. William Michael Harnett, *Still-Life:
Violin and Music*, Metropolitan Museum of Art,
1888. © Metropolitan Museum of Art.

historic associations remain, his wife's associations are better known. While
Malouf seems to associate Maud Plunkett with Molly Bloom, Burnett suggests
that the predominant Irish association for Maud Plunkett is Maud Gonne, the
famous stage actress of *Cathleen ni Houlihan*, who despite her English birth
personified the struggle of the emerging Irish nation and Irish revolutionar-
ies involved in the Easter Rising of 1916.[33] Gonne was reportedly a stunningly
beautiful woman and the muse of the Irish poet William Butler Yeats. Maud
Plunkett's origin in "Glen-da-Lough . . . Wicklow" remains central to her character formation.[34] The name springs from the Irish *Gleann dá locha*, or "glen of
the two lakes", the location of a ruined medieval monastery in County Wicklow
that was started by St Kevin and is now a tourist attraction.

There is another level of resonance for Maud's Irish origin that Walcott uses
rather subtly in *Omeros*. The *Airs from Erin* that she plays at her piano include
"Bendemeer's Stream".[35] This traditional Irish folk song appears in Thomas
Moore's collection *Irish Melodies*, published in 1807 and 1835.[36] Moore's *Melodies*
were remarkably popular and dramatically influenced William Michael Harnett,
a renowned painter from County Cork.[37] Installed just steps away from Winslow
Homer's *The Gulf Stream* in the Metropolitan Museum of Art (see figure 8.1),

Harnett's *Still-Life: Violin and Music* includes in its painted background, on a piece of paper behind the violin, "Moore's original note on the melody . . . 'This ballad is founded upon one of the many stories related of St Kevin, whose bed in the rock is to be seen at Glendalough, a most gloomy and romantic spot in the county of Wicklow.' "[38] Cullen explains:

> The song is indeed a tale of St Kevin who is attempting to find peace and isolation as a hermit in a cave above one of the lakes at Glendalough. He is endlessly tempted by Kathleen whose eyes are "of the most unholy blue". In anger, the indignant saint "hurls" her from a height into the lake but soon regrets his action and can only be comforted . . . by Kathleen's ghost which "was seen to glide, / Smiling, o'er the fatal tide".[39]

Not only has Walcott's portrait of Maud been shaped by the tale of Kathleen and St Kevin in Moore's *Melodies*, portrayed in the Harnett painting, he has returned Maud to the lake – as a spectre much like St Kevin's Kathleen. Kathleen is both a specific object of desire for St Kevin and more generally a representation of Ireland as an incarnation of Cathleen ni Houlihan, and thus Maud Gonne. Kathleen's death portends not only Maud Plunkett's end in St Lucia, across the Atlantic, but also her absence of progeny and her desperate attempts to embroider birds in flight on fabric that ultimately serves as her own funeral shroud. Walcott's Plunkett searches for his lost Maud late in *Omeros*, after her death from cancer. He goes to Ma Kilman, who envisions Maud in Ireland: "I see flat water, like silver. I see your wife walking there / in a white dress with frills and pressing her white hat / with one hand in the breeze by a lake".[40] Ma Kilman's depiction of Maud in the afterlife seems to emerge out of the Kathleen and St Kevin myth captured by Harnett and Moore; Kathleen and Maud glide by the lake as spectres that evoke loss. The references that surround Walcott's Maud textually are drawn from a museum work (Harnett's *Still-Life*) that captures the pain of exile and a longing for return. Maud in St Lucia is a woman in an archipelago that seems not her own, with an enduring longing to go home.[41]

The actress Maud Gonne also had a connection with the early twentieth-century museum complex in Dublin, for she supported public display of the photographs of Dublin photographer William Lawrence. While the Lawrence in *Omeros* remains an obscure presence – a black waiter who serves Plunkett at the club and whose characterization is somewhat thin – his allusive resonance is thick with possibilities. Perhaps the most well-known referent for him, and one supported overtly in the text through allusions to North Africa and the Middle East, is T.E. Lawrence, who was born in Wales the illegitimate son of an Anglo-Irish baronet, Sir Thomas Robert Tighe Chapman, and a Scottish governess, Sarah Junor or Junner (also known as Lawrence), who had been working for the Chapman family.[42] After the First World War, T.E. Lawrence worked in Paris for the British, negotiating the division of the Middle East among British, French and Arab interests, and published a memoir, *The Seven Pillars of Wisdom*, in 1926. His final publication was a translation of *The Odyssey* in 1932, which is respected because of Lawrence's archaeological expertise in the Bronze Age eastern Mediterranean. Thus Lawrence, the character in *Omeros*, is most obviously not only part Irish in his cultural resonance but also, playfully, by allusion a translator of *The Odyssey*; he operates at once as an embodiment of everyday folk, an avatar of the imperial endeavour and a figure of cultural translation.

While this Irish paternity remains intriguing, there is in fact a secondary Lawrence whose work, not as a writer or translator but as a kind of cultural archaeologist and a visual artist, affords an even greater cultural connection or reference. This Lawrence's work was central to the Dublin museum headed by the various Plunketts and was overtly supported by Maud Gonne. William Lawrence opened his photography studio at 5, 6 and 7 Upper Sackville Street (now O'Connell), across from Dublin's General Post Office, in 1865. It was a part of "Lawrence's Great Bazaar and Photographic Gallery", destroyed by fire during the Rising in 1916.[43] His studio was renowned not only for producing images of the Dublin museum but also for documenting evictions in Ireland in the 1890s. According to Cullen,

> The Lawrence photographs are ... part of a fascination with recording the new cultural institutions of the expanding urban scene. ... what becomes apparent in the Lawrence photographs of the Dublin Museum and given their great number is how the new public museum featured as a statement on the potential state of a nation's cultural richness. Thus it can be said that the museum as a phenomenon becomes as much a national or a civic space as it was an actual functional storage and display area for art.[44]

Indeed, the storage and display of Irish culture through the work of Lawrence's studio were not to be relegated to museum interiors but were "used as a political propaganda tool against Queen Victoria: during the Queen's Jubilee celebrations in 1897, Maud Gonne orchestrated public displays of images of evictions and deaths from starvation by projecting them on to the exterior of a building in [what is now] Parnell Square in Dublin city centre".[45] Gonne organized the visual projections at the event. She highlighted the Lawrence photographs, and

Figure 8.5. William Lawrence, *The Battering Ram Has Done Its Work*, 1888. © National Photographic Archive at the National Museum of Ireland.

particularly his eviction scene from County Clare, *The Battering Ram Has Done Its Work*, with statistical slides that detailed the number of Irish dead, courtesy of Queen Victoria.[46] Cullen explains:

> The display can only have been visually effective after darkness had fallen which was late, as it was 22 June. . . . James Connolly and some of his Corporation contacts had, in defiance of the jubilee, arranged, as Gonne tells us, "for the cutting of wires to prevent the display by the Unionist shops of their electric decorations". Not surprisingly, the police turned up and were angered by the sabotage on the loyalist lights and the clear popularity of the anti-monarchical display on the very evening of the sixtieth anniversary of the Queen's coronation. A riot ensued. . . . By using the Lawrence slides to attack English imperialism and in particular to attack the very person of Victoria, whom Gonne was later to refer to as "The Famine Queen", the nationalists of the 1890s were following a recent trend in the public use of lantern slides to aid political propaganda.[47]

Lantern slides, unlike small photos, could be projected on an extremely large scale, so that the image and message were exponentially increased. Maud Gonne's connecting of Dublin museum culture with the harsh realities of everyday life in Ireland through the lantern slides of William Lawrence evokes Walcott's juxtaposition of high and low culture – the heroic with the common – in *Omeros*. Maud Gonne advocated for the Irish peasants forced off their land, whereas Maud Plunkett embroiders birds on a cloth as a symbolic gesture of escape because she longs to return to her land.

The "Lawrence of St Lucia" in *Omeros* is clearly not simply this Irish photographer from the late nineteenth century, nor is he a clear rendition of T.E. Lawrence, the British colonial war hero. However, in his multiple associations with visual images, Walcott does reference these historical figures: when Lawrence is present, mirages appear and shadows repeatedly fall on paper in his wake. Walcott writes of this waiter that he "frowned at a mirage" and "came staggering up the terrace / with the cheque finally, and that treaty was signed; / the paper was crossed by the shadow of her face".[48] Lawrence himself is identified with a visual phenomenon and Maud's face is put in shadow by his arrival. Lawrence the waiter seems to have a visual power that belies his status as a mere server. It is possible that Walcott is humorously undermining the imperial agency of T.E. Lawrence by referencing the visual records of a much less well-known Irishman, one whose work overtly countered British management in Ireland and supported the indigenous Irish against enduring exile in their own land. William Lawrence's photographs were featured in the National Library of Ireland's *Notice to Quit* show, which displayed records of the land evictions of the nineteenth century. They seem, as Walcott notes keenly, "framed forever in the last century, / as was much of Ireland".[49]

Ireland for Walcott functions as a location of complex nostalgia and cultural exile, a display in a case or, as he writes, in a frame. Part of the unique reticulation of the exhibitionary complex is as a subtle force which promotes causes and organizes social relationships "to coordinate an order of things and to produce a place for people in relation to that order".[50] Walcott's exhibitionary complex in *Omeros*, particularly that surrounding his cataloguing of Irish characters, broadly defined, serves to critique the very notion of high and low, of official versus popular culture, and even the conception of linear, progressive history that the exhibitionary complex commonly attempts to reify. From Colonel Plunkett to Joseph Mary Plunkett, from Maud Gonne to Moore's *Melodies* and Harnett's *Still-Life*, from T.E. Lawrence to William Lawrence, Walcott's cataloguing of Irishness seems to rest upon an inclusive vision that pairs the revered saints of an Irish nation at home with the troubled practitioners of imperialism abroad. Major Plunkett's attempt to reimagine the past and create progeny anew reflects a critique of just such a complex. Walcott's highly allusive and circular catalogue produces a dynamic and imaginative continuum that reveals the limits of personal and cultural narrative when it is framed in a singular linear progression.

The spectacle that is Ireland in Walcott's textual museum *Omeros* is directly related to Dublin's emerging museum culture at the turn of the previous century, and its more contemporary exhibitions in public spaces that question boundaries of self and nation and conceptions of ethnic and cultural histories. Walcott's complex exhibition of Ireland in *Omeros* relies on a systemic matrix of allusion whose references show the intimate affiliations between questions of exile and indigeneity. Perhaps when Walcott acknowledges "There was Plunkett in my father, much as there was / my mother in Maud", he offers a lens into why his catalogue of Ireland is so sympathetic.[51] Walcott suggests that the Irish Caribbean connection in *Omeros* is profoundly intimate and familial. When he collects the Plunketts and Lawrence and places them in his gallery of Irish identity, this act becomes not merely one of a museum curator exhibiting artefacts for visitors but rather a personal collection that reveals Ireland as a striking element of St Lucian identity. While Maud embroiders a symbolic flight away from St Lucia, she becomes in fact part of the fabric of St Lucian society. Finally, then, as he seeks from Ma Kilman a vision of his late wife, Walcott's ancestor-of-a-kind Major Plunkett imagines "the knolls and broken castles of Ireland. / Plunkett never thought he would ask the next question. / 'Heaven?' He smiled. [Ma Kilman replies:] 'Yes, if heaven is a green place.'"[52]

Notes

1. See cover image: Derek Walcott, *Seascapes with Figures* (June Kelly Gallery, 2002).
2. Derek Walcott, "Another Life" (1st manuscript), University of the West Indies, Mona, Jamaica, 59.
3. Ibid.
4. Didacus Jules, ed., "Selected Writings of Harold Simmons Manuscript", Folk Research Centre, Castries, St Lucia, 115.
5. Ibid.
6. Irene Martyniuk, "The Irish in the Caribbean: Derek Walcott's Examination of the Irish in *Omeros*", *South Atlantic Quarterly* 32 (1999): 138.
7. Derek Walcott, *Another Life: Fully Annotated*, ed. Edward Baugh and Colbert Nepaulsingh (Boulder: Lynne Rienner, 2004), 106.

8. Derek Walcott, "Reflection on *Omeros*", *South Atlantic Quarterly* 96 (1997): 239.

9. Tony Bennett, "The Exhibitionary Complex", in *Culture, Power, History*, ed. Nicholas B. Dirks, Geoff Eley and Sherry B. Orther (Princeton, NJ: Princeton University Press, 1994), 129.

10. Ibid.

11. Ibid., 135.

12. Burton Benedict, "The Anthropology of World's Fairs", in *The Anthropology of World's Fairs: San Francisco's Panama Pacific Exposition of 1915*, ed. Burton Benedict (New York: Scholar Press, 1983), 53–54.

13. Lara Kriegel, "After the Exhibitionary Complex: Museum Histories and the Future of the Victorian Past", *Victorian Studies* 48 (2006): 681–704.

14. Derek Walcott, *Omeros* (New York: Farrar, Straus and Giroux, 1990), 43.1 [page 43, line 1], 91.12.

15. Ibid., 80.23, 87.20, 197.16, 183.26.

16. Ibid., 182.16–21.

17. Ibid., 183.26–184.3.

18. Winslow Homer, *The Gulf Stream*, 1899 (New York: Metropolitan Museum of Art).

19. Walcott, *Omeros*, 26.7–9.

20. Ibid., 43.1.

21. Ibid., 43.12.

22. Ibid., 87.20.

23. Ibid., 197.16–18.

24. Paula Burnett, "Walcott's Intertextual Method: Non-Greek Naming in *Omeros*", *Callaloo* 28, no. 1 (Winter 2005): 173.

25. Ibid.

26. Fintan Cullen, *Ireland on Show: Art, Union, and Nationhood* (Burlington, VT: Ashgate, 2012), 32–33.

27. Michael Malouf, *Transatlantic Solidarities: Irish Nationalism and Caribbean Poetics* (Charlottesville: University Press of Virginia, 2009); Maria McGarrity, *Washed by the Gulf Stream: The Historic and Geographic Relation of Irish and Caribbean Literature* (Newark: University of Delaware Press, 2008).

28. James Joyce, *Ulysses: The Corrected Text*, ed. Hans Walter Gabler, Wolfhard Steppe and Claus Melchior (New York: Random House, 1986), 15.1703–5.

29. Cullen, *Ireland on Show*, 32.

30. Kathleen St Peters Lancia, "The Ethnographic Roots of Joyce's Modernism: Exhibiting Ireland's Primitives in the National Museum and the 'Nestor' Episode", *Irish Modernism and the Global Primitive*, ed. Maria McGarrity and Claire A. Culleton (New York: Palgrave Macmillan, 2009), 89.

31. Ibid., 89–90.

32. Patrick F. Wallace and Raghnall ó Floinn, eds., *Treasures of the National Museum of Ireland: Irish Antiquities* (Dublin: Gill and Macmillan, 2002), 9.

33. Malouf, *Transatlantic Solidarities*, 150; Burnett, "Walcott's Intertextual Method", 174.

34. Walcott, *Omeros*, 24.9.

35. Ibid., 56.11.

36. Moore's collection is mentioned with some mockery in the opening section of James Joyce's final story in *Dubliners*, "The Dead".

37. Cullen, *Ireland on Show*, 143–47.

38. William Michael Harnett, *Still-Life: Violin and Music*, 1888 (New York: Metropolitan Museum of Art).

39. Cullen, *Ireland on Show*, 144.

40. Walcott, *Omeros*, 306.16–19.

41. "Ireland and a [displaced] existence, or what Joe Cleary has called 'an exilic consciousness', is implied by Harnett's seemingly haphazard depiction of objects in space"; Cullen, *Ireland on Show*, 147.

42. Lawrence, who had limited professional options because of his birth, was Oxford-educated, spoke Arabic and worked in the Middle East as an archaeologist for the British Palestine Exploration fund before the First World War. During the war he provided the British with critical knowledge of the area and became involved in the taking of Aqaba, a location vital to protecting British naval interests and the Suez.

43. The Lawrence Collection, "About William Lawrence", http://www.lawrencecollection.com/about, accessed 29 March 2013.

44. Cullen, *Ireland on Show*, 34–35.

45. National Library of Ireland, "*Notice to Quit*, 26 June–30 September 2003, National Photographic Archive", http://www.nli.ie/en/udlist/programme-and-events-previous-exhibitions.aspx?article=a8dec9c1-e3c8-47d3-8ed6-fbe2d2b27028, accessed 29 March 2013.

46. William Lawrence, *The Battering Ram Has Done Its Work* (Bandeleur evictions, 1888), National Library of Ireland, Lawrence Photographs, R1772.

47. Cullen, *Ireland on Show*, 104.

48. Walcott, *Omeros*, 23.10–18, 32.1–3.

49. Walcott, *Omeros*, 303.16–17.

50. Bennett, "Exhibitionary Complex", 130.

51. Walcott, *Omeros*, 263.16–17.

52. Ibid., 307.3–5.

Chapter 9

Pamela Colman Smith's Performative Primitivism

ELIZABETH O'CONNOR

ALTHOUGH TODAY SHE IS PRIMARILY REMEMBERED FOR designing the Rider-Waite tarot deck, Pamela Colman Smith was a highly regarded artist, poet, folklorist, editor, publisher and stage designer who was active from the mid-1890s through the 1920s. Her drawings and watercolours were the first non-photographic art to be exhibited in Alfred Stieglitz's Little Galleries of the Photo-Secession in New York. She also edited and published a small magazine, the *Green Sheaf,* which appeared for thirteen issues from May 1903 to May 1904 in London; beginning with the seventh issue it was also sold in Brentano's bookstore in New York.[1] The magazine marks the culmination of her long-time interest in both Irish myth and Jamaican folktales, which stemmed from her close collaborations with both Jack and William Butler Yeats and a childhood spent primarily in Jamaica.[2]

Colman Smith's interest in moving across and between these cultural resources is shown in her 1896 journal essay and two book-length illustrated collections of Jamaican folktales: *Annancy Stories*, published in 1899, and *Chim-Chim: Folk Stories from Jamaica*, in 1905. It is also demonstrated by the fact that she would often regale family, friends and, increasingly, paid audiences by performing these stories, as well as several of her own compositions and a few of W.B. Yeats's plays, using handmade models in front of the elaborate sets of her miniature theatre.[3] In this way, Colman Smith, who went by the nickname "Pixie", was an early disseminator of Jamaican folk culture. She seems to have

Figure 9.1. Pamela Colman Smith.

styled both her private and public personae as a distinctive fusion of the Jamaican trickster figure Anansi and the Irish pixie, both of which she appears to have been drawn to because of their gender indeterminacy, unconventionality and fearlessness.

In a July 1907 piece in the *Craftsman* magazine – one of her rare essays on the role of the artist – Colman Smith laments that too many US artists are overcome with doubts and afraid to embrace new ideas. "Each one has a great fear of himself, a fear to believe, to think, to do, to be, to act", she claims; in order to combat this trend, she urges young art students to draw on real life, to exhibit fearlessness and freedom of thought, and to work tirelessly to eradicate "those mawkish weeds of sugar-sweet sentimentality".[4] In her two folktale collections, this drive towards independence can be seen in the changes she made to several well-known tales to give female characters more agency and to transform the patriarchal tiger into a gender-indeterminate spider. Colman Smith's own hybridity – she appeared to be of mixed race, born to white American parents – set her apart and seemingly shaped her attraction to other outsider figures such as Anansi and the pixie.

Colman Smith's lifetime refusal to toe the line and follow societal and artistic conventions captivated a diverse group of friends, patrons and admirers, from Stieglitz and Yeats to Ellen Terry and Mark Twain, earning her increasingly wide acclaim in the early years of the twentieth century. However, by the end of the 1920s Colman Smith had stopped publishing and exhibiting her work, and as a result had faded from public view both in New York, the site of her four major exhibitions, and in England, her adopted home. Originally based in London, she eventually moved to the Lizard, at the tip of Cornwall, where she operated a vacation home for Roman Catholic priests. She died, penniless and forgotten, in 1951.[5]

Like the later years of her career, her early life is also filled with gaps and silences. What we do know is that Corinne Pamela Colman Smith was born on 16 February 1878 in the Pimlico area of London, to Charles Smith and Corinne Colman.[6] Shortly thereafter the family moved to Manchester, where Charles Smith, who was an auditor, worked for an upholstery manufacturer.[7] When Colman Smith was ten, the family moved to St Andrew parish, near Kingston, Jamaica, because her father had been engaged with the West India Improvement Company.[8] She remained there until 1893, when she travelled to New York, returning to Jamaica in 1895 to nurse her sick mother, who died the following year. With the exception of some relatively brief trips to New York, Colman Smith lived in Jamaica until early 1899, when she sailed to England with her father.

Colman Smith was very close to her father, whom she affectionately nicknamed "Pig".[9] However, a 1903 article in the *Reader* credits her mother with having the biggest impact on her work, stating that it was "from her mother [that] she derived an intense, individual creative desire, which very early in life began to satisfy itself in a curious sort of drawing".[10] Both parents came from prominent American families that were based primarily in New York.[11] It is unclear why the couple settled in England or how long they had been living there before Colman Smith's birth. On her father's side she was related to the stage actor William Gillette, who debuted the role of Sherlock Holmes on the New York stage and of whom she would make several drawings.[12] Her maternal grandmother, Pamela Chandler Colman, was an author of children's books, and her maternal uncle, Samuel Colman, was a noted landscape artist of the Hudson River School.[13] Through her mother, Colman Smith was also related to Joel Chandler Harris, the author of the Br'er Rabbit stories, and she reportedly read the Uncle Remus tales obsessively as a child.[14] Once she reached Jamaica, this interest fused with and was eventually supplanted by her fascination with the rich Jamaican folklore tradition.

Despite her well-known relatives, Colman Smith was, as Kathleen Pyne notes, "a woman of mysterious origins, who to contemporaries seemed part Asian or part African or of some indeterminate 'mixed blood'".[15] Rather than attempting to distance herself from this difference, Colman Smith appears to have embraced it, creating an "identity as an authentic primitive and childlike voice that spoke the truth of the inner self against the restrictions of cultural convention".[16] Her exposure to both Jamaican folktales and pirate lore as a teenager, her friendship with several members of the Yeats family, and her interest in Irish mythology during her early adult years appear to have been key factors in the development of that voice.

Her artistic life began in 1893 when she travelled to New York City with her father at the young age of fifteen and enrolled at the Pratt Institute in Brooklyn, where she studied composition, drawing and painting. At Pratt she was widely regarded as a "child wonder" and was befriended by the noted photographer Gertrude Kasebier.[17] Although Colman Smith remained at the Brooklyn art school until June 1897, she did not take a degree. The *Reader* article states that she studied at the Pratt for only two years; "[a]s no noticeable change showed itself in the character of her work under this tutelage, and as she became more determined to work out her own problems in her own way, she ended her connection with the school".[18] While Colman Smith's resolve to do things her own way seems to be a hallmark of her personality, part of the reason for her failure to take a degree can be attributed to the fact that she spent most of 1895–98 in Jamaica, initially helping to nurse her sick mother, who died in 1896, and then helping to run the family's estate, Ambersgate, in the parish of St Andrew.[19]

While it is impossible to know how much (if any) of the cultivation of this free-spirit persona was intentional, we do know that Colman Smith adopted the name "Pixie Pamela", which – at least for a time – seems to have supplanted "Pamela" entirely. Colman Smith signed her new name to a 7 December 1899 letter to her cousin Mary ("Bobby") Reed, adding in parentheses, "That's my name ET gave me."[20] "ET" is Dame Ellen Terry, the famous British Shakespearean actress, who was a long-time friend and mentor of Colman Smith.[21] In return she contributed illustrations of Terry for an 1899 Lyceum Theatre brochure, and later illustrated (and possibly ghostwrote) Terry's 1913 book *The Russian Ballet*.[22] In subsequent letters to Reed, Colman Smith does not elaborate on why Terry gave her the name or why she decided to keep it. However, in the twelve extant letters that predate this one, Colman Smith signed with either a wide range of nicknames or "Con", which is probably a shortened form of her given name, Corinne. Almost regardless of what initially inspired it, Colman Smith created an identity for herself through Pixie Pamela.

Her interest in fairies, especially in their indeterminate gender, freedom and fearlessness, seems to have taken root after she arrived in Jamaica in 1888. In a 1912 *Craftsman* article, Irwin MacDonald notes that "from childhood she has had the gift of the 'second sight'".[23] In Jamaica Colman Smith listened with rapt attention to the folktales and legends told by firelight, "but she visualized nothing in that place of romantic and horrible memories, although she felt intensely the oppression and excitement of its psychic atmosphere".[24] It was only when she first visited Ireland in 1899 "that the power to see clearly the invisible realm", which she claimed to have possessed in early childhood, returned to her.[25] Through these visions and by reading a wide variety of Irish myths and legends, Colman Smith became well versed in Irish mythology, learning to distinguish between "the gnomes, goblins, wraiths, leprechauns, pixies, salamanders, and people of the sea".[26]

Even before Colman Smith visited Ireland, she became somewhat familiar with the island's rich folk culture by reading the works of W.B. Yeats and others.[27] One of her first pieces commissioned by the New York publisher R.H. Russell was a triptych illustration of W.B. Yeats's 1894 play *The Land of Heart's Desire.*[28] Colman Smith's illustration, which appeared in 1898, is notable for the free movement of her riotously dancing female subjects. In the centre image, one of the two lone males in the composition is a black-frocked priest who is being physically restrained by two women, ostensibly because of his horror over the indecorous merrymaking. The second male, Shawn Bruin, tries to restrain his wife, Maire, from romping with the barefoot red-headed fairy child who is leading the white-gowned pixies dancing in the side panels. Shawn implores his now energized wife, who was previously withdrawn and listless, to remain with him in the real world instead of giving in to the false escape of the laughter and dancing of fairies. However, she succumbs to the spirit's charms and dies in his arms. The play marks the first time that Yeats drew on Irish folklore as a living mythology, an idea which greatly influenced Colman Smith and resonated with her own growing interest in Jamaican folklore and legends.

The 1895–98 period, which she spent primarily in Jamaica, was an extremely prolific time for Colman Smith; it saw the emergence of her interest in both folklore and theatre. Letters to her cousin Bobby Reed in Brooklyn reveal that in 1896 Colman Smith staged a Christmas-season performance of her play *Henry Morgan,* based on the life of the legendary seventeenth-century Jamaican pirate, at the Infant Trees kindergarten in Kingston, where she worked as head teacher for a time.[29] The play was enacted in her miniature theatre, which was equipped with elaborately painted sets and cut-out figures that were moved by means of grooves and strings, all made by Colman Smith.[30]

Two years later she performed the same play for her fellow students and teachers as part of a Pratt Institute fundraiser. The *Pratt Institute Monthly* states that the performance netted ninety-five dollars and terms *Henry Morgan's* thirteen acts and fifteen scenes "a most original and charming entertainment".[31]

The unnamed writer goes on to explain: "Whether one sees the interior of the heroine's chamber, or the blue waters and sunny hillsides of the tropical island, each is a delicately-balanced harmony, constructed on the most refreshingly-original lines, yet so simply and unerringly true that one feels a new faculty for seeing life, though it be that of two centuries ago."[32] Thus the writer seems to equate Colman Smith's primitivism with her originality – something that was extremely common in early assessments of her work and which probably influenced her cultivation of the mystical pixie persona. After her return to England in mid-1899, she frequently dressed as a Jamaican peasant to recite Anansi tales.

During her stay in Jamaica, Colman Smith composed several plays, including *The Magic Carbuncle*, which she told Reed she wrote in one day, and *Herne the Hunter*, which she created after designing advertisements for a Kingston restaurant that featured a young woman carrying a tureen of steaming turtle soup.[33] The texts of these plays have not been preserved but an account of the plot of *Henry Morgan*, included in letters to Reed, reveals comic as well as tragic elements. The play features a swashbuckling hero, a beautiful heroine, a wicked witch, corrupt police and an almost farcical (albeit true) happy ending in which Morgan is knighted for his service to the colony and then becomes governor of Jamaica.[34] However, despite the stereotypical nature of much of the plot and characters, there are some unexpected, even subversive elements. Most strikingly, these include the fact that Morgan's success stems far less from his own feats of bravery than from those of his dark-skinned housekeeper, Martha, who hides him from treacherous pirates, and the duplicity of Julia Bogle, who alone recognizes Morgan in disguise and through her quickness and ingenuity allows him to escape undetected.[35] As Colman Smith revealed to Reed in her letters, she would generally "act" these plays herself but would be accompanied by others. In early performances in Jamaica, at home and at local schools, her father would read brief inter-titles between scenes, while servants would create special effects such as claps of thunder and the clashing of swords.[36] For the Pratt performance, a fellow student read the play's script.[37]

After Colman Smith's return to England in 1899, her focus seems to have shifted away from the elaborate sets and towards her own self-stylization. This shift is at least partly due to the fact that for several years her miniature theatre remained in New York while she travelled between England and Ireland.[38] Initially she would perform these tales for friends as part of weekly salon parties in her London studio.[39] However, in 1903 she began to advertise, in the back pages of her *Green Sheaf,* the services of "Gelukiezanger" – a name which, as I detail below, she appears to have made up and which appears to carry much personal significance – who would entertain guests with Anansi tales.[40] Gertrude Moakley notes: "For these performances she dressed in flowing orange and red robes with coral beads and feathers arranged in her hair. She sat cross-legged on a little platform in a room lit only by candles and began her recital in Jamaican dialect, 'Once in a long before-time, before Queen Victoria come to reign o'ber we.' "[41]

By 1907 Colman Smith had moved back to New York and was enchanting America with her storytelling. A contemporary newspaper account notes that she delivered these "fairy folk-tales . . . in the weird dialect of the Jamaican negroes – a sort of cockney English with Spanish colouring, a rhythmic rising inflection at the end of each sentence, and barbaric words and idioms sprinkled through it that must have come directly from the voodoo worshippers of the African jungle".[42] Mark Twain was in the audience at one of these performances and "was so delighted that he laughed like a child the whole time".[43] Unfortunately, the writer does not note exactly what had reduced Twain to laughter, but the piece strongly implies that the hilarity lay in Colman Smith's "rhythmic rising inflection" and her choice of "barbaric words and idioms" borrowed "directly from the voodoo worshippers of the African jungle" as much as from the content of her tales.

Colman Smith's early experiences as both playwright and performer seem to have influenced her work as an illustrator. She contributed designs to at least four books in 1899, as well as compiling, writing and illustrating folktales for her *Annancy Stories*. Her twelve full-colour illustrations for a book of old English ballads, *The Golden Vanity and the Green Bed*, are representative, highlighting her interest in the sailors, nautical themes and pictorial representations of Jamaica that were to remain consistent themes in her work.[44] She based illustrations for both the *Broad Sheet,* the publication she co-edited with Jack Yeats, and the *Green Sheaf,* the little magazine that she edited and published by herself, on several of these images. An example is Colman Smith's illustration of a pirate ship toppling in the waves that accompanied an untitled poem detailing the exploits of Henry Morgan in the April 1902 *Broad Sheet,* as well as almost all her drawings for the October 1906 "Pirate Issue" of the *Green Sheaf.*

Colman Smith's book of folktales, *Annancy Stories,* which she wrote as well as illustrated, was also published during this prolific year. Her depictions are the first known published drawings of Anansi, a trickster figure who can assume the forms of both a man and a spider. While *Annancy Stories* contains only line drawings rather than the hand-coloured illustrations that are far more typical of her work, Colman Smith's second book of Jamaican folktales, *Chim-Chim: Folk Stories from Jamaica,* published in 1905 by her Green Sheaf Press, does contain colour illustrations. Of the eight stories in the collection, six of them are slightly expanded versions of tales from *Annancy Stories.* The remaining two, "Turkle and Pigeon" and "Kisander", are very similar to other published variants of these tales.[45] However, several of the others, as well as additional stories that appear only in the *Annancy Stories* collection, do include quite striking differences from other collected variants of the tales, especially in relationship to the role of women and the Tiger character. In her introduction *Chim-Chim,* Colman Smith presents herself as a transcriber who "tried to write down [the stories] exactly as I heard them from many different people and in different parts of the island, where they vary more or less".[46] This focus on transcription is important, as it gives credence to her use of Jamaican Creole. However, this claim to transcription also allows her to minimize, if not gloss over entirely, the changes she made to several of the tales.

Figure 9.2. *Chim-Chim* illustration.

These changes are most evident in the evolution of her three different versions of "Annancy and the Yam Hills". The first version, which is not illustrated, was published, along with "De Story of de Man and Six Poached Eggs", in Franz Boas's *Journal of American Folklore* in 1896.⁴⁷ Although this was an American publication, the journal frequently published folk stories from around the globe. Colman Smith's first version is quite short; however, it does include a key difference: the animal that tricks Anansi into saying "five", the Obeah Queen's name, and thus falling down dead, is a female guinea fowl rather than the male monkey that is Anansi's traditional adversary in most versions of the tale.⁴⁸ In still other versions, Anansi emerges unscathed after tricking a variety of animals into saying "five".⁴⁹ In Colman Smith's *Annancy Stories* version, "Annancy an' de Nyam Hills", Guinea Fowl eats Annancy after he falls down dead.⁵⁰ It concludes with the moral "Dis story show dat 'greedy choke puppy'!"⁵¹ Interestingly, Colman Smith's title illustration depicts six dark-skinned women in Jamaican peasant dress yelling and shaking their fists at a shrugging Annancy.⁵² This dimension of the tale is not readily apparent in the text of this version but is much more readily visible in *Chim-Chim*. Now titled "Five Yam Hill", the story closely follows the text in *Annancy Stories* with the exception that the closing motto is "Dis show how man stupid!"⁵³ Guinea Fowl is also far more overtly feminine. She is called Mrs Guinea Fowl – in the previous versions she is referred to without the honorific – and wears a bonnet and frilly shawl, while Annancy is crouching in the corner and appears to be wearing a long-sleeved, high-necked black dress.⁵⁴

Another key difference between Colman Smith's Anansi retellings and those of other transcribers is in the character of Tiger. As the king of the jungle, Tiger is fierce and warlike; he is one of the chief rivals of Anansi, who is regarded as the weakest but also the cleverest of all the animals.⁵⁵ The biggest difference is that in Colman Smith's versions Tiger is not a tiger but rather a humanoid spider that looks very similar to Annancy.⁵⁶ Annancy frequently bests Tiger, who has slightly more feminine features despite the fact that both are referred to as male. The *Chim-Chim* collection offers an explanation for these differences: Colman Smith writes in "Chim-Chim", the first story in the collection, that Tiger "is anoder Spider".⁵⁷ This brief explanation does much to clarify the relationship between the two and seems to relegate it to one of friendly rivalry rather than mortal combat.

A possible reason for this change can be found in the *Annancy Stories*. "Paarat, Tiger an' Annancy" contains some elements of the more common "Anansi and Monkey" but is essentially a different story. Colman Smith's tale begins with a famished Parrot, Tiger and Anansi agreeing to play a game. They travel to each of their mothers, asking if the mothers know their new names. Of course Anansi cheats and secretly informs his mother that his name is now Checherebanja; she survives, while the other two mothers fall victim to the game and are eaten.[58] However, even more interestingly, Tiger's new name is "Gelukiezanger", the name Colman Smith picked to advertise her Jamaican storytelling performances. While the reason for this is never explained – and the name appears to have been invented by her – it does seem to imply a link between Tiger and herself, most likely due to their shared image as trickster figures.

Colman Smith's drawings for *Annancy Stories* bear several similarities to her illustrations for Yeats's *The Land of Heart's Desire* and for Seamus MacManus's *In Chimney Corners: Merry Tales of Irish Folklore*, offering a complicated matrix of cultural overlap via indeterminacy. For example, her final illustration of three sisters seemingly bewitched by Anansi's fiddling in "How Annancy Win de Five Dubbloon" is very similar to the riotous dancers in her illustration for Yeats's play. Even more surprising are the similarities between her drawings of Jamaica's Anansi – who seems to lack a clear gender identity – and the Irish giant that she includes in multiple illustrations for MacManus's book.[59] Both works were completed in 1898–99, so it stands to reason that there is some overlap. However, the fact that Anansi and the giant both have large ears and a diminutive stature does seem to indicate that she created a trans-cultural representational code in which both are seen and signified as trickster figures.

Trying to capitalize on her illustrations for MacManus's collection, in June 1899 Colman Smith and her father travelled to London, where they contacted William Butler Yeats in hopes of selling him stage designs for his 1892 play *The Countess Cathleen*.[60] She had regularly performed the play as part of the repertoire of her miniature theatre, both in New York and Jamaica, creating her designs within a few months of the play's first publication in 1895.[61] W.B. was in Ireland at the time and asked his father, John Butler Yeats, to meet with them instead. He describes the pair in a letter to his son:

> Pamela Smith and father are the funniest-looking people, the most primitive Americans possible, but I like them much. Pamela (Miss Smith her father always said even when addressing her) is bringing out a book of Jamaican folklore. Her work whether a drawing or the telling of a piece of folklore is very direct and original and therefore sincere – its originality being its naïveté. I should feel safe in getting her to illustrate anything. She does not draw well, but has the right feeling for line and expression and colour. . . . She looks exactly like a Japanese. Nannie says this Japanese appearance

comes from constantly drinking iced water. You at first think her rather elderly, you are surprised to find out that she is very young, quite a girl. . . . I don't think there is anything great or profound in her, or very emotional or practical.⁶²

John Yeats's lengthy assessment reflects both his paternalism and his biases against "primitive" Americans, especially those whom he assumes to be a class below him and whose racial origins he has trouble ascertaining. However, his comments also highlight the difficulty that so many white Anglo-Americans appear to have encountered when trying to discern basic details about Colman Smith, such as her age and ethnicity (she was twenty-one at the time of the visit). This difficulty of readily "placing" her age, ethnicity and class translates into a tendency both to exoticize her background and to depict her as simple and naive. Similar impulses can be seen in Arthur Ransome's description of Colman Smith, whom he refers to as "Gypsy" in his 1907 *Bohemia in London*, where he terms her a "strange little creature" and states that upon welcoming him into her London salon she described herself as a "goddaughter of a witch and sister to a fairy".⁶³ While it is impossible to know whether Colman Smith actually uttered these words or they are Ransome's own contribution, it does seem in keeping with her tongue-in-cheek response to Anglo-American prejudice. For example, in response to John Yeats's narrow-minded comments, she created a sketch of herself in a kimono drinking ice-water. Thus, rather than directly confronting or combating these biased views, Colman Smith seems to have celebrated her position as a marginalized outsider, which her Pixie persona would only strengthen.

When Colman Smith and William Butler Yeats finally met in March 1901, it was her turn to look a bit askance at the eminent poet. In a letter to Albert Bigelow Paine she writes of her encounter with Yeats at a studio tea in a stable:

W.B.Y. was there and he is a rummy critter! Seemed most stupid and had on a tea party air and posed about and looked bored – And when all the ladies with ermine collars had gone, who all told him how very much they liked his bloomin poetry, which probably they had never read or heard of . . . then WB began to talk! Folklore – songs, plays, Irish, language, and lots more – reciting a sort of folksong which was splendid.⁶⁴

What is striking about her hard-headed account – even more than her preference for Yeats's folklore over his poems – is that it is hardly that of a naive child. Shortly after this initial meeting, Yeats saw her stage designs for *The Countess Cathleen* and watched parts of a performance of the play in her Henrietta min-

iature theatre, with which he was "much pleased".[65] Later that year, with his
help, Colman Smith joined the Urania Temple of the Order of the Golden
Dawn, and later still the Irish Literary Society. She frequently discussed plans
for a projected illustrated edition of Blake – someone they both admired – and
suggested that she design a book of Gaelic mythology for children, but nothing
came of either plan.[66] She collaborated on stage designs and costumes with Edith
Craig, Ellen Terry's daughter and a close friend of Colman Smith's during this
period, for Yeats's *Where There Is Nothing*, in a production that premiered at
the Royal Court Theatre in London in November 1904. Yeats termed parts of
these designs "impressive" and wrote to Lady Gregory shortly after the play's
opening that "Pixie Smith . . . alone seems to understand what I want".[67]

Colman Smith's involvement with the Yeats family was not limited to William
Butler. She contributed Christmas card, lace, wallpaper and other designs to
the Dun Emer Press, run by Elizabeth and Lilly Yeats and Evelyn Gleeson.[68] She
also collaborated with Jack Yeats on *A Broad Sheet* for eleven monthly issues
in 1902, which seems to have introduced her to the world of little magazines.
Colman Smith struck up a friendship with Jack and his wife, Cottie, cultivated
by their shared love of miniature theatre. In June 1901 she visited them at their
cottage in Devonshire, watched Jack Yeats's performance of his miniature circus,
and reportedly dressed up in native costume and regaled them with Jamaican
folktales.[69] Notable highlights from Colman Smith's tenure at *A Broad Sheet*
include her illustration of the "blood bond" passage of George Moore and W.B.
Yeats's *Grania,* her illustration of George Russell's "The Gates of Dreamland"
and her own "A Cobweb Cloak of Time".

Colman Smith's reasons for ending her affiliation with *A Broad Sheet* are
unclear but were most likely tied to her desire for a little magazine over which
she had exclusive control. A 15 December 1902 letter from Jack Yeats to John
Quinn hints at personal discord between the co-editors:

> Between you and me and the wall, as they say, Miss Pamela Smith (though I think her
> a fine illustrator with a fine eye for colour and just the artist for illuminating verse)
> is a little bit lazy, and she being a woman I can't take a very high hand with things,
> so there is often a lot of fuss about the numbers, and I don't like to be responsible for
> anything that I have not got absolute control of.[70]

A Broad Sheet continued until December 1903 and the two remained friendly.

In January 1903 Colman Smith launched her own little magazine after lengthy
discussions with Yeats during the planning stages; ultimately, however, she did

not incorporate many of his suggestions. She replaced his choice of *Hour-Glass* with the *Green Sheaf* for a title and dedicated it not to "the Art of Happy Desire", as he suggested, but more simply to "pleasure".[71] Where Yeats wanted the subject matter to be confined to dreams of an ideal state, "beautiful or charming or in some other way desirable", Colman Smith chose to have her title page proclaim "pictures, verses, ballads, of love and war; tales of pirates and the sea . . . ballads of the old world".[72] In addition to content by Yeats, contributors to the *Green Sheaf* included Russell, Synge, Lady Gregory, Lady Alix Egerton, Cecil French and Christopher St John.

While the first few issues did roughly follow the dreamy, optimistic lead that Yeats had outlined, by the fourth issue the tone had dimmed. This is best seen in Colman Smith's poem "Alone", which is accompanied by her illustration of a woman in a long cloak standing near barren trees:

> Alone and in the midst of men,
> Alone 'mid hills and valleys fair;
> Alone upon a ship at sea;
> Alone – alone, and everywhere.
>
> O many folk I see and know,
> So kind they are I scarce can tell
> But now alone on land and sea,
> In spite of all I'm left to dwell.
>
> In cities large – in country lane,
> Around the world – tis all the same;
> Across the sea from shore to shore,
> Alone – alone, for evermore.[73]

Despite being surrounded by "many folk" wherever she goes, the speaker is unable to accurately assess their kindness, finding herself isolated and adrift. Colman Smith was an only child who never married; her father died in 1899, and she is not known to have returned to Jamaica. She also found herself increasingly at odds with William Butler Yeats and his family. The break began over an advertisement she included on the back page of the *Green Sheaf*, promoting prints of a portrait she had made of W.B. and, evidently, did not obtain his permission to sell.[74] This compounded existing strains in their relationship over her decision to advertise her services as "Gelukiezanger", who entertained audiences with lilting Jamaican Anansi tales, in the pages of her little magazine.

When the Order of the Golden Dawn split in 1904 over conflicts between Aleister Crowley, whom Yeats initially supported, and the scholar Arthur Waite, whom Colman Smith followed, the break was consolidated. Colman Smith remained active in the temple until at least 1909, when she contributed the designs for the tarot deck for which she is now arguably best known. During this period she began to create paintings that were inspired by visions she had while listening to works by Schumann and others.[75] Her artistic career seems to have reached its apex with these synaesthetic paintings, which were exhibited three times during 1907–09 at Alfred Stieglitz's Little Galleries of the Photo-Secession in New York. However, as a brief mention in the *New York Times* illustrates, her final Stieglitz exhibition was cut short when patrons were put off by her decision to appear in traditional Jamaican costume and declaim Jamaican folktales, as well as poems by W.B. Yeats, in the middle of the gallery.[76]

Thus audiences who were initially drawn to her otherness in her guise of Gelukiezanger were now repelled by her public displays of primitivism. In response, Colman Smith seems to have stopped telling Jamaican Anansi stories, at least publicly, shortly after her last Stieglitz show; she also did not publish any more folktale collections. Her art became increasingly based on synaesthesia and lost the vibrancy and vitality that characterized so much of her early work as she retreated almost completely into the mythical world of Irish fairies, pixies, mermaids and the *sidhe*. However, unlike many of the artists and writers of the Modernist movement, Colman Smith did not create a symbolic system by which to help viewers unlock the "meaning" of her work.[77] As a result, and compounded by the horrors of the First World War that drew audiences away from more fantastic creations, she and her unique fusion of Jamaican and Irish folk culture easily slipped into obscurity.

Notes

1. Kathleen Pyne, *Modernism and the Feminine Voice: O'Keeffe and the Women of the Stieglitz Circle* (Berkeley: University of California Press, 2007), 47–61. See also George Heard Hamilton, "The Alfred Stieglitz Collection", *Metropolitan Museum Journal* 3 (1970): 371–92.
2. Untitled anonymous article in the *Reader: An Illustrated Monthly Magazine* 2 (September 1903): 331.
3. Melinda Boyd Parsons, *To All Believers: The Art of Pamela Colman Smith* (Newark: University of Delaware Press, 1975), 4.

4.   Pamela Colman Smith, "A Protest Against Fear", *Craftsman* 11, no.6 (March 1907): 728.

5.   Stuart Kaplan, *The Artwork and Time of Pamela Colman Smith: Artist of the Rider-Waite Tarot Deck* (Stamford, CT: US Games Systems, 2009), 92–95; Parsons, 17.

6.   Parsons, *To All Believers*, 4; Pyne, *Modernism*, 47–48; Kaplan, *Artwork and Time*, 5–8.

7.   Parsons, *To All Believers*, 4; Kaplan, *Artwork and Time*, 5–6.

8.   Kaplan, *Artwork and Time*, 5–6.

9.   Letter from Pamela Colman Smith to Mary ("Bobby") Reed, 2 November 1896, Bryn Mawr College Library Special Collections, box 1, folder 5. I would like to thank Eric Pumroy and the Special Collections staff for their help and for allowing me to quote from the collection.

10.   *Reader*, 331.

11.   Kaplan writes that Corinne Colman Smith "was believed to have also been from Brooklyn, but may have been of Jamaican descent" (*Artwork and Time*, 5). He does not offer a source for this assertion.

12.   Pamela Colman Smith, *William Gillette as Sherlock Holmes* (New York: R.H. Russell, 1900).

13.   Pamela Chandler Colman, *The Mother's Present: A Holiday Giftbook for the Young* (Boston: S. Colman, 1847). For more on Samuel Colman, see Grace Guleck, "The Poetic Landscapes of Samuel Colman", *New York Times*, 14 May 1999, http://www .nytimes.com/1999/05/14/arts/art-in-review-the-poetic-landscapes-of-samuel -colman.htm.

14.   Kaplan, *Artwork and Time*, 5; Parsons, *To All Believers*, 12.

15.   Pyne, *Modernism*, 47.

16.   Ibid.

17.   Ibid; Kaplan, *Artwork and Time*, 8.

18.   *Reader*, 331.

19.   Letters from Pamela Colman Smith to Bobby Reed, 25 July 1896 and 17 September 1896, Bryn Mawr College Library Special Collections, box 1, folder 1. The 25 July letter references her mother's recent death; the 17 September letter reveals that "I make waffles for breakfast and everybody was so slow. . . . You know I pay all the wages now and market money."

20.   Letter from Pamela Colman Smith to Bobby Reed, 7 December 1899, Bryn Mawr College Library Special Collections, box 1, folder 14.

21.   Parsons, *To All Believers*, 2, 8.

22.   Ibid., 14; Kaplan, *Artwork and Time*, 85–86.

23.   Irwin M. MacDonald, "The Fairy Faith and Pictured Music of Pamela Colman Smith", *Craftsman* 23, no. 1 (October 1912): 32.

24.   Ibid.

25. Ibid., 33.

26. Ibid.

27. Parsons, *To All Believers*, 3.

28. W.B. Yeats, *The Land of Heart's Desire*, illustrated by Pamela Colman Smith (New York: R.H. Russell, 1898).

29. "Christmas Performance", *Gleaner* (Kingston, Jamaica), 14 December 1896, 3.

30. I.A. Haskell, "The Decorative Work of Miss Pamela Colman Smith", *Pratt Institute Monthly* 6, no. 3 (December 1897): 67.

31. "Teachers, Students, and Things", *Pratt Institute Monthly* 6, no. 5 (February 1897): 148.

32. Ibid.

33. Pamela Colman Smith, letters to Bobby Reed, 17 September 1896 and 19 October 1896, Bryn Mawr College Library Special Collections, box 1, folders 2 and 4.

34. Pamela Colman Smith, letter to Bobby Reed, 17 September 1896, Bryn Mawr College Library Special Collections, box 1, folder 2.

35. Ibid.

36. Pamela Colman Smith, letter to Bobby Reed, 5 October 1896, Bryn Mawr College Library Special Collections, box 1, folder 3.

37. "Teachers, Students, and Things", 148.

38. Parsons, *To All Believers*, 3.

39. Ibid., 5.

40. "Gelukiezanger", *Green Sheaf* 6 (October 1903): 16.

41. Parsons, *To All Believers*, 5; *Reader*, 332.

42. "Mofussilite", "Weekly-Whispers", *Nelson* [New Zealand] *Evening Mail*, 4 May 1907, 2.

43. Ibid.

44. Pamela Colman Smith, *The Golden Vanity and the Green Bed: Words and Music of Two Elizabethan Ballads* (London: Elkin Matthews, 1903).

45. Pamela Colman Smith, *Chim-Chim: Folk Stories from Jamaica* (London: Green Sheaf Press, 1905), 30–40, 48–52.

46. Ibid, n.p.

47. Pamela Colman Smith, "Two Negro Stories from Jamaica", *Journal of American Folklore* 9, no. 35 (October–December, 1896): 278.

48. Martha Beckwith, "Yam Hills", *Jamaican Anancy Stories* (New York: American Folklore Society, 1924), http://www.sacred-texts.com/afr/jas/jas031.htm.

49. Pascale de Souza "Creolizing Anancy: Signifyin(g) Practices in New World Spider Tales", in *A Pepper-Pot of Cultures: Aspects of Creolization in the Caribbean*, ed. Gordon Collier and Ulrich Fleischmann (Amsterdam: Rodopi, 2003), 360–61.

50. Pamela Colman Smith, *Annancy Stories* (New York: R.H. Russell, 1899), 59.

51. Ibid.

52. Ibid., 60–61.

53. Ibid., 62.

54. Ibid., 23.

55. Philip M. Sherlock, *Anansi: The Spider Man* (London: Macmillan Caribbean, 1979), 1–2.

56. Colman Smith, *Chim-Chim*, 13.

57. Ibid., 14.

58. Colman Smith, *Annancy Stories*, 52.

59. Seamus MacManus, *In Chimney Corners: Merry Tales of Irish Folklore* (Garden City, NJ: Doubleday, 1899).

60. Parsons, *To All Believers*, 5.

61. Joan Coldwell, "Pamela Colman Smith and the Yeats Family", *Canadian Journal of Irish Studies* 3, no. 2 (November 1977): 28–29.

62. J.B. Yeats, *Letters to His Son W.B. Yeats and Others, 1869–1922*, ed. Joseph Hone (New York: E.P. Dutton, 1946), 61.

63. Arthur Ransome, *Bohemia in London* (New York: Dodd, Mead, 1907), 56–57.

64. Coldwell, "Pamela Colman Smith", 29.

65. Alan Wade, ed., *The Letters of William Butler Yeats* (London: Hart Davis, 1954), 444.

66. Parsons, *To All Believers*, 11; Coldwell, "Pamela Colman Smith", 29.

67. Wade, *Letters*, 444.

68. Nicola Gordon Bowe, "Two Early Twentieth-Century Irish Arts and Crafts Workshops in Context: An Túr Gloine and the Dun Emer Guild and Industries", *Journal of Design History* 2, no. 2/3 (1989): 193–206.

69. Hilary Pyle, *Jack B. Yeats: A Biography* (London: Routledge and Kegan Paul, 1970), 66–67.

70. William Michael Murphy, *Family Secrets: William Butler Yeats and His Relatives* (Syracuse, NY: Syracuse University Press, 1995), 288.

71. Wade, *Letters*, 389.

72. This description is on the title page of each of the thirteen issues of Colman Smith's *Green Sheaf*.

73. Pamela Colman Smith, "Alone", *Green Sheaf* 4 (August 1903), 9.

74. Parsons, *To All Believers*, 9–10.

75. MacDonald, "Fairy Faith", 20–32.

76. Pyne, *Modernism*, 53.

77. MacDonald, "Fairy Faith", 20–34.

Chapter 10

The Final Fortress

The Redlegs *and Bajan-Irish Abjection*

HARVEY O'BRIEN

THE REDLEGS IS A TELEVISION DOCUMENTARY FIRST broadcast in Ireland in December 2009, on the Irish-language television station TG4. The film has two components: a historical overview of the seventeenth-century human traffic between Ireland and Barbados and an inside look at the Irish-descended Barbadian community living in Martin's Bay today, people who still bear the name "Redlegs". Portions of the material had previously been seen in *Barbado'ed* (2009), a shorter programme broadcast exclusively on BBC Two (Scotland) earlier in the year; it featured Scots author and broadcaster Chris Dolan[1] exploring the same routes and connections from a Scottish point of view. Though both pieces were produced by the Irish-based Moondance Productions (Lydia Conway, producer), *The Redlegs* was more widely distributed. The film in this longer form was subsequently nominated for both the pan-European Prix Europa, in the category of multicultural programme of the year, and the Ireland-based Radharc Awards, recognizing films that portray positive human values and challenge the moral conscience of the audience.

The challenge to the moral conscience presented by *The Redlegs* runs deeper and wider than may first appear evident. The tenuous hold on the dimension of local ownership of history embodied in its bifurcated presentation does not negate its potential to provoke discussion on ethnic visibility, particularly given the emphasis the film places on tracing direct lines of interconnection between the Caribbean and two European countries that profess a strongly Celtic identity. *Barbado'ed* personalizes this visibility through Dolan's physical presence as presenter, narrator and interviewer. *The Redlegs* assumes a more consciously dispassionate "historical" position by using a neutral, invisible narrator who recites many of the same observations that Dolan delivered in a personal manner (and a Scots accent) in the earlier film. Though both films locate the fundamental injustice of Cromwellian transportation within a familiar historical and political framework of imperial oppression, they complicate this frame with the living and present conditions of contemporary descendants of the original colonial deportees, linked in one case with Scotland and in the other with Ireland. The evident cultural and economic deprivation and isolation of this "white race of poor people", as photographer Sheena Jolley describes them in the film, is not easily incorporated within a postcolonial or post-racial conception of either Scotland or Ireland in the twenty-first century.[2]

Estimates of how many so-called sugar slaves were transported from Ireland to the Caribbean in the seventeenth century vary with different historical accounts, but certainly tens of thousands of men, women and children from the Celtic isles, dispossessed of their lands, were sent "to Hell or Barbados" before, during and after the Cromwellian conquest (1649–53). Richard Dunn states that from the 1650s the colonies evinced "a distinctive social and economic formula by which they and theirs lived and died".[3] Karl Watson, who appears as an interviewee in the film, delineates this formula by enumerating three constituent classes of planters: the planter elite, the merchant class and the poor whites, this last group identifiable partly by income level but also by insufficient ownership of land to enfranchise them with voting rights. This was, according to Watson, the largest single group among the white population, one which, particularly following emancipation, "sank to lower depths of poverty and degradation than they had experienced earlier".[4] The living descendants of the original Redlegs (so named, according to lore, because their pale skin burned quickly below the hem of their kilts) represent a potentially troubling metahistory of emigration and diasporic identity politics. As Édouard Glissant poignantly observes,

The marginal and the deviant sense in advance the shock of cultures; they live its future excess. The rebel paves the way for such a shock, or at least its legibility, by refusing to be cramped by any tradition at all, even when the force of his rebellion comes from the defense of a tradition that is ridiculed or oppressed by another tradition that simply has more powerful means of action. The rebel defends his right to do his own surpassing: the lives of marginal and deviant persons take this right to extremes.[5]

When President Barack Obama visited Ireland in May 2011, Taoiseach Enda Kenny used the occasion to assert: "If there's anyone out there who still doubts that Ireland is a place where all things are possible; who still wonders if the dream of our ancestors is alive in our time; who still questions our capacity to restore ourselves, reinvent ourselves and prosper, today is your answer."[6] The appeal of restoration and reinvention in the face of crippling recession, spiralling debt and sinking public morale would appear evident. Claiming Barack Obama as an exemplar of Irish ancestral dreaming was certainly convenient, but what of this "largest Irish tribe to be forgotten", as the documentary puts it, which still exists to some degree today with neither reinvention nor prosperity in evidence? What of their ancestral dreams?

The documentary portrays this community of Irish descent in Barbados today as a dejected, abject and impoverished marginal group. Though more creolized in reality than the framework of the documentary presents, these descendants of the original "poor whites" retain some degree of ethnic visibility but do not constitute a typical diasporic demographic. No one comes to them seeking support for political and cultural causes in the "home" country, as routinely happens with Irish diasporic communities. Neither does anyone seek to tell their story as an exemplar of the restorative trajectory of a formerly enslaved ethnicity with strong cultural roots, as celebrated by Obama and Kenny and described by Diane Negra in Irish-American terms in *The Irish in Us*: "using Irishness as an ethnic code for reinstating social values perceived to be lost in millennial American culture".[7] In fact, notwithstanding the existence of this documentary, plus another made in 1976 by Radharc Productions titled *The Black Irish*, some charitable intervention recorded by the newer film in its closing section, and one or two key books, including Sean O'Callaghan's *To Hell or Barbados: The Ethnic Cleansing of Ireland*,[8] this diaspora has gone largely unclaimed. The introductory narration to the documentary goes so far as to say these people have been "hidden by history".

The Redlegs seem doubly dejected by their status in Barbados. As the documentary makes clear, members of the community proclaim their Bajan identity proudly. "I was born here. This is my little island", says Martin's Bay resident Eustace Norris in an accent recognizably both Hibernian and Bajan. Yet the economic and professional standing of this group in Barbados is entirely marginal. The film documents the largely insular subsistence-based existence of these people, complete with a localized barter system for food and supplies that is virtually indistinguishable from a model of village life associated with eighteenth-century peasantry. In the film, members of the community speak of a sense of repression and rejection by other Barbadians. "They try to keep you down", says Richard Bailey, a member of the community. The conditions in which they live are evidently underdeveloped; even geographically, Martin's Bay is shown in the film to be a remote, unvisited part of the island, away from the tourist routes. Sheena Jolley describes her first encounters with the Redlegs in the early 2000s – they are seen "walking up the road, barefooted, obviously poor, and hauling coconuts" – and how this isolated, suspicious community allowed her access to photograph them as if they were an exotic tribe discovered by an explorer.

Debates rage in the Barbadian press and online about the health and status of the Redlegs, some of it directly inspired by the screening of the film and by a subsequent article in the *Irish Times* by Sheena Jolley. This article was abstracted online by Barbados Free Press, juxtaposed with remarks by social scientist Peter Simmons from the *Daily Nation* to the effect that mixed marriages could lead to greater health and social prospects for children from this community. One blogger, identified only as "KJK01", responded:

> What an amazing community and an amazing chapter in human history. These little pockets of diversity should be welcomed and celebrated, not have people making plans for their assimilation. Here is a community that has survived on the brink for almost 400 years, and now people are trying to determine what is best for their "survival". Maybe just leave them alone and stop trying the [*sic*] "help" them. They've survived for this long without our help, maybe they know something we don't.[9]

There is, however, a disconnect between such conclusions and what seems to be the lived experience of the Redlegs today. Eric Bailey, a young man with the pale skin and freckled features of a stereotypical Irish tourist, states in the film, "I wasn't born four hundred years ago", and "I don't know about slavery. I come into the free days." The question naturally arises: what is the nature of these post-emancipation, postcolonial "free days" in a community that seems not to have assumed an active place in the culture and economy of Barbados, let alone a broader Caribbean identity? For a subculture with low literacy and little sense of history beyond rumours of the "old ancestors", does the ethnic and racial connection with Ireland (or Scotland) alone constitute justification for a measure of separateness, and with what meaning for how (and, indeed, why) a community professes an identity at all? Richard Bailey describes the difficulty of extracting information from his forebears: they would fail to specify points of origin, saying only *dem say* (which the film's subtitles translate as "Dempsey", as if it were a proper name instead of a colloquialism for rumour and conjecture). At the end of the day it is difficult to assess the degree to which this community has a desire, or a need, to trace its roots, apart from provocation by the documentary and the documentarians.

The film begins by framing the story of the Redlegs as concealed history, in which they are "forgotten casualties" of Cromwellian victimization. As Brian Winston has persuasively argued, Griersonian documentary tends to conflate complex causative contexts to narrative binaries of problem and resolution that make victims of any subject, and this does characterize the position here. From the outset the film uses the familiar historical frame of suffering under colonialism to define Ireland's past. There is some irony to this insofar as we might consider the aggressive political reframing of exactly this paradigm – through the Irish visits of President Obama and Queen Elizabeth II in 2011 – a "moving on" or "going forward", in the parlance of post–Celtic Tiger Ireland. Revisiting the tropes of anti-colonial rebellion in the context of a neglected diaspora is simultaneously comforting and ennobling, without threatening the privilege of twenty-first-century Irish post-nationalism.

The film recounts the basic facts of known history, explaining and contextualizing the deportation of men, women and children to Barbados and other colonies in the early to mid-1650s. Sean O'Callaghan's book delves more deeply into this purge and more fully explores the successive waves of emigration from Ireland to the Caribbean. According to O'Callaghan there were two distinct migrations. Initially, in the first wave of indentured servitude, the Irish who signed voluntary contracts of three to seven years' duration became part of a colonial subclass of household servants distinct from African slaves. Others were sent wholly as "slaves", when the anti-Catholic purges intensified following Cromwell's departure from Ireland as its conqueror. Though reference to this distinction is made in the documentary, it is not significantly directive in contextual terms without prior knowledge or further reading, opening the film to criticism for totalizing the experience of Irish immigrants as entirely equal to that of African slaves.

The Black Irish, the 1976 Radharc film, also offers this conflation. Though that film focuses more on Montserrat, it also refers in part to Barbados when it

states: "Irish and African negro shared a common suffering, a common griev-
ance, and for the most part lived together in peace and common understanding."
The conflation of African and Irish slave experiences has been both debunked
and rebuked by scholars, including Michael Malouf, in his reading of Sinéad
O'Connor's appropriation of Rastafarianism; Thomas Byrne, in tracing the
Hooke family's economic benefits that accrued from settlement in the Caribbean
colonies; and in the most detail by Donald Akenson, in his treatise on the Irish
managerial class as Fanonian postcolonial mimics, *If the Irish Ran the World:
Montserrat, 1630–1730*.[10] As he notes,

> None of this is pleasant to record. But if the self-replicating cycle of abuser-abused-
> abuser-abused is to be broken, the Irish polity, through the historians who are keepers
> of its collective memory, must cease to view the emigrants from Ireland as forever-pas-
> sive victims, and therefore as persons who are incapable of hard dealing. One of the
> fundamental stories of the Irish diaspora is of Irish emigrants choosing to do unto
> others what others had already done unto them. In neither case was that a matter of
> kind and tender mercies.[11]

As a film produced by Radharc – a company with a religious ethos – *The
Black Irish* can be understood to frame its figuration of black/white relations
and inter-slave solidarity in broader Catholic terms within the ethos and the
ethic of universal brotherhood; indeed, the film does emphasize the religious
nature of the deportations and the legacy of that religious heritage. If anything,
religion is a notably absent element in *The Redlegs*, other than the concluding
section, in which Father Jim Finn sets out to support the community through
charity work.

As Catherine Eagan notes, the so-called Irish racial project is still a power-
fully emotive and divisive matter, hotly debated in education and in scholarship.
Eagan reports on the academic fallout from Lawrence Osborne's forceful rejection of Irish claims of non-hegemonic cultural legitimacy through experiences
of slavery and prejudice. Osborne stated:

> Speaking the language of Athens hardly made Alexander the militaristic barbarian
> or Aristotle the provincial Thracian a mutilated buffoon, any more than speaking
> English made Joyce a traumatized "nigger". The construal of either as prototypes of
> Third World iconoclasm and oppression, as traumatized subjectivities grappling with
> the ripple effects of cultural imperialism, is a deft romanticism. And as far as the Irish
> in particular are concerned, it skips over the delicately tricky but rather obvious fact
> that they are not, when all is said and done, black.[12]

This comment triggered a wave of academic outrage and response from Irish post-colonialists, including, notably, Luke Gibbons. Gibbons's emotive evocation of the Irish famine as a thinly veiled instance of ethnic cleansing, Eagan reports, "threatened to eclipse his careful differentiation of the Irish experience from that of colonized people of color".[13] The point is that the argument can quickly collapse from the particular to the general, with the underlying issue being the formation of identity through an experience of (historical, racialized, arguably sectarian) trauma. The most interesting question raised by *The Redlegs* is the degree to which these experiences were particular to those who – even once upon a time – claimed or actually possessed an Irish or Celtic identity.

The film does seek to specify elements of the Irish experience of colonial Caribbean life with reference to distinctions of race, politics and culture. Historian Nicholas Canny of the National University of Ireland, Galway, recounts in the film the role played by former Irish rebels as leaders in plantation uprisings, which involved combined forces of African and European slaves. This is confirmed and discussed by Hilary McD. Beckles, who records petitions made by English planters that Irish rebels no longer be sent to Barbados in the wake of the 1692 slave uprising, in which the Irish played a key role.[14] The political context of the Cromwellian deportations, with roots in the earlier Irish rebellions, is undoubtedly one of its defining features, borne out as a particular element of a local historical experience by this thread of the documentary's narrative. However, it is not necessarily a kind of Irish exceptionalism – something Akeson in particular is at pains to debunk, even given his use of the Irish as a particular subject. For example, in the film reference is made to a demand for Irish women by English colonists who did not wish to consort sexually with native or African women. O'Callaghan goes into this in even greater detail in his book, describing, with the aid of records from the Public Archives of Barbados, the use of Irish women to breed children of mixed race for use in the big houses of the plantations and the brothels of Bridgetown.[15] What is evinced by these two separate but related aspects of the Caribbean Irish experience is the root of misrecognition of what was by the late 1600s becoming a new generation of Irish Caribbean people, and of their kinship not so much with the dispossessed but with the colonists themselves.

By the 1660s, the film reports, inherent mistrust of the Irish by English plantation owners – reinforced, as interviewee Michael D. Higgins explains, by former alliances of the Irish with the French against the English – was forcibly mitigated by the legal requirement in Barbados to employ one white militia man per thirty acres. This made the dejected, unruly Irish an important colonial buffer between the now minority white population and the black labour force and underclass. Beckles argues: "Planters wrote of their Irish servants as constituting a special problem. Their discussions suggest that long-standing tensions and hostilities in English-Irish relations threatened the stability of white communities and the accomplishments of the English colonizing mission in general."16 Provided with chattel-house dwellings and some measure of "authority", such people began to band together into a community of their own, defined by intermarriage and some sense of fidelity to an ancestral (racial) separateness from African slaves. However, one significant effect of this caste system, the film argues, was the sense of privilege assumed by the militia tenants that led to their refusing to acquire specialized skills such as carpentry or millinery, which was "slave work". As the film details, this was instrumental in their drift into poverty after emancipation. Partly out of an assumption of kinship with the landlords rather than with the emancipated slaves – a kinship that was entirely illusory and based on pride – the film's voiceover states that the Barbadian Irish were "willing to chose race over class in regard to identity".

This familiar mode of assimilation and mimicry corresponds with a Fanonian model of postcolonial social development, where the pathology of colonization becomes visible through the distorted reflection that the postcolonial society, upon achieving independence, mirrors back towards its former colonizer. This recalls Akeson's comment about the cycle of victimization in Montserrat, although in the case of Barbados it is more misrecognition that leads to abjection, given the status of this "buffer class" after the devolution and development of political power following emancipation. As Fanon concludes, "colonialism forces the people it dominates to ask themselves the question constantly: 'In reality, who am I?' "17 While the centre of political and social momentum gradually shifted from freed slaves to skilled artisans and farmers and through to nineteenth- and twentieth-century capitalist government, the film argues (supported by Karl Watson) that the descendants of the Irish and Scots deportees began to drift into a liminal space between community and nationality, where in some sense they remain. As Watson notes, "Poor whites or 'Redlegs' have been portrayed usually in rather generalized terms. This is because little attention was paid to them by officials and it was only as oddities that they caught the passing eye of the traveler, who naturally recorded only the most striking defects or aberrations."18 In contrast to patterns of emigration and migration to the United States, where geographical mobility and the overall racial profile favoured further migration and greater assimilation – and ultimately the forging of an expatriate ethnic identity relating to the "home country" – the Caribbean Irish simply went into an implosive decline.

Author Des Geraghty locates the psychic disinheritance that begins to define the Redlegs as they are now within the broader context of classical colonialism, whereby "the Empire" consciously sought to sever the connection with the originating culture, producing a rootless people owing allegiance only to itself. Barbadian historian Ronnie Hughes describes this even more cynically, arguing that because they were ill-adapted to the "deadly heat", the Irish servants and slaves were considered comparatively disposable and barely worth the mental effort of applied ethnic extermination or repression. Groundsman Winston Gill, charged with maintenance of St Nicholas Abbey Mill in St Peter, anecdotally asserts the same history, based again on colloquial oral tradition. He states that the Irish workers were driven from the mill because they were less efficient producers. This implies that the evolution of this subculture becomes a sort of side effect or afterthought of colonialism, an almost forgotten sociopolitical drift from the middle to the margins, rooted both in class and in race.

The film makes some effort to delve into physical evidence to unpack these kinds of broad assumptions, but, as it notes, "the poor rarely leave evidence of their existence", and the Redlegs have not kept written histories. Watson notes: "In writing a history of these people then, one has to proceed in a fashion rather like that of one assembling a jigsaw puzzle, selecting bits of information at random and hoping to make a whole picture."[19] Anthropologist Fred Smith of Virginia's College of William and Mary is seen throughout the film excavating former dwellings of residents of a different part of the island, describing the construction of slave quarters and types of buildings shown to have contemporary analogues in the western Barbadian habitations of the modern Redlegs.

The ancestral predilection for alcoholism and laziness still attributed to the community today is discussed in the film by Karl Watson. He argues that many of the historically recorded accounts of drunken Irish servants and slaves can be explained as symptoms of diseases caused by parasitic infections, to which the natives of colder northern climes were particularly susceptible. However, this argument is complicated by images of the interviewees from Martin's Bay with empty or partly empty alcohol bottles in view. Questions must be raised, inevitably, about the historical discontinuity between colonial and postcolonial paradigms of poverty and deprivation, and the nature of the culture today in relation to its roots. Is the sociobiological explanation even relevant to understanding the relationship between alcoholism and poverty today? And how does this chime with the film's own evocation of the Irish tourists' quest for what it calls "sun and rum punch" when they visit the island on holiday?

Throughout the film, the theme of Celtic displacement and alienation is continually reinforced by references to the climate. It begins with the image of paradise represented by Barbados as a holiday destination, but invites the viewer "behind the veil" of the "magical island" to find the "final fortress" of an Irishness that has endured in this "hellish" environment. This is actually a rather startling juxtaposition, and one at the heart of the real challenge that this film represents. Can it be argued that this abject, dejected community of "poor whites" can be seen as a kind of primordial remnant of a "pure but lost" Irish generation, one defined – as nationalist mythology would always have it – by resistance to assimilation? Is the film saying that the paradigm has shifted so much that Ireland has lost touch with its own rebel past, and has here the opportunity to confront its abject doppelganger: a return of the repressed by way of the wretched of the earth? In the brogue-tinged accents, white faces and familiar features of these impoverished Bajans, what does the Irish viewer see? As evidenced by the debate around teaching of the Great Famine as described by Eagan – was it ethnic cleansing? – nothing is incidental when it comes to formation of a sense of nationality with reference to history and education. It is all too easy to slip into a comfort zone of a "temporary inhabiting of other-ness"[20] that invites an image of solidarity while maintaining privileged distance.

Any historical documentary must grapple with the frame within which it places the past. As Pierre Sorlin once wrote, "history is a society's memory of its past, and . . . the functioning of this memory depends on the situation in which the society finds itself".[21] This is equally true of all historical films, be they documentary or fiction. And so, bearing in mind the project of reconstructing this "concealed" history while Ireland confronts its sense of self in the wake of the Celtic Tiger, this film inevitably calls into question the epistemological and rhetorical roots of its argument. It can be said that the film represents an ethically informed intercession in debates about identity, and in this context offers a real challenge to the position of privilege from which the contemporary Irish viewer confronts this distant present. Like Jacob Riis's *How the Other Half Lives* (1890) or even Fanon's *The Wretched of the Earth* (1961), it is a provocation to its viewers to confront truths about themselves as they look at others who are like and yet not like them.

There is certainly something of this message in the O'Callaghan book, which concludes with an account of his visit to Barbados in the 1990s and his encounters with "the Red Legs today" under Newcastle Hill. He concludes: "It was a melancholy outing, and although I was glad to get back to the gaiety and bustle of the hotel, I could not get the Red Legs out of my mind. Perhaps somebody, somewhere will do something to ease their plight"; he exhorts Irish Catholics to "band together and do something for their long forgotten brethren".[22] This rhetorical shift to a mode of religious missionary engagement is perhaps problematic, calling to mind another genus of colonialism and an overarching ethos that is itself facing question in Ireland today.

The film follows the same line and, in accession to a Griersonian problem-resolution structure, closes out its presentation with an answer to O'Callaghan's call. Its last scenes are wholly concerned with redemptive interventions. We follow the charitable missionary work of Father Jim Finn and of David Shirley, an Anglo-Irish descendant of English planters. Shirley accounts for his charitable activities as a type of postcolonial reparation for his ancestors' legacy. He says of the "sugar slaves" that "they died without an identity: any identity", and the voiceover speaks of the "cultural jungle" in which the Irish became this "ghostly community". In its last minutes, the documentary becomes a safer space in which to encounter the Redlegs – as a victimized Other for whom "something is being done" in our name but without our involvement.

The film's very last frames are spent with Anne Banfield, a Redleg whose interracial marriage, decried by her conservative father, is presented as the ultimate solution. "Black or white, we are all one", she says, a sentiment which echoes *The Black Irish* and is hard to dispute in purely humanistic terms, but which is also an echo of a much more troubling ongoing debate. In recent years the aforementioned social scientist Peter Simmons has played a significant part in this debate; O'Callaghan quotes extensively from Simmons in his closing chapter. He also quotes Lionel Hutchinson's 1971 novel *One Touch of Nature*, in which racial mixing is proffered as a means of moving "up the hill" and away from poverty and marginalization. It is arguably an uncomfortable analogy with the very past that is being confronted to suggest that biology alone can settle this matter. It does nonetheless again force us as viewers to confront what constitutes the experience of an identity, and to deal head-on with the manner and degree to which skin and features create a sense of commonality – but also contribute to a reaction of abjection. Are the Redlegs an Irish Other or a refracted mirror of a lost past? In reading that past, should their history be understood as integral or parenthetical, and how should we understand the threads of multiculturalism, migration and nationality relative to both past and present? Provocative questions indeed. The issue is to what degree viewers of the documentary will feel invited to ask them.

Notes

1. Dolan would later author the novel *Redlegs* (Glasgow: Vagabond Voices, 2012).
2. This paper focuses substantially on the Irish version of the film – *The Redlegs* – not least because, at the time of its most recent revision (June 2014), *Barbado'ed* appeared to have been removed from the various websites that hosted it, including Moondance Productions' home page, http://www.moondance.ie. However, it was only ever intended for local television broadcast, whereas, as noted, *The Redlegs* was widely distributed. At the same time, *Barbado'ed* is readily available online at YouTube, whereas a recent search for *The Redlegs* yielded no results.
3. Richard Dunn, *Sugar and Slaves: The Rise of the Planter Class in the English West Indies, 1624–1713* (London: Jonathan Cape, 1973), 335.
4. Karl Watson, "Walk and Nyam Buckras: Poor-White Emigration from Barbados, 1834–1900", *Journal of Caribbean History* 34 (2000): 133.
5. Édouard Glissant, *Poetics of Relation*, trans. Betsy Wing (Ann Arbor: University of Michigan Press, 2009), 156.
6. Enda Kenny, public address, College Green, Dublin, 24 May 2011.
7. Diane Negra, "The Irish in Us: Irishness, Performativity, and Popular Culture", in *The Irish in Us: Irishness, Performativity and Popular Culture*, ed. Diane Negra, 1–19 (Durham, NC: Duke University Press, 2006), 4.
8. Sean O'Callaghan, *To Hell or Barbados: The Ethnic Cleansing of Ireland* (Dublin: Brandon, 2000).
9. "KJK01", 30 May 2011, comment on Sheena Jolley, "Remnants of an Indentured People", *Irish Times*, 12 December 2009, republished by Barbados Free Press, 29 December 2009, http://barbadosfreepress.wordpress.com/2009/12/28/irish-times-most-barbados-red-legs-have-bad-or-no-teeth-many-blind-without-limbs/.
10. Michael Malouf, "Feeling Éire(y): On Irish-Caribbean Popular Culture", in *The Irish in Us: Irishness, Performativity and Popular Culture*, ed. Diane Negra, 318–53 (Durham, NC: Duke University Press, 2006); Thomas Byrne, "Banished by Cromwell?: John Hooke and the Caribbean", *Irish Migration Studies in Latin America* 5, no. 3 (November 2007): 215–20; Donald Akeson, *If the Irish Ran the World: Montserrat, 1630–1730* (Liverpool: Liverpool University Press, 1997).
11. Akeson, *If the Irish*, 175.
12. Lawrence Osborne, "The Uses of Being Irish", *Village Voice*, 3 June 2008, http://

www.lawrenceosborne.net/2008/06/the-uses-of-bei.html, accessed 28 November 2013.

13. Catherine Eagan, "Still 'Black' and 'Proud': Irish America and the Racial Politics of Hibernophilia", in *The Irish in Us: Irishness, Performativity and Popular Culture*, ed. Diane Negra, 20–63 (Durham, NC: Duke University Press, 2006), 42.

14. Hilary McD. Beckles, "A 'Riotous and Unruly Lot': Irish Indentured Servants and Freemen in the English West Indies, 1644–1713", *William and Mary Quarterly* 47, no. 4 (1990): 503–22.

15. O'Callaghan, *To Hell or Barbados*, 114–16.

16. Beckles, "Riotous and Unruly", 504.

17. Frantz Fanon, *The Wretched of the Earth*, trans. Constance Farrington (New York: Grove, 1963), 250.

18. Watson, "Walk and Nyam Buckras", 136.

19. Ibid.

20. Eagan, "Still 'Black' and 'Proud'", 53.

21. Pierre Sorlin, *The Film in History: Restaging the Past* (New York: Barnes and Noble, 1980), 16.

22. O'Callaghan, *To Hell or Barbados*, 225–26.

Part 3

Comparative Readings and Critical Encounters

Chapter 11

Water Songs

"The Lake Isle of Innisfree" and Jamaican Poetry

LEE M. JENKINS

I will arise and go now, and go to Innisfree,
And a small cabin build there, of clay and wattles made:
Nine bean-rows will I have there, a hive for the honey-bee,
And live alone in the bee-loud glade.

And I shall have some peace there, for peace comes dropping slow,
Dropping from the veils of the morning to where the cricket sings;
There midnight's all a glimmer, and noon a purple glow,
And evening full of the linnet's wings.

I will arise and go now, for always night and day
I hear lake water lapping with low sounds by the shore;
While I stand on the roadway, or on the pavements grey,
I hear it in the deep heart's core.[1]

IN HIS INFLUENTIAL STUDY OF CARIBBEAN CULTURE *The Repeating Island*,
Antonio Benítez-Rojo discerns in the archipelago "the features of an island that
'repeats' itself, unfolding and bifurcating until it reaches all the seas and lands
of the earth". The reader, he explains, should understand *repeats* in "the almost
paradoxical sense with which it appears in the discourse of Chaos [theory]",
in which "every repetition is a practice that necessarily entails a difference".[2]
This chapter attempts to reconfigure Ireland and the Caribbean as repeating

islands by tracing the contours of a repeating *isle*: W.B. Yeats's "The Lake Isle of Innisfree", published in 1890, and its reception and revision – its repetition with a difference – in Jamaican poetry from the 1910s to the 1990s.[3] Late in his life, Yeats would complain that, forty years after he had written it, "The Lake Isle of Innisfree" still "pursued him around the world"; for more than a century its ripple effect would be felt in Jamaica, an island Yeats never visited.[4] Nonetheless, Jamaican poets Claude McKay, Una Marson and Lorna Goodison have all revisited Yeats's poem, customizing a West Indian "island imaginary" from his island in the west of Ireland.[5]

Collectively, the Jamaican response poems to "The Lake Isle of Innisfree" comprise an intertextual island tradition that as such is set apart from the reception of Yeats elsewhere in the Caribbean. The Barbadian poet and critic Kamau Brathwaite, for instance, is interested less in the early lyricism of a poem like "The Lake Isle of Innisfree" than in the modernist metaphysics of the later Yeats; indeed, Brathwaite has analogized the arcane system of Yeats's *A Vision* (1925, 1937) to the experiments in "cultural cosmology" which have defined the later stages of his own oeuvre.[6] Taking as its less ambitious remit the transatlantic transposition of "The Lake Isle of Innisfree" into the Jamaican poetic imaginary, this chapter moves from a consideration of Yeats's poem itself to assessments of its early Jamaican revisions in McKay's "The Hermit" (1912) and Marson's "Nostalgia" (1937). The chapter concludes with an extended appraisal of Goodison's "Country, Sligoville" (1994), the last link in the chain of repeating island poems, in which Yeats himself is inducted into Jamaican poetic and folkloric traditions. From McKay's early experiments with "nation language" (to use Brathwaite's preferred term for dialect) through Marson's poetics of exile to Goodison's postcolonial celebration of island cultures, the Jamaican redactions of "The Lake Isle of Innisfree" chart the decolonization of the island's poetry.[7]

"The Lake Isle of Innisfree" itself is caught in the binary between the great and little traditions of colonizing centre and colonized hinterland, the poem's polarized geographies reflecting the "schizoid" nature of Anglo-Irish identity.[8] Yeats's formative experience was that of the declining and liminal Protestant Ascendancy class as he moved with his immediate family back and forth between Dublin and London, meanwhile spending his childhood summers in County Sligo (Innisfree is on Lough Gill, not far from the town of Sligo, the home of Yeats's mother's family, the Pollexfens). "The Lake Isle of Innisfree" is a product of that polarity, as Yeats would recall in *Autobiographies*: "when walking through

Fleet Street very homesick I heard a little tinkle of water and saw a fountain in a shop-window which balanced a little ball upon its jet, and began to remember lake water. From the sudden remembrance came my poem 'Innisfree' ".[9]

In the discussion of "Yeats and Decolonization" in his *Culture and Imperialism*, Edward Said argues that "if there is anything that radically distinguishes the imagination of anti-imperialism, it is the primacy of the geographical element".[10] Drawing on Said, Stephen Regan suggests that Yeats's poem "encourages us to think again about the function of the imagination in relation to geography and to reconceptualise homesickness and nostalgia as political desire".[11] "The Lake Isle of Innisfree" was written five years after the Second Home Rule Bill of 1893, which had proposed a bicameral parliament to control domestic affairs in Ireland; passed by the House of Commons, the bill was subsequently defeated in the House of Lords. If Yeats's poem is read in its contemporary context, either his cabin on the lake isle provides the poet with pastoral consolation for the political desire frustrated in the British upper house, or the cabin, "of clay and wattles made", is the seat of domestic Home Rule of a grassroots kind, the isle a site of solitary maroonage in its remoteness from the imperial centre.[12] "Innisfree" is insular in a double sense: its credo of self-reliance has been parsed both as a coded declaration of Irish autonomy and as an articulation of the concept of individual freedom which, as Michael North points out, "lies at the very basis of English liberalism": "The poem wraps its freedom in layers of insulation: it is to be found only in the 'deep heart's core,' at the very center of the person, who is alone on an island, encircled by a lake, which is itself on another island, isolated by a sea from the starting point of the poem."[13]

Yeats had been drawn from childhood to the lake isle's "legended past" and even into his early twenties was clinging to his "dream" of living "on a little island called Innisfree".[14] In the local lore of County Sligo, the isle is the home of the Tuatha Dé Danann, or fairy people; in *Autobiographies* Yeats recalls "a story in the county history of a tree that had once grown upon that island" and bore "the food of the gods".[15] As he notes elsewhere, the berries of this "enchanted tree" were, "according to one legend, poisonous to mortals, and, according to another, able to endow men with more than mortal powers".[16]

Yeats was working on his own collection *Fairy and Folk Tales of the Irish Peasantry* (1888) when "The Lake Isle of Innisfree" was conceived. Yet the autochthonous Irishness of the island is mediated in the poem by its speaker's physical distance from the place and by Yeats's allusions to classical and New World versions of pastoral, from Virgil to Thoreau: the "hive for the honey-bee" adverts to the apicultural theme of the fourth book of the *Georgics*, while the "nine bean-rows" have been transplanted to the lake isle from the "Bean-Field" chapter of *Walden*.[17] North is right to argue that "Yeats sees Sligo through the prism of a sophisticated primitivism".[18] According to his account of the poem's provenance, Yeats sees Innisfree through plate glass, too, the fountain-and-ball window display in the London shop window operating as a mechanical proxy for the natural environment of the lake isle itself. Even the name of the place is refracted: *Innisfree* is an English phonetic transcription of the Irish *Inis Fraoigh*, which means "island of heather", and so, paradoxically, it is the anglicized version of the place name which sanctions the poem's association of *island* (*inis*) with *free*dom. North puts it nicely: "How much more compactly could the divided allegiance of the poet be expressed than in this necessity to bring into a different language a place name from his home country in order to express its freedom? The place name occupies the exact divide, the hyphen, between the two halves of the Anglo-Irish experience."[19] "Innisfree" thus bears an equivocal relationship, both to the cartographic impulse of cultural nationalism, as defined by Said, and to "the old Gaelic *dinnseanchas* tradition of place-name poems" – represented in the poetry collected in the twelfth-century Book of Leinster, for example – to which Regan claims it "harks back". [20]

Yeats's own appraisal of "Innisfree" as "my first lyric with anything in its rhythm of my own music" stresses individual talent ("my own music") over tradition, whether Irish or English.[21] Countermanding Yeats, however, Irish revolutionary and poet-critic Thomas MacDonagh judges that "Innisfree" belongs to the "Irish Mode" (as opposed to the "Celtic Note", which is tainted by imperial stereotypes), since the poem resists scansion according to English metrical norms.[22] Conjoining prosody and anti-colonial nationalism, MacDonagh's Irish Mode prefigures Brathwaite's theory of a Caribbean "rhythm which approximates the *natural* experience, the *environmental* experience".[23] Equal to if in gentler measure than Brathwaite's "tidalectic" island rhythm, Yeats's "lake water lapping with low sounds by the shore" breaks the English pentameter.[24]

By contrast, Claude McKay's "The Hermit" is "imprisoned in the pentameter".[25] The poem is an example of "pentameter dialect", its English metre policing the disruptive vernacular in which one of the voices of the poem speaks.[26] Of the three Caribbean responses to "Innisfree" considered here, McKay's is the closest in date to Yeats's original; "The Hermit" appeared in 1912 in *Songs of Jamaica*, the first of two collections of McKay's dialect or nation language poetry to be published in that year. "The Hermit" echoes "The Lake Isle of Innisfree" and is McKay's indigenous version of the poem, in which Yeats's island idyll is transposed to the linguistic and physical environment of rural Jamaica. "Dere by de woodland" McKay reassembles Yeats's small cabin, replicating both the semiotic and the structural stresses and strains of "Innisfree" in his Jamaican simulacrum:

> Far in de country let me hide myself
> From life's sad pleasures an' de greed of pelf,
> Dwellin' wid Nature primitive an' rude,
> Livin' a peaceful life of solitude.[27]

The linguistic double consciousness of McKay's poem is exposed in its clunky code-switching between local language and a stock poetic lexicon, clichéd phrases such as "life's sad pleasures" offering a bland foretaste of the bitter oxymorons which lace his sonnets written in Standard English.[28]

It is to "hide" from these "sad pleasures" that the hermit resorts to the Jamaican countryside, far from the "pelf" with which the city is synonymous.[29] McKay knew all about pelf (theft) from his experience as a "bobby" in the Royal Jamaica Constabulary, but his dialect poems more often unsettle the ethical polarity maintained in "The Hermit" between the corruption of the city and the tonic properties of the countryside. In the preface to *Constab Ballads*, his second book of Jamaican verse, McKay even confesses to a "most improper sympathy with [the] wrongdoers" he encountered when he pounded the pavements of Spanish Town and the Half-Way Tree district of Kingston.[30] Of course, his hermit speaker may, by way of Yeats's "Innisfree", be meditating on pelf in the sense not of petty theft but of the historical grand larceny of slavery and colonialism. Like his countryman Marcus Garvey, McKay linked the struggle for black self-determination in the Americas to Irish resistance to British colonial rule; his cultural and political affinities with the Irish earned him the moniker "Black Murphy".[31] But "The Hermit", like "The Lake Isle of Innisfree", retreats from whatever ideological critique it may also moot. "Far in de country" the hermit makes his abode in the inaccessible fastness of the mountainous Jamaican interior, once the habitat of fugitive slaves led by Nanny of the Maroons.

Like Yeats's poem, however, McKay's invokes symbolic freedom in terms of solitary sanctuary:

> An' in my study I shall view de wul',
> An learn of all its doin's to de full;

List to de woodland creatures' music sweet –
Sad, yet contented in my lone retreat.³²

McKay may have insisted that "the peasant's passion for the soil possesses me, and it is the strongest passion in the Irish revolution", but in his "lone retreat" McKay's recluse is hardly in a position to proselytize on behalf of a new vision of Jamaican society, much less one of its postcolonial nationhood; in fact, in 1912, the year the poem appeared in *Songs of Jamaica*, McKay left the island, never to return.³³ That said, in Brathwaite's view, Caribbean "native literature begins with McKay the exile".³⁴ In his "home thoughts from abroad" poems, McKay the exile would return to "The Lake Isle of Innisfree"; for instance, in "The Tropics in New York", the familiar Jamaican fruits "[s]et in the window" of a Manhattan storefront, like Yeats's Fleet Street window display, stop the poet in his tracks on the city sidewalk.³⁵

Caribbean migration to the mother country is the subject of the "Poems Written from England" sequence in Una Marson's 1937 collection *The Moth and the Star*.³⁶ The last of these, "Nostalgia", is her rewriting of "The Lake Isle of Innisfree". Marson's poem, the opening line of which is "I will arise and go again to my fair Tropic Isle", appears at first to be as nostalgic for the Yeatsian original as it is for her own island home. But Marson's Jamaican "Innisfree" is not an example of what Jahan Ramazani would call "weak" transnationalism.³⁷ Rather, the poem is a complex instance of the subversive mimicry which Alison Donnell has identified in Marson's seemingly derivative verse.³⁸ Invoking her native land and home by way of "The Lake Isle of Innisfree", Marson co-opts Yeats to an anti-colonial poetics – decades before Said would do so – in a poem in which, to recur to Regan's reading of "Innisfree", nostalgia serves as a foil for "political desire": "I must leave this lovely country for one that's lovelier far, / I would leave the land of glow-worms and seek again the star".³⁹

A quarter-century before Jamaican independence, Marson is singing the praises of her "country", her first-person speaker taking imaginative possession of "my fair Tropic Isle" at a date when Jamaica was still a British dominion. Marson's island, which is "basking in the sun", represents a new day, in contrast to the waning power of the British Isles; "the land of glow-worms", England's day is almost done. The poem's speaker asserts that on her return to Jamaica she will "dream" not only of "the by-gone days" but also of "days that are to be"; Marson's island reverie, although nominally nostalgic, harbours a vision of the future for the poem's speaker and Jamaica alike.⁴⁰ Indeed, the lignum vitae tree under which Marson's speaker says she will sit would, after 1962, become a symbol of independence, the tree's flower the national flower of Jamaica.

In "Nostalgia" Marson signifies on McKay as well as on Yeats, offsetting her recourse to the latter by carrying forward the Little Tradition instanti-ated by her Jamaican predecessor. Like "The Hermit", "Nostalgia" is writ-ten in quatrains and rhyming couplets; a fourteen-liner, Marson's poem also makes a formal allusion to McKay's post-Jamaican sonnets. Marson echoes the formal and thematic circularity of "The Lake Isle of Innisfree" by adapt-ing the conventions of the Shakespearian sonnet, topping her poem as well as tailing it with a rhyming couplet. The opening lines of "Nostalgia" – "I will arise and go again to my fair Tropic Isle / And sit beneath the palm trees that there forever smile" – are repeated with a difference in the couplet with which the sonnet concludes: "Oh, I'll arise and go again to my fair Tropic Isle / For I hear voices calling and I'm so sad meanwhile." The pleasures of exile are lost on Marson's "sad" speaker.

The poem's prosody contributes to its treatment of colonial nostalgia: "My loving friends with eager eyes are waiting for the day / When I'll come and hold their hands and ever with them stay."[41] Like "The Lake Isle of Innisfree", "Nostalgia" employs the figure of hyperbaton or inversion – alteration of the usual word order – found in Yeats's "of clay and wattles made" and in Marson's "ever with them stay". Poets resort to inversion as a means of placing a rhyming word at the end of a line, but Yeats and Marson also use hyperbatic word order as a strategy of emphasis, Yeats's archaic diction complementing the antiquated method of his cabin-making, and Marson's registering her poem's strategic recuperation of Yeats's 1890s island imaginary.[42]

Like McKay's "The Hermit", Marson's "Nostalgia" is an indigenous West Indian version of "The Lake Isle of Innisfree" which substitutes for the "purple glow" of Yeats's Heather Island the "purple hills" of Marson's own "Tropic Isle". McKay's hermit dwells in a landscape of "tropic roses" and "wild cane", and Marson's poem likewise features local flora such as the lignum vitae, known as the "tree of life" because of its medicinal properties.[43] Unlike McKay's and Yeats's poems, however, which are versions of pastoral, Marson's is a vision of island *communitas*. Her speaker would gladly exchange the solitude of met-ropolitan exile for the company of "loving friends" at home. Human "voices calling" draw her back to the island, not McKay's "woodland creatures' music sweet", nor Yeats's "lake water lapping". Moreover, Marson's female and feminist reinscription of "The Lake Isle of Innisfree" contests the patriarchal premise which Yeats's poem takes from the parable of the prodigal son: "I will arise and go to my father" (Luke 15:18).[44]

An accomplished exponent of the Caribbean women's tradition which emerges in Marson's verse, Lorna Goodison has traced a matrilineal island genealogy in poems which praise Jamaican women, from historical figures such as Nanny of the Maroons to the poet's birth mother. In "Country, Sligoville", from her 1999 collection *Turn Thanks*, Goodison takes up from Marson the conversation between Yeats and Jamaican poets: "I arise and go with William Butler Yeats / to country, Sligoville".[45] In this performative utterance, Yeats's vision of Innisfree is both brought into being and changed utterly: Yeats's dream may be to live alone in the bee-loud glade, but Goodison declares that she is going with him to its Jamaican counterpart, "in the shamrock green hills of St. Catherine".[46] The co-ordinate at which the colonial trajectories of Jamaica and Ireland intersect, Sligoville was named for the Anglo-Irish Marquess of Sligo. As governor of Jamaica between 1834 and 1836, Sligo facilitated the transition to the apprenticeship system which obtained between the Slavery Abolition Act of 1834 and full emancipation in 1838.[47] Established in 1835, Sligoville was the island's first free village, the earliest settlement to be established for former slaves; as such, although its residents were bound to work as apprentices on local plantations, it "embodied the utopian promise of a free black Jamaica".[48]

Goodison's poem analogizes Sligoville to Innisfree, Yeats's own "country" embodiment of freedom. This makes Yeats, in his imagined sojourn there, a surrogate of sorts, both for the rebellious native Irish who, under Cromwell's orders, were transported to Jamaica as indentured labourers in the 1650s, and for Lord Sligo, the Anglo-Irish representative of the colonial planter culture who was a friend of poets, if not a poet himself.[49] For her part, Goodison, even if she did learn elements of her trade from Yeats, is no apprentice mage to his arch-poet.[50] Instead she discovers common ground with Yeats, in a place where the colonial legacy to which both poets are heir is in some degree redeemed: "We walk and palaver by the Rio Cobre / till we hear tributaries / join and sing, water songs of nixies."[51] The river flows through Bog Walk Gorge, a topographical marker of the long-standing presence in rural Jamaica of bog-trotting Irish peasantry. Brought together at Bog Walk by their islands' interconnected histories of colonialism, slavery and resistance, Goodison and Yeats "swap duppy stories" and trade "Dark tales of Maroon warriors" who are "bush comrades of Cuchulain", pooling the myths and folklore which are the sources of the two poets' "water songs".[52]

The confluence of Jamaican and Irish legacies is a family matter for Goodison, whose great-grandfather George O'Brian Wilson "jumped ship in the Lucea Harbour at the sight of the magnificent blue-green mountains of Western Jamaica".[53] Wilson married a propertied creole but fell in love with a local girl, Leanna Sinclair, who would become the "Guinea Woman" muse of Goodison's poems and stories. Leanna reappears, this time with the Irish father of her child, in "O Pirates Yes They Rob I", from the 2005 volume *Controlling the Silver*. Here Goodison acknowledges that her gift is a bequest not only of her "griot" great-grandmother's songs of freedom but also of Wilson's "Irish / airs": "O to hear him sing the lake Isle of Innisfree / now become Harvey River, near Lucea".[54]

"Country, Sligoville", Goodison's own rendition of "The Lake Isle of Innisfree", mixes Irish airs with Jamaican songs. Her poem alludes both to Yeats's "Down by the Salley Gardens", from his 1889 collection *The Wanderings of Oisin and Other Poems*, and to ring songs like "Little Sally Water", the Jamaican version of which was recorded by Louise Bennett in 1957:

> Little Sally Water sprinkle in the saucer
> Rise Sally rise, and wipe your eyes.
> Sally turn to the east
> Sally turn to the west
> Sally turn to the one you love the best.[55]

The ring song and Yeats's lyric both derive from the folk tradition. As Bennett remarks in the liner notes to her 1957 LP *Children's Jamaican Songs and Games*, ring songs and folksongs "have no personal authorship but have been handed down from one generation to another".[56] Originally titled "An Old Song Re-sung", Yeats's "Down by the Salley Gardens" was his "attempt to reconstruct an old song from three lines imperfectly remembered by an old peasant woman in the village of Ballysadare, Sligo, who often sings them to herself".[57] "Salley Gardens" returned to the oral tradition from which it came when it was set to music in 1909: "My mother used to sing that song", Goodison recalls in her memoir of her mother and her island.[58] In "Country, Sligoville" the two Sall[e]y songs join in a composite elegy for the poet's "dead mother": "Sally water will go down / to the Sally gardens with her saucer / and rise and dry her weeping orbs."[59]

Goodison splices Yeats's early lyric of love and loss with the vernacular culture of her Jamaican childhood, fusing the music of "Innisfree" with the phonic properties of her own island's ring songs. Her poem thus evinces the qualities of both "strong" and "elegiac transnationalism". In moving proof of Ramazani's point that the "poetry of mourning can be made to serve both nation-specific and cosmopolitan ends", Goodison makes the master of modern elegy her confidant, as she calls the "late" Yeats into the centre – the deep heart's core – of her own visionary poem: "William Butler, I swear my dead mother / embraced me. I then washed off my heart / with the amniotic water of a green coconut."[60]

The epiphany Goodison shares with Yeats shows her fellow folklorist that, like his legended Innisfree, the home of the Tuatha Dé Danann, Jamaica is a duppy island. Among its more benevolent *genii loci* are ancestral spirits such as the River Mumma, who dispenses remedies from "her underwater clinic".[61] The water in which the poet washes her heart is just such a remedy: in Jamaica, green coconut water is valued as a heart tonic. Like the lignum vitae, the coconut palm is a Jamaican tree of life, the "amniotic" water of its young fruit the life-giving source and symbol, for Goodison, of her poetic genesis and her matrilineal island inheritance alike. Goodison's relationship to Ireland, and thus to Yeats, is through the female line; accordingly, her response to "The Lake Isle of Innisfree" draws not on the patrimonial pedigree of his progenitor poem but on the maternal embodiment of Yeats's island dream, the lake waters lapping in the poet's heart. "Country, Sligoville" is her "turn thanks" both to "The Lake Isle of Innisfree" and to the island mother whose "birth water sang like rivers" in Goodison's own early signature poem "I Am Becoming My Mother".[62]

Yeats's lake isle has traversed the Atlantic, multiplying as a repeating island in the Caribbean poetic imaginary as a geography of desire, as a site of symbolic and of solitary or non-aligned freedom, and as a signifier of exile and return. As an "inter-colony contact" point between Ireland and the Caribbean, "Innisfree" is a point from which the full measure of Yeats's "international achievement in cultural decolonization" may be gauged.[63] In the nexus between "The Lake Isle of Innisfree" and its Jamaican response poems, colonial and postcolonial island traditions "join and sing".[64]

Notes

1. W.B. Yeats, *The Variorum Edition of the Poems of W.B. Yeats*, ed. Peter Allt and Russell K. Alspach, 3rd ed. (London: Macmillan, 1966), 117.

2. Antonio Benítez-Rojo, *The Repeating Island: The Caribbean and the Postmodern Perspective*, 2nd ed. (Durham, NC: Duke University Press, 1992), 3.

3. "The Lake Isle of Innisfree" first appeared in the *National Observer* on 13 December 1890. The poem was published in book form in 1892, in *The Countess Kathleen and Various Legends and Lyrics*.

4. R.F. Foster, *W.B. Yeats: A Life*, vol. 1, *The Apprentice Mage, 1865–1914* (Oxford: Oxford University Press, 1997), 79.

5. Maria McGarrity, *Washed by the Gulf Stream: The Historic and Geographic Relation of Irish and Caribbean Literature* (Newark: University of Delaware Press, 2008), 111.

6. See Kamau Brathwaite, *Magical Realism*, 2 vols (New York: Savacou North, 2002), n.p.

7. Brathwaite distinguishes "standard, imported, educated English" from local language which reflects "the African aspect of experience in the Caribbean", and recommends the term *nation language* in place of *dialect* because of the "pejorative overtones" of the latter. See Edward Kamau Brathwaite, *History of the Voice: The Development of Nation Language in Anglophone Caribbean Poetry* (London: New Beacon, 1984), 13.

8. R.F. Foster, *Modern Ireland, 1600–1972* (Harmondsworth, UK: Penguin, 1990), 170.

9. W.B. Yeats, *Autobiographies*, ed. William H. O'Donnell and Douglas N. Archibald (New York: Scribner, 1999), 3:139. Yeats refers to the epiphany, although he alters its location, in his 1891 novella *John Sherman*: "Delayed by a crush in the Strand, he heard a faint trickling of water near by; it came from a shop window where a little water-jet balanced a wooden ball upon its point. . . . It made him remember an old day-dream of his" – the dream of going to "a little islet called Innisfree. . . . and building a wooden hut there". W.B. Yeats, *The Collected Works of W.B. Yeats*, vol. 12, *John Sherman and Dhoya*, ed. Richard J. Finneran (New York: Macmillan, 1991), 56–57.

10. Edward Said, *Culture and Imperialism*, 2nd ed. (London: Vintage, 1994), 225.

11. Stephen Regan, "W.B. Yeats: Irish Nationalism and Post-Colonial Theory", *Northern Irish Studies* 5, no. 1 (2006): 90–91.

12. Yeats, *Variorum Edition*, 117.

13. Michael North, *The Political Aesthetic of Yeats, Eliot, and Pound* (New York: Cambridge University Press, 1991), 24.

14. Yeats, quoted in Russell K. Alspach, *Yeats and Innisfree* (Dublin: Dolmen, 1965), 74; Yeats, *Autobiographies*, 71–72.

15. Yeats, *Autobiographies*, 71–72.

16. Yeats, *Variorum Edition*, 742. According to the version of the legend which Yeats recounts in *Autobiographies*, the tree was guarded by "some terrible monster": "A young girl pined for the fruit and told her lover to kill the monster and carry the fruit away. He did as he had been told, but tasted the fruit; and when he reached the mainland where she had waited for him, he was dying of its powerful virtue. And from sorrow and from remorse she too ate of it and died" (*Autobiographies*, 85).

17. See W.B. Yeats, *Writings on Irish Folklore, Legend and Myth*, ed. Robert Welch (Harmondsworth, UK: Penguin, 1993).

18. North, *Political Aesthetic*, 24.

19. Ibid., 25.

20. Stephen Regan, "The *Fin de Siècle*, 1885–1897", in *W.B. Yeats in Context*, ed. David Holdeman and Ben Levitas, 25–34 (Cambridge: Cambridge University Press, 2009), 30. With reference to Yeats's 1899 collection *The Wind among the Reeds*, C.L. Innes remarks that Irish place names "are used and specified as belonging within a whole system of rooted Irish culture and identity. In these early poems Yeats is remapping Ireland as a possession of a distinctively Celtic people"; C.L. Innes, "Modernism, Ireland and Empire: Yeats, Joyce and Their Implied Audiences", in *Modernism and Empire*, ed. Howard J. Booth and Nigel Rigby, 137–55 (Manchester: Manchester University Press, 2000), 145. In his sophisticated analysis of Yeats, nationalism and postcolonialism, David Lloyd likewise comments on Yeats's early poetry's "desire to rename and reappropriate the geography of Irish landscapes, to imbue an anglicized culture with myth and folklore that is distinctively Irish"; David Lloyd, "Nationalism and Postcolonialism", in *W.B. Yeats in Context*, ed. David Holdeman and Ben Levitas, 179–92 (Cambridge: Cambridge University Press, 2009), 181.

21. Yeats, *Autobiographies*, 139.

22. Thomas MacDonagh, *Literature in Ireland* (1916; reprint, Tyrone: Relay, 1996), 6.

23. Brathwaite, *History of the Voice*, 10.

24. Yeats, *Variorum Edition*, 117. In *History of the Voice*, 9–10, Brathwaite notes: "What English has given us as a model for poetry . . . is the pentameter"; despite attempts to break it, "the pentameter remained, and it carries with it a certain kind of experience, which is not the experience of a hurricane. The hurricane does not roar in pentameters." "Tidalectics" is "like the movement of the ocean . . . coming from one continent/continuum, touching another, and then receding"; Kamau Brathwaite, *ConVERSations with Nathaniel Mackey* (New York: We Press and Xcp, 1999), 34.

25. Brathwaite, *History of the Voice*, 20.

26. Charles Bernstein, *My Way: Speeches and Poems* (Chicago: University of Chicago Press, 1999), 127.

27. Claude McKay, *Complete Poems*, ed. William J. Maxwell (Urbana: University of Illinois Press, 2004), 34.

28. Ibid.

29. Ibid.

30. Ibid., 294.

31. Claude McKay, *The Passion of Claude McKay: Selected Prose and Poetry, 1912–1948*, ed. Wayne Cooper (New York: Schocken, 1973), 57.

32. McKay, *Complete Poems*, 35.

33. McKay, *Passion*, 59; McKay, *Complete Poems*, 35.

34. Brathwaite, *History of the Voice*, 42.

35. McKay, *Complete Poems*, 154.

36. Marson reverts to the theme of exile, and to Yeats, in "Home Thoughts": "And I am

here in London", she tells us, in a poem in which "bees, hungry for hidden honey, / Swarm"; Una Marson, *The Moth and the Star* (Kingston: Marson, 1937), 22.

37. Marson, *Moth*, 24; Jahan Ramazani, *A Transnational Poetics* (Chicago: University of Chicago Press, 2009), 81.

38. See Alison Donnell, "Sentimental Subversions: The Poetics and Politics of Devotion in the Work of Una Marson", in *Kicking Daffodils: Twentieth-Century Women Poets*, ed. Vicki Bertram (Edinburgh: Edinburgh University Press, 1997), 113–24.

39. Marson, *Moth*, 24.

40. Ibid.

41. Ibid.

42. Yeats would reconsider his recourse to inversion in "The Lake Isle of Innisfree", noting that at the time of the poem's composition, "I only understood vaguely and occasionally that I must for my special purpose use nothing but the common syntax"; *Autobiographies*, 153.

43. Marson, *Moth*, 24.

44. Ibid.; McKay, *Complete Poems*, 35; Yeats, *Variorum Edition*, 117. Yeats recalls in *Autobiographies*, 47: "My father had read to me some passage out of *Walden*, and I planned to live some day in a cottage on a little island called Innisfree."

45. Lorna Goodison, *Turn Thanks* (Urbana: University of Illinois Press, 1999), 47.

46. Ibid.

47. Howe Peter Browne, second Marquess of Sligo (1788–1845), piloted the apprenticeship system on the coffee and sugar plantations his family owned in Jamaica.

48. Michael Malouf, "Duppy Poetics", in *Ireland and Transnational Poetics: Essays in Honor of Denis Donoghue*, ed. Brian G. Caraher and Robert Mahoney, 191–204 (Cranbury, NJ: Associated University Presses, 2007), 200. Nini Rodgers notes, however, that apprenticeship was "a compromise solution unpalatable to both sides": despite being called the emancipator of Jamaica, Lord Sligo's "apprentices had difficulty in believing in his commitment to their emancipation as he himself had been a slave owner" (of some 286 slaves); *Ireland, Slavery and Anti-Slavery, 1612–1865* (London: Palgrave Macmillan, 2007), 92.

49. The Irish comprised the largest ethnic group in Jamaica after Africans. Lord Sligo was a friend of Byron.

50. Goodison has said that she learned from Yeats's 1936 edition of the *Oxford Book of Modern Verse*, which she read and reread, "to love poems for their danger and power". Yeats omitted "The Lake Isle of Innisfree" when he selected his own work for this anthology, choosing instead the poems "Symbols", "Sailing to Byzantium" and "In Memory of Eva Gore-Booth and Con Markiewicz". See Lorna Goodison, "How I Became a Writer", in *Caribbean Women Writers: Essays from the First International Conference*, ed. Selwyn R. Cudjoe (Wellesley, MA: Calaloux, 1990), 291.

51. Goodison, *Turn Thanks*, 47.

52.   Ibid. See Goodison's "On Becoming a Mermaid", from her 1986 volume *I Am Becoming My Mother*, and Yeats's lyric "The Mermaid", from the sequence "A Man Young and Old" in his 1928 collection *The Tower*.

53.   Lorna Goodison, *From Harvey River: A Memoir of My Mother and Her Island* (Toronto: McClelland and Stewart, 2007), 39.

54.   Lorna Goodison, *Controlling the Silver* (Urbana: University of Illinois Press, 2005), 36; Goodison, *From Harvey River*, 39.

55.   Louise Bennett, *Children's Jamaican Songs and Games* (Folkways, 1957, 33-1/3 rpm), liner notes, p. 6. Another version of this ring song was recorded circa 1940 by the Andrews Sisters; "Little Sally Walker" and "Little Sally Saucer" are among its numerous transatlantic variants.

56.   Bennett, *Children's Jamaican Songs and Games*, liner notes, 1.

57.   W.B. Yeats, quoted in A. Norman Jeffares, *A New Commentary on the Poems of W.B. Yeats* (London: Macmillan, 1984), 12. Yeats would complain in a 1935 letter to Dorothy Wellesley that the army of the Irish Free State was marching to the tune of "Down by the Salley Gardens", a tune that was "first published with words of mine, words that are now folklore"; ibid.

58.   Goodison, *From Harvey River*, 39.

59.   Goodison, *Turn Thanks*, 47. In her memoir, Goodison recalls "crying in Papine Market [in Kingston] because my mother was dead", only to find herself surrounded by women: "I stand in that loving circle of women, like Sally Water of the children's ring game, with weeping eyes"; *From Harvey River*, 269.

60.   Ramazani, *Transnational Poetics*, 81, 72; Goodison, *Turn Thanks*, 47. Ramazani, 81, argues that the intertextuality which is a defining feature of modern elegy makes the genre "weak transnationalism" in contradistinction to more aggressive varieties of transnational poetries which flaunt their "discrepant cultural materials". Goodison's version of elegy arguably collapses Ramazani's Bloomian weak/strong distinction. Certainly "Country, Sligoville" comprises a stronger misreading in Bloom's sense of Yeats than the definition of it as "cultural dovetailing" suggests. See Lamia Tewfik, "'I arise and go with William Butler Yeats . . .': Cultural Dovetailing in Lorna Goodison's *Country Sligoville*", *Irish Migration Studies in Latin America* 5, no. 3 (2007): 225–29.

61.   Goodison, *Controlling*, 53.

62.   Lorna Goodison, *I Am Becoming My Mother* (London: New Beacon, 1986), 38.

63.   McGarrity, *Washed by the Gulf Stream*, 19; Said, *Culture and Imperialism*, 288.

64.   Goodison, *Turn Thanks*, 47.

Chapter 12

The Haunted Ocean

Mourning Language with J.M. Synge and Derek Walcott

LEIF SCHENSTEAD-HARRIS

> There is no politics without an organization of the time and space of mourning.
>
> — Jacques Derrida, *Aporias*

IN A FAMOUS 1979 INTERVIEW WITH EDWARD Hirsh, Derek Walcott speaks candidly about his respect for John Millington Synge. Walcott particularly stresses the influence of Synge's play *Riders to the Sea* (1904) on his own early play of a half-century later, *The Sea at Dauphin* (1954). On reading *Riders to the Sea*, Walcott says, "I realized what he had attempted to do with the language of the Irish. He had taken a fishing-port kind of language and gotten beauty out of it, a beat, something lyrical. Now that was inspiring, and the obvious model for *The Sea at Dauphin*."[1]

Along with their linguistic similarities, the two one-act plays share a significant formal structure, a "beat": the lyrical rhythm of mourning work performed by a small family or community responding to loss. In *Riders to the Sea* an Irish family, made up of Maurya and her two daughters, contends with the drowning of two of the family's sons, Michael and Bartley. In *The Sea at Dauphin*, fishermen Afa and Augustin face the suicide of Hounakin, Augustin's relative, and the past deaths of a number of fellow fishermen at sea, Afa's friend Bolo in particular. Both plays are disturbed by spectral emanations of loss; both impoverished groups of mourners are haunted by memories of those lost at sea. The lyric power of their language reflects a melancholic fascination with the dead. Both writers' relation to dominant English discourses in language and culture redoubles the intensity which mourning brings to language. Walcott, a St Lucian writer, and Synge, an Irish writer, illustrate the paradigmatic power of minoritarian writers making intensive and even politically revolutionary use of mourning language. This chapter explores methods of linguistic intensification to examine how the plays achieve similar effects in their respective literary traditions. It investigates how they create "beauty" – a beat – in what Walcott deemed "a fishing-port kind of language" by turning on the figure of the ghost, not a Gothic figure made of bedsheets but the living memory of a person lost to the sea.

Synge's and Walcott's languages are deeply influenced by each writer's minoritarian pose. The closeness of this position and its considerable effect on dramatic expression serves as a point from which to compare their work. Paul Breslin argues that the "surge" of language is common to both plays, "the sense of releasing lyrical possibilities in the speech of people whose lives might seem, to an unsympathetic observer, as hard and barren as the rocks of Aran or Dauphin themselves".[2] Minoritarian writing demonstrates language's ability to release marginalized perspectives on consciousness. Languages used in a normative way by dominant political multiplicities can be reshaped from their geographical or cultural peripheries. Writers who form minorities within a language used by a clearly defined majority of speakers, such as anglophone Irish or Caribbean writers enmeshed in English imperial discourses, can effect drastic change.[3] Thus Caribbean and Irish anglophone speakers have the power to disrupt and restructure the English language in similar ways. If dominant English is a kind of imperial mainland, these writers trace its heterogeneous and changing shore. Along this border are the regional dialects, creoles, and creative admixtures which constitute the contact zone between English and other languages, and from which new expressive potentials are released.

The peripheral or "fishing-port" position of writers such as Synge and Walcott creates opportunities for linguistic revivification, if ones fraught with challenge. In this regard Synge's dramatic influence is famous. Pascale Casanova observes that the Irish playwright popularized "a new, free, modern idiom, impertinent in its rejection of the usages of a written language that was fixed, dead, rigidified".[4] Montserratian poet and scholar E.A. Markham notes that West Indian writers similarly modify English with distinctive stresses and imagery; the ensuing language, in Kamau Brathwaite's judgement, possesses the power of "a howl or a shout or a machine-gun or the wind or a wave".[5] Minoritarian changes to dominant languages effectively intensify language. They reject calcified meanings, expose dead metaphors and, on the whole, stretch normative expectations about linguistic possibilities.[6] Intensity, a property of difference, individuates language. The principle of dynamic reversibility dictates that where intense pressure exists, so too does the potential for change. As language is intensified and individuated it becomes open to radical alteration. In this regard, at least, the tense stance of the minoritarian writer torn between linguistic heritages is only with difficulty distinguished from the creative if solipsistic generation of an avant-garde idiolect.[7]

Like other literary traditions across the reaches of a post-imperial landscape, Irish and St Lucian linguistic spaces situate writers in a complex relationship with normative English, whether it is spoken next to Irish Gaelic, as in Ireland, or the French and English creoles of St Lucia. Each is far from the received pronunciation of metropolitan London and yet they are similar in their contested and thus creative use of the English language. In Africa, Chinua Achebe famously advocated "an English which is at once universal and able to carry [an African writer's] peculiar experience".[8] Divorced from its imperial prospects, this "new English"[9] oscillates between a desire for global intelligibility and local expressions of minoritarian cultures. Only in this always contested fashion is English "a world language for poets, or at least a semiglobal conduit through which poets encounter, advance, and redirect cross-cultural flows of tropes and words, ideas and images".[10] Minoritarian writers, including those from Ireland and the Caribbean, inhabit this conduit as they negotiate different linguistic cultures and reshape language for their own uses.

Although written under very different circumstances, Synge's and Walcott's plays reveal similar transformations in their literary cultures. Both playwrights' dramatic work emerged from the margins of dominant culture and, especially in their early days, was performed by small theatrical movements that coped with limited resources. These plays also challenged conservative assumptions about aesthetic validity. First performed by the Irish National Theatre Society, *Riders to the Sea* confused and repelled its first Dublin audiences. "There are some things which are lifelike and yet quite unfit for presentation on the stage", an early review commented. "*Riders to the Sea* is one of them."[11] A half-century later, in 1953, *The Sea at Dauphin* was initially read by the University College of the West Indies Drama society; the next year Errol Hill produced it for the Trinidadian New Company. Revealingly, one of the first reviews of Walcott's play is titled "Not the Stuff for a West Indian Theatre".[12] St Lucian priest Charles

Jesse, another reviewer, objected to the play's 1954 performances with complaints similar to those lodged against *Riders to the Sea*: "all that is true of life is not fit for human eyes and ears".[13] Although as natural as colloquial language, these plays were considered offensively unfit as art. Such disruptions are often normalized; deterritorializations are re-territorialized. *Riders to the Sea* became an Abbey Theatre staple often paired with Synge's later *Playboy of the Western World* (1907). Similarly, *The Sea at Dauphin* settled into the role of minor classic and subsequently won the Best West Indian Play award at Jamaica's 1956 Adult Drama Festival.

Despite challenges to the dramatic companies that staged them, *Riders to the Sea* and *The Sea at Dauphin* proved to be formative in their respective literary movements. Synge's participation in the Abbey Theatre is widely recognized as crucial to the rebirth of Irish drama in the twentieth century. In 1905 Synge's reputation was already well established. Hogan and Kilroy observe that, for then-contemporary audiences, "it was Synge, rather than Lady Gregory or [William] Boyle or Padraic Colum, who seemed to typify in the minds of Dubliners the Abbey Theatre".[14] But such typicality also occasioned conservative disdain. Writers at the nationalist paper *An Claidheamh Solusis* ("The Sword of Light"), for instance, saw the unsettled and even spectral nature of Synge's plays as indicative of their author's failings. "While the Anglo-Irish dramatic movement has now been in existence for ten years", the writers observed, "its net result has been . . . the generation of a sort of Evil Spirit in the shape of Mr J.M. Synge".[15] Outside Ireland, assessments by drama critics such as Arthur Walkley spoke positively of Synge's innovations in dramatic speech. Walkley admiringly characterized the language of Synge's plays as one "spoken with watchful care and slightly timorous hesitation. . . . These Irish people sing our language – and always in a minor key." Quoting John Milton's "Il Penseroso", he complimentarily deems the play's language "most musical, most melancholy".[16] Not only was Synge perceived as one of the foremost dramatists of the revolutionary Abbey Theatre. Admirers and detractors both sensed that his work bore the unsettling imprint of melancholic grief.

Walcott's contribution to Caribbean theatre is equally influential. Speaking broadly but in no uncertain terms, Kole Omotoso argues that Walcott's early plays "redeem Caribbean drama and theatre" in the 1950s.[17] For Christopher Innes, "at least until the 1980s, Walcott was the sole Caribbean dramatist of any stature, while his Trinidad Theatre Workshop remained the only company with extensive expertise".[18] Like the Abbey, the Trinidad Theatre Workshop broke new ground for emergent theatrical companies and for linguistic expression. In particular, *The Sea at Dauphin* is an early example of hybridization of French Creole in anglophone theatre.[19] In the context of a broad resurgence of interest in folk culture, Walcott drew from marginalized local culture and St Lucian colloquialisms while adopting a few English (or Anglo-Irish) dramatic conventions in his early plays.[20] Characters from fishing communities such as Dauphin "speak for themselves and express their communal predicament and vibrancy more or less in their own terms", Edward Baugh writes; they use "a language derived from their native creole, with its homegrown poetic imagery and phrasing, its own earthy and proverbial authority and eloquence". After Walcott, Creole became an accepted (or at least precedented) medium for dramatic expression.[21]

Synge's plays also draw on folk tradition as a marginal discourse with the potential to upset dominant discourses and normative expectations.[22] However, Synge's peasantry, inspired by the Inishmaan islanders, proved too weird, too intensely grotesque for urban nationalists. Daniel Corkery, Irish revivalist and author of *The Hidden Ireland*, argues that the Irish peasantry stands unchanging, almost outside of time. To him Synge perverts folk culture, as if the playwright had intended to invert Shakespeare's famous injunction "Hold the mirror up to nature". Instead, Corkery wryly suggests, Synge's plays "[h]old the mirror, not up to nature, but up to nature's freaks!"[23] He thoroughly rejects the intensity of Synge's presentation of Irish folk culture on the stage, deeming it abnormal and destabilizing. What Corkery sees as freakish, however, reflects affective intensities in the mourning language of Synge's play.

The theme of mourning holds consistent across Synge's and Walcott's plays, and it effectively redoubles their minoritarian linguistic intensities. Confronting the irruption of loss into a marginal community, both plays stretch language to the limit of its expressive capacity. At moments of pure grief, language becomes a wordless keening or (in the word's Irish origins) *caoinim*: a lament, a cry.[24] In his account of time spent on Inishmaan, Synge discerned in the islanders' grieving a sound of pain in which "the inner consciousness of the people seems to lay itself bare for an instant . . . all outward show of indifference or patience is forgotten, and they [mourners] shriek with pitiable despair before the horror of the fate to which they are all doomed".[25] Synge recognized that language's confrontation with loss occupies a powerful threshold. By staging the moment of loss a play gains a high coefficient of intensity, for as grief reveals itself in the mourning actor, language reaches towards what it cannot provide: access to the lost object of desire. At this threshold mourners seek to keep the dead from oblivion; through language, the living are haunted by the absent presence of the dead. Like all mourning work, however, this language risks melancholic obsession, a danger it avoids only by dissolving memory's obsessions into phantasmal images. Although staged, language's power holds true. Precisely this mournful use of language brings these plays to an intensity which contributes to their minoritarian disruption of normative English, granting them dramatic power as they rapidly – in one act – stage the dissolution of obsession and hold close the ghosts of loss.

Significantly, the dead of both plays are fishermen who have been lost to the sea. This topographical gesture places the works in a tradition of island writing that foregrounds the ocean's nearness as "a vital component of island identity".[26] Maurya, the primary character of *Riders to the Sea,* knows that the sea is closer to spectral unsettlement than spiritual consolation. She rejects a young priest's interference as she mourns her sons. "It's little the like of him knows of the sea", she says.[27] Maurya is perhaps echoing a folk belief that considered a priest's intrusion into the fishing world unlucky.[28] More trenchantly, she understands the sea's power to swallow loss and forestall consolation. While the sea takes in and hides the bodies of the dead, it leaves their vanishing place unmarked and unremarkable. There are, in Robert Pogue Harrison's words, "no gravestones on the sea. . . . It closes over rather than keeps the place of its dead."[29] Such inscrutability disturbs mourners' attempts at memory. Thus, like some vast and unreadable archive, the sea engenders melancholy. "Where are your monuments", Derek Walcott asks in "The Sea Is History" – only to answer, "The sea / has locked them up."[30] Facing this oceanic emblem of oblivion, both plays examine how shore dwellers inhabit a threshold that mediates topography and perception, the ocean and the mainland: between the living, who are present, and the lost, who are drowned.

Afa, the main character of *The Sea at Dauphin,* offers two hypotheses for interpreting the sea while he mourns his friends: "Some say this sea is dead fisherman laughing. Some say is noise of all the fisherwoman crying. Sea in Dauphin never quiet. Always noise, noise."[31] Laughing and crying are both too intense for figurative representation in words which simply cannot stretch to accommodate their affective intensity. These expressions of disquieted grief establish a bond between the ungrounded place of the dead and the living who, haunted by those lost at sea, cry out without consolation at its edges.[32] Kept by such grief are the ghosts who occupy living thresholds of loss. Harrison reminds us that mourners who grieve those lost at sea "suffer a special form of anguish. . . . Their grief is unceasing in that it lies at an enormous, untraversable remove from [the dead's] remains."[33] This distance is temporal as much as physical, a psychological yearning refuted by implacable material absences. It can be crossed by a ghost, the medial figure of disjointed time. Such grief suggests that "the intimacy of human time at the heart of natural time depends on keeping one's dead close by, within an earthly realm of presence".[34] Intimacy may well be the watchword of the ghost, the secret-sharer whose haunting power is at times unwelcome and unchosen. A ghost's asemic message bears an urgency current to human time, and is carved from inhuman oblivion in the sea's timeless archive just as the fishermen dredge their livelihoods from its living riches. Yet as the mute figures of Synge's play show, ghosts have exactly nothing to say.

The ocean's influence suggests why neither play entirely allows the efficacy of traditional mechanisms for coping with loss. Embittered Afa suggests that consolation is a false hope. "If compassion you want talk to the sea", he says, "ask it where Bolo bones, and Rafael, and friends I did have before you even born".[35] Absence with no promise of amelioration has usurped consolation's place. Standard syntax has been similarly disrupted. Ghosts – phantoms of language – figure these alterations, just as they resist consolatory gestures. The plays' ghosts dwell by the sea, the disappearing point of loss. "There does be a power of young men floating round in the sea", Maurya reminds us.[36] Thus, as Maria McGarrity writes, "the deep ocean functions as a depository, an entity that takes, preserves, and yields matter up to the poet in altered form".[37] Ghosts are kept hidden in language through the names spoken by the living, even when the proof of death – the corpse – is sometimes visible, as in Synge's play. The word's spoken half-life is a dramatic invocation but not quite a definitive presence. Susan Cole argues that themes of mourning are one of tragic drama's oldest markers. She defines the genre, in fact, as a "performance of ambivalence on behalf of an absent presence".[38] For Cole, and for my present argument, tragedy's ghosts are "a concession to the fact of death but not to the prospect of annihilation".[39] The fishermen are lost to the sea, but not lost entirely. Once they are given over to the place of loss, they cannot be found to be dead. In this ambivalent state they can be neither wholly forgotten nor entirely remembered. Their names remain to haunt the living.

Unsurprisingly, the most powerful speeches of either play are those in which phantasmal absences riddle the fabric of expression. When Maurya and Afa burst into eloquent recitations of those they have lost, they reach linguistic peaks of intensity characterized by repetition, catachresis and a catching rhythm. Maurya's speech in *Riders to the Sea* deserves full quotation:

> I've had a husband, and a husband's father, and six sons in this house – six fine men, though it was a hard birth I had with every one of them and they coming to the world – and some of them were found and some of them were not found, but they're gone now, the lot of them. . . . There were Stephen, and Shawn, were lost in the great wind, and found after in the Bay of Gregory of the Golden Mouth, and carried up the two of them on the one plank, and in by that door. [There is a noise, as of a "crying out by the seashore", but Maurya continues.] There was Sheamus and his father, and his own father again, were lost in a dark night, and not a stick or sign was seen of them when the sun went up. There was Patch after was drowned out of a curagh that turned over. I was sitting here with Bartley, and he a baby, lying on my two knees, and I seen two women, and three women, and four women coming in, and they crossing themselves, and not saying a word. I looked out then, and there were men coming after them, and they holding a thing in the half of a red sail, and water dripping out of it – it was a dry day, Nora – and leaving a track to the door.[40]

The door opens at this point and women enter, uncannily re-enacting the events in Maurya's remembrance speech. Entranced by memories of the men she has named, Maurya asks, "half in a dream", "Is it Patch, or Michael, or what is it at all?"[41] At a threshold where time and place lose their shape, the names of the dead merge with images of the living to gain ghostly substance. The ocean's water uncannily enters the home, as does its prophecy of loss. Caught in spectral repetition and interrupted only by the cry of breaking language, Maurya does not distinguish among certain dead of the past (Patch), the present disappearing before her eyes (Michael), and the future's uncertainty. With her is the audience, caught in her incantatory vision. Maurya now sees time as accretionary instead of linear, built up equally of presences and absences. Chronological time is momentarily suspended and ghosts (rather characteristically) begin to "appear in a time to which they do not belong".[42]

In *The Sea at Dauphin,* Afa gives a structurally analogous speech that, like Maurya's, recites the names of the dead and disjoints time and syntax. In contrast, however, his speech gains intensity by stretching itself over a grimace and a threat.[43] Clearly angry, and undeterred by his shipmate Augustin's pleas for calm, Afa delves into the gruesome fate of the drowned. "[E]very night it getting whiter", Afa says, describing the sea's increasing uncanniness.

> Since Bolo drown. Everybody say Boileau would never drown. And Habal, Habal drowning there last year. And in September is not Annelles, Gacia brother they find

two mile behind Dennery, one afternoon a boy catching crab, walking, see him on sand, when all the *maitre* boat looking for him by Trou Pamphile, his body swell, and the boy turn this thing with his foot and when he finish it was Annelles, drown like what, like Raphael, and Boileau. Ay, Augustin behind![44]

From the memory of lost friends to the swollen corpse that was and is not Annelles, Afa's speech propels clipped clauses towards an explosive yet ominously predictable revelation of death. Shortly after, in the same tone, Afa will ask another character, "Where is Habal, Raphael, Annelles, Boileau? Sun breaking, papa, talk fast."[45] Unlike Maurya's visionary trance, Afa's speech is characterized by anger and interrogation. Constant to both is a telling repetition of names and an absence of words that would make the syntax grammatically normative; constant, then, is an intensity of minoritarian language that comprehends loss.

Maurya and Afa's speeches interrupt conventional stories of living through loss. Their mournful invocations draw on the inaccessible and melancholic archive of the ocean. The haunted logic of naming loss holds open a linguistic threshold across which ghosts pass, and it colludes with the minoritarian position of formal estrangement to endow these plays with linguistic intensity. The effect, abstracted, is audible as a sound, a keening lament or an angry shout, in which the actors destabilize dominant uses of language through strangeness and a forbidding intimacy with the dead. Language reaches towards the asemic ocean for a sound resembling "dead fisherman laughing . . . fisherwomen crying . . . noise, noise". *Riders to the Sea* goes so far as to stage the *caoine* or keen, a cry of sorrow for the dead that Eavan Boland describes as "an art of the dispossessed . . . part a fresh-spoken grief and part an age-old formula".[46] The lament was so disconcerting to Synge's actors that they were uncomfortable witnessing and performing it.

The ghosts haunting *The Sea at Dauphin* and *Riders to the Sea* are neither Synge's *púca*-like grey horse nor Walcott's absent fishermen per se. They take shapes unfamiliar to the Irish Gothic and foreign to the folkloric duppies and bugaboos described by earlier colonial writers in the West Indies such as Edward Long and Matthew Gregory Lewis.[47] In Synge's and Walcott's works, ghosts are haunting reminders of loss embodied by the proper names kept current in the plays' circulating, changing, even keening language. Rather than settling for conventional Gothic tropes, these plays keep open the haunted space of a proper name after its owner's disappearance. In this way they include the absent or lost in their communities through a political language of dispossession and inheritance. Jacques Derrida forcefully argues that any politics requires an "organization of the time and space of mourning" and, more, "an anamnesic and thematic relation to the spirit as ghost . . . an open hospitality to the guest as *ghost*, whom one holds, just as he holds us, hostage".[48] Reframed as a question of the theatre, politics becomes a double responsibility towards tragedy and towards the ghost carried inside the gesture of the name. The theatre's political function, besides presenting questions of ideology, is communal: tragedies exemplarize forms of identity and ways of addressing loss. In doing so they build and reinforce transhistoric communities.[49]

In this context, mourning work redoubles its own unsettling power to transform grief into a formative social discourse. Grief's language might "make and unmake the world".[50] Elaine Scarry argues that loss and language are intimately linked, and heavy with pain: "To witness the moment when pain causes a reversion to the pre-language cries and groans is to witness the destruction of language; but conversely, to be present when a person moves up out of that pre-language and projects the facts of sentience into speech is almost to have been . . . present at the birth of language itself."[51] Staging this moment when language is stretched almost beyond recognition, cast into grief and dwelling beside the reticent ocean deeps, *Riders to the Sea* and *The Sea at Dauphin* dramatize the threshold where language dies to be reborn. Dramatic events shape the use and history of an English language extended beyond its usual subject matter, context and even syntax. The imperial English language does not "die" in these haunted anti-colonial plays; rather, it is staged at an intensified threshold of acculturation. However insubstantial, these ghosts remain, linguistic equivalents to memorials such as Jason deCaires Taylor's underwater sculpture *Vicissitudes* (2006) – a circle of shackled figures holding hands and facing outwards – off the coast of Moilinere Bay, Grenada. The plays' names, like the sculpture's figures, host the ghosts of the lost, whether intending to do so or not.[52] Synge's and Walcott's plays stage the moment when the memory of loss is committed to language through mourning. They demonstrate one type of linguistic change: the intense expression of grief by a minoritarian writer.

Elaine Scarry's identification of pain's linguistic threshold helps to describe mourners who, feeling themselves haunted, break into cries and laments. The funerary lament traditionally divides the *eikon* from the phantasm, the body from the ghost and, ultimately, the living from the dead.[53] The lament abandons the already absent corpse to instead address images of loss which are neither recognizable human beings (bodies washed out to sea do not always return) nor a perfect representation (an *eikon*; memory's ideal form), but rather an erratic and flickering apparition: the image as phantasm, its haunting power the sign of memory's investment. In mourning, the lament separates obligations from desires. Registering loss, it inaugurates a separation of names and corpses. Death is a singular end and yet it repeats, so that with each death "the whole world is lost, and yet with each we are called to reckon our losses".[54] Through this reckoning among desire, names and corpses – all of which survive the loss of a person and so continue to gesture towards something more that they cannot contain: a life – ghosts emerge to shadow the living. What is not certain, however, is whether the grieving lament will remake the world so as to exclude and forget the spectral figures who take shape in the imaginings of language, or if another accommodation is possible, another form of community and another configuration of consciousness in which ghosts might find a home.[55] The lament, in other words, does not properly distinguish between mourning and melancholia.[56]

Riders to the Sea and *The Sea at Dauphin* provoke linguistic and political renewal by engendering twin blossomings of cultural activity. However, neither play allows its characters any consolatory recompense. They find only the resolve to continue. "They're all gone now, and there isn't anything more the sea can do to me", Maurya exhales at the play's end.[57] Afa speaks some of his last lines pensively looking out on the water. "Last year Annelles, and Bolo, and this year Hounakin", he says. "And one day, tomorrow, you Gacia, and me."[58] Grief neither festers nor heals, and if mourning has become "modern" and no longer normatively Freudian, as in Jahan Ramazani's analysis, it is also not unresolvedly melancholic.[59] The plays transform their characters' losses through melancholy's creative potential.[60] To adapt Walter Benjamin, the phantasms of the work of art translate "an appreciation of the transience of things" into a "concern to rescue them for eternity".[61] From its dramatic crucible, minoritarian language emerges new but empty-handed, fresh from its mourning watch beside the haunted ocean. Like the characters who speak it, language expresses only its own survival in the face of a spectral *memento mori*. And yet, in performing the work of art, language changes and readies a new expressive potential for Irish and Caribbean speakers.

What do the tragedies of Walcott and Synge achieve? They are, to be sure, short and even somewhat isolated plays, trial pieces in the early phase of each playwright's career. Nonetheless, they exemplify how to derive artistic influence from such fragility: the power of the minoritarian writer and the power of the voice in the face of death. These plays construct compelling and intimate dramatic homes for their audiences and ghosts alike. In Anne Carson's words,

> watching unbearable stories about other people lost in grief and rage is good for you – may cleanse you of your darkness. Do you want to go down to the pits of yourself all alone? Not much. What if an actor could do it for you? Isn't that why they're called actors? They act for you. You sacrifice them to action. And this sacrifice is a mode of deepest intimacy of you with your own life.[62]

Mourning with ghosts by carrying their names, drama's intimacy is shared among the audience, the actor and the felt presence of the lost. "Paradoxical as it may sound", Susan Cole reminds us, "a representation of loss in theatre, *itself* a transient-as-life mode, is already an enactment of some kind of triumph over loss".[63] Once described, loss is accepted. Yet this is enough; the act politically reorganizes the space of loss without hastily supplanting it with meaning. In this ambivalent but intensified space, language transforms, stretching to shape a new social and individual consciousness and social identity. It speaks *to the* audience from the stage but also, using a familiar shape, tries in some way to open a space *for* them to speak.

The minoritarian writers' task is to reshape the language given to them, "to make a minor or intensive use of it, to oppose the oppressed quality of this language to its oppressive quality".[64] Such is the work of mourning language in a minoritarian context, and its redoubled intensities are staged by the haunted early plays of John Millington Synge and Derek Walcott. One play takes place in the home of an Irish family that has lost its sons. The other turns to St Lucian shores to portray a man who has lost his friends. Both are concerned with the powers of grief and lamentation. These plays do not only provide their respective audiences in Ireland and the Caribbean with a way of comprehending loss and absence. They also model similar patterns of intensity and change for writers across the anglophone world, and reveal in their distinct minoritarian languages the universal human experience of life's ultimate rhythm: the ghost's beat.

Notes

1.   Edward Hirsh, "An Interview with Derek Walcott", *Contemporary Literature* 20, no. 3 (1979): 288.
2.   Paul Breslin, *Nobody's Nation: Reading Derek Walcott* (Chicago: University of Chicago Press, 2001), 89.

3. Think of Franz Kafka's deracinated fables – the work of an Ashkenazi Jew writing in German – or James Joyce's overflowing excesses and Samuel Beckett's stark humanity stripped of all affectation, both latter examples the work of Irish writers in English. Gilles Deleuze and Félix Guattari offer these modernist examples to demonstrate that minoritarian writers estrange dominant uses of language, and thus open new forms of consciousness and community; *Kafka: Toward a Minor Literature*, trans. Dana Polan (Minneapolis: University of Minnesota Press, 1986), 17–18. This is possible in the "language arts" since, as Deleuze and Guattari argue: "there is no language in itself, nor any universality of language, but a discourse of dialects, patois, slangs, special languages. There exists no ideal 'competent' speaker-hearer of language, any more than there exists a homogenous linguistic community. … There is no mother tongue, but a seizure of power by a dominant tongue within a political multiplicity"; Gilles Deleuze and Félix Guattari, *A Thousand Plateaus: Capitalism and Schizophrenia*, trans. Brian Massumi (London: Continuum, 2003), 7. Accordingly, the minoritarian use of language demonstrated here by an Anglo-Irish writer and an anglophone St Lucian writer can be judged a political disruption – a sudden shout, a violent break – of the existing imperial seizure of linguistic power.

4. Pascale Casanova, *The World Republic of Letters,* trans. M.B. DeBevoise (Cambridge, MA: Harvard University Press, 2004), 310.

5. E.A. Markham, "Ireland's Islands in the Caribbean: Poetry from Montserrat and St Caesare", in *The Cultures of Europe: The Irish Contribution*, ed. James P. Mackey (Belfast: Queen's University of Belfast, 1994), 138; Edward Kamau Brathwaite, *History of the Voice: The Development of Nation Language in Anglophone Caribbean Poetry* (London: New Beacon, 1984), 13.

6. A "disjunctive use of the faculties" creates linguistic intensity at thresholds of disruption and sensorial distortion, according to Bogue's gloss on Deleuze's use of *intensity*; Roland Bogue, *Deleuze and Guattari* (London: Routledge, 1989), 63.

7. Modernist, surrealist or Dadaist work comes to mind. See Ronald Bogue, *Deleuze's Wake: Tributes and Tributaries* (Albany: State University of New York Press, 2004), 69; David Lloyd, *Nationalism and Minor Literature: James Clarence Mangan and the Emergence of Irish Cultural Nationalism* (Berkeley: University of California Press, 1987), 19–26.

8. Chinua Achebe, "English and the African Writer", *Transition* 18 (1965): 29.

9. Chinua Achebe, *Morning Yet on Creation Day: Essays* (London: Heinemann, 1975), 62.

10. Jahan Ramazani, *A Transnational Poetics* (Chicago: University of Chicago Press, 2011), 20.

11. "Irish National Theatre Society", *Irish Times*, 26 February 1904, 5.

12. J.S. Barker, "Not the Stuff for a West Indian Theatre", *Trinidad Guardian*, 5 August 1954, 4.

13.   Bruce King, *Derek Walcott: A Caribbean Life* (Oxford: Oxford University Press, 2000), 112.

14.   Robert Hogan and James Kilroy, *The Abbey Theatre: The Years of Synge, 1905–1909* (Dublin: Dolmen Press, 1978), 55.

15.   *An Claidheamh Solusis*, 9 February 1907, 7.

16.   Arthur Walkley, "The Irish National Theatre", *Times Literary Supplement*, 8 May 1903, 146.

17.   Kole Omotoso, *The Theatrical into Theatre: A Study of the Drama and Theatre of the English-Speaking Caribbean* (London: New Beacon, 1982), 62.

18.   Christopher Innes, "Dreams of Violence: Moving beyond Colonialism in Canadian and Caribbean Drama", in *Theatre Matters: Performance and Culture on the World Stage*, ed. Richard Boon and Jane Plastow (Cambridge: Cambridge University Press, 1998), 76.

19.   St Lucian Creole's orthography would later be standardized by Daniel Crowley, although Bruce King finds this academic standardization less than successful: "the results were visually grotesque and thought unusable by many"; *Derek Walcott*, 144. Paul Breslin draws attention to Walcott's use of echoing dramatic lines to translate Creole from francophone St Lucian to a language the playwright found more useful: "[since] the most commonly used form of St. Lucian creole has a French rather than an English lexicon, Walcott's first task of translation was a literal one. But an English creole also exists in St. Lucia, so Walcott did not have to invent one entirely from scratch. To help linguistic outsiders, Walcott often makes his characters paraphrase their French creole phrases with English creole equivalents"; *Nobody's Nation*, 85.

20.   King, *Derek Walcott*, 111; Mary Lou Emery, *Modernism, the Visual and Caribbean Literature* (Cambridge: Cambridge University Press, 2007), 194. While Walcott's interest in folk culture intensified in his work with the Trinidad Theatre Workshop that followed *The Sea at Dauphin*, his interest in English or Anglo-Irish dramatic models lessened considerably.

21.   Edward Baugh, *Derek Walcott* (Cambridge: Cambridge University Press, 2006), 3, 68.

22.   Seán Ó Súilleabháin, "Synge's Use of Irish Folklore", in *J.M. Synge: Centenary Papers, 1971*, ed. Maurice Harmon (Dublin: Dolmen Press, 1972), passim.

23.   Daniel Corkery, "Mr Yeats in Cork", *Leader*, 30 December 1905, 314.

24.   Edward O'Reilly, *An Irish–English Dictionary* (Dublin: James Duffey, 1864), 101.

25.   John Millington Synge, *Collected Works*, vol. 2, *Prose*, ed. Alan Price (London: Oxford University Press, 1962), 75.

26.   Elizabeth DeLoughrey, "Island Writing, Creole Cultures", in *The Cambridge History of Postcolonial Literature*, ed. Ato Quayson (Cambridge: Cambridge University Press, 2011), 803. See also Rod Edmond and Vanessa Smith's edited collection *Islands in*

History and Representation (London: Routledge, 2003) and Greg Dening's *Islands and Beaches* (Honolulu: University Press of Hawaii, 1980).

27. John Millington Synge, *Collected Works,* vol. 3, *Plays,* ed. Ann Saddlemyer (London: Oxford University Press, 1968), 21.

28. Declan Kiberd, *Synge and the Irish Language* (London: Macmillan, 1979), 164.

29. Robert Pogue Harrison, *The Dominion of the Dead* (Chicago: University of Chicago Press, 2003), 12.

30. Derek Walcott, "The Sea Is History", in *The Star-Apple Kingdom* (New York: Farrar, Straus and Giroux, 1979).

31. Derek Walcott, *The Sea at Dauphin,* in *Dream on Monkey Mountain and Other Plays* (New York: Farrar, Straus and Giroux, 1970), 57.

32. Walcott's play foreshadows later works that adopt ghosts as a central figure such as David Dabydeen's long poem *Turner* (1995), Fred D'Aguiar's novel *Feeding the Ghosts* (1997) and M. NourbeSe Philip's poem sequence *Zong!* (2008). All grieve the spectral presences haunting the Atlantic, legacies of the *Zong* atrocity of 1781 and of the Middle Passage. Meanwhile, the confluence of ghosts, water and the gothic in Irish theatre has surged to recent prominence in plays such as Marina Carr's *Portia Coughlan* (1996), Sebastian Barry's *The Steward of Christendom* (1996) and Conor McCarthy's *The Weir* (1997), and in Neil Jordan's *Sunrise with Sea Monster* (1994), *Shade* (2005), and *Ondine* (2009).

33. Harrison, *Dominion,* 12.

34. Ibid.

35. Walcott, *Sea at Dauphin,* 53.

36. Synge, *Plays,* 23.

37. Maria McGarrity, *Washed by the Gulf Stream: The Historic and Geographical Relation of Irish and Caribbean Literature* (Newark: University of Delaware Press, 2008), 98.

38. Susan Letzler Cole, *The Absent One: Mourning Ritual, Tragedy, and the Performance of Ambivalence* (University Park: Pennsylvania State University Press, 1985), 1.

39. Ibid., 11.

40. Synge, *Plays,* 21.

41. Ibid.

42. Alison Rudd, *Postcolonial Gothic Fictions from the Caribbean, Canada, Australia, and New Zealand* (Cardiff: University of Wales Press, 2010), 173.

43. Paul Breslin argues that the plays' dramatic gestures echo perspectival differences in their primary characters, specifically Maurya's trancelike behaviour and Afa's volatility. See *Nobody's Nation,* 87, where he observes that gestures in "*Riders to the Sea* express grief or agitation but not anger", while those of *The Sea at Dauphin* "become increasingly charged with barely restrained violence". C.L. Innes argues that this difference stems from the plays' differently gendered characters and settings, thus Maurya's home and Afa's fishing boat; see C.L. Innes, "Postcolonial

Synge", in *The Cambridge Introduction to J.M. Synge*, ed. P.J. Mathews (Cambridge: Cambridge University Press, 2009), 127.

44. Walcott, *Sea at Dauphin*, 58.

45. Ibid., 62.

46. Robert Kilroy and James Kilroy, eds, *The Abbey Theatre: Laying the Foundations, 1902–1904* (Dublin: Dolmen Press, 1976), 115, passim; Eavan Boland, *A Journey with Two Maps: Becoming a Woman Poet* (New York: W.W. Norton, 2011), 53–54.

47. On the general subject of the Irish Gothic, see W.J. McCormack's seminal "Irish Gothic and After (1820–1945)", in *The Field Day Anthology of Irish Writing*, ed. Seamus Deane (Derry: Field Day Publications, 1991), 2:831–53; also McCormack's *Dissolute Characters* (Manchester: Manchester University Press, 1993). For colonial West Indian writers, see Edward Long's (infamously racist) *The History of Jamaica* (London: Lowndes, 1774), 2:416, passim. See also Matthew Gregory Lewis's *Journal of a West-India Proprietor* (London: John Murray, 1834), 98; Lewis is notable for his novel *The Monk* (1796) and play *The Castle Spectre* (1797). The Gothic here is more akin to Walcott's "West Indian Gothic" in *Another Life* (New York: Farrar Straus and Giroux 1973).

48. Jacques Derrida, *Aporias*, trans. Thomas Dutoit (Stanford, CA: Stanford University Press, 1993), 61–62.

49. As Jane Plastow observes in her introduction to *Theatre Matters*, "a people without some sense of communal identity become fundamentally disempowered and negated at a profound level of their personal sense of being. . . . theatre not only examines the resultant sense of loss . . . but also attempts to take part in the healing process of asserting culture and identity"; Richard Boon and Jane Plastow, eds, *Theatre Matters: Performance and Culture on the World Stage* (Cambridge: Cambridge University Press, 1998), 1–2. Ngũgĩ wa Thiong'o deems such power a way to resist the "culture bomb" of dominant and imperial cultures that otherwise threatens to "annihilate a people's belief in their names, in their languages, in their environment, in their heritage of struggle, in their unity, and ultimately in themselves"; *Decolonising the Mind* (London: James Currey, 1986), 6. Hence the stark argument that Abdul R. JanMohamed and David Lloyd put forth in "Toward a Theory of Minority Discourse", in their *The Nature and Context of Minority Discourse* (Oxford: Oxford University Press, 1990), 6: for minoritarian communities "culture is not a mere superstructure; all too often . . . the physical survival of minority groups depends on the recognition of its culture". Constructing and changing the discourses that shape identities, a community's *language* is crucial to its survival.

50. Ramazani, *Transnational Poetics*, 85.

51. Elaine Scarry, *The Body in Pain: The Making and Unmaking of the World* (Oxford: Oxford University Press, 1985), 6.

52. Both Taylor and America's Black Holocaust Museum have said that *Vicissitudes* is

not a sculpture about the Middle Passage. "I was just making sculptures of different kids holding hands", Taylor says; "Portfolio: Jason Taylor", *X-Ray Mag* 18 (August 2007): 92. See also America's Black Holocaust Museum, "*Vicissitudes*: NOT Sculptural Homage to Victims of the Middle Passage", 23 May 2012, http://www.abhmuseum .org/2012/05/vicissitudes-sculptural-homage-to-victims-of-the-middle-passage/. Despite such disavowals, the Middle Passage haunts this sculpture-turned -monument; its images are simply too strongly associated with the place and the bodies of African slaves murdered during the Atlantic crossing.

53. Harrison, *Dominion of the Dead*, 147.
54. Pascale-Anne Brault and Michael Naas, introduction, in Jacques Derrida, *The Work of Mourning*, ed. Brault and Naas (Chicago: University of Chicago Press, 2001), 15.
55. While minoritarian writing may change language and influence consciousness, for Brault and Naas, languages used for mourning perform a similar function. See ibid., 5: "we find ourselves at a loss, no longer ourselves, *as if* the singular shock of what we must bear had *altered the very medium in which it was to be registered*". The disconcerting shock of loss returns language to its aleatory point of pure intensity (once again) Afa's cries and laughter. As Derrida writes, even if speech seems impossible while mourning, "so too would be silence or absence or a refusal to share one's sadness" (*Work of Mourning*, 72). While Derrida, Brault and Naas are concerned with the im/possibilities of speech, I am here concerned with the *as if* they offer: *as if* language changes under pressure, *as if* language on the haunted threshold of loss becomes intense, stretched beyond capacity . . . almost. Such a theoretical provocation returns to the question of grief at the moment of articulation and raises the question of the communities in which this language circulates.
56. See Sigmund Freud, "On Mourning and Melancholia", in *Freud: The Standard Edition of the Complete Psychological Works of Sigmund Freud*, ed. and trans. James Strachey (London: Hogarth, 1973), 14:243–58. Contrary to Freud's insistence, however, scholars still admit confusion over his distinction between mourning and melancholy. As Michael Ann Holly writes, "despite Freud, it is difficult to tell them apart"; *The Melancholy Art* (Princeton, NJ: Princeton University Press, 2013), 3.
57. Synge, *Plays*, 23.
58. Walcott, *Sea at Dauphin*, 76.
59. Jahan Ramazani, *Poetry of Mourning* (Chicago: University of Chicago Press, 1994), 4.
60. Giorgio Agamben traces a history of melancholy's creative potential, "something at once positive and negative", in his *Stanzas: Word and Phantasm in Western Culture*, trans. Ronald L. Martinez (Minneapolis: University of Minnesota Press, 1993), 11–15.
61. Walter Benjamin, *The Origin of German Tragic Drama*, trans. John Osborne (London: Verso, 1998), 223.

62.   Anne Carson, "Tragedy: A Curious Art Form", in *Grief Lessons: Four Plays* (New York: New York Review of Books, 2006), 7.

63.   Cole, *Absent One*, 166.

64.   Deleuze and Guattari, *Kafka*, 27.

Chapter 13

Que diga perejil / Abair broagh

A Comparative Study of Shibboleths, Security and Violence

K. BRISLEY BRENNAN

THIS CHAPTER INQUIRES INTO LINGUISTIC SHIBBOLETHS IN Ireland/Northern Ireland and Haiti/the Dominican Republic in order to more broadly investigate their uses and results. I tentatively define a linguistic shibboleth (hereafter simply a shibboleth) as a social and cultural language-based test that aims to collect empirical data in order to determine how someone conforms to the delineated boundaries of belonging within a group. While shibboleths may have more innocuous applications, they are often close to violence as they can be used to police borders.[1] The differentiating potential of shibboleths corresponds to the boundaries drawn by their use, bounds such as the weak forward slashes bifurcating the names of the island nations above.

My comparative study examines the use of *perejil* ("parsley") during the massacre of Haitians in the Dominican Republic in 1937, as well as the linguistic divisions used to reinforce sectarianism in Northern Ireland and Ireland. This Caribbean Irish connection, then, is an analytic construct rather than a connection made via migration, trade, biographic figures or cultural contact and exchange. Because of the constitution of this connection, my comparative case study is an analytically valuable method only inasmuch as it resists the possibility that an additional case would change the outcome of the study, in the event that the additional case were overly dissimilar. Thus this chapter uses cases that are neither wholly similar nor dissimilar.

By examining the linguistic structures and socially determined concepts at work in a shibboleth, I will demonstrate how a shibboleth can be a means of establishing and maintaining security; I will also describe the role of violence. At times a shibboleth may be benign but in other cases the accompanying violence cannot be ignored.[2] In writing about the poetry of Paul Celan, Jacques Derrida draws out the parallel between state-sponsored violence and the violence of invasive languages – for example, colonial languages such as German, French, Spanish and English.[3]

Shibboleths and violence are mediators. Whether they mediate perfectly or imperfectly is a matter not of value judgement but of completion and incomple-tion, like the perfect and imperfect aspects of verbs described by grammarians of English. In the perfect aspect, a completed action and its results are emphasized; it cannot be reversed. For example, "I have done the work" emphasizes how work was done and that the work is done. The imperfect indicates a mediation that is in process and the process is emphasized. For example, "I was working" emphasizes how the work was ongoing and does not provide a clear indication that the work was or is finished. Clearly distinguishing between perfect and imperfect mediation will help to clarify the function of a shibboleth, which can seem chaotic, especially when it manifests with violence.

Edwidge Danticat's *The Farming of Bones* and Seamus Heaney's "Broagh" demonstrate an acute understanding that language can and has been used to enact violence, but that it can also be used to redress injury. In a 2008 interview, Heaney was asked how the conflict in Northern Ireland shaped his writing, to which he replied: "No matter how well-disposed you are, no matter how per-sonally irreproachable your political or religious attitudes, you dwell in a place which is troubled. You're answerable to that, especially when violence erupts, and lives are being lost, and lives are being taken."[4] For Heaney, writing can redress harm by outstripping the conditions that enable and sustain violence. Unsurprisingly, "Broagh" works towards softening the rigidity of linguistic divisions between Scottish, Irish and English. Danticat's novel also performs a softening, between Haitian and Dominican. In a January 2012 interview, Danticat was asked what writing and writers accomplish against the forces of violence, to which she responded that writers bear witness in concert with other witnesses.[5] Effectively Heaney and Danticat demonstrate that writing and language can be used to "re-tune" the world in which witness circulates by "creating dangerously".[6]

There is a degree of consensus within linguistics that shibboleths are language tests of phonemic differences attributable to social groups that determine how satisfactorily the demands for membership within a group are met. Hannes Kniffka describes shibboleths as verbal behaviours in which a shibboleth is employed to determine the prompted language-user's pronunciation ability based on the user's pronunciation performance. The utterance of a shibboleth acts as a determination of the speaker's identity, however accurately or errone-ously judged. According to Kniffka's formulation, the limited and circumstantial data of a language-user's pronunciation in one instance can be generalized and then imposed on the user's total verbal behaviour and ability.[7] The judgement of the user's ability is then jointly a judgement of the user's status as member or non-member of the group. This helps to explain how the boundaries of belong-ing to social groups defined by language use are obscure from the standpoint of verbal behaviour, prompting one to investigate what a shibboleth accomplishes rather than how a shibboleth works.

Shibboleth comes into English from the biblical book of Judges.[8] On the whole, Judges recounts the Hebrew acquisition of territory and a succession of military leaders called judges, of whom Deborah is the only judge in the sense of an arbiter. Like the shibboleth, a judge might seem to be a figure of judge-ment, but both are, more or less, ways of acquiring and securing territory. Still generations from establishing a formal nation, the Hebrew proto-nation goes through a cycle of obedience and disobedience as they push to gain and control new territory. Jephthah is called to be a judge and to defend Israel against the Ammonites, who are attempting to regain territory along the Jordan River lost to Israel. Jephthah leads Israel to victory through the power of Yahweh, but the Ephraimite tribe of Israel does not participate. The Gileadites, Jephthah's tribe, target the Ephraimites for punishment by using the word *shibboleth* to detect Ephraimites as they attempt to cross the Jordan. Although *shibboleth* in the Hebrew Bible שִׁבֹּלֶת is usually best understood to mean an ear of grain, in this story it can be more appropriately understood as its less common mean-ing: a channel or torrent of water, like that of a river or flood. As the logic goes, anyone who says "sibboleth" is an Ephraimite, who is known to be unable to utter "shibboleth".

The voiceless fricative *sh* appears to have caught its prey, according to the story, but by no means would the linguistic test have caught every Ephraimite. Like any shibboleth, this test would not have been entirely accurate in identi-fying Ephraimites, as it actually detects people who do not make the voiceless fricative in the instance of testing. The Gileadites use a feature of their Hebrew in order to secure their territory, first by guarding the border of the Jordan River and then by excising the Ephraimites, who did not join the rest of Israel. In this story, geographical place and communal belonging are linked by a particular grammar in which spoken language bolsters a territorial claim while also determining the criteria for communal membership. Similarly in Danticat's novel, Trujillo's soldiers use a phonemic feature of Spanish in order to secure the boundary between Haiti and the Dominican Republic by exterminating ethnic Haitians in the border area, and anyone who threatens the security of the white Dominican elite. In contrast, as will be seen, in Heaney's poem the usual suspects of linguistic differences between Scottish, Irish and English are undone by the poet, which is an act of resisting the territorial claims that partially fuel conflict. In these ways, the stories of the book of Judges, the Haitian massacre and the violence on the island of Ireland render linguistic features that can be used to justify violence and to mark the boundaries of territory such as that along a river, whether it is the Jordan, the Dajabón or a *bruach* (Irish for "bank", like that of a river).

This grammar of belonging, geography and nation is implemented by a social group of language-users to secure territory and membership. The obscure boundary of belonging, in attempting to clarify and impose itself as a geographical border, necessarily employs a sense of community. To use the formulation of Stanley Cavell, claims to reason are themselves claims to community, and reflexively, claims to community are claims to reason.[9] Communities establish the criteria and standards according to which meaning is understood and according to which candidacy for inclusion is determined.[10] In Kniffka's formulation, a shibboleth is a verbal behaviour used to over-generalize a person's total speech ability, or a mechanism of language in which one instance of a person's ability to pronounce a word is used as an overall indication of their pronunciation and language ability. But Kniffka's formulation neglects the social function of a shibboleth in favour of linguistic empiricism. Cavell's formulation of claims to community can supplement Kniffka's formulation of a shibboleth by emphasizing how criteria and standards are used in evaluation. The criteria and standards that govern knowledge, intelligibility and communal belonging are inherent in any grammar, including the grammar of belonging, geography and nation that sustains the shibboleth.[11] Its endgame is security, never mind its fundamental malfunction – language use in one instance is hardly a reliable indicator of a person's total language ability, let alone of belonging to a nation partly defined by geographical boundaries. Hence, any judgement derived should be subject to scepticism.

There could have been an Ephraimite capable of pronouncing the *sh* in *shibboleth*, just as there were likely Haitians capable of trilling the *r* in *perejil* during Trujillo's 1937 dictatorship-sponsored genocide of Haitians along the border area with the Dominican Republic – popularly known as the Parsley Massacre, El Corte ("the cutting" in Spanish) or Kout Kouto ("the stabbing" in *kreyòl*). In Danticat's novel, Amabelle states that she could have pronounced *perejil* had she the chance and the will.[12] The linguistic border established between Haitian and Dominican was used to impose a geographical border between the two countries. Even though the linguistic border seemed clear for the purpose of separating Haitians from Dominicans, the *perejil* shibboleth was remarkably effective in identifying persons who did not satisfy the criteria established for what it meant to be Dominican, even if they were Dominican. The "parsley" test was useful for classifying a person as insufficiently Dominican in order to keep Haitians and Dominicans of Haitian descent – many of whom were also of African descent – from mixing with lighter-skinned Dominicans. Haitians and Dominicans in the border area, like many of the characters in Danticat's novel, conducted business with each other, especially as many Haitians worked in the cane fields of the Dominican Republic, and they sometimes intermarried or cohabited. This border space remained outside the control of both governments at the time of the state-sponsored genocide, as Lizabeth Paravisini-Gebert explains.[13] However, by 1937 the United States had ended its occupation of Haiti, and the Dominican government – run by Trujillo, who was backed by the United States – was in a much better position to make a grab for control of the border once the US Marines had gone.

In this context, the *perejil* shibboleth was a military exercise provoked by a Dominican nationalist reflex of aggression against cooperation and cohabitation by Haitians and Dominicans along the border. It was even used by the Dominican state before the genocide in 1937, in order to collect migration taxes. Richard Lee Turits explains how the test was "rigged. It served largely as a pretext, a mock confirmation of the presumptions and fantasies of an inherent and radical distinction between ethnic Dominicans and Haitians *clung to by outside* [Dominican] *officials and elites*."[14] The epicentre of Dominican nationalism in Santo Domingo had become anti-Haitian by 1937, whereas before then "Dominican national identity was far from uniformly imagined as antithetical to or exclusive of Haitians and Haitian culture", and "a largely bilingual frontier population remained indifferent and even hostile to urban visions of Dominican nationality".[15] While it attempted to secure territory, the shibboleth and massacre were also an exercise in securing urban Dominican nationalism as anti-Haitian by ridding the Dominican Republic of anyone who was deemed to be insufficiently Dominican.

In basing her novel on historical events, Danticat frames a critique of nationalism and nationalist judgements that are based on the criteria and standards of belonging described by Cavell. Additionally, her novel critiques nationalist visions of belonging by drawing alliances through the characters' shared experiences. For Amabelle, the shared experiences of surviving the massacre and surviving loved ones allow her to constitute a community. Even before the massacre, Amabelle loses her parents, who drown in Rio Dajabón, a river in the Dominican Republic that borders Haiti in the north. Without the conventional community constituted by a family of blood relations, Amabelle's only recourse is to create her own family and community; her ancestors are "revenants, shadows, ghosts".[16] She eventually finds Sebastien Onius, but when she loses him during the massacre, he disappears into the same state as her ancestors. She is left to "wish at least that some of the dust of his bones could trail [her] in the wind".[17]

Left alone again, Amabelle can only dream Sebastien from out of the void. "[M]ore like flesh than air", Amabelle's memories of Sebastien repeat like the declarative statement that belies its certainty: "*His name is Sebastien Onius. Sometimes this is all I know. My back aches now in all those places that he claimed for himself*", Amabelle reflects, "arches of bare skin that belonged to him, pockets where the flesh remains fragile, seared like unhealed burns where each fallen scab uncovers a deeper wound".[18] With only memories of Sebastien and of her parents, Amabelle attaches herself to Yves and his mother, Man Rapadou. Her experiences of the massacre shared with Yves draw her to him, and they use their relationship to help each other to forget and to mourn.[19]

The story of the Valencia twins, Rafael and Rosalinda, is a foil to Amabelle's story and to her constructed community based on shared experiences. Rafael and Rosalinda share blood relations and in utero experiences, but they do not share skin tones. On one level, the difference in their skin tones critiques notions of familial belonging that rely on socially inscribed racial categories. On another level, the difference in their skin tones critiques notions of national belonging that depend on race. The twins are the children of Pico Valencia, an unwavering Trujillo supporter. Rosalinda has darker skin and Rafael has lighter skin, which aligns with Señor Valencia's favouritism for Rafael. Though it initially seems that Rosalinda will die from illness, she recovers and Rafael suddenly dies – the text inverts the merits of the pigmentocracy. On yet another level, as a para-testimony, Danticat's text critiques the single story of official history (the master narrative) by exposing the limits of storytelling. Her novel transcribes the stories of its characters, but the vast majority of Danticat's fictional characters are restrained from registering their stories with the Haitian government, presumably like the testimonies of actual people killed or silenced during and after the massacre.[20]

The Valencia twins' mother, Señora Valencia, worries that Rosalinda might be mistaken for Haitian because her skin is dark (read: too African).[21] One might expect Rosalinda to die because of her difficult birth, resulting from a badly placed umbilical cord. Doctor Javier gives weight to this foreshadowing when he carries on about how many people begin as twins in utero but kill off their twin, or their stillborn twin is sacrificed for their survival.[22] But it is Rafael who ultimately dies.[23] The different skin tones of the twins and Señora Valencia's concerns indicate that dark skin is a threat. This indication is tuned according to the Dominican elite's obsession with tracing ancestry back to the Spanish conquistadors. In all of these ways, Danticat's novel challenges nationalist and imperial paradigms of belonging, and it offers an alternative paradigm based on shared experiences. Lynn Chun Ink describes how Danticat's novel challenges definitions of community that are dependent on national borders by "exposing nationalism's prohibition of collective alliances across national lines", and by obscuring the border between Haiti and the Dominican Republic through rendering the borderlands as a space of commingled living and working.[24]

Danticat furthermore challenges the grammar that undergirds the *perejil* shibboleth by including the story of Jephthah as an epigraph to her novel. This comparative context places the stories of the book of Judges and Danticat's novel in tension, such that the faults of the shibboleth exposed in one help to expose the faults of the shibboleth in the other. Israel struggles to figure out its leadership and its covenant with Yahweh long before it establishes a formal Israel nation-state. That narrative of state formation finds an echo in Haiti's and the Dominican Republic's long struggles to establish democratic leadership after centuries of imperial rule and American occupation.

The use of a shibboleth to identify an enemy to control or to exterminate is a tactic both long practised and commonly known. In that context, Heaney's "Broagh" seems something apart, because there is no apparent violence on the surface of the poem. An anglicized place name derived from the Irish word *bruach*, the shibboleth *broagh* is rendered as a "low tattoo" – an identifying sound heard from beneath the foliage of *boortrees* (Scottish, meaning "elders") and among the *rigs* ("seedbeds") that end in *docken* ("docks").[25] Moreover, John Wilson Foster reminds readers that while the velar fricative *gh* is a sound native to the Irish language, it was also a sound native to English which disappeared at the beginning of the Modern English period.[26] In that light, Heaney's poem can be read as an allegory about lost common ground.

Daniel Tobin contextualizes the import of this linguistic history when he writes: "If *broagh* is a threshold to origins it is also a threshold to the complex cross-cultural history of Irish and English. In a word, *broagh*, meaning *river-bank*, bespeaks the instability of origins and, in essence, the fundamental (and fortunate) impurity of language."[27] If nationality is taken to be defined almost wholly by a language and if sectarian boundaries are drawn by the borders of a nation, Heaney's linguistic topography indicates a glaring problem with such formations: linguistic purity is more a tale than a truth, such that the uncertain linguistic boundaries weaken national boundaries. His poem renders a linguistic history that directly and convincingly challenges sectarian divisions, exposing the shared history of Irish, Scottish and English. As Tobin further writes, "what Heaney's poem rehearses in imaginative terms is the political and historical reconciliation of two hostile communities into one and not the elevation of the native community over the colonizer".[28] Thus it is more appropriate to speak of the relationship among the Irish, Scottish and English languages as cohabitants of an ecosystem marked by a *longue durée* of linguistic interculturation.

Sectarian division is simply not present in the linguistic geography of Heaney's poem, even if the strangers in Heaney's poem, who are neither Irish nor English, struggle with that last *gh* in *broagh*.[29] Instead there is a shared linguistic ground for which nationalist descriptors are inadequate. This common ground can be found in the Scottish, Irish and English linguistic ancestry of *gh*, as well as in the use of Scottish words that co-populate the lexicon of Northern Ireland along with Irish and English words. That does not mean, of course, that the Scottish, Irish and English languages are of the same lineage; rather, it demonstrates that these languages developed among one another and that the linguistic borders between them are more porous than might be initially assumed. If Heaney's poem were to reinscribe sectarian divisions, then one would expect "Broagh" to wilfully obscure the history of linguistic interculturation in favour of nationalist rhetoric. "Broagh", however, cannot be said to do anything of the sort.

Heaney's poem and its shibboleth *broagh* invoke a history of violence in the poem's critique of sectarian platforms, despite its apparent placidity. His poem, then, can be read as a poetic intervention into the sectarian conflict, born out of his sense of responsibility. "In a war situation or where violence and injustice are prevalent, poetry is called upon to be something more than a thing of beauty", Heaney said when asked how violence in Northern Ireland shaped his poetic craft.[30] One can see this poetic vocation of intervention in Heaney's oeuvre from the shared linguistic ground of "Broagh" to his repeated appeals in other poems to victims of violence rather than to perpetrators of violence.[31]

In comparing Danticat's and Heaney's renditions of shibboleths, it becomes clear that belonging to a nation is fraught with tension between inclusion and exclusion, a tension that can be exacted as a means of establishing security by way of policing and enforcing borders and by way of acquiring territory, as well as security by other means and in other senses. In this context, membership in a nation is far from an either/or construction (either Irish or British, either Haitian or Dominican). While Heaney's poem remains broadly inclusive, it challenges the linguistic boundaries between Irish, Scottish and English. On the whole, "Broagh" is populated by lexical artefacts of a shared history of linguistic interculturation.

The mythical lore of Ireland and its topography can be seen in the *dinnseanchas* (literally, "topography") genre.[32] Heaney defines *dinnseanchas* as "poems and tales which relate the original meanings of place names and constitute a form of mythological etymology".[33] Clearly his definition is more literary than literal. When the word *dinnseanchas* is broken down, it becomes easy to see the strong sense of belonging therein denoted. *Dinn* is a conjugated preposition meaning "of us". *Sean* (as well as *shean*) means "old" and *chas* can mean "a turn" or "a story" or "a song". Even though *chas* (also *cas*) has many applications, underlying its literary use is a persistent sense of shifting ground, such that stories and songs wind and turn like rivers etching themselves into the land. In *dinnseanchas* and Heaney's "Broagh", geography and belonging coalesce into a kind of grammar – one in which meaning and signification are structured by peoples and places, as opposed to a conventional grammar of syntactical and morphological manipulations of language.[34] The ancestry of *broagh*, in Heaney's excavation of a topographical lexicon shared among the Irish, Scottish and English languages, directs readers to work through the entanglement of language, culture and place.

In the case of *perejil*, the shibboleth operates as a means to achieve an end – securing Dominican urban nationalism – and in Heaney's poem, the shibboleth mediates the fault lines of sectarian politics by destabilizing the linguistic boundaries among Irish, Scottish and English, which is a means of securing a peace. The endgame of these shibboleths is the establishment of security, but *security* itself is an increasingly ubiquitous word – as in equity securities, "cyber-security", "national security", "social security", "securitization" and "home security systems", to name a few examples. I defer to John Hamilton's recent work on *security* and add some emphasis to his philological study of the term. Going back to the Latin source, *securitas* can be translated as a state of being apart from care, concern or worry; as Hamilton demonstrates, the term implies a threat.[35] The implicit threat in *security* is pivotal in understanding the incentive behind using a shibboleth.

In the case of Ireland and Northern Ireland in Heaney's poem, continued sectarian politics threaten the peace process. It is commonly acknowledged that one's pronunciation of the letter *h* could be used to identify (however accurately or inaccurately) someone who says "haitch" as a Catholic and someone who says "aitch" as a Protestant. During the Troubles, this was a method used to determine whom to assault and whom to let pass.[36] In the case of Haiti and the Dominican Republic, the developing racial hybridity and comingling among rural Haitians and Dominicans threatened the elitist urban nationalism of Santo Domingo which practised a policy of *blanqueamiento* ("whitening"). If *security* can be said to mean anything certain, response to a perceived threat is a primary criterion, especially as *security* does not necessarily mean prevention of or protection from harm (as was the case for victims of the 1937 massacre and the Troubles), nor does it necessarily mean freedom, as its invocation can be used to justify oppression or repression of a perceived enemy. Even more systematic in its definition, Michel Foucault argues that the apparatus of security (*le dispositif de sécurité*) is one of the complexly entangled mechanisms of biopower, in which the characteristics and features of human life are used as objects of a political strategy.[37] According to Foucault, the apparatus of security is an index of perceived degrees of danger which are judged against a series of all probable events.[38] His formulation of security as a biopolitical mechanism provides another iteration of the context of threat implicit in the notion of security, again demonstrating that security measures such as shibboleths are reactionary instruments, and that shibboleths and their accompanying violence are essentially lacking in informed and critical examination.

Given the reality that shibboleths have been and can be used to establish security, especially through violent means, my inquiry turns now to violence:

sometimes the alter ego of a shibboleth. Given the history of European and American imperialism that altered the islands, I look to Frantz Fanon's theory of violence. Understanding Fanon's theory of violence crucially depends on an anti-colonial context. He describes the violence as a dialectical denouement, an unravelling of the colonial paradigm. In this process, colonizers exert control through violence and colonized subjects resist through violence, because violence is the only effective means available for liberation and because colonial violence is already totalizing, in the sense that it is outside the control of subjugated peoples and in the sense that the violence is perpetrated in a number of registers. Out of the meeting of colonial and anti-colonial violence, liberation emerges. Violence is a perfect mediation, according to Fanon, because decolonization requires violence and nonviolent anti-colonial methods are ineffective. It is a perfect mediation because it is appropriate in the sense that it meets the requirements of ending colonialism, which, in the context of Fanon's time and place, could be overcome and countered only by a totalizing anti-colonial violence. He argues that violence perfectly mediates colonial oppression because it works to establish the dream of decolonization as a reality; the motivation of this violence is the completion of decolonization.

Richard Philcox translates Fanon's *médiation royale* as "perfect mediation".[39] In the French, Fanon plays on the political sense of *royale*, an adjective meaning "regal" or "royal", and its more familiar sense, meaning "total". The linguistic play that encapsulates the dialectical denouement is lost in the English translation, but not to the discredit of Philcox. *Perfect* certainly has its issues, especially given its sense of faultlessness, but to translate Fanon's words as "total violence" might give a reader the impression that he advocates a stereotypical anarchy or violence for violence's sake, which is not the case. Furthermore, *perfect* does carry a sense of totality, which is concomitant with the achievement of total decolonization essential to Fanon's theory of violence.

For Fanon, violence is not an end in itself; it is not its own objective. Yet violence is integral to an anti-colonial political programme which resists the power structures that enable colonial violence, and it is integral to re-forming the colonized person into a liberated person. Like the violence that enforces an imposed colonial language, the violence that resists colonial domination demands language. My point here is to reaffirm that language and violence can be close in kind, and, moreover, to indicate how a shibboleth – itself a veneer that can bond language and violence – can be a perfect and an imperfect mediation. Philcox's translation (*perfect* for *royale*) is largely a matter of translating how the anti-colonial violence that Fanon advocates is suited to combating colonial violence, in that it satisfies the requirements for transforming the state of colonization into a state of decolonization. The violence that Fanon advocates is a mediator. When accompanying a shibboleth, a mediator that can be used to broker the boundaries of belonging so as to establish security, violence is an auxiliary mediator that can be used to enforce the verdict of the shibboleth. In the sense that the accompanying violence is designed to achieve an irreversible enforcement of the verdict, it is a perfect mediation.

In the grammatical sense, "perfect violence" describes a completed and irreversible mediation wherein emphasis is placed on the results of the completed action, whereas "imperfect violence" describes a mediation that is in process and has not been completed. My readings of Danticat's novel and Heaney's poem demonstrate these perfect and imperfect mediations. On one hand, *The Farming of Bones* renders a historical reality and performs its titular work of loosening the silence that buried the massacre. In this way Danticat's novel exposes the violence of the *perejil* killings and the resulting destruction of life and distortion of cultural and historical memory; it emphasizes the loss of life and the results of the massacre – completed actions that cannot be reversed but may be unearthed. On the other hand, Heaney's poem renders an imperfect mediation: a negotiation that is still in process and that his poem continues and pushes. Unlike a number of his other poems, "Broagh" does not feature victims of violence and the results of violence; instead, it challenges the discriminatory work of the shibboleth through the same medium in which the shibboleth operates – language. The poem's sedimentation of a shared linguistic ancestry emphasizes how peace in Northern Ireland is in process, a process that the poem wants to secure. This critical lens of perfect/imperfect helps to clarify the stakes of the mediation and inversely parallels the "terrifying ambiguity of the shibboleth, sign of belonging and threat of discrimination" of which Derrida speaks.[40] The shibboleth and its auxiliary violence are a tragic inversion in which language that is inclusive and protective can also be exclusive and aggressive; the shibboleth and its violence are an inversion of security as protection and security as oppression.

Danticat's novel and Heaney's poem present shibboleths which disrupt any notion that they are merely linguistic tests; they emerge as methods for securing an objective, such as Dominican urban nationalism or peace in Northern Ireland. The state-sponsored violence of El Corte/Kout Kouto is eponymous to the violence perpetrated; the sectarian and state-sponsored violence in Ireland

and Northern Ireland, though not a formal feature of Heaney's pastoral *broagh/brogue*, can be read into his poem as the addressee of the poem's apostrophe. The violence accompanying these shibboleths functions as perfect or imperfect mediation, a binary that elucidates how quickly language as protection and nourishment can be inverted into the language of peril and affliction. Continued studies and analyses of nonviolent shibboleths will clarify the grounds of their appropriation, but my analysis demonstrates that any inquiry into phenomena that can be found globally – such as a shibboleth and its accompanying violence – must be simultaneously comparative in scope and attentive to particular milieux in order to initiate and complete the task of analysing the functions and consequences of the phenomena, a process which itself is necessary for understanding how to prevent the deleterious effects of its presence, especially when accompanied by violence. Furthermore, the Caribbean–Irish comparison I draw here offers scholars another vantage point from which to imagine future projects that do not necessarily depend on biographical figures, trading routes or diasporas and migrations, as well as from which to reimagine those projects which are, and how those projects might be brought into comparison with subjects outside their initial scope.

Notes

1. For example, Torontonians typically pronounce *Toronto* by shortening the initial *o* sound and dropping the final *t* sound, whereas recent immigrants to the city and outsiders tend to pronounce the initial vowel as long and the final consonant as hard. As for shibboleths unaccompanied by violence, literary or other appropriations seem to have a smattering of functions, from in-group/out-group discrimination, humour and humiliation to the practical matter of determining that North Americans in the United Kingdom might mean a pair of trousers when they say "pants".

2. For example, Appalachian cultures in the United States pronounce *Appalachian* with a *ch* sound in the final syllable, like the *ch* in *church*. Pronouncing the final syllable as *sh*, as in *shoot*, reveals one to be an outsider. This can be a rather innocuous shibboleth.

3. See "Shibboleth: For Paul Celan", in Jacques Derrida's *Sovereignties in Question: The Poetics of Paul Celan* (New York: Fordham University Press, 2009).

4. Hyung W. Kim, "15 Questions with Seamus Heaney", *Harvard Crimson*, 8 October 2008.

5. Kimberley Nagy and Lauren McConnell, "Create Dangerously: A Conversation with Edwidge Danticat", *Wild River Review* (January 2012).

6. For "re-tuning", see Seamus Heaney, "Crediting Poetry", Nobel Lecture, 7 December 1995. Danticat borrowed the phrase "creating dangerously" from the final public lecture of Albert Camus for her collection of essays by the same name.

7. Hannes Kniffka, *Working in Language and Law* (New York: Palgrave Macmillan, 2007), 89.

8. Judges 12:6.

9. Stanley Cavell, *The Claim of Reason: Wittgenstein, Skepticism, Morality, and Tragedy* (New York: Oxford University Press, 1979), 20.

10. Ibid., 11.

11. Ibid., 14.

12. Edwidge Danticat, *The Farming of Bones* (New York: Soho, 1998), 193.

13. Lizabeth Paravisini-Gebert, *Literature of the Caribbean* (London: Greenwood, 2008), 88.

14. Richard Lee Turits, *Foundations of Despotism: Peasants, the Trujillo Regime, and Modernity in Dominican History* (Stanford, CA: Stanford University Press, 2003), 165 (emphasis added).

15. Richard Lee Turits, "A World Destroyed, A Nation Imposed: The 1937 Haitian Massacre in the Dominican Republic", *Hispanic American Historical Review* 82, no. 3 (August 2002): 593.

16. Danticat, *Farming of Bones*, 278.

17. Ibid., 281.

18. Ibid., 281 (emphasis added).

19. Ibid., 274.

20. Ibid., 236. For more information on testimonies of survivors of the massacre, see Lauren Derby and Richard Lee Turits, "Temwayaj Kout Kouto, 1937: Eyewitnesses to the Genocide", in *Revolutionary Freedoms: A History of Survival, Strength and Imagination in Haiti*, ed. Cécile Accilien, Jessica Adams and Elmide Méléance (Pompano Beach, FL: Educa Vision, 2006).

21. Danticat, *Farming of Bones*, 12.

22. Ibid., 19.

23. Ibid., 87.

24. Lynn Chun Ink, "Remaking Identity, Unmaking Nation: Historical Recovery and the Reconstruction of Community in *In the Time of the Butterflies* and *The Farming of Bones*", *Callaloo* 27, no. 3 (Summer 2004): 790, 800.

25. For "low tattoo", *boortrees*, *rigs* and *docken*, see lines 10, 11, 1 and 2 respectively in Seamus Heaney, "Broagh", in *Wintering Out* (London: Faber and Faber, 1972), 27 (italics added). For the Scottish meanings, see Daniel Tobin, *Passage to the Center: Imagination and the Sacred in the Poetry of Seamus Heaney* (Lexington: University Press of Kentucky, 1999), 76.

26. See note 9 in John Wilson Foster, "The Poetry of Seamus Heaney", *Critical Quarterly* 16, no. 1 (1974): 48.

27. Tobin, *Passage*, 76.

28. Ibid., 77.

29. Heaney, "Broagh", line 4.

30. Kim, "15 Questions".

31. Kieran Quinlan also makes this observation. See "Unearthing a Terrible Beauty: Seamus Heaney's Victims of Violence", *World Literature Today* 57, no. 3 (Summer 1983): 365. Recall also Heaney's *Government of the Tongue*, in which he describes the poet as a witness who "represents poetry's solidarity with the doomed, the deprived, the victimized, the under-privileged"; Seamus Heaney, *The Government of the Tongue: Selected Prose, 1978–1987* (London: Faber and Faber, 1988), xvi.

32. *Dinnseanchas* may be also spelled *dinnsheanchas*, which is more indicative of its pronunciation in standard Modern Irish.

33. Heaney, "The Sense of Place", in *Preoccupations: Selected Prose, 1968–1978* (London: Faber and Faber, 1980), 131–32.

34. A conventional understanding of linguistics – particularly that of grammarians of English, Irish, French and Spanish – holds that meaning and signification are rendered in a matrix of syntax (word order), morphology (parts of speech and structures such as prefixes and roots) and phonology (sounds such as syllabic emphasis and rhyme). "Broagh" supersedes this conventional understanding of grammar, as poetry often does, by prompting its audience to read the words of the poem along the seam that holds together language, language-users and the place of the language-users.

35. John T. Hamilton, *Security: Politics, Humanity, and the Philology of Care* (Princeton, NJ: Princeton University Press, 2013), 5.

36. Shane Alcobia-Murphy, *Governing the Tongue in Northern Ireland: The Place of Art / The Art of Place* (Cambridge: Cambridge Scholars Press, 2005), 115.

37. Michel Foucault, *Security, Territory, Population: Lectures at the Collège de France, 1977–1978* (New York: Macmillan, 2009), 1.

38. Ibid., 7.

39. Frantz Fanon, *Les damnés de la terre* (Paris: La Découverte, 1985), 60; Frantz Fanon, *The Wretched of the Earth*, trans. Richard Philcox (New York: Grove Press, 2004), 44.

40. Derrida, *Sovereignties*, 27. See also Tim McNamara, "Language Assessments as Shibboleths: A Poststructuralist Perspective", *Applied Linguistics* 33, no. 5 (November 2012): 564–81.

Chapter 14

Medbh McGuckian's *Shelmalier* and Dionne Brand's *Inventory*

Elegiac Ecopoetics

ELAINE SAVORY

Let us not invoke the natural world,
it's ravaged like any battlefield, like any tourist
island, like any ocean we care to name,
like oxygen[1]

If they destroyed all the words like electric light,
put them in a grave beneath branches,
could trees be expected to heal
without inherited things?[2]

IT IS NOT ONLY NEW, ODDLY, TO think about Irish and Caribbean poetry together, but even more so to frame that thinking by ecocritical concerns – the history of poetics in a particular environmental space. Medbh McGuckian and Dionne Brand began their professional careers as poets at roughly the same time.[3] Both are usually read in the context of their particular national and regional affiliations, McGuckian's Ireland and Brand's Caribbean and Canada. McGuckian was educated in Ireland (Queen's University, Belfast) and has stayed in Ireland, whereas Brand has long lived in Canada. It could be argued that they are quite different, because Brand's vision is more global and McGuckian's more national.

They certainly have very different individual voices, each having discovered her own contemporary postcolonial poetics. But reading them together affirms important correlations and opens the reader to apprehending each poet more fully.

Obviously they are both women poets who in their work represent gender in original ways. Then there are the complex historical connections between Ireland and the Caribbean, both of which saw a long and brutal English/British occupation. Because of this, though English retains dominance in the anglophone Caribbean and Ireland and is the language that both poets use, it occupies a complicated space, altered by both colonizer and colonized.[4] Both poets are aware of language as complex and often untrustworthy, and the history of colonialism and language in both Ireland and the Caribbean has to contribute to this. But they have other important commonalities which are the subject of this chapter, namely the ways in which their formal poetics have developed to express an awareness of the nature of death, grief and joy as deeply interconnected with a complex sense of environment. They have both broken new ground with regard to poetics, and reading them together provides an opportunity to see parallels and to think about them in relation to the histories of the Caribbean and Ireland.

Thinking about the environment in both Ireland and the Caribbean recalls that British colonialism dominated not only people but land. In both the anglophone Caribbean and Ireland, a single crop became a symbol of suffering under colonialism, and at times a focus for resistance to it. In Ireland the failure of the sustenance crop, potatoes, caused the Great Famine and mass emigration; in the Caribbean the production of sugar cane was supported by slavery and indentured labour. Both sugar cane and the potato are associated with exploitation of both land and people, which means that mass suffering and death are part of the stories of these two important crops.[5] Brand and McGuckian do not write explicitly about sugar cane and the potato, but their consciousness of the environment is complex, and far from politically quiescent "nature writing".

Both McGuckian and Brand make death a central concern in the collections discussed here, which represent loss and survival thrust against each other. As their poetic practice evolved, both poets have found ways of employing new poetic strategies, such as juxtaposition, irony and a refusal to tell linear tales. They have both created their own aesthetic paths and found ways to bear elegiac witness to a complex present and a painful collective past. By *elegiac* I do not mean simply sadness or longing for what is lost, but a tough-minded awareness of the complex relationship of life and death. When John Elder makes the useful point that "many Irish writers from the nineteenth century to the present have sought to escape from the elegiac mode in their depictions of Ireland's deeply rooted culture and history",[6] he means they escaped unconflicted Romantic affirmation of landscape and nature. But the elegiac in the work of Brand and McGuckian is anything but Romantic – *Romantic* implying an inheritance from the English colonialism that has had such a great impact on both Ireland and the Caribbean. Instead, their elegiacs are feisty and determined, edgy, full of the life which is fullest at the very edge of death. Their individual but parallel searches also necessarily brought both of them to inhabit the English language with a great resistance to old maps of the relations among feelings, thoughts and words.

Both poets employ voices in these poems which conjugate the relation of individual and collective. Recent work on cultural trauma and its connection to collective identity is helpful here.[7] In his *Cultural Trauma: Slavery and the Formation of African American Identity*, Ron Eyerman argues that though many African American subjects he interviewed did not necessarily directly experience "forced servitude and ... nearly complete subordination to the will and whims of another" (the definition of slavery), yet collective cultural trauma is the foundation of their sense of identity and culture. He goes on to say: "Slavery formed the root of an emergent collective identity, one that signified and distinguished a race, a people, or a community, depending on the level of abstraction and point of view being put forward." But he distinguishes between the immediate trauma for slaves of plantation life and the long memory of slavery, intensified by systematic racism, which inspired African American collective action. One important example of this is the founding of the National Association for the Advancement of Colored People in 1909. Thus slavery is "mediated through recollection and reflection, and, for some, tinged with some strategic, practical, and political interest" – still traumatic, but in a different way.[8]

Caribbean and Irish collective identities have also been strongly informed with regard to a brutal history, and in each case, as in the American South, exploitation of the land is a critically important part of that history.[9] Terry Eagleton calls the Great Famine the Irish Auschwitz, noting that for some in Ireland, denial is the only possible response.[10] Plantation slavery in the Caribbean has left a deep shadow of racial inequity; the struggle for full opportunity for the majority of people of African and Indian descent is ongoing, necessarily contributing to a strong sense of collective identity based in racial history. Those Irish people who emigrated to the Caribbean involuntarily, as political prisoners, had to find another conjugation of collective identity in their new locations: most of them worked the land. Land, and the working of land, are as crucial in Irish as in Caribbean collective memory, which records the suffering of the majority at the hands of an elite few.

Whether and how poetry might speak about mass trauma, whether experienced or remembered, has been debated since the Holocaust, and since 9/11 it has become more visible. As Rukmini Bhaya Nair argues, "Reading terror is undoubtedly one of the great preoccupations of the twentieth century."[11] She places poetry at the centre of resistance, arguing that it is as strong against terror as a state might be. This is a very provocative statement, but Nair supports it by arguing that poetry and song and story are enduring elements in all human cultures, because they "constitute evolutionary safeguards against that fatal terror of 'the other' that has, paradoxically, always caused the species to wage war against itself".[12] But poetry can rarely afford direct statement, although a strong political consciousness is often tempted to replace layered wordplay and multiple options of meaning with something immediately accessible by the reader. However, this negates poetry's highest mission of cleansing language of misuse and making words new again. Brand and McGuckian have found ways to make language new without abandoning political and social insight.

The reason that both might be expected to turn to direct statement is that they both experienced political turmoil. McGuckian grew up amid sectarian violence in Northern Ireland; Brand knew the politics of anti-colonialism and of race and class while growing up in Trinidad, and she was deeply engaged in the political upheavals in Grenada in the early 1980s.[13] Thus each might be considered likely to be a poet who directly accesses political issues. On the other hand, it is clear to any reader that something new is going on in terms of language use and poetic form. Most critics have focused on either their politics or their aesthetics, without realizing how they are organically connected. Brand's sense of the environment has been noticed, but that is unusual. Michaela Schrage-Früh points out that McGuckian's poetry "has generally been labeled as 'non-political' . . . all the more amazing for a Catholic poet who has lived all her life in Belfast and has thus had firsthand experience of the euphemistically named 'Troubles'".[14] Though Edward J. Mallot admits a political dimension to the work in its embracing of opposites – "empowered and helpless, North and South, men and women, self and non-self" – he thinks McGuckian not easy to understand politically, as she sometimes claims "political import for apparently innocuous pieces". But he quotes McGuckian's admission that she has felt like doing violence to the "tyrannical" English language, a statement made shortly after *Shelmalier* appeared, demonstrating how passionately anti-colonial she can feel.[15] Heather Clark's review of McGuckian's *The Currach Requires No Harbours* admits that though the poems are "virtually indecipherable", they "begin to unveil themselves when read in their historical context".[16] For *historical*, read *political*.

The work of Martin Heidegger (1889–1976) has been employed as a way into McGuckian's work. Shane Alcobia-Murphy demonstrates a McGuckian poem as intertextual with Heidegger's commentary on Hölderlin's poetry and poetry in general.[17] McGuckian's famously dense and difficult poetry does generally seem to relate to Heidegger's representation of language as highly complex and poetry as something which "awakens the illusion of the unreal and of dream as opposed to the tangible and clamorous reality, in which we believe ourselves to be at home".[18] Many of her poems move between a dreamlike state and full consciousness. McGuckian's sense of the connection between the fate and agency of people and the fate of their environment also relates to Heidegger, who is often cited by environmental critics. Timothy Clark, in his survey of ecocriticism, argues that Heidegger thought "that no facet of the universe, no plant or animal, can ever be mentioned without, by that very act, becoming part of the discriminations and significances of a human cultural world".[19] And Timothy Morton has remarked, significantly, that "deconstruction . . . searches out, with ruthless and brilliant intensity, points of contradiction and deep hesitation in systems of meaning. If ecological criticism had a more open and honest engagement with deconstruction, it would find a friend rather than an enemy."[20]

Both Brand and McGuckian embrace the inconsistencies and contradictions of language, and both entirely avoid making nature into a simple, entirely comprehensible entity. But Brand has more often been seen as political. Writing on *Inventory*, Carrie Dawson says: "I believe that Brand's insistence that we 'leave nature' and instead take stock of the myriad differences collapsed under the banner of 'nature' might help us shape a scholarly practice attentive to the relationship between questions of social and environmental justice in this country" – but by "this country" she means Canada, not the Caribbean.[21] Jim Hannan begins his discussion of *Ossuaries*, which is more recent than *Inventory*, by saying that Brand's entire poetry "merges a questioning, passionate, often lonely sensibility with a commitment to political activism and justice for historical and recent wrongs".[22] As to her aesthetic, he finds her paratactics "maddening", because connections between items in Brand's lines are not "explicitly" communicated to the reader,[23] something similar to early responses to McGuckian's poetry.

In *A Map to the Door of No Return* it is helpful to see how Brand makes a personal map of the world which is explicitly connected to the complications of language and of memory after collective trauma. The Door of No Return is a metonym, for all the separate doors in slave castles on the West African coast – which opened only to facilitate passing into captivity on the slave ship and then on the plantation – come to mean the final separation of the slave from ancestry, family, culture, language and, most significant of all, freedom. Brand rightly argues that the Door of No Return "makes the word *door* impossible and dangerous, cunning and disagreeable".[24] No wonder Brand finds that "[l]anguage can be deceptive" and, as a corollary, that all words need to be questioned and revisioned. She meditates on the nature of the passage through that door between worlds, and the inadequacy of words to represent that experience: "What language would describe that loss of bearings or the sudden awful liability of one's own body?" (p. 21).

The Door of No Return, that sinister archway, is a place of "irrecoverable losses" (p. 24) and, as the title of this book, helps to focus us on her meditation on place and on memory. She begins with a conversation with her grandfather, when she was thirteen and curious about ancestries. It is frustrating because he cannot remember enough ancestral history for her. But the reader also needs to understand that loss of memory, or burial of memory, is a common aftermath of trauma, and that this trauma is not only her grandfather's but that of all slaves and their descendants. Brand imagines "pulling the word off his tongue if only I knew the first syllable" (p. 4). Disruption of language is disruption of memory and therefore of a sense of place – which is, of course, strongly related to the significance of maps drawn by those who know, remember or recreate place. But for those for whom ancestral language and memory are, in an important way, left behind the Door, collective trauma continues down the generations. Her childhood memory of Trinidad is that "everyone here was unhappy and haunted in some way", though she did not know what haunted them (p. 11). She had, at a young age, awareness of "a wound much deeper than the physical" (ibid.) signifying trauma, a remaining damage experienced by a whole community if not articulated as a shared identity, needing to be addressed and acknowledged so that healing could begin.

The book is essentially about mapping, both personal and official, about Brand's journeys and those of the ancestors. Some of those journeys are by land and some by sea – a sea which is complex and powerful and deeply contradictory, both bearing the slave ships to the Caribbean and being able to "wash away blood and heal wounds" (p. 10). Brand writes: "Water is another country" (p. 56). She writes of the Grenadian coup and its consequences, and her witness strongly relates place and violence: a "murderous incline" in St George's, the capital, breadfruit "bashing themselves on the concrete steps" (p. 157). Nature itself is acting a part in the human drama. But trauma in the Caribbean is lived alongside the loveliness of the sea and undeveloped land, another deeply contradictory experience. In Trinidad and Tobago Brand sees lovely flamboyant trees and the "Atlantic and the Caribbean in a wet blue embrace" (p. 197).

McGuckian has not provided an equivalent text to help in apprehending her poetics. But the growing field of postcolonial ecocriticism helps us understand the work of both Brand and McGuckian, because it encourages a complex and multifaceted critical approach, with the environment being another complex subtext. Elizabeth DeLoughrey and George Handley, in their introduction to *Postcolonial Ecologies*, argue that "Western discourses of nature and the environment have been shaped by the history of empire".[25] In terms of Ireland and the anglophone Caribbean, that empire was the same, namely the British Empire. The British managed to sustain a great pride in their empire (and their cultural productions, most importantly literature) along with amnesia about what had been done to maintain empire, power and financial profit. Irish cultural theorist Terry Eagleton insightfully imagines Ireland as "Britain's unconscious", where in the nineteenth century "the British were forced to betray their own principles";[26] the same might be said of the Caribbean's place in the British imperial psyche.

The British love of horticulture turned sinister on the plantation and during the Great Famine: the welfare of powerless people was ignored in the pursuit of development of crops which provided more wealth and control to the few. Then, from the end of the eighteenth century on, as empire became ever more central to the country's economic success, the British love of poetry turned increasingly towards wanting to erase uncomfortable political realities. That meant that landscape and the environment became largely about the pastoral, the nostalgic embrace of lovely nature, and working people became only accessories in a carefully manicured view. Eagleton says: "The English tend to think of paintings first and farms second – just as Jane Austen tends to look at a piece of land and see its price and proprietor but nobody actually working there."[27]

But *ecocriticism* and *ecology* are terms which embrace a great many positions, from conservative to radical. In Ireland until recently, ecocriticism has been rather conservative.[28] More conservative readings tend to focus on "nature writing", which celebrates the beauty of unspoiled place and is politically opposed to urban development. But there is something naive about expecting to cherish something (rural beauty) almost as a relic when rural hardship destroyed so many lives for so long. Tim Wenzell's *Emerald Green: An Ecocritical Study of Irish Literature* and Eamonn Wall's *Writing the Irish West: Ecologies and Traditions* make the case that Irish poetry has often expressed a protective love of nature.[29] Wenzell points out that an early name for Ireland was "the Isle of Woods" but that forty-five thousand acres of forest were destroyed between 1841 and 1881, during the height of colonial intrusion.[30] His chief concern is the rise of urban sprawl in Ireland, which will undermine both Ireland's richly green landscapes and "nature writing", long an important part of Irish literary culture. He deplores both Ireland's recent turn to land development (for housing) and that at the same time nature has recently been "ignored in the literature of Ireland's writers".[31]

For Wall, Patrick Kavanagh, Louis MacNeice, Seamus Heaney and Michael Longley, who all have strong connections to Northern Ireland, are inspired by Ireland's so-called wild west – areas where Gaelic survived somewhat better. These poets matured in an Ireland that was still mostly rural, Kavanagh and MacNeice being born in the first decade of the twentieth century and Heaney and Longley on the brink of the Second World War. Wall points out that Kavanagh objected to Yeats's take on nature, calling him (along with Synge and Lady Gregory) an "agricultural-poetic tourist".[32] But Wall reads all these poets as loving "nature". MacNeice he locates as embracing the "same Irish pastoral ideal that ultimately accepts the presence of the natural world, despite the hardships it poses on humanity".[33] As for Heaney, Wall argues that "he comes to accept the natural world as part of being",[34] which is disappointingly bland, though he does see that in later work Heaney moves closer to embracing nature in all of its reality. Michael Longley is also uncritically seen as a nature poet.

Wall includes three poets in his study of the literary representation of the Irish west: Anglo-Irish Richard Murphy from County Mayo, Mary O'Malley from County Galway and Maya Cannon from County Donegal. After 1969 Murphy isolated himself to write on a small island off Ireland's west coast; Wall says he had to "seek to reshape both his personality and his art by listening carefully to nature rather than to the human voice".[35] Wall sees O'Malley as somewhat like Heaney in her response to the environment, most particularly in her poem "Tracing Wall", which complements Heaney's well-known poem "Digging" in the sense of exploring connections between a father's work and a child's turn to writing. Wall comments that for both Heaney and O'Malley, "poetry is not only connected to the physical world, but it is also an integral part of it",[36] though O'Malley is aware of overdevelopment around Galway City,[37] which signifies some political consciousness about the environment. As for Cannon, Wall allows her a "strong ecological consciousness",[38] but all he seems to mean is a passionate love of nature, despite his attempt to define her work as relating to "deep ecology", which requires humans to live on equal terms with all of nature. Indeed, Wall argues generally that interest in nature in Irish poetry has been ecological for a very long time, taking *ecological* to signify "absorption with place".[39] However, ecocriticism in Ireland is now diversifying and including more complex perspectives. *Out of the Earth: Ecocritical Readings of Irish Texts* includes explicitly political topics such as ecofeminism, the place of animals in the human world, and the ecological dangers of tourism.[40] McGuckian's complex apprehension of environment leads Irish poetry in the direction of the postmodern as a tool for thoughtfully experiencing our contemporary reality.

In the anglophone Caribbean there was a strong early pastoral tradition; British love of landscape (and erasure of plantation realities) was reflected in such poems as the Englishman James Grainger's "The Sugar-Cane", which has no issue with slavery, and Frank Collymore's "Hymn to the Sea", which is a kind of nature poem.[41] The dominance of the metre in Grainger emphasizes his acquiescence to prevailing norms among whites about slavery.[42] A special edition of *Caribbean Quarterly* celebrating John Figueroa is titled "At Home the Green Remains". It includes several poems by Figueroa which wonderfully celebrate nature – "Now leaves have fallen I can see / the architecture of tree / how dark earth pumps sap slowly to / the sun and skies" – but remain late Romantic.[43]

Caribbean poetry from the mid-twentieth century has often been deeply politically engaged, written at a time of strong movements against colonial rule, such as Martin Carter's "University of Hunger" and more recently David Dabydeen's "Coolie Odyssey".[44] These benefit from a postcolonial ecological reading, for their vision of the natural world is inseparable from that of the fallen world of man. *Caribbean Literature and the Environment* demands that an ecocritical reading be considered essential for Caribbean literature. The editors declare that "probably no other region in the world . . . has been more radically altered in terms of human and botanic migration, transplantation, and settlement than the Caribbean", and cite Edouard Glissant's determination that Caribbean culture and nature have not been brought into productive rela-tion.[45] Caribbean writers have clearly been aware for a considerable time that the environment is part of the political space of struggle against first colonialism and then neo-colonialism. As in the case of race- or gender-based criticism, ecocriticism shows critics both catching up with and then performing their critically important task of demonstrating how to read a text with new awareness.

In both Ireland and the Caribbean, ecocriticism is a new development, and within both, new readings of long-standing images of place and culture have emerged. Ian Gregory Strachan's *Paradise and Plantation: Tourism and Culture in the Anglophone Caribbean* establishes ways in which contemporary tourism renews old inequities.[46] Strachan critically explores work by V.S. Naipaul, Derek Walcott, Paule Marshall, Jamaica Kincaid and Michelle Cliff, investigating complexities and shortcomings in their representations of paradise, the prevailing Eurocentric trope. With regard to Ireland, Eóin Flannery critiques the representation of Ireland as "backward, lethargic and anachronistic". He concludes: "there is a historical genealogy within which Ireland, its landscape and its fractious colonial history have become aestheticised into passivity".[47]

McGuckian and Brand constantly undermine old, established clichés of the environment. McGuckian presents us with a "May apple" – far more complicated than the usual image of the apple as a healthy and commonplace fruit, or even as a prevalent element in Gaelic and other mythology. The lines are immediately haunting and mysterious: "All is moving inwards and redder-appearing / than the innermost third of my May apple, filled from clear to black with old blood."[48] The May apple (or Mayapple) is native to forests in North America and Asia; its fruit is pale green and almond shaped and it turns yellow when ripe. McGuckian's fruit is rotting from the core with the memories of old conflicts, a new kind of "fruit". Brand's image of nerve endings stored "in coloured bottles on a tree near the doorsteps" follows images of women coping with extreme violence and stress while they try to bring back some sort of normalcy, imaged in the fruits of the earth: bread, honey, figs, baked yams.[49] Those "nerve endings" were, surreally, gathered up from the street, spilled and counted "like rice grains".[50]

McGuckian explains the title of her collection, *Shelmalier*: as a Victorian word "with a beautiful coalescence of Irish and English, its sense of a lost and all but forgotten tribe, its being both a place name for a barony in Wexford and a battalion of seabird hunters, [it] seemed an evocative title".[51] Wexford was central in the 1798 Irish rebellion.[52] Though William Pratt, in a largely negative review, cannot fathom the title and accuses McGuckian of "straining for originality",[53] the multiple meanings of the word *shelmalier* warn us not to try to turn the collection into narrative, and to remain vigilant about the complexity of language. McGuckian, like Brand, loves constant juxtaposition, and the challenge of interpreting the same words in different locations. Three sets of words reoccur in many of the poems, having to do with death, with flora and fauna, and with water. Life (often expressed as sexual love) and death can have a kinetic relationship:

> Your arms are a living robe of earth you halve
> with me so death is a quarantine – only half a death.[54]

> My heart in your mouth is a tan-coloured telephone
> that hears your near-dying voice everywhere.[55]

The personae of the poems often have very close identification with the natural world: "my pine-wooded mind";[56] "I wish that sea-water would abstain from me now";[57] "I was the set-faced silence under / the breast-moulding sparkle and airy system / of the mile-high branches."[58] The unusual images remove all possibility of cliché, making the words set against each other fresh, if often ambiguous. What is not ambiguous is the sense of the elegiac, in which both great loss and grief and great love are complexly expressed. In this elegiac, the long-dead who fought for their cause in 1798 and the living female personae of these poems connect across time, embracing life and death, fertility and growth, and the long stillness of historical memory:

> *The leaves are tongues whose years of blood are locked*
> *in the wrong house, time feels unclocked*

> *or has been dead too long by now to cast*
> *its freshly slaughtered shadow from the past*[59]

In "Feastday of Peace", "the long, long dead / steer with their warmed breath / my unislanded dreams" because the dead are in "overcrowded soil", buried together, and from the earth comes growth. In the same poem, "The wound-open / window" seems to frame their "View-thirsting". They send a "kind of springtime / through the air we will breathe" – life is sustained by the dead. They speak and are "lace-curtain Irish", the would-be respectable, living quiet behind their conventions. For the living now, they seem to "anchor the moon-lines", but their language also chafes "like a boat in a sky-voyage". Finally, their language is English and their apprehension by the narrator is in English, which is so far away from being able to capture their significance that "the English meaning so unlike language". McGuckian's linguistic collisions allow language to be disrupted from beneath, not only by the dead and the political significance they carry, but also by the living who are trying to reach the dead without falling back into tired ways of using words. So war and death and sexuality and hope and a curious despair are tangled together, as are the human and the nonhuman world:

> As summer's funeral
> in the deceitful wane of the war
> is like a paper bride
> in an unwomanly room
> touching her mildly widowed
> newlywed body –

Something is both lost and promising: "were death fore-experienced, though all the leaves were there".[60]

These poems express a complex sense of emotional ecology in which the power of life embraces the power of death, which then turns back to the power of survival, as in the cycle of nature, though this version is far more visceral, mysterious and challenging than the usual representation of passage of the seasons in poetry:

> If they destroyed all the words like electric light,
> put them in a grave beneath branches,
> could trees be expected to heal
> without inherited things?[61]

Freedom is bound up with an unusual apprehension of context: "Would we be freed again like a view / seeing deep into gardens";[62] "I prayed to my imperfect idol freedom / till roads and rivers moved, limousine lanes tilted into roadlessness".[63] Similarly, familiar religious and political symbols are destabilized here:

> Crosses look like missiles
> the rose-coloured blotches
> of feeble Republican bombings
> embroider a Liberal flag[64]

Though Pratt accuses McGuckian of not being sufficiently politically cogent and understandable, she is performing – extraordinarily well – a necessary cleansing of old oppositions and titles, in the very language (English) which is so tainted with a history of dividing and ruling Ireland: "*the English words refuse to breathe*".[65]

In "Brownstone Bride", joyous love and death are again close: "Not a death-night touching / my sleeve, but my active operational germ of self / lacerated and untended on the peopled-enough sea."[66] The words *active* and *operational* reverberate with "germ of self", germ as living source, as in bacteria or seeds which have germinated. The self is painfully cut and as if abandoned in a space – the sea – where there are all-too-many people, who presumably ignore that self. McGuckian employs many images of water, in sea, river, rain and lake. They have multiple meanings: the equivalent of tears; a place to which to flee; the basis of all life; spaces where nothing is certain; vehicles of pain. This is far from the uncritical adoration of most nature poetry. In "The Word-Thrower", the persona swims out to sea "as though bitten by the past"; the sea does not seem to offer any consolation.[67] But in "Rathlin Road", "Always and only rain freed me", and after that the persona can "lie like new water".[68] "Green Crucifix" opens with "A month and a half of rain" which seems to bring a lover, " a joyful fighter", but there is also a "remembered / blue of the river" which the persona is unwilling to remember, perhaps because of pain.[69] In "Circle with Full Stop" the persona is at war, lying with a pistol "when I could have been swimming / under fire across the Danube", and then, "to bring out the taste of the month / I've had my dive into your head". Though she was August in the "dance of the months", now she is in winter, "a March sea".[70]

Living is complicated, full of consciousness of death and the possibility of future growth, both elegiac and hopeful. Though the collection has many first-person statements, it also is a collective, with a sense of history and of nation. The title poem, "Shelmalier", marks a man's death and a woman's desire for his speech; between them they are history and the present for Ireland, that which is dead and gone and that which is alive but aware of the past. Thus we can talk of an ecology here, a tight-knit system in which dead and living interact, in which there is consciousness of a difficult and violent past which breathes life into the present, and in which the individual is part of something much larger, in mourning and in joy, and language itself is required to go through some trauma in order to live again: "He has left me a fresh-robbed word, a small flat gift; an old word unsoftened by sun."[71]

In "Man Dressed as a Skeleton", at the opening the persona has just left a valley where the necessary corrective of fire has cleansed the forest, leaving a "cropped golden end" where a" black rainbow" occurs in "a church's ground". A "moon-responsive day" has "white-inside hinges" which keep blushing "where melted silver is poured down the throat of a subject race" – a brutal image of colonization in which the loveliness of the moon is fused with the ability of people to pervert natural resources into agencies of power.[72] McGuckian's taut language becomes entirely comprehensible once we realize that she is subverting the usual images of Irish landscape to include the violence of colonial occupation. Far from being apolitical, McGuckian draws on collective trauma and grief, as well as the sheer joy of being alive and capable of love, to make a brilliant collage of being in Ireland in the era of the Good Friday agreement and the hope of defeating past violence (this collection is drenched in Christian symbols).

Like McGuckian, Brand chose one word for the title of her collection – *Inventory* – and though printed in sections, it is really one long poem. It interweaves the human and the natural world, demonstrating how power has wounded both nature and those people who cannot protect themselves. There is no nature left here outside human culture; the tone is very elegiac, mindful of loss and pain and thoughtful about it. Brand's poem begins with the way Westerners "buried themselves in our chests", "acidic as love": the learning of violence and oppositions over territory. It is very difficult to understand "the whole immaculate language of the ravaged world".[73]

Brand's long lists of places where atrocity happened are reminiscent of Barbadian poet Kamau Brathwaite's brilliant postmodern elegy after 9/11.[74] However hard it is to live, people will hold onto hope: "the tap's dripping precious, / the electricity will soon come back".[75] As in McGuckian's work, the natural and the human are dislocated in their being by violence, bound into a wounded ecology. Houses "are on the edge of rotted dreams"; a persona says, "I'm waiting / to step into another life" but there will be found "without rivers, without hopes, without nails, without anything we know now" (III, pp. 35–36) – also without bruises, bullet-holed walls, serial killers or lost brides. The poem sequence inventories human destructiveness of other humans and of the planet, often referencing a collectively responsible *we*:

> the forests we destroyed,
> as far as
> the Amazonas' forehead
> the Congo's gut,
> the trees we peeled of rough butter,
> full knowing, there's something wrong
> with this.
> (I, p. 7)

A woman weeps in front of a television, witnessing suffering in wars (III, p. 21), seeing more and more items of horror on network news: "two, two in collision near Khallis, council member / in Kirkuk, one near medical complex, two in / Talafar, five by suicide bomb in Kirkuk" (III, p. 23). Women suffer in marriages, with pregnancies; they still struggle to survive and wish to hear "all that noise poets make about / time and timelessness" (III, p. 33). Brand's irony is often savage. Death is so pervasive that the persona even requests, "let us all celebrate death" (III, p. 35). But in the midst of death and violence there is always life as well, the need to "remember that cat we used to have", and "to buy lemons" (III, p. 28). Until "the planet is ruined", somehow things will go on, and a woman will fill an old basket with daylilies (III, p. 32). It is not a sentimental resolution, but a realization that death and life nibble at each other constantly.

Brand can be metapoetic, mocking the need to smooth sounds to make them rhythmic, as when, at the end of another list of casualties – "child on bicycle by bomb / in Baquba" – a question follows: "why does that alliterate on its own, why / does she observe the budding of that consonant" (III, p. 38). As for McGuckian, for Brand our uses of language are likely to be suspect and to require a tough cleansing. The elegiac tone of much of this long poem mourns the failure of humanity to protect its own and its habitat equally, and if there is a collective identity here, it is that of owning that failure while being conscious of and regretful about it. Nostalgia for easier images is attacked:

> where's their life of green oranges,
> of plums and dates, of papayas ripening
>
> forget it we can't speak of nature in that breath any more,
> the earth is corroding already with cities.
> (III, p. 40)

The planet has "withered lungs" (III, p. 41), and the natural world is ravaged as if it is a battlefield (III, p. 42). Though the poem urges "we" to admit meaning harm to one another, "whatever language we might have spoken is so thick with corrupt intentions, it persuades no one" (III, p. 43). Our very words are already rotten.

In Brand's poem, destruction and survival intertwine, as does despair at human stupidity and destructiveness and hope that something might be learned other than evasion and denial. We do not understand our environment well enough to take care of it, "like what billions of rainless universes do we kill /

just stepping through air, what failing cultures / submerge under a breath". In this part of the poem, Hurricane Katrina has just hit New Orleans. The storm is imagined as a great bird whose "wet wing flapped, dishevelled / against the windows like great damp feathers". "She" ends up "a ruffed foot, a quilled skirt trailing off" (VI, p. 83). Nature is as destructive as humans. Though the narrator knows "we're fucked" (VI, p. 84), she cannot tell certain of her kind, but the "birds of the world know this". The list which follows is rich in sound and image: "the banded pitta, the mangrove pitta, the bulbul, / the iora, the red-naped and scarlet-rumped // trogan, the fire-tufted barbet, flame back, philentoma". Brand revels in describing them, as in "the alliterative blue-bearded bee-eater". They are not all innocents, being capable of "the feathered work of greed" (VI, p. 85). Humans – "wingless, flightless" – have made "how many vows of death or endless death for endless peace" (VI, p. 86). So is there no hope of happiness? Cynically, the answer is "tennis matches and soccer games, / and river song and bird song and / wine naturally and some Sundays". But "fresh snapper and wild salmon", the food of choice of the fastidious middle classes, requires "killing something" (VII, p. 89).

Yet the very earth "keeps springing back" (ibid.). Somewhere there are people who can make "a music / come out of nothing" (VII, pp. 91–92). There is someone "who says, / don't worry, when you need it, rain, / rain is the happiest of weathers" (VII, p. 92). This is a list of joyful experiences and possibilities, even though the persona says to ask others about happiness, "not me, why should I know how to dance and sing in the middle of it all" (VII, p. 94). The list includes animals:

> squirrels in the eaves of a house going about
> their business,
> ground doves fluttering from tree to lemon tree
>
> all this, black butterflies and flying ants.
> (VII, p. 96)

There are many more: hummingbirds, beavers, one-inch pandas, "not simple // not simple as the ways to kill them, far more / complicated" (ibid.). In the end, "happiness is not the point, really, is a marvel / an accusation in our time". Indeed, the persona has "atomic openings in my chest / to hold the wounded", for the poet's job is not to soothe: "that's not my job, / my job is to revise and revise this bristling list" (VII, p. 100).

Brand's collection, then, is a mourning for the devastation "we" are making on the earth, and yet it is an affirmation, not of the logic of language but of its capacity, in the right hands, to shake up the complacent who may be looking for evasive comfort in a poem. Her apocalyptic world is, however, not hopeless (nor is her apocalyptic language about pitching one side against another). There is survival, though she offers a warning: "but let's leave nature for a while / how can we, yes, let's not essentialize the only / essential thing" (VII, p. 96). Her language is marvellously ordinary and at the same time tough-minded and resistant to reduction. It is also rhythmical, with heightened sound patterns such as alliteration, assonance and repetition, but Brand never lets the comfort of pattern overcome the need to ask questions and know complex feelings.

Brand and McGuckian have adopted postmodern poetic strategies in order to release themselves from evasive and complacent poetics which cannot discover collective engagement with a traumatic past or present. In the work of these two poets, love and grieving, which we think we know, must be practised anew, as both visceral and cerebral at the same time. A commodified society has a price for everything and turns everything into something to sell. Brand writes: "the wars' last and late night witness, / some she concluded are striving on grief / and burnt clothing, bloody rags, bomb-filled shoes" (p. 21). The word *striving* marks the way careers are built on televising suffering; it sits between two sets of alliteration (*w* and *b*) so that it is very evident. Human love has a choice: ignore its contexts or be aware and be threatened by them; the ruin of human concern for other humans, a colossal failure of love, leads to a place where "the planet is ruined, the continent / forlorn in water and smoke" (p. 31). McGuckian's lover embraces both sexual desire and the connection to death and burial in earth: "Your newly relaxed / muscles ripple towards bitterness, the first / oddly lit colour of the first spadeful."[76] A bride contemplates:

> Not a death-night touching
> my sleeve, but my active, operative germ of self
> lacerated and untended, on the peopled-enough sea,
> a life led in trees by the sore and sterile
> unresting imagination, trapped in vigilance forever.[77]

Once again alliteration makes "unresting" the more noticeable. There is no time for easy assumptions, because the sustaining trope in this collection is that love is shadowed by death and war (the uprising in Wexford), so that even the self is lacerated.

Brand and McGuckian have produced poetry which embraces a difficult present informed by a brutal past and reinvents poetics. If their poetry is difficult and frustrates us in our desire to be soothed or entertained or have our questions answered, it certainly offers us proof that extraordinary imaginations and wordsmiths are reimagining the postcolonial experience on both sides of the Atlantic.

Notes

1. Dionne Brand, *Inventory* (Toronto: McClelland and Stewart, 2006), III, 42.
2. Medbh McGuckian, "The Rose Trellis", in *Shelmalier* (Winston-Salem, NC: Wake Forest University Press, 1998), 24.
3. Brand published *Fore Day Morning* in 1978. In 1979 McGuckian won a prestigious poetry competition; she published two brief collections the following year and her first full-length book of poems, *The Flower Master,* in 1982.
4. Irish English is inflected by Gaelic, just as Caribbean English creoles are informed by African languages (and, in Trinidad and Tobago and Guyana and to a lesser extent across the Caribbean, by Indian languages as well).
5. I must thank my research assistants, Brittany Fowle, Brian McGrath and Xenia Ellenbogan, for their excellent help in the initial research for this chapter. For important insights into the Irish Famine and potato horticulture, see Peter Gray, *The Irish Famine* (New York: Harry N. Abrahams, 1995); David Nally *Human Encumbrances: Political Violence and the Great Irish Famine* (Notre Dame, IN: University of Notre Dame Press, 2011); and D.R. Glendinning, "Potato Introductions and Breeding up to the early 20th Century", *New Phytology* 94 (1983): 479–505. For sugar cane horticulture, see H. Galloway, *The Sugar Cane Industry: An Historical Geography from Its Origins to 1914* (Cambridge: Cambridge University Press, 2005). Cane was highly interbred to prevent disease, whereas the Irish potato came from a limited gene pool. The intersection of horticultural practice and the political and social implications of both sugar and the potato are of critical importance in the histories of Ireland and the Caribbean.
6. John Elder, "Introduction", in *Out of the Earth: Ecocritical Readings of Irish Texts*, ed. Christine Cusick (Cork: Cork University Press, 2010), 1–4.
7. Jeffrey Alexander offers this definition of cultural trauma: it occurs "when members of a collectivity feel they have been subjected to a horrendous event that leaves indelible marks upon their group consciousness, marking their memories forever and changing their future identity in fundamental and irrevocable ways"; "Toward a Theory of Cultural Trauma", in *Cultural Trauma and Collective Identity*, ed. Jeffrey C. Alexander, Ron Eyerman et al., 1–30 (Berkeley: University of California Press, 2004), 1.

8. Ron Eyerman, *Cultural Trauma: Slavery and the Formation of African American Identity* (Cambridge: Cambridge University Press, 2001), 1–2.

9. But not all Irish emigrants to the Caribbean were indentured labourers. Some became overseers or managers of sugar plantations, such as the notorious Thomas Thistlewood. See Sean O'Callaghan, *To Hell or Barbados: The Ethnic Cleansing of Ireland* (Dublin: Brandon, 2000), for the history of Irish people transported to Barbados.

10. Terry Eagleton, *Heathcliff and the Great Hunger* (London: Verso, 1995), 13.

11. Rukmini Bhaya Nair, *Poetry in a Time of Terror* (Oxford: Oxford University Press, 2009), xxii.

12. Ibid., xii.

13. The Grenadian revolution in 1979 was a coup which established a much more radically left-wing government, led by Maurice Bishop. In 1983 Bishop was executed, along with others, by a group led by Bernard Coard; six days later the United States invaded Grenada.

14. Michaela Schrage-Früh, "An Interview with Medbh McGuckian", *Contemporary Literature* 46, no. 1 (Spring 2005): 2.

15. J. Edward Mallot, "Medbh McGuckian's Poetic Tectonics", *Eire/Ireland* 40, no. 3–4 (Fall–Winter 2005): 249–50.

16. Heather Clark, "*The Currach Requires No Harbours* by Medbh McGuckian", *Harvard College Library* 35 (2008): 225.

17. Shane Alcobia-Murphy, " 'The Name Flows from the Naming': The Key to Understanding Medbh McGuckian's Poetry", *Estudios Irlandes* 3 (2008): 1–9. The McGuckian poem is "The Self-Concealing", from *Had I a Thousand Lives* (Oldcastle, Ireland: Gallery Press, 2003).

18. Martin Heidegger, *Elucidations of Hölderlin's Poetry*, trans. Richard Hoeller (New York: Humanity Books, 2000), 70.

19. Timothy Clark, *The Cambridge Introduction to Literature and the Environment* (Cambridge: Cambridge University Press, 2011), 58.

20. Timothy Morton, *Ecology Without Nature: Rethinking Environmental Aesthetics* (Cambridge, MA: Harvard University Press, 2007), 6.

21. Carrie Dawson, "How Does Our Garden Grow?", *Canadian Literature* 204 (Spring 2010): 110.

22. Jim Hannan, "*Ossuaries*", *World Literature Today* 84, no. 5 (September/October 2010): 70.

23. Ibid., 71.

24. Dionne Brand, *A Map to the Door of No Return: Notes to Belonging* (Toronto: Vantage, 2002), 19. Subsequent references to this work appear parenthetically in the text.

25. Elizabeth DeLoughrey and George B. Handley, "Introduction: Towards an Aesthetics of the Earth", in *Postcolonial Ecologies: Literatures of the Environment* (Oxford:

Oxford University Press, 2011), 10.

26.   Eagleton, *Heathcliff*, 9.

27.   Ibid., 4.

28.   The Glotfelty-Fromm reader on ecocriticism asks how literary studies are changed in a time of environmental crisis. Ecocriticism is often interdisciplinary, but as a solely literary approach it needs to ask what contribution literature makes, has made or could make to apprehension of the danger of climate change and environmental depredation. There are parallels with the history of feminist, Marxist and other politically focused literary critical approaches: at an early phase they asked questions about the status quo of criticism and of writing, helping set the stage for new approaches and new texts. See Cheryll Glotfelty and Harold Fromm, eds, *The Ecocriticism Reader: Landmarks in Literary Ecology* (Athens: University of Georgia Press, 1996). Greg Garrard provides a good basic introduction to terminologies and practices (such as *pastoral*, *wilderness*, *apocalypse* and *environmentalism*) in *Ecocritism: The New Critical Idiom* (New York: Routledge, 2004). The work of Lawrence Buell has been foundational in US environmental criticism, exploring connections between human history and the environment in texts; see *The Environmental Imagination: Thoreau, Nature Writing, and the Formation of American Culture* (Cambridge, MA: Harvard University Press, 1995); *Writing for an Endangered World: Literature, Culture, and the Environment in the United States and Beyond* (Cambridge, MA: Harvard University Press, 2001); and *The Future of Environmental Criticism: Environmental Crisis and Literary Imagination* (Malden, MA: Blackwell, 2005). However, as DeLoughrey et al. point out, there is an emphasis on male alienation from the environment in Anglo-American ecocriticism; see Elizabeth DeLoughrey, Renee K. Gosson and George Handley, eds, *Caribbean Literature and the Environment: Between Nature and Culture* (Charlottesville: University of Virginia Press, 2005), 4. Early Irish ecocriticism has broadly agreed with Anglo-American ecocritical concepts: "the interconnections between nature and culture, specifically the cultural artifacts of language and literature" (Glotfelty and Fromm, *Ecocriticism Reader*, xix). At its least provocative, such ecocriticism focuses on the pastoral – that nostalgic apprehension of the countryside by urban dwellers from Theocrititus on – or on landscape or specific flora and fauna in particular literary works.

29.   Tim Wenzell, *Emerald Green: An Ecocritical Study of Irish Literature* (Newcastle-on-Tyne: Cambridge Scholars, 2009); Eamonn Wall, *Writing the Irish West: Ecologies and Traditions* (Notre Dame, IN: University of Notre Dame Press, 2011).

30.   Wenzell, *Emerald Green*, 7.

31.   Ibid., 3.

32.   Wall, *Writing the Irish West*, 110.

33.   Ibid., 116.

34.   Ibid., 120.

35. Ibid., 57.

36. Ibid., 75.

37. Ibid., 80.

38. Ibid., 170.

39. Ibid., 52.

40. Christine Cusick, ed., *Out of the Earth: Ecocritical Readings of Irish Texts* (Cork: Cork University Press, 2010).

41. James Grainger, "The Sugar-Cane", in *The Penguin Book of Caribbean Verse*, ed. Paula Burnett (Harmondsworth, UK: Penguin, 1986), 104–5; Frank Collymore, "Hymn to the Sea", in *Collected Poems* (Bridgetown: Advocate, 1959).

42. Grainger's poem demonstrates that when blank verse (or any regular metre) is too regular, it provides a comforting containment of the subject matter of the verse, as in "On festal days; or when their work is done; / Permit thy slaves to lead the choral dance" ("The Sugar-Cane", 105).

43. Esther Figueroa, ed., "At Home the Green Remains: Caribbean Writing in Honour of John Figueroa", *Caribbean Quarterly* 49, nos. 1–2 (March–June 2003), 126.

44. Martin Carter, "University of Hunger", in *University of Hunger: Collected Poems and Selected Prose* (Newcastle: Bloodaxe Books, 2006); David Dabydeen, "Coolie Odyssey", in *The Oxford Book of Caribbean Verse*, ed. Stewart Brown and Mark McWatt (Oxford: Oxford University Press, 2005), 299–303.

45. DeLoughery, Gosson and Handley, *Caribbean Literature*, 1.

46. Ian Gregory Strachan, *Paradise and Plantation: Tourism and Culture in the Anglophone Caribbean* (Charlottesville: University of Virginia Press, 2002).

47. Eóin Flannery, "Ireland of the Welcomes: Colonialism, Tourism and the Irish Landscape", in Cusick, *Out of the Earth*, 106.

48. McGuckian, *Shelmalier*, 26.

49. Brand, *Inventory*, 46.

50. Ibid., 30.

51. McGuckian, *Shelmalier*, 13.

52. This uprising against the British was led by the Society of United Irishmen, who sought to unite Catholic and Protestant and were inspired by the French Revolution. After the Irish joined with the French, who unsuccessfully tried to invade Ireland in 1796, the British responded with extreme violence and the rebellion was suppressed. Rebels had massacred prisoners loyal to the British in Wexford, which gave the British an excuse for severe retaliation against the leaders. See Thomas Pakenham, *The Year of Liberty: The Great Irish Rebellion of 1789* (London: Abacus, 1998). McGuckian indirectly references the conflict in the title poem, "Shelmalier" (75), and also by many references such as "war", "army", "battles", "weapons" and "a bomb". She makes a parallel between old and new conflict by referencing "Republican bombings" (99).

53. William Pratt, "Book Review: *Shelmalier*", *World Literature Today* 73, no. 4 (1999): 744–45. Pratt is most irritated by McGuckian's treatment of history: "these poems are too personal for a juncture with history" (745). But this seems to be because he expects a linear sense of history to be prominent.

54. McGuckian, "Shoulder Length, Caged Parrot Earrings", in *Shelmalier*, 48.

55. McGuckian, "Clearing out the Workhouse", in *Shelmalier*, 30.

56. McGuckian, "Dream in a Train", in *Shelmalier*, 17.

57. McGuckian, "Pass Christian", in *Shelmalier*, 18.

58. McGuckian, "Mass Read by Night in the Open Air", in *Shelmalier*, 54.

59. McGuckian, "Script for an Unchanging Voice", in *Shelmalier*, 16.

60. All quotations in this paragraph from McGuckian, "Feastday of Peace", in *Shelmalier*, 23.

61. McGuckian, "Rose Trellis", 24.

62. Ibid.

63. McGuckian, "Their Word for Harvest Freedom", in *Shelmalier*, 42.

64. McGuckian, "The Sickness of the Cloth", in *Shelmalier*, 99.

65. Ibid., 85.

66. McGuckian, "Brownstone Bride", in *Shelmalier*, 93.

67. McGuckian, "The Word-Thrower", in *Shelmalier*, 29.

68. McGuckian, "Rathlin Road", in *Shelmalier*, 41.

69. McGuckian, "Green Crucifix", in *Shelmalier*, 46.

70. McGuckian, "Circle with Full Stop", in *Shelmalier*, 31.

71. McGuckian, "The Birthday of Monday", in *Shelmalier*, 117.

72. McGuckian, "Man Dressed as a Skeleton", in *Shelmalier*, 66.

73. Brand, *Inventory*, 11.

74. See Brathwaite's elegy for 9/11, "Hawk", in *Born to Slow Horses* (Middletown, CT: Wesleyan University Press, 2005), 92–117. Brathwaite broadens the grief for the dead of 9/11 by listing many names which are metonyms for mass death across the world, such as "as in Bhuj. In Grenada.Guernica.Amritsar. Tajikistan" (101).

75. Brand, *Inventory*, III, 48. Subsequent references to this work appear parenthetically in the text.

76. McGuckian, "A Light Form of War", in *Shelmalier*, 73.

77. McGuckian, "Brownstone Bride", 93.

Chapter 15

"Two Tunes"

Settler-Colonist Worlds in Elizabeth Bowen's The Last
September and Jean Rhys's Voyage in the Dark

RICHARD McGUIRE

ALTHOUGH THERE ARE MARKED DIFFERENCES IN THE positioned colonial histories and socioeconomic and strategic imperial prerogatives in the colonization of Ireland and Dominica, there is, nonetheless, a strikingly parallel narrative of settler/colonial experience to be found in Elizabeth Bowen's Anglo-Irish novel of declining Ascendancy, *The Last September,* and Jean Rhys's diasporic Dominican colonist novel of return to the metropolis, *Voyage in the Dark.* Analysing the two novels, I will show comparatively how these harmonies are constructed. In each text, an orphaned female protagonist less than twenty years old expresses estrangement from her colonizing plantocratic extended family. She identifies with the colonized peoples rather than her own society. Furthermore, she exploits narrative tropes of fire in wishing for physical destruction of the "Big House" society within which she was raised.

First, however, it is necessary to attend to the contexts of positioned colonial histories in Ireland and Dominica. In the two decades before September 1920, the period in which *The Last September* is set, Anglo-Irish Protestant society's obliviousness or denial of the impending force of republican feeling and nationalist aspiration is clearly evident, both in secondary historical accounts of the Troubles and critical commentaries on the primary evidence of autobiography and memoir. In a careful narrative of the decline of the Ascendancy, McConville demonstrates that famine caused many landlords of the Anglo-Irish Big Houses built in the eighteenth century to take out bank loans to keep up appearances and deny decline, even while their estates displayed signs of dilapidation and a slow, inexorable fall towards genteel poverty.[1] Following political advances by the Land League's campaign seeking to redistribute colonial lands, he continues, John Redmond's Irish Parliamentary Party successfully introduced into Asquith's Liberal British government a third Home Rule bill in 1912. This was met the following year by Unionist resistance, occasioning paramilitary defence of Protestant Ulster.

The year 1913 also saw the formation in the north of Ireland of the Ulster Volunteer Force, which was countered by the National Volunteers, who merged with the Irish Republican Brotherhood to form what eventually became the Irish Republican Army. Although the Home Rule bill was passed in 1914, it was postponed by the outbreak of the Great War. A failed uprising by nationalists, impatient for a republic and total severance from Britain, began in Dublin on Easter Monday, 1916.[2] The uprising, Cottrell believes, was not widely supported by the majority of the Irish population, until British courts martial and reactionary executions of many of the key conspirators turned opinion almost completely in the nationalist republicans' favour. Sinn Féin, a nationalist party formed in 1905 by Arthur Griffith that developed strong links with republican paramilitarism, comprehensively defeated the Irish Parliamentary Party in elections during 1918; it then claimed that it had a mandate to govern Ireland as a united sovereign nation, in spite of Unionist resistance in Ulster. Attacks by the Irish Republican Army against the Royal Irish Constabulary intensified until Britain sent auxiliary troops (including the Black and Tans, so called because of their makeshift uniforms: part police black and part military khaki) to assist the force under attack.

At this point, and by September 1920, McConville argues, many Anglo-Irish Big Houses effectively became garrisons under threat of republican attack and paramilitary land grabs. British soldiers, war weary and shell-shocked after the horrors of the Great War, defended large Anglo-Irish estates where – as McConville's summary of Anglo-Irish autobiographer Nora Robertson's memoir, *Crowned Harp*, seems to suggest – its inhabitants socialized and revelled in a cultural and historical vacuum, decidedly oblivious of the inevitable tide of independence and the imminent decline of their caste. McConville notes Robertson's youth of "endless dinner parties and balls" and "country house parties" where the Anglo-Irish of Big House society mimicked the opulent splendour and social confidence of its late eighteenth-century apex, all the while relying for its maintenance on the very British support that at the summit of its powers it had, in a nationalist spirit, resisted.[3]

Hermione Lee, in her 1983 introduction to Elizabeth Bowen's memoirs of Anglo-Irish Ascendancy life at the beginning of the twentieth century, *Bowen's Court & Seven Winters*, remarks upon the Bowen family's dynastic Protestant landlord society. In her view, Bowen's Court, an archetypal north-eastern Cork Big House which flourished in the pre-Union eighteenth century and maintained dominance over rural peasant tenants until the Troubles, can be read as metonymical of the aspirant, established and then declining fortunes of the Ascendancy as a whole.

> To an extent, the history of the Bowens is the history of the Anglo-Irish family, and of a class which came to flower in the late eighteenth century, went into decline thereafter and was, by the 1920s, an isolated minority cut off from the country it had once dominated. . . . The Big House builders' obsession with self-aggrandizement and self-perpetuation, the orgies of hunting and drinking, the lawsuits and deeds of sale, the notorious eccentrics . . . many of these clichés are facts of the Bowen family history.[4]

It would perhaps be over-reductive to conflate the Bowen family history comparatively with that of Jean Rhys in the context of discussion of Dominica. However, when one considers Dominica's positioned colonial history and the role within it that Rhys's forebears played, one can begin to spot biographical contexts that converge and admit parallels between the two novels. Without going into detail about the power struggles between France and Britain over control of slave trading, planter/settlers, and coffee and sugar producing in Dominica, suffice it to say that by the time Britain achieved unequivocal political control over the island in 1815, after the Napoleonic Wars, many among the slave population still spoke predominantly French Creole. Pigmentocracy also played a crucial part in Dominican society. The hierarchical social structure in the Caribbean was predicated upon and privileged the notion that the whiter a person's lineage and appearance were perceived to be, the more elevated their status. Planter/settlers entered into concubinage or intermarried with Afro-Dominicans to a degree that any commonplace Western, imperial concept of a binary between the semiotics of whiteness and blackness became unworkable in the face of such complex stratification of race and caste.

Henry Hesketh Bell became the colonial administrator of Dominica in 1899.[5] He set about the task of constructing the new so-called Imperial Road into the interior and encouraging settler/planters to come from Britain to the island. Dominican historian Lennox Honychurch notes that between 1904 and 1905, Dominica's white settler population grew from a handful to more than four hundred.[6] This new population struggled to grasp the complex racial caste system and pigmentocracy of Dominica. In Rhys's *Voyage in the Dark*, the protagonist Anna Morgan's stepmother, Hester, represents one of this new wave of colonists, expressing her distaste at (or a lack of sophisticated understanding of) Anna's creolized accent, mannerisms and, implicitly, heritage. While there is no exact corollary of this in Bowen's *The Last September*, I shall discuss later in this chapter how the old Anglo-Irish Ascendancy, as represented by Myra Norton, seeks to differentiate itself as an Irish caste from the new English military colonial castes at the Danielstown estate. Within the colonial societies of both novels are tensions between successive generations of arrivals from Britain.

While mindful of the historical specificities of the Irish and Dominican settler/colonist worlds, one nonetheless starts to note striking correspondences between the colonial biographies of Elizabethan Bowen and Jean Rhys that provide context for the confluent experiences of Lois Farquar and Anna Morgan, the respective protagonists of *The Last September* and *Voyage in the Dark*. Both writers were born in the 1890s, although not on the colonial estates which provided source material for their respective novels. Bowen's ancestral home, Bowen's Court, in North Cork, was constructed in 1776 at the height of the Anglo-Irish Ascendancy; Rhys's maternal ancestral home, Geneva, dates from 1700. Although neither house was burned down by anti-imperial rebels, widespread torching of colonial houses inspired Bowen's destruction by fire of the Danielstown estate at the close of *The Last September*. There are also intimations of destruction by fire of the Costerus estate in the climax of *Voyage in the Dark*, in which kerosene drums are struck percussively and ominously around the house; of course, a reader of *Wide Sargasso Sea* might link this with the destruction of the Coulibri estate in that novel.

Bowen and Rhys departed for England in their youth. Although the two writers unquestionably identified with their former colonial homes, as they provided settings for their novels, both formulated a complex, nuanced sense of identification with their colonized territories instead of identifying with Britishness. Importantly, Bowen's sense of Irishness was not of the popular neo-Gaelic mode adopted by the Irish literary revivalists; rather, she was aware of herself as a member of the Protestant Ascendancy. Rhys's adverse reaction to the lack of colour and warmth in English weather and manners reinforced her sense of being a Dominican, or West Indian; this idea of a complex counter-British self-imagining rather than embrace of a colonized island and peoples has been explored by Gregg.[7] Carr's critical study of Rhys also considers this issue in further detail.[8]

Having suggested a comparative method of reading the colonial worlds provided by the two novels, and having considered positioned histories relating to the contexts of each author and her novel, I now supply a close reading that demonstrates remarkable confluences between the worlds of the texts in play. Some analysis of the texts referring to structuralist and formalist consideration of narrative form will show a close harmony between the represented worlds of the eighteen-year-old protagonists Lois Farquar and Anna Morgan in the declining years of their plantocratic societies.

Seymour Chatman, in his structuralist analysis of text, argues that narrative is constituted of two major elements: story, which comprises the actions, happenings, major and minor events, setting and characters in a text, and discourse, which comprises the voice, mood and temporal arrangement of the story's events.[9] If we venture further and apply Russian formalist textual analysis within this configuration of narrative, we might reduce the basic elements of the story, the actions and happenings, to the element of *fabula*. It is when we look comparatively at aspects of the *fabula* across *The Last September* and *Voyage in the Dark* that we see a surprisingly extensive list of parallels, many of which have profound implications for representation of settler/colonial lived experience across Ireland and the Caribbean. Lois Farquar and Anna Morgan are both eighteen years old at the start of the two novels. Each has been raised mainly on a colonial estate at which her ancestors have been based for several generations. Each is an orphan, having lost her parents in perhaps tragic circumstances.

Lois Farquar is revealed in the heterodiegetic narration of *The Last September* as the orphaned daughter of Ulster Protestant Walter Farquar and his wife, Laura, sister to Sir Richard Naylor, landlord of the Anglo-Irish estate of Danielstown, County Cork. In her childhood, Lois was raised in Leamington, England, where she also boarded as a scholar. Sir Richard and his wife, Myra, are now Lois's legal guardians and she resides with them, having completed her English schooling, in Danielstown. We understand from a conversation between Hugo and Francie Montmorency – visitors to the estate whose stay is depicted in the book's first part, "The Arrival of Mr and Mrs Montmorency" – and through Francie's focalized free, indirect thought that Lois's mother, Laura, was "very remote", and that Laura had died suddenly "without giving anyone notice of her intention", though we do not learn the cause of her death.[10] Likewise, the nature of the "terribly sad" fate of Lois's father, Walter, to which Myra refers as "what we always expected", is inferred but never revealed.[11]

Anna Morgan is also eighteen when she first documents herself, through homodiegetic narrative, as the orphaned daughter of an unnamed woman of the Costerus family, landed for five generations on the Constance estate in Dominica, and Gerald Morgan, a first-generation Dominican planter/settler whose gambling, "Folly" and bad debts – at least in the implied opinion of his surviving second wife, Hester – appear to have contributed to the premature death of "a brilliant poor man buried alive you might say yes it was a tragedy a tragedy".[12] Anna and Hester have sold up their last Dominican property, the unsuccessful Morgan's Rest, and migrated to Ilkley, Yorkshire, with their depleted inheritance before Anna leaves to pursue a career as a chorus girl in the provincial towns of Great Britain.

Lois and Anna each have an elderly relative with distinct views on settler/colonial identity, caste and difference. For example, Lois's uncle and aunt, Sir Richard and Lady Myra Naylor, throughout the novel demonstrate self-identification with a kind of Anglo-Irish Ascendancy mentality that closely resembles the eighteenth-century anti-English, proto-Republican separatism of the Protestant Irish typified by politician Henry Grattan. In Anglo-Irish society such typification of cultural separateness is rife: Sir Richard Naylor demonstrates belief in an Irish national character that is something distinct from the English. He attributes to Englishness the negative qualities of hysterical fear. When Francie Montmorency worries that the Danielstown party might be shot if they sit outside on the house's steps too late into the dark evening, Sir Richard replies, "You're getting very English, Francie! Isn't Francie getting very English? Do you think maybe we ought to put sandbags behind the shutters when we shut up at nights?"[13]

Lady Naylor first ascribes to Englishness a bland anonymity: "Practically nobody who lives in Surrey ever seems to have been heard of."[14] Second, she bemoans their annoying "disposition . . . to be socially visible before midday".[15] Even the "Honourable Mrs Carey", who attends a Danielstown tennis party fortified by representatives of the local garrison and their English wives, adds her view of polite disgust at the English. In reply to military wife Betty Vermont's exclamation that "Your scrumptious Irish teas make a perfect piggy-wig of me", she replies with a sublimely stilted "Does it really?" while musing internally on "a tendency, common to most English people, to talk about her inside".[16] It is thus unsurprising that she sabotages her niece Lois's wish to marry the British soldier Gerald Lesworth, in order to prevent her from redefining a generationally established sense of Anglo-Irish identity and distinction.

Anna's stepmother, Hester Morgan, also has a strong sense of colonial identity, but in her case it is constructed not after the model of a settler/colonist of several generations, which might provide a neat corollary to the Naylors, but rather as a new arrival in Hesketh Bell's Dominica, with a fresh nationalistically and racially shaped view of her Englishness. She refers to Anna's creolized qualities – un-Englishness that might in a general sense have been praised by Myra Naylor – with disdain. Furthermore, Hester sabotages Anna's attempts to redefine her sense of status and identity by squandering Anna's paternal inheritance on herself.

Hester's conceptualization of cultural and racial difference appears superficially, on a textual reading of *fabula*, to correspond with *The Last September*'s Myra Naylor, but she differs from Myra inasmuch as she is not a settler/colonist of several generations but a first-generation, English-born immigrant. She maintains a perspective that is at times decidedly antithetical to the settler viewpoint of the long-established Costerus family of Anna's childhood Constance estate (the near equivalent of Bowen's Naylors). Hester fails to realize how the mixed racial identity of colonist and colonized castes alike evolved as a historical process, beginning with concubinage between slave masters and African female slaves during a period of low birth rates, high death rates and a need to perpetuate slave stock at a low price; sexual congress between colonizer and colonized and the increasing heterogeneity of Dominican identity and community persisted into Anna's childhood. For Hester, Ramsey Costerus's propensity to father children of variant castes is an index of his moral degeneration; she fails to regard it as a cultural norm in Dominican society. She disdains "illegitimate children wandering about all over the place called by his name – called by his name if you please".[17] She remarks, "Uncle Bo! Uncle Boozy would be a better name for him."[18] An English ideology of racial and social norms informs her view of a "slack" colonial class corrupted by spending too much time in the colonies. In overly racist dialogue, Hester criticizes Anna's creolized mannerisms: "you growing up more like a nigger every day. Enough to drive anybody mad."[19] She furthermore intimates, through condescendingly suggestive phraseology, her assessment of Anna's mixed background, remarking, "I always thought that considering everything you were much to be pitied."[20]

There are, as I say, historical nuances between many confluences in the texts that should be understood in order to prevent overworlding or over-textualizing rather parallel peripheral settler/colonial narratives which are writing back to metropolitan constructions of British colonial expansionist identity and experience. Recognizing such nuances protects against reducing a comparative reading of two novels from specific geographical and historical locations into a neat narratological formula. Materialist critics such as Aijaz Ahmad have voiced deep suspicion of Western academic, theory-based study of postcolonial anglophone literatures. He sees a tendency towards de-historicizing and over-textualizing postcolonial literatures as a way of silencing the lived anti-colonial struggles that motivate decolonizing texts and assimilating them into a neo-colonial hegemonic formula.[21] I seek to counter such a risk by noting how textual similarities are moderated by specificities of historical context.

In *The Last September*, before the destruction of Danielstown by Republican forces, fire is a symbol of repressed desire for destruction of constraints within the stultifying Anglo-Irish society. Lois Farquar and Anna Morgan both employ the trope of fire to express anti-colonial resistance: Lois's fire dreams operate at the fringes of her conscious thought, through metaphor, while Anna uses the physical sensation of fire in a bedroom interior to catalyse her sensual memory of Dominican childhood. However, the ways in which fire is articulated differ because of historically positioned context and ideological implications. Fire in the Anglo-Irish imagination is a symbol of the destruction by Irish republican forces of the Anglo-Irish Big House – a widespread act of paramilitary vandalism intended to dispossess the Ascendancy in a nationalist land grab, or a symbolic gesture of anti-colonial triumphalism – during and following the War of Independence. John Dorney notes that the Big House, or country mansion of the Anglo-Irish landed class was a target of republicans throughout the Irish revolution of 1919–23: "A total of 275 were burned out, blown up or otherwise destroyed between 1920 and 1923. Of these, by far the greatest number, 199, were destroyed, not during the conflict against the British, but in the period of intra-nationalist civil war between 1922–1923."[22]

Lois's desire for destruction runs counter to the security and perpetuation of her caste. But she appears unable to formulate and overtly articulate her wish for Danielstown to be destroyed by fire, or to admit to identification on any significant level with Irish republican sentiment. Not so the Oxford-educated Laurence, who has no difficulty informing Hugo Montmorency, "I should like to be here when this house burns. . . . And we shall all be so careful not to notice."[23] Montmorency sardonically asks if Laurence's remarks are indicative of "the undergraduate of today", at least, the undergraduate shipped to an Oxford relatively autonomous from the Ascendancy. It becomes clear that Lois, who remains based in Danielstown until the conclusion of the novel, is unable to express her incendiary anti-colonial wishes to escape the ideological and physical confines of the Big House, except via a figurative eruption of fire imagery almost on the periphery of her consciousness. Indeed, the first point at which the reader interprets prolepsis of Danielstown's destruction by fire is via focalization from Lois's perspective. In chapter twelve of the novel, when Lois visits Marda Norton's guestroom on the pretext of showing her a book of drawings, Lois's complex, sexually ambiguous and passionate response to Marda's apparent lack of interest in her precipitates another example of violently inflammatory focalization that again allows Lois's unconscious – or the textual unconscious shared between narrator and focalizer – to will the destruction of her caste.

Since Marda Norton is due to leave Ireland to marry Leslie Hawe in Kent, she represents for Lois simultaneously a symbol of escape from the parameters of the Anglo-Irish estate and also imprisonment within the patriarchal confines of provincial middle England, to which colonial women seem inexorably drawn to return diasporically in pursuit of economic and gender definition. Michael McConville remarks that "Irish peers tended to look for a cash element in their marriages".[24] It was always a part of the colonial project in the Caribbean, and an inevitable effect of dwindling colonialism, that for economic reasons settler/colonists returned to the centre of empire to maintain wealth and social status. Marda Norton is one of these emigrants; in *The Last September* she chooses marriage in England as her prerogative. Lois is desperate to transcend this colonial activity and mentality: "She wanted to go wherever the War hadn't"; "She liked unmarried sorts of places"; "Could one travel alone?"[25] Yet it is through psycho-narration that her most subversive desires are figuratively rendered. Lois fixates upon the bedroom carpet with its "strange pink fronds" and meditates upon fire's emancipatory potential:

> Lois thought how in Marda's bedroom, when she was married, there might be a dark blue carpet with a bloom on it like a grape, and how this room, this hour would be forgotten. Already the room seemed full of the dusk of oblivion. And she hoped that instead of fading to dust in summers of empty sunshine, the carpet would burn with the house in a scarlet night to make one flaming call upon Marda's memory. Lois again realized that no one had come for her, after all. She thought, "I must marry Gerald."[26]

The perspectival and ideological implication of psycho-narration is that, by including narratorial obtrusion into the discourse ("Lois thought"; "And she hoped"), Lois's thoughts and emotions are to an extent framed in the narrator's own phraseology, and thus, implicitly, her viewpoint.[27] Therefore ambiguities surface in the language, implying the narrator's and focalizer's shared authorship in proleptically ensuring, at the periphery of diegesis and through metaphor, an unspeakable narrative presaging a wish for the destruction of Danielstown. For example, is "Marda's bedroom, when she was married" her marital bedroom in Kent or the bedroom in Danielstown at a time when Marda is married? This semantic ambiguity is not clarified by reference to how Marda might in time forget "this room, this hour"; the blue carpet with its grape-like bloom might, for instance, symbolize Lois's own attendant adult desire for Marda's beauty. This ignition of desire and fear that the fate of Lois – and, for the narrator, all young females of the later Ascendancy – might be confined to colonial socioeconomic restrictions on social and gender definition causes her to wish that "instead of fading to dust in summers of empty sunshine, the carpet would burn with the house in a scarlet night to make one flaming call upon Marda's memory".

Again, there is semantic ambiguity. Is Lois fantasizing that Marda will die a sacrificial death in her marital house at the peak of her sensuality, rather than age and fade to mundanity and married middle age? Or is she wishing for Danielstown to burn somehow to create a psychic echo that will invade Marda's memory and remind her of Lois and her vibrant but abandoned offer of escape from settler/colonial life and the provincial English diasporic life which succeeds it as a matter of course? The lexis and syntax of the discourse, shared by narrator and focalizer, resist a definitive construction of meaning and, in Derridean terms, defer a unitary response. What leads me to argue that Lois wishes for the destruction in flames of Danielstown is her thought, "I must marry Gerald." Throughout the text, Gerald occupies a tenebrous, nebulous and shape-shifting presence between colonial Self and disruptive colonized Other. The Englishwoman Betty Vermont likens him, in othering, orientalist terms, to a Bedouin.[28]

For the diasporic Dominican Anna Morgan, fire is a primarily a symbol of warmth, sensation and prelinguistic physical connection – in almost Kristevan semiotic terms – with nature, as opposed to the cold, grey, anonymous world of England, whose social norms and mores are promulgated through language and through ideological precepts of propriety and order. At the start of *Voyage in the Dark*, Anna cannot conceive of her immediate environs emotionally. In

England an experiential divide falls, gloving Anna's tactile, memorial sense apprehension of her previous lived experience of Dominica. She constructs a binary opposition of "heat, cold; light, darkness; purple, grey" between her former Dominican and current English locations. While she seeks to construct a hybridizing third space for reconstructing Dominican experience, sense perception and consciousness, through meditating on the glow of a bedsitter fireplace to evoke an idealized dream memory of "looking down Market Street to the Bay" with the sun-illumined sea "millions of spangles", this strategy can be conducted only in solipsistic isolation, with her eyes closed and with no active engagement in her new migrant environment.[29]

Anna drifts through this metropolitan heart of colonial darkness, psychologically imprisoned behind the "high, dark wall" of an English social mindset.[30] She is anaesthetized or shut out from her childhood sense-identity, and she has only her increasingly disjointed recollections of home to provide floundering snatches of opportunity, defining herself by pale echoes of the warmth of the Afro-Caribbean community and the Dominican climate she knew as a child. Anna's fire strategy to define herself by her remembered Caribbean sensations is materially and historically positioned in the psycho-geography of her childhood climate, which proves almost fatally irreconcilable with the cold patriarchal, consumerist and exploitative rationalism of England. The pillow on which she lies, on her first meeting with Walter Jeffries, "is as cold as ice"; it offers Anna, through her impending life from bed to bed in a life of sexual commodification, no substitute warmth, no physical connection with her Dominican sensuality.[31]

There is also confluence between Bowen's and Rhys's intimation of the anti-colonial destructive capacity of fire when one considers the climactic end of part four of *Voyage in the Dark*. In her swirling, anaesthetized state of befuddlement as Anna succumbs to unconsciousness during a spontaneous abortion, the text fragments into a cacophonous dialogic synchronicity: of overheard disembodied voices, of Anna's own queasy and repeated cry of giddiness, and of her narrated analeptic childhood recollection of a masquerade enacted by the local Afro-Dominican community outside the Costerus estate. Writing about the evolution of Carnival in Trinidad, Bridget Brereton asserts that "sometime between 1939 and 1945, old oil drums were made into musical instruments . . . steelbands hit the city streets, and Trinidad and Tobago – and the world – had a whole new kind of music".[32]

However, if we consider *Voyage in the Dark* for its intertextual relevance in contributing to historical documentary readings of Caribbean society and culture, we can see that, as far back as the 1890s, Dominican carnival is represented as having adopted the tin drum as part of its musical instrumentation. More important, we might read a radically subversive and incendiary symbolism behind the Afro-Dominicans' choice of instrument: "banging the kerosene-tins".[33] These tins, struck in an implicitly menacing carnival where Afro-Dominicans use the semiotics of hybridity to mimic and mock in masks their white masters, are indexical signifiers of the explosive material they conventionally contain; as they are struck they are figuratively ignited around the perimeter of the Costerus estate.[34] Further support for the symbolic potential of this ritual is evidenced by Brereton's observation about Trinidadian carnival and the street procession known as *canboulay* (a creolization of the term *cannes brûlées*, translated as "burnt cane"). Crown authorities were so nervous about the parade of lighted torches through the streets of Port of Spain – and its implications for inflammatory revolution and the torching of colonial properties – that the practice was banned, albeit "not without a riot".[35] The banging of kerosene tins by Afro-Dominicans wearing white masks to taunt their oppressors inevitably reflects Rhys's own experiences – and, by extension, historical experiences of anti-colonial resistance in Dominica – of two attacks upon her maternal antecedents' Geneva estate in Grand Bay, in 1844 and 1930.

While fire symbolizes warmth, it also invokes destruction of colonial lands, the latter joining Rhys's novel with Bowen's. And as with Bowen's Lois Farquar, who subtly identifies with the fire of republican revolt, Rhys's child Anna Morgan remains fascinated, peering from a window of the Costerus estate at the masquerade and enchanted by the implication of the masked revellers that she is, ancestrally, the creolized "Brown Girl in the Ring". She understands instinctively "why the masks were laughing" at their satirized colonial target, and identifies with not only the seditious power of the spectacle but also the inner feelings of the people behind the masks, people who appear white to outsiders but who harbour anti-colonial anger and opposition to the doctrine of white colonial control from within, quick to identify with the flame of inflammatory rebellion as a destructive expression of the revolutionary will to freedom from imperial control.[36]

History, therefore, decides the contrastive manner in which apparently confluent narrative articulations of settler/colonial malaise in early Ireland and in Dominica write in a nuanced, specifically positioned course towards the metropolitan and dominant discourse. Their differences confirm the heterogenization and incorrigible plurality of colonial discourses of identity, community and relationship with the colonial centre. However, their very nuances do not confirm cultural difference between variations of lived Anglo-Irish or colonial Caribbean settler experience. They demonstrate rather how the historical, socioeconomic, environmental and even meteorological processes which have shaped colonialism in Ireland and the Caribbean produce variations on similar narrative forms and themes that decolonize authoritative discourses on English expansionist identity in the colonies.

A reading of parallel narrative and thematic features in the novels leads to the following conclusion. The protagonists Lois Farquar and Anna Morgan are young, plantocratic but bohemian girls from a society and hegemony that is profoundly anxious about its declining role in the land over which it has for generations presided as the landowning elite. They emerge from planter/settler communities that are fraught in regard to their relationships with the imperial centre of England and its people, who in the latter stages of colonial power have recently arrived in their respective islands. They struggle to classify their own identities in relation to their caste and the English imperial society of which they are historically, and putatively, an expansionist limb. Their unconscious desires erupt through similar narrative applications of the trope of fire, to suggest their repressed but uncontrollable identification with the Other of their colonized peoples. Bowen's and Rhys's texts are most demonstrative in understanding comparatively how the Irish novel in English best represents, in its generic form and extended prose length, the historical contexts, narrative forms and themes of collapse of colonial rule, identity and a sense of future purpose in planter/settler Anglo-Ireland and Dominica.

Notes

1. Michael McConville, *Ascendancy to Oblivion: The Story of the Anglo-Irish* (London: Quartet, 1986).
2. Peter Cottrell, *The Anglo-Irish War: The Troubles of 1913–1922* (Oxford: Osprey), 2006.
3. McConville, *Ascendancy*, 249.
4. Hermione Lee, "Introduction", in Elizabeth Bowen, *Bowen's Court & Seven Winters* (London: Vintage, 1999), x.
5. Peter Hulme, "Islands and Roads: Hesketh Bell, Jean Rhys and Dominica's Imperial Road", *Jean Rhys Review* 11, no. 2 (2000): 23–51. Further references are given in the text.

6. Lennox Honychurch, *The Dominica Story: A History of the Island* (Roseau: Dominica Institute, 1975), 9.

7. Veronica Marie Gregg, *Jean Rhys's Historical Imagination: Reading and Writing the Creole* (Chapel Hill: University of North Carolina Press, 1995).

8. Helen Carr, *Jean Rhys* (London: Northcote House, 1996).

9. Seymour Chatman, *Story and Discourse* (Ithaca, NY: Cornell University Press, 1980).

10. Elizabeth Bowen, *The Last September* (1929; reprint, London: Vintage, 1998), 19.

11. Ibid., 17.

12. Jean Rhys, *Voyage in the Dark* (1934; reprint, Harmondsworth, UK: Penguin, 2000), 53.

13. Bowen, *Last September*, 23.

14. Ibid., 58.

15. Ibid., 193

16. Ibid., 46.

17. Rhys, *Voyage*, 55.

18. Ibid., 53.

19. Ibid., 54

20. Ibid., 56.

21. Aijaz Ahmad, *In Theory: Nations, Classes, Literatures* (London: Verso, 1992).

22. John Dorney, "The Big House and the Irish Revolution", The Irish Story [website], http://www.theirishstory.com/2011/06/21/the-big-house-and-the-irish-revolution/, accessed 7 July 2011.

23. Bowen, *Last September*, 44.

24. McConville, *Ascendancy*, 249.

25. Bowen, *Last September*, 99.

26. Ibid., 98.

27. Dorrit Cohn, *Transparent Minds: Narrative Modes for Presenting Consciousness in Fiction* (Princeton, NJ: Princeton University Press, 1983).

28. Bowen, *Last September*, 36.

29. Rhys, *Voyage*, 7.

30. Ibid., 127.

31. Ibid., 21.

32. Bridget Brereton, *An Introduction to the History of Trinidad and Tobago* (Harlow, UK: Heinemann, 1996), 90.

33. Rhys, *Voyage*, 157.

34. Homi K. Bhabha, "Cultural Diversity and Cultural Differences", *The Post-Colonial Studies Reader*, ed. Bill Ashcroft, Gareth Griffiths and Helen Tiffin (London: Routledge, 2006), 155–57.

35. Brereton, *History of Trinidad and Tobago*, 89.

36. Rhys, *Voyage*, 156–57.

Chapter 16

Mutual Obsessions

Walcott, Beckett and Brathwaite

JEAN ANTOINE-DUNNE

IN AN INTERVIEW IN IRELAND IN 1991, Derek Walcott made the following observation when asked how he saw his work in relation to Irish writers such as Samuel Beckett. He noted that Beckett's writing was "still baroque" and that his use of the O as in the mouth of *Not I* resonated with the pessimism that still pervaded European writing. In the Caribbean, however, according to Walcott, the O is an O of exuberance rather than finitude.[1] Walcott's focus on that O contains certain distinct ideas. In the first instance, the O is an exclamation that emerges from shock or awe. It also represents a space that surrounds the utterance and, by the force of this containment, causes a resonating echo. The O is then potentially representative of both joy and the extreme despair or shock that causes pain and sadness, but it is also the sign of an enclosure that forces reverberations to echo within the psyche of an individual. It is by its very inscription a sign of contradictory imagining.

The cavern or constricted space that is so often an image in the work of writers such as Beckett, Walcott and Brathwaite suggests that to be born into a place where history is a constraining presence, and where the land itself speaks of a relationship of servitude, is to be born with a desire for somewhere else. For Walcott, Port of Spain is "A silent city, blest with emptiness / like an engraving".[2] His work becomes increasingly fraught with contradiction, tinged with residues of colonial upbringing and equally with the necessity for new ways of seeing. The trope of journeying facilitates the figuration of layers of constriction while beckoning to limitless possibilities. Many Irish and Caribbean writers thus view themselves as inevitable travellers. This chapter seeks the reasons for shared and recurring images and ideas in the work of two Caribbean writers, Walcott and Brathwaite, and the Irishman Beckett.

Beckett attaches himself to a long tradition of storytelling and commentary in his appropriation of the lonesome figure of the bard as incarnated in the figure of the tramp. The tramp also pervades Walcott's writing, where he increasingly transmutes into the wanderer, best epitomized perhaps in the trope of the prodigal. But Walcott's use of the wanderer is also attributable to the *omowale* of Kamau Brathwaite's *The Arrivants: A New World Trilogy* and to his interest in oral performance.[3] In "The Muse of History", Walcott notes the universal continuities in oral traditions.[4] The adherence to a bardic tradition, whether of the *seanachie* (a wandering poet who told stories and thus maintained the history of his people) or, in the case of Walcott, the calypsonian or griot, allows each poet and writer to access the ineffable.

Interestingly, Beckett, Walcott and Brathwaite are also equally occupied with a sense of history as simultaneity. In Beckett's works the timelessness of recurring phenomena and the trauma of relationships are evoked in the minimal image or shape of the utterance of pure pain and in the visceral effect on the body of the listener, for example, in the isolated moving mouth and lips of *Not I* on stage. Walcott speaks of the simultaneity of great art, and for him there are "simultaneous concepts, not chronological concepts. . . . If you think of art merely in terms of chronology, you are going to be patronizing to certain cultures."[5] One might then suggest that Walcott, Beckett and Brathwaite respond to similar – if culturally and historically different – experiences, and that as great artists their intuitions go beyond historical or chronological logic into a realm of shared human responses.

There is an analogous concern with form in the work of these three writers, born of an intuition that human communication is in essence deeply flawed. In each instance the writer moves towards modes of communication derived not from words but from a distillation of belief in an unworldly and spiritual domain that finds space and time of little relevance. Ghosts from Walcott's past hover in Italy, and the resident dead emit their screams as he hovers over the Alps.[6] In *Omeros*, Achille hears the leaves "talk a dead language"[7] and "Stone-faced souls" peer "through the pomme-Arac tree"[8] as the dead and decimated defy time and space to make their presence felt in the contemporary world. Brathwaite in the *X/Self* of *Ancestors* points to narratives that ensure power over the deluded as he sees Rome echoed in the Caribbean, in Julia, who is "caesars young mulatto sister" and also a drug-addicted television star.[9]

For Beckett the artist "can't go on" yet "must go on"[10] despite the "incoercible absence of relation"[11] between self and other, and despite the failure of art. This perceived gap in communication is more than a reprise of modernist angst. It is evidence of a contradictory truth that there is an inner reality that cannot be expressed but that nonetheless demands a constant will to express. His struggle with language and art is to free language from its enthralment in time and give it a fluidity that leads ultimately to an idea of God or "Worm"[12] or Mahood. This desire and this failure lead to unfathomable works such as *Quad*, where the movement to and fro shapes a complex of linear movements that, as Deleuze has read them, suggest the exhaustion of human possibility.[13] For Beckett there are too many voices, too much repetition, too many competing experiences in time and in the fixated memory of any individual. The most cogent example of such tyranny is in his late play *That Time*, in which the flow of words emerges as individual acts of remembering in three voices, each of which emanates from the one self but all of which are locked in specific images of the past.[14] Words become incapable of representing the tyranny of the past and the competing influences of that past on the present. Form, as in *Not I*, then becomes the vehicle through which the impact of that past is felt on the psyche. In *Murphy* Beckett had experimented with a form of distortion as a way of disrupting the power of words and images in their creation of stereotypes.[15] His manoeuvres in this and *Three Novels* include bawdy swipes at sexual repression, censorship, religious conformity, habits of worship (the Catholic Mass), pub-crawling and the reification of the peasant and the folk. By creating distorted figures who combine several of the stereotyped notions of what it is to be Irish, Beckett locates the self within a confining frame that has been created by the historical experiences of a specific place and a particular people. Beckett's personal quest for non-being or the core of being becomes ultimately a search for silence and the end of it all: habit, history, perceiving of the other, enthralment by the other.

For writers such as Walcott and Brathwaite, for whom the pressure of history on the body, mind and psyche of the New World individual is felt in language, to be rid of it all becomes in a very real sense the duty of the writer, as vocalizer and as representative of a people weighed down by the past. Beckett is relevant to our interpretation and understanding of Caribbean writing because his works are in search of a self that is beyond history and the construction of others. His work is also, nonetheless, emphatically about the impact of history on the body, so that to be true to oneself as a writer is to realize the shaping of the past as a concrete presence and to move beyond it to a personal freedom. What is interesting is that Beckett, Walcott and Brathwaite all arrive at similar points in their creative confrontations with their pasts.

Beckett's *The Unnamable* points us towards the Caribbean at a most crucial stage in the text. One can thus argue that from his earliest writings Beckett sensed a communion of ideas and shared experiences: "I'm Worm, that is to say I am no longer he, since I hear. But I'll forget that in the heat of misery, I'll forget that I am no longer Worm, but a kind of tenth-rate Toussaint L'Ouverture, that's what they're counting on. Worm then I catch this sound that will never stop, monotonous beyond words and yet not altogether devoid of a certain variety."[16] It is no coincidence that Beckett should reference the leader of the 1791 Haitian revolt, in particular in a novel written in French. Beckett was a close friend of Nancy Cunard, who compiled the massive *Negro* anthology in 1933.[17] Moreover, he translated the work of André Breton, a friend of Aimé Césaire, and other French surrealists for Cunard and Titus.

The inclusion of the francophone rebel Toussaint suggests an abiding admiration and connection with the French Antilles and with the cause of black rights. Toussaint further elaborates and intensifies the themes of isolation and resistance and is an eternal symbol of possible victory of the enslaved over their masters. For Beckett, a decorated Resistance fighter of the Second World War, Toussaint seems to represent a stage in the process towards selfhood outside the narratives of history. Toussaint also represents the value of failure, something Beckett made iconic in his own work. Beckett's novel *Murphy* was famously rejected forty-seven times before it was finally published, and after the failure of the 1956 Miami production of *Waiting for Godot* he wrote to Alan Schneider: "Success and failure on the public level never mattered much to me, in fact I feel much more at home with the latter, having breathed deep of its vivifying air all my writing life up to the last couple of years."[18] Failure is in fact the key determining idea of much of his work, both in terms of the thematic content and in his use of stylistic patterning which causes the reader to forget rather than remember, since the language constantly seems to go around or back on itself.

Further, Toussaint's imprisonment speaks metaphorically to Beckett's own sense that the presence of others is a form of imprisonment. Words and the constant pressure of words become increasingly aligned to the idea that the perception of others, their relentless presence and insistence on speaking, is a form of un-freedom. In *Play*, bodies are incarcerated in urns and voice their versions of the same reality without recourse to the perceptions of the other. They are doubly imprisoned, for despite their solipsism, their need chains them to the other protagonists even beyond death, hence the repeated refrain "Am I as much as . . . being seen?"[19]

As a way of exhuming historic vestiges, the works of Brathwaite, Beckett and Walcott demonstrate an increasing tendency to use language as a kind of invocation and incantation to summon the dead. The incantatory rhythms of Brathwaite's *Born to Slow Horses* and his use of Sycorax text formatting in this work parallels, though it does not mimic, the graphing and contouring elements of Beckett's work.[20] These writers share a desire to grapple with the dead or the unknowable through their struggles with the shape of language. Brathwaite's inventive use of fonts and video techniques simulates sound as a carrier of historic resonance and attempts to create a physical impact in its visual patterning. This acts in concord with his constant revisions of earlier works, when the original seems to burgeon into a newer version and the older texts become vehicles to a past that the writer summons into being, as he also invokes his wife, Doris (renamed "Zea Mexican"), in *Dreamstories* and *Elegguas*.[21] The later Brathwaite is no longer simply concerned with history as something to react against, or with the creation of counter-narratives or language in opposition to an imperial culture, but rather with a web of connections which he as a Caribbean writer must make visible as concrete enactments on the body and mind of the present.

Declan Kiberd's *Inventing Ireland* suggests a Caribbean–Irish interface relevant to this argument. Kiberd argues that Irish writers "anticipated" the writings of theorists and writers such as Frantz Fanon, Aimé Césaire, George Lamming and C.L.R. James. The Caribbean as a theoretical framework and the writings that emanate from it hold up the arguments of *Inventing Ireland*. However, disappointingly, the end result is that the Caribbean is perceived not so much as a place of original thought but as a place where ideas already established in nucleus form by Irish writers develop into specific and intoxicating theories.

For Kiberd, C.L.R. James is first and foremost a figure who deconstructs English writing, and in his use of the figure of Caliban – also effectively deployed by George Lamming – demonstrates that "*outsiders* had always been the decisive agents in history and holders of the keys to their changing worlds", since they were on the edge of things and saw far more clearly "what man as a creature truly is".[22] For Kiberd, James is the theorist who can outplay the conqueror in subtle ways. Kiberd links James's overturning of the traps of language to Beckett's own awareness of "the language of the enemy" that "comes freighted with historic meaning".[23] He quotes Beckett's "I use the words you taught me. If they don't mean anything any more, teach me others. Or let me be silent"[24] to argue that for Beckett, ridding oneself of language becomes the path to uncovering the "dark side as the 'commanding side of [his] personality' ".[25] *The Irish Writer and the World* claims that oppositional movements failed to recognize that "[t]o invert, rather than abolish, colonial hierarchies would never be enough: . . . The corresponding identity, whether calling itself *Négritude* or *Irishness*, would simply remain a label *to have* rather than a way *to be*."[26] He argues that Beckett is the quintessential Irish writer, since his works go beyond the rhetoric of certain postcolonial thinkers and the reproduction of cycles of dominance and servitude. The trope of national essence was replaced by the need for "expressing the individual" and the search for what Soyinka, quoted in Kiberd, called "the essence of himself".[27]

Kiberd's argument and his use of Caribbean theorists point to shared obsessions and images in the works of certain Caribbean and Irish writers. Beckett's experiments in freeing words from layers of experience, intimacy, gender constructions and history parallel experiments by Caribbean writers who seek to renounce the thing that cannot be spoken with words that are too full of the meanings and perceptions of others. To this end the cavern as a vehicle of inner resonance becomes a key motif in Beckett's work: "But now he knows these hills, that is to say he knows them better, and if ever again he sees them from afar it will be I think with other eyes, and not only that but the within, all that inner space one never sees, the brain and heart and other caverns where thought and feeling dance their Sabbath, all that too quite differently disposed."[28]

This is similar to Walcott's image at the start of *The Prodigal,* of the tunnel through which the past echoes and which through associational logic leads ultimately to a beckoning to spectres that inhabit other enclosed spaces. The poem develops an image of a tunnel linked to an idea of seeing or myopia. The whites of America see only the colour of a black man's skin and construct their "idea of America" through "the tunnel's skin".[29] This tunnel vision moves to a connection with travelling that recalls Brathwaite's lonely travelling exiles of *Rights of Passage*[30] in the reiteration of ideas and images such as "gripped face" and the man who "contains many absences".[31] Travel exposes an internalized sense of inferiority to other places, especially Europe, and references images of beauty and imagination linked to Western mythologies such as "The Ice

Maiden", whose apotheosis is rendered complete in the image of a woman on a train whose racist attitude is shrouded beneath an exterior of calm and gentle beauty.[32] Ideas and images of beauty and superiority that reside in the poetic imaginary therefore also constitute a kind of "tunnel vision" from which the poet must escape. Movement in space, across continents, becomes a way of uncovering the layers of narratives and imported and untrue myths that have led to the poet's myopic vision. The past as encircling lines that lock in an individual psyche becomes the cavern or psychic terrain within which echoes reverberate, as ghosts that haunt the imaginary of both old and new worlds:

> I saw the walled city early in the morning
> with its sprinkled streets; under the arcades
> the beggars slept, unshifting as History.
> There was the city, then there was the magical
> echo of the city's name and the same sulphurous
> mirage of its double created by history,
> by the shade of the rusting almonds, by the galvanized sea
> whose ruts were left by the galleons, Cartagena
> and the ghost of Cartagena . . .[33]

In Beckett's plays and prose pieces one can also discern the importance of a silence that reverberates, similar to the many silences in *Omeros* which seem to suggest that the void into which the writer looks, whether sea or death, is never the end but a possibility. This possibility echoes not in space but in the mind and psyche of the writer. Beckett's novella *Imagination Dead Imagine* foregrounds the importance of vibration and relates it to fluctuating light and dark, both as systems of projection on the body of the victim (the protagonist) and as a mechanism for transmitting sense or emotion.[34] Walcott's writing also courts echoes and resonances. Their works seek, through the use of visual motifs, music and discordant sounds and movement, to harness these reverberations and get beneath the surface of words. Beckett attempts to disintegrate the object through the play of light – which is another form of vibration – as in *A Piece of Monologue*. Each object takes on an identity and each part of the body becomes a separate, sensuous fact of existence but not of certainty of being. The disintegration or fracturing of the body[35] works in accord with the fragmentation of each concrete object through the play of light:

> There in the dark that window. Night slowly falling. Eyes to the small pane gaze at
> that first night. Turn from it in the end to face the darkened room. There in the end

slowly a faint hand. Holding aloft a lighted spill. In the light of spill faintly the hand and milk white globe. Then second hand. In light of spill. Takes off globe and disappears. Reappears empty. Takes off chimney. Two hands and chimney in light of spill. ... Fade. Birth the death of him.[36]

A *Piece of Monologue* describes the flickering of perception and the occasional, if relentless, illuminations of the external world in a mind always faced by death and unknowing. Language becomes more than words and avails the representational potential of light, dark, colour, play, where every facet of the work is made a vehicle of possible projection. What Brathwaite and Walcott share with Beckett is the desire to make language a graph of the artistic pursuit of self-expression, and equally to engage with aesthetic mechanisms that allow illumination of the pressure of the past on the human psyche.

In Brathwaite's early work, the quarrel with history first takes the shape of a particular use of language and form in which folktales, myths and very existence at the edge of despair, as in "Dust" (1962), make words and sound and music living testimony to the vital lives of those who have been marginalized. In his *History of the Voice* he theorizes the need for a new language system to evoke the ways in which both land and past have uniquely shaped the stories and sound systems of the Caribbean and the Americas. The hurricane, he says, "does not roar in pentameters".[37] His work later begins to fret with words and even with sound as being inadequate for the task of poetry, so he shapes a poetic which has its antecedents in George Herbert and certain African American poets but most specifically is influenced by contemporary media practices in its use of the principle of montage – interesting since both Beckett and Walcott also use montage concepts to fashion their work.[38] Beckett's use of light, for example, is based on Eisenstein's theory of the mutual impact of sound and light vibration in the projection of a film.[39] His use of distortion is even more closely affiliated to the use of the close-up, which fragments and focuses on part of an object for psychological effect in the creation of a montage ensemble and in the development of a tendentious line. All three writers reference the idea that film montage creates an impact on the body that bypasses cerebral thought, through what Sergei Eisenstein, drawing on kabuki, called a monistic ensemble.[40] *Omeros* deploys the senses as a way of intensifying the affective response of the body of the reader. Seven Seas, the blind fisherman, sees "with his ears" and moves "by a sixth sense".[41] The poem embraces a theory of audiovisual affect in its constant refusal of any one sense and in its valorization of this sixth sense.

Brathwaite, having explored sound systems as in *Islands*, in which jazz can form the structuring principle as well as the central image, and reggae, calypso and the drum shape the thematic content of the poems, moves beyond this towards appropriation of a montage sensibility. Here the conflict of sound, line and silence becomes a mechanism for enabling a clash of memory and myth.

.

sing

.

clink of the chains
and the dungeon of

drums

drink
dark

damp.
ness

sing[42]

The spaces in between the individual words represent the silences of the Middle Passage, while the repetition of *d* shapes the sound and rhythm of the drum. But there is a difference, in that now the font creates a demonstrable change of tone through its visual impact. The "lines" too are conflictual: they shape a dissonance similar to the movement of oppositional lines in a montage sequence. Brathwaite appears to be haunted by words, not only because words recur and resurrect in successive poems but also because they evoke a haunting presence at the interstices or gaps, as if the dead are forever behind them. His development of a depleted language, rendered subservient to shape and the visual, seeks to escape from words and to call the dead in a manner similar to (though not indebted to) Beckett, who writes in *The Unnamable*: "I'm in words, made of words, others' words, what others, the place too, the air, the walls, the floor, the ceiling, all words, the whole world is here with me, I'm the air, the walls, the walled-in one, everything yields, opens, ebbs, flows . . .".[43] For Brathwaite, silence breeds ghosts.

is when the bamboo from its clip of yellow groan and wrestle
begins to glow
and the wind learns the shape of its fire

and my fingers following the termites drill
find their hollows
of silence. shatters of echoes of tone .

that my eyes close
all along the wall . all along the branches . all along the world
and that that creak of spirits walking these graves of sunlight

spiders over the water. cobwebs crawling in whispers[44]

Here Brathwaite courts the echoes of multiple histories "all along the world", in search of a lost time in his regret and remorse as he contemplates yet again the death of his wife. Titled "fflute (s)", this poem is a meditation on the past as it enters language, but that language in its sounds issues from the very body of the poet – he plays on it as if it were an instrument. The body becomes a hollow space through which painful remembrance is given expression, replicating the impact of events of a distant past on the mind, soul and physical being of the poet. "Spiders" suggests an African vestige, also recalled in "the shape of its fire", reminiscent of the making of the drum in *Masks*. The body, hollowed out by suffering, is forced into a rhythm that mimics both the suffering of the enslaved, whose memory of an ancestral past is a faint echo, and the trauma of a more recent death. The movement here recalls that of the traveller-poet, whose traversing of the land enables him to speak its history and chronicle the layers of that history. He seems to ask whether as a poet he can articulate an idea of freedom – personal and communal — and answers without pause, again repeating a technique from *The Arrivants*, that this is only the beginning of possibility. The "it" repeated at the start of four verses creates a stutter that is a movement to birth or an emerging idea that has not yet found fruition:

it is the gurgle pigeon dream the ground dove coo
it is the sun approaching midday listening its splendour
                    it is your voice alight with echo

w/the birth of sound.[45]

The echo then proves to be a point of entry into the psyche and a site of both recollection and freedom. To be is to court the past in faint tremors that exist as ghosts, and these spirits must find a space for utterance. But these ghostly presences are also part of a history that threatens to imprison the mind and that reside in the land as memories of uneven relationships and servitude. This pervasive sense of presence is part of the inheritance of African-based religions and belief systems. Interestingly, in works such as Walcott's "The Loupgarou", a draft for a film,[46] and in *Omeros* these presences take centre stage. Caribbean and Irish writers seem to be haunted by the past, a fact that Walcott foregrounds in his epic poem *Omeros* and in so doing conjoins the land, ancestral beliefs and his vision in images of La Sorcière, the mountain and Ma Kilman, the healer.

In *Omeros* Walcott asks: "Who will teach us a history of which we too are capable?"[47] He then initiates a process of examining similarities and differences between the Caribbean and Ireland as he explores the Irish obsession with history as a way of exploring the Caribbean's sense of historylessness. This becomes a demonstration of the value of such remembering and the trauma that a failure to forget can bring and ultimately the idea that the past is always existent in the present. Irish recollection and Ireland's inability to let go of the past have led to wars of attrition: brother against brother in civil strife. The question of the self or the true *is* of being is therefore not to be answered by simply excavating the past or following its echoes; courting memory is no sure way to find peace or sense of self. *Omeros*, as a question posed and then answered, pivots around this search for the true *is* of being that is the *is* of the Antilles. This poem expresses the truth that too much history and too much remembering are a curse, as in the often quoted "The Muse of History", in which history is seen as a "medusa".[48] Both Walcott and Beckett have a profound intuition that if one could only jettison the past then life could in fact begin anew, but both see history as a tunnel which poet and thinker must deliberately enter and traverse before arriving at something different, that is, the idea of self.

Walcott's contemplation of Ireland leads to a meditation on the many silences that are also part of Irish history. These silences as gaps are both positive and negative. As a memory of a deep and sustaining faith, silence is "in flower", but this faith generates doubt in the poet and is also a sign of division caused by that very adherence to dogma and to history:

> . . . but which faith, in a nation
> split by a glottal scream, by a sparrow's chirrup,
>
> where a prayer incised in a cross, a Celtic rune
> could send the horse circling with empty stirrup
> from a sniper's bolt?[49]

The echoes of history or the "weight of the place"[50] that Walcott finds in Ireland are different from the silence at the water's edge in *Omeros*, where a space opens up and Helen has a vision shaped by multiple histories. But both suggest that history is a series of fictions or a way of seeing the past from a particular psychological or ideological perspective. Ireland for Walcott is a place to be reverenced not because its writers have been part of his unending list of influences, but because he sees similarities that are startling and lead to a leap of recognition, and also differences that must be accounted for and that he must understand. It is history, its effects and its echoes, which gives Walcott pause.

There are many similarities in aesthetic responses to the past in the work of these writers. However, while Beckett's project has been to fictionalize the human as a series of caricatures shaped over time by habit and internalized ideas, Walcott's solution has been to show that history itself is a mirage or hallucination born of the hauntings of the past, but amenable to myth making. In *Omeros* echoes emanate from the spaces between different cultures and times,[51] and these generate multiple and overlapping effects that he then uses to shape a visionary poetry. Helen's refusal to take "shit / from white people"[52] triggers successive memories of shipwreck, migration, the destruction of a city, of those who come by ship so that "a beach burns their memory";[53] but here, as in the 1965 essay "The Figure of Crusoe",[54] the detritus of the past is burned and transformed into a creative and renewing process. The echoes that exist at the interstices between several superimposed worlds link, through their burgeoning meaning, to the idea that the perceived silence of New World history and its peoples – whose tongues are silenced like the conch shell – is not loss but a reverberating presence. This is already signalled at the start of the poem, in the secret that Philocte does not tell to the tourist but pours down the mountain, the waterfall and the echoing brooks, down to the sea.[55] It is also made manifest in the figure of the silent woodsman.

The woodsman is oddly positioned between the narratives of Maud and Plunkett, two resident expatriates (one an Irishwoman, the other a figure representing Walcott's own father's European lineage) whose narratives form part of the polyphonic weave of *Omeros*. Maud and Plunkett are strangely ambivalent about the island, its dialect and its beauty. The woodsman's appearance and its situation within the text act as a rebuke to Plunkett, who rationalizes his need to write a history of St Lucia to give it complexity and significance. He suggests that the reality of native life is as "flat" as a postcard because of the residues of a "swinish" empire.[56] However, the secret knowledge in the signs from Africa that the silent old woodsman makes qualifies and indeed renders superfluous

Plunkett's desire to write this history. The signs become part of that movement of echoing silence which engages the idea that multiple histories, narratives, lives and ghosts inhabit the silent spaces of the Antilles. The actual meaning of the poem *Omeros* emerges from burgeoning echoes, or the space between two lines and the conflict between two movements, all of which evoke a zero, a nothing that is everything. The ghost of Walcott's father says: "O Thou, my Zero, is an impossible prayer, / utter extinction is still a doubtful conceit. / Though we pray to nothing, nothing cannot be there."[57] That silence and that zero issue in echoes that shape the pattern of Walcott's poetry. Rhythm as the movement between sound and silence beckons not to a simple formula but to the idea that poetry must assume "the shape of that hurt".

These three writers, coming from quite different traditions and backgrounds, have all recognized the need to find a poetic system to approximate the conflicting experiences and residues of history. Walcott's sense of entrapment evolves into the concept that courting the echoes of an oppressive past, as opposed to being locked into that past, generates a leap to new understandings and ways of seeing. The wound carries the cure; the swift brings the seed from Africa, then becomes "bleached bone" which after "all that motion" becomes "a pile of fragile ash" that "grew its own wings", from which emerged the ants, "the ancestors of Achille, / the women carrying coals after the dark door / slid over the hold".[58] This is further transformed in the antithetical movement of *The Prodigal*, where the "flare of the flame tree" and the clattering parrots appear as "small wild souls returning" and suggest a transformative process:

> Flare of the flame tree and white egrets stalking.
> Small bridge, brown trace, the new fire station.
> And the clatter of parrots at sunrise
> and at dusk their small wild souls returning
> to the darkening trees, . . .[59]

In other words, the summoning of echoes, through an aperture similar to Beckett's many tunnels and caverns, bids resurrection and transfiguration of the dead. The actual compression of time and space evokes an image of the past, but equally an image of future possibility.

As Caribbean writers, Walcott and Brathwaite have sought an image that is both concrete and abstract in their quest for a material and spiritual reality. Their ideologies and emphases are, however, different. Walcott courts correspondences and moves between Europe, America and the Caribbean with an ease inflected only by a sense of self-induced betrayal. He remains committed, in his recent play *O Starry Starry Night*,[60] to drawing correspondences between his vocation and that of Western artists such as Gauguin and Van Gogh. But his work remains rooted in a tradition of textuality, despite his many incursions into film, painting, sound systems and silence. Brathwaite, however, not unlike Beckett, increasingly dismantles language and the very form of writing. His Afrocentricity has led to movement into a labyrinth of spirit and even spirit possession. For Brathwaite, language is a vehicle for entering the realm of spirits and the dead. For Walcott, it is an act of "exorcism"[61] and of evocation that summons an image of a "simply decent race".[62]

Beckett, because he is an Irish writer, comes with a certain knowledge and inheritance of ideas and processes which he has acknowledged in the often quoted line that he would "give the whole unupsettable applecart for a sup of the Hawk's Well or the Saints', or a whiff of Juno, to go no further".[63] In citing Yeats, Synge and O'Casey, he situates himself in a tradition of Irish writing and drama. But while his work retains many features of what has become a signature of the Celtic Revival – its belief in another life and in its own mythologies – hovering over it all is a veneration of the dead, not unlike the sense of the dead that one finds in the Caribbean, where those ancestral presences interact and communicate with the living in everyday existence. This may be the legacy that Yeats bequeaths to Beckett in plays such as *Purgatory* and *The Words upon the Window-Pane*,[64] in which the dead infiltrate and have a greater presence than the living in a profound courting of spirits.[65] But then that foregrounds a further possibility: that what Yeats, Beckett, Brathwaite and Walcott share is a desire to communicate with the dead. In a real sense they see spirits. These spirits are present as potent forces laboriously unearthed and made visible because of the very scepticism of these writers and their quarrels with history.

The prose piece "Ill Seen Ill Said", no matter from what perspective one looks at it, is a ghost story, in which the author attempts to transmit the ephemeral presence of a woman wrapped up in her past and her memories:

> Yes within her walls so far at the window only. At one or the other window. Rapt before the sky. And only half seen so far a pallet and a ghostly chair. Ill half seen. And how in her faint comings and goings she suddenly stops dead. And how hard set to rise up from off her knees. But there too little by little she begins to appear more plain. Within her walls. As well as other objects.[66]

The idea of a life or being beyond the material world conjures a determined process of self-excavation. The blank spaces of history become filled by presences. But this is no romantic escapism.

Irish writing and Caribbean writing come to resemble each other not because Walcott and Brathwaite are mimics and write with a great debt to Europe and Ireland, but because as Caribbean poets they walk on the threshold of another world in a manner similar to writers such as W.B. Yeats and Beckett. The difficulty in this statement is that it suggests mysticism, occultism and the stereotypes generated by those who constructed the colonies as impractical and thus in need of governance. Perhaps the difference may be conjured as a double vision which sees beyond the windowpane and into a glass darkly, but also with an ironic and often sardonic perception of what being Irish or Caribbean means in the context of a world dominated by layers of historic narrative. All three writers, Brathwaite, Walcott and Beckett, are concerned with peeling away the self from such accretions while recognizing the impact of these many narratives and voices. That their works echo each other is a fact not of influence but of recognition. Beckett and, to an extent, Walcott create systems whereby laughter can be directed at the self even as they pursue their own vital being. One finds little laughter in Brathwaite but rather a continuing process of self-scrutiny and determined self-criticism – even pessimism. All seek to peer beneath and beyond the surface of everyday reality to uncover the truth of their own existence.

Notes

1. "Derek Walcott in Conversation with Jean Antoine", *Poetry Ireland Review* 34 (Spring 1992): 72–85.
2. Derek Walcott, *Tiepolo's Hound* (New York: Farrar, Straus and Giroux, 2000), 5.
3. Edward Kamau Brathwaite, *The Arrivants: A New World Trilogy* (Oxford: Oxford University Press, 1973). See Gordon Rohlehr's explication in *Black Awakening in The Arrivants of Edward Kamau Brathwaite* (Port of Spain: Rohlehr, 1981).
4. Derek Walcott, "The Muse of History", in *What the Twilight Says: Essays* (New York: Farrar, Straus and Giroux, 1998), 47.
5. Derek Walcott, "Reflections on *Omeros*", *South Atlantic Quarterly* 96, no. 2 (1997): 240–41.
6. Derek Walcott, *The Prodigal* (New York: Farrar, Straus and Giroux, 2004).
7. Derek Walcott, *Omeros* (London: Faber and Faber, 1990), 162.

8.   Ibid., 164.

9.   Edward Kamau Brathwaite, "Julia", in *Ancestors: A Reinvention of Mother Poem, Sun Poem, and X/Self* (1977; reprint, New York: New Directions, 2001), 400–403.

10. Samuel Beckett, *Three Novels: Molloy, Malone Dies, The Unnamable* (1951, 1953; reprint, New York: Grove Press, 1991), 414.

11. Samuel Beckett, *Proust and Three Dialogues with George Duthuit* (London: John Calder, 1965), 125.

12. Beckett, *The Unnamable,* in *Three Novels,* 347–49.

13. Gilles Deleuze, *The Exhausted,* trans. Anthony Uhlmann, *SubStance* 24, no. 3, issue 78 (1995), 3–28, http://www.jstor.org/stable/3685005.

14. Samuel Beckett, *That Time,* in *The Complete Dramatic Works* (London: Faber and Faber, 1990), 385–95.

15. Samuel Beckett, *Murphy* (1938; reprint, London: Picador Pan, 1973).

16. Beckett, *The Unnamable,* 343.

17. See James Knowlson, *Damned to Fame* (London: Bloomsbury, 1996), 137, 168.

18. Maurice Harmon, ed., *The Correspondence of Samuel Beckett and Alan Schneider* (Cambridge, MA: Harvard University Press, 1998), 9.

19. Beckett, *Play,* in *Complete Dramatic Works,* 317.

20. Edward Kamau Brathwaite, *Born to Slow Horses* (Middletown, CT: Wesleyan , 2005).

21. Edward Kamau Brathwaite, *Dreamstories* (London: Longman, 1994); *Elegguas* (Middletown, CT: Wesleyan University Press, 2010), 109.

22. Declan Kiberd, *Inventing Ireland* (London: Jonathan Cape, 1995), 276 (emphasis added).

23. Ibid.

24. Ibid.

25. Quoted ibid., 459.

26. Declan Kiberd, *The Irish Writer and the World* (Cambridge: Cambridge University Press, 2005), 139 (emphasis in original).

27. Ibid., 142.

28. Samuel Beckett, *Molloy,* in *Three Novels,* 10.

29. Walcott, *Prodigal,* 3–4.

30. Brathwaite, *Rights of Passage,* in *The Arrivants.*

31. Walcott, *Prodigal,* 4.

32. Ibid., 15, 19.

33. Ibid., 47.

34. Samuel Beckett, *Imagination Dead Imagine* (1965; reprint, London: Calder and Boyars, 1971).

35. See Anna McMullan for an in-depth analysis of disintegration of the body (dehiscence) in *Performing Embodiment in Samuel Beckett's Drama* (London: Routledge, 2010).

36. Samuel Beckett, *A Piece of Monologue*, in *Complete Dramatic Works*, 427.
37. Edward Kamau Brathwaite, *History of the Voice: The Development of Nation Language in Anglophone Caribbean Poetry* (London: New Beacon, 1984), 10.
38. Jean Antoine-Dunne, "Overtones of the Visual Imagination", in *Interlocking Basins of a Globe: Essays on Derek Walcott* (Leeds: Peepal Tree, 2013), 135–52.
39. See Jean Antoine-Dunne, "Beckett, Eisenstein and the Image: Making an Inside an Outside", in *The Montage Principle: Eisenstein in New Cultural and Critical Contexts*, ed. Jean Antoine-Dunne and Paula Quigley (Amsterdam: Rodopi, 2005), 191–211.
40. S.M. Eisenstein, *Sergei Eisenstein: Selected Works*, vol. 2, *Towards a Theory of Montage*, ed. Michael Glenny and Richard Taylor (London: British Film Institute, 1991).
41. Walcott, *Omeros*, 11–12.
42. Edward Kamau Brathwaite, *Jah Music* (Mona, Jamaica: Savacou Cooperative, 1986), 51.
43. Beckett, *The Unnamable*, 386.
44. Brathwaite, *Elegguas*, 109.
45. Ibid., 110.
46. "The Loupgarou", no. 343, box 5, typescript (ca. 1972). Walcott Special Collection, Alma Jordan Library, University of the West Indies, St Augustine, Trinidad and Tobago.
47. Walcott, *Omeros*, 197.
48. Walcott, "Muse of History".
49. Walcott, *Omeros*, 199.
50. Ibid., 198.
51. Ibid., 34.
52. Ibid., 33.
53. Ibid., 164.
54. Derek Walcott, "The Figure of Crusoe: On the Theme of Isolation in West Indian Writing" (1965), in *Critical Perspectives on Derek Walcott*, ed. Robert D. Hamner (Boulder: Lynne Rienner, 1997).
55. Walcott, *Omeros*, 4.
56. Ibid., 63.
57. Ibid., 75.
58. Ibid., 239.
59. Walcott, *Prodigal*, 75.
60. Derek Walcott, *O Starry Starry Night* (London: Faber and Faber, 2014). The world premiere took place at the University of Essex, April 2013; the St Lucian premiere was on 8 August 2013.
61. Walcott, *Omeros*, 294.
62. Ibid., 297.

63.   Quoted in Linda Ben-Zvi, ed., *Women in Beckett: Performance and Critical Perspectives* (Urbana: University of Illinois Press, 1990), 89.

64.   W.B. Yeats, *The Collected Works of W.B. Yeats*, vol. 2, *The Plays*, ed. David R. Clark and Rosalind E. Clark (New York: Simon and Schuster, 2001).

65.   See Katherine Worth, *Samuel Beckett's Theatre: Life Journeys* (Oxford: Clarendon Press, 2001).

66.   Samuel Beckett, "Ill Seen Ill Said", in *Nohow On* (London: John Calder, 1989), 62–63.

Chapter 17

Rewriting Heathcliff

Irishness, Creolization and Constructions of Race in Brontë and Condé

EMILY TAYLOR

THE ACT OF WRITING BACK TO THE empire is by now a widely recognized feature of postcolonial literature around the world. In the Caribbean, beginning in the middle of the twentieth century in the midst of independence movements and the call for full enfranchisement, writers such as Aimé Césaire and Jean Rhys returned to the European colonial canon to rewrite imperial representations of the colonized Other. Rhys's novel *Wide Sargasso Sea* is perhaps one of the most well-known examples; in it she attempts to write a new life for poor Bertha, the mad creole wife from *Jane Eyre*.[1] Rhys intertwines Bertha's story with a rewriting of Rochester's character that depicts the vulnerability and weakness of the English male colonizer. In another example, Césaire, George Lamming and Elizabeth Nunez all return to Shakespeare's last play to reclaim Caliban from his brutish status and represent him as colonized subject, with Prospero recast as the colonizer.[2] In this chapter I want to consider a somewhat more curious rewriting: Maryse Condé's 1995 novel *La migration des cœurs*. Translated into English by her husband, Richard Philcox, *Windward Heights* offers us a postcolonial re-vision of Emily Brontë's English novel *Wuthering Heights*.

What is curious about *Windward Heights* is that Condé does not have any clear business rewriting *Wuthering Heights*. What does nineteenth-century rural England have to do with the story of an emerging Guadeloupian nation-space? What does the romance of Cathy and Heathcliff have to do with the rise of the Socialist Party and the demand for equal rights from the French state? In other words, how is the tale of Heathcliff, an anonymous child who disrupts the agrarian aristocracy of the moors, useful to a writer such as Condé? Unlike Rhys's text, which seeks to offer a more direct corrective to a colonial narrative penned by a Brontë sister, Condé in her novel lifts the plot of *Wuthering Heights* in order to narrate the history of post-emancipation Guadeloupe. She marks this difference by dedicating her novel "To Emily Brontë / Who I hope will approve of this interpretation of her / masterpiece. / Honour and respect."[3] Condé suggests with this dedication that her narrative is an interpretation of a great work, not necessarily a rejection of it or a call to reconsider its place in the cultural register. We do not have the uneasy task of deciding, after Condé is done with it, whether we should go on loving *Wuthering Heights*. In fact Condé seems to amplify the novel's mythical status as one of the most iconic, and tragic, love stories.

But, as with many of Condé's works, we cannot completely accept this dedication at face value; there is something about the narrative that goes beyond inspiration or admiration. In fact Heathcliff's character is the foundation for *Windward Heights*. Rewritten as the creole character Razyé, he becomes the national hero of our tale and a reluctant agent of decolonization. What about the love story, and what about Heathcliff in particular, makes this postcolonial narrative possible for Condé? Here I draw on the hypothesis that Brontë's Heathcliff is Irish, and ask how Condé uses his Irishness to recreate him as a creolized character in *Windward Heights*.

Ireland, one of the initial sites of English colonization, echoes throughout the British literary canon; it becomes a testing ground for representing the "dark" Other, the subject of colonization. Strategies of racializing the Irish, and theories of physiognomy fleshed out in representations of the Irish in English fiction, helped to create and sustain a discourse that justified colonial oppression and imperial rule. The case of the Irish seems to be where the Manichean logic of modern conceptions of race is most strained. Because there were relatively few phenotypical distinctions between the English and Irish populations, a convoluted thesis emerged that the savagery of the Irish could be observed in their characters, and recast the Irish as apelike wild men and women beyond the pale, and perhaps beyond the reach, of English "civilization".[4] The strategies employed by the English to reduce the Irish to colonized subjects was replicated as the British Empire expanded its global reach.

Perhaps Condé was drawn to her revisionary project because the Irish case exposes so clearly the constructed nature of European notions of race. This exposure allows Condé to playfully critique this constructed nature in her representation of Guadeloupe as a creolized nation. Heathcliff is a mixed character, torn between the culture of the moors and the idea of his past. Never fully able to assimilate, his origins haunt him and ultimately lead to his tragic end. In this chapter I explore what Heathcliff's "Irishness" lends to Condé's representation of creole subjects, and how the colonial construction of Irishness is important for understanding postcolonial narratives in the Caribbean. By reading Heathcliff as he is recreated in Condé's novel of creolization, we may also be able to call him a prototypical creole. Thus Condé's novel gives us both a new story and a new way of considering an old tale.

Wuthering Heights is fraught with all sorts of anxieties, including a central concern, common in English fiction of the British Empire, with articulating an idea of Englishness that could withstand the taint of colonial contact with the non-English abroad.[5] One of the uncanny aspects of the novel is that the colonies wash up on the English shore in the form of a dark little boy with no name, no discernable language and no clear place of origin. Nelly, the housekeeper, describes her first glimpse of Heathcliff when Mr Earnshaw brings him home after finding him on the streets of Liverpool: "I had a peep at a dirty, ragged, black-haired child; big enough both to walk and talk ... yet, when it was set on its feet, it only stared round, and repeated over and over again some gibberish, that nobody could understand."[6] Heathcliff is dark and at least partially inhuman; Nelly seems to consider him more an animal or an object than a human child – not *he* but *it*, with nothing to recommend him to the society in which he finds himself. Nelly and the Earnshaws literally cannot place him, and so Earnshaw passes him off to Cathy as a plaything, significantly substituting this new toy for the whip she was promised from Liverpool. They name him Heathcliff after a son who died in childhood, but he never takes the Earnshaw surname.

Heathcliff's outsider status in relation to the family structure of the Heights and Thrushcross Grange imbues the narrative with tragic power and provides its central conflict. Mr Earnshaw's decision to adopt Heathcliff into the family, although never a fully realized gesture, means that Cathy's love for Heathcliff is both incestuous and a transgression of the established social order. Understanding Heathcliff's status as Other within the novel has been a central concern for literary scholars. Placing the novel in a historical context, both materially and ideologically, has led a number of them to suggest that Emily

Brontë may have been thinking of the Irish when she created Heathcliff. Terry Eagleton and Elise Michie both read Heathcliff as Irish-based, on the biographical evidence of Brontë's Irish heritage and because Branwell, Emily's brother, most likely witnessed the first wave of mass Irish immigration to England. Branwell visited Liverpool during the summer of 1845, just months before Emily began writing her novel. Both Eagleton and Michie cite Emily Brontë's biographer Winifred Gérin, who suggests that Branwell's time in Liverpool would have coincided with the "the first shiploads of Irish immigrants . . . landing at Liverpool and dying in the cellars of the warehouses on the quays. Their images, and especially those of the children, were unforgettably depicted in the *Illustrated London News* – starving scarecrows with a few rags on them and an animal growth of black hair almost obscuring their features."[7] Emily and Branwell may have been more attuned to the plight of the Irish because their father, Patrick, was an Irishman. He managed to transform himself from an illiterate weaver into a Cambridge-educated clergyman, changing his surname in the process from Prunty to Brontë.[8]

It is also possible Emily had her father in mind when she created Heathcliff. The character is likened many times over to Satan or the devil, and Michie argues that the literary figure associated with Heathcliff's social and economic advancement is Milton's Satan. Apparently Patrick Brontë was reciting *Paradise Lost* in a field when he was discovered by a minister and taken under his care to be educated and made a gentleman. According to Michie, Patrick's leap upward in class was like Satan's flight from Pandemonium to Eden.[9] But although he ascended a class hierarchy, his Irishness remained a marker of racial difference, albeit sublimated, as Michie explains: "Questions of race remain, however, denied or repressed in writings about Patrick Brontë and in his own stories about his life which emphasize instead the way he overcame class difference."[10] Michie explains how contemporary accounts of Patrick reference his supposedly violent Irish nature, scan his speech for traces of Irish language and report on his features, which, in the case of Mrs Gaskell, report no hint of his "Celtic descent".[11] Although suppressed, these representations of Emily Brontë's father reveal the imperial mechanisms used to scan physical features and actions as evidence of a colonized subject's "true" nature.

Heathcliff's own nature seems predetermined by his darkness, and Eagleton likens him to Shakespeare's prototypical Other: "It is clear that this little Caliban has a nature on which nurture will never stick; and that is simply an English way of saying that he is quite possibly Irish."[12] Eagleton does admit that it is possible to read Heathcliff otherwise; he also suggests that he could be a creole character, or "any kind of alien".[13] In *Heathcliff and the Great Hunger*, *Wuthering Heights* serves Eagleton as evidence of Irish history filtered through an English consciousness. His psychoanalytic and historical reading of the novel is less concerned with aligning Heathcliff with a precise chronology of historical events and more concerned with understanding this character's place in the way the English conceived of the Irish as "natural" subjects, which allowed them to construct the idea of English culture.[14] Eagleton reads Heathcliff as a split subject: although he tries to undermine the ruling order, he remains obsessed with it because of his desire for Catherine. He thus remains Irish and ultimately less successful than his real-world counterpart, Patrick Brontë, in assuming an English identity. His trajectory is mapped onto Irish history, as Eagleton describes: "Heathcliff starts out as an image of the famished Irish immigrant, becomes a landless labourer set to work in the Heights, and ends up as a symbol of the constitutional nationalism of the Irish parliamentary party."[15]

The colonial strategy of racializing the colonized by proposing an inherent nature, marked by physical characteristics and particular forms of language, circulated throughout the British Empire and at home in the colonial centre. So while Heathcliff may or may not be literally Irish, both Eagleton and Michie reveal how the strategies employed to racialize Patrick Brontë resurface in Emily's novel in relation to Heathcliff. Heathcliff may not be identifiably Irish in name, but he is Irish to the English characters inasmuch as his outsider status is reinforced by his "blackness" and disregard for social order. When Mr Earnshaw first introduces him to the family, he tells his wife, "you must e'en take it as a gift of God; though it's as dark almost as if it came from the devil".[16] Like Nelly, Mr Earnshaw calls him "it" and describes him in terms of his blackness. Despite this darkness that signifies Heathcliff's difference, Mr Earnshaw insists that the family take him in as if he were a gift from God or otherwise destined to appear in their midst. Hindley, Cathy's brother, accepts neither Heathcliff nor Mr Earnshaw's suggestion that he comes to them from heaven. He reiterates the comparison between Heathcliff and Satan when Heathcliff tricks him into giving up his horse: "Take my colt, gipsy, then! . . . And I pray that he may break your neck: take him, and be damned, you beggarly interloper! and wheedle my father out of all he has: only afterwards show him what you are, imp of Satan."[17] Hindley, as the biological son and rightful heir, can see Heathcliff's presence only as a curse. His acquisition of the horse is the first of many illicit property exchanges he will orchestrate in his takeover of both houses.

In Brontë's novel, Heathcliff may be ideologically constructed as Irish but he is an elastic figure, coming to typify and seemingly embody a wide spectrum of colonial Others over the course of the narrative. Susan Meyer and Maja-Lisa von Sneidern both read him in relation to African slaves, noting Liverpool's role as one of the major ports for the slave trade.[18] Heathcliff collectively embodies the colonial Others of the British Empire: he is alternatively termed a Lascar (an Indian seaman), a gypsy, "an American or Spanish castaway", Chinese, African and Irish.[19] Carine Mardorossian cites the portrayal of Heathcliff's racial difference as one of Brontë's most radical interventions in the discourse of her time: "she made racial mixing an incontrovertible and lived reality at home in England rather than just the result of questionable but distant sexual practices in the colonies".[20] Heathcliff's danger is predicated not just on his dark Otherness but also on his sexual threat, both to Catherine and to Isabella Linton, a threat associated mythically and stereotypically with black masculinity. He is the dark stranger whose reproductive capabilities could undo the white families' genealogical claims to their land and wealth.

Wuthering Heights is itself a mixed form: Northrop Frye reads it as both romance and novel.[21] Similarly, Heathcliff is a mixed character, both formally and racially, in that he draws on the conventions of both the Gothic hero and the Gothic villain; as readers we are compelled both to identify with his character and to reject him. We identify with him because he resists his subjugation, but we are shocked at his treatment of Isabella and the younger Catherine and his unwavering passion for Cathy and for revenge. Unlike other Gothic heroes who seem to be the demon lover but turn out to be the right man, Heathcliff is undoubtedly the demon lover, the dark lover, the brother with whom Cathy falls in love.

Brontë's text, however radical, is only able to describe the tragedy of English adherence to notions of a "pure" subject. Heathcliff never becomes an acceptable suitor. Rejected by Catherine, he claims Isabella through deception and keeps her through force. *Wuthering Heights* is not a celebration of racial mixing. It posits the possibility, and does seem to write against the ideologies of racial purity that underlie prohibitions against miscegenation, but it never fully represents an interracial sexual relationship. Heathcliff may or may not actually have sex with Catherine – certainly their affair is extramarital to the extent that they are clearly more than "brother and sister" – and they never have children. His tragic marriage to Isabella produces one son, Linton, whom Heathcliff intends to make an instrument of revenge in his plot to take over both Thrushcross Grange and

Wuthering Heights. Von Sneidern asserts that although Brontë uses Heathcliff to critique the "myth of Anglo-Saxon superiority", with Linton Heathcliff she "reimposes the taboo against miscegenation".[22] Linton, she argues, embodies all the characteristics associated in colonial discourse with the mulatto, as he "manifests most of the worst accidents and mistakes mixed blood could represent for mid-century England: disease, viciousness, treason, cowardice, duplicity, unmerited power, shiftlessness".[23] Again Heathcliff poses a duality: he is both a rebel fighter, a voice for justice, and a source of "biological" contamination. His love for Catherine is transcendent as long as it remains unconsummated. Brontë stops just short of the most horrifying prospect for the national dream of a racially homogeneous, "pure" England. She destabilizes the categories of the social order but does not go so far as to suggest new ones that could accommodate a stranger – and the hybrid issue of strangers – into the social sphere. The genealogical impulse of the novel demonstrates how power operates but does not create a new order from the disorder Heathcliff creates. Linton dies, Heathcliff's line ends and the original white English families reunite in Cathy and Hareton's romance.

Wuthering Heights stages the drama of penetration of the foreign in all its masculine connotations. Heathcliff's presence destabilizes the national order, leaving us with a text that demonstrates how gender and sexuality in part determine race and national identity, and vice versa. Heathcliff is a threat because he can claim the women, inherit property and begin a new family line. *Wuthering Heights* persists in the literary imagination because it leaves the tensions between the national and the foreign unresolved. Heathcliff remains a figure both inside and outside, both hero and villain, a Gothic composite that challenges national identity and the boundaries of Englishness in the context of British colonial enterprises.

This crisis of national identity is perhaps the element of *Wuthering Heights* that is most useful for Maryse Condé's revisionary project. Heathcliff's Irishness assists in Condé's representation of an emerging Guadeloupian national identity because it models a stranger who is never fully at home. One of the most famous women in the field of francophone Caribbean writing, Condé grapples not only with the legacies of French colonial representations of *les Antilles* but also with the legacies of male nationalist rhetoric that often entirely neglects gender and alternative sexualities. Aimé Césaire and Frantz Fanon are her theoretical forebears, key figures in establishing discourses (such as Négritude) that were crucial in decolonization movements both within the Caribbean and throughout the colonized world. Condé's contemporaries, including Édouard Glissant and the writers known as the Créolistes (Jean Bernabé, Patrick Chamoiseau and Raphaël Confiant), continue to insist on uniquely Caribbean identities, despite the francophone Caribbean's status as pseudo-independent overseas departments of France. Most important to all these writers is the articulation of a particular type of cultural nationalism, one that continues to construct the Caribbean subject as fully equal but not identical to the French one.

Condé's main critique of Césaire, Fanon and the Créolistes is that they continue to posit that subject as male. While Césaire and Fanon have been criticized for being too essentialist in their use of Africa as the only sanctioned touchstone for Caribbean identities, the Créolistes value mixed subjects but continue to formulate them as male, claiming that all are Césaire's sons.[24] A. James Arnold argues that the *"créolité* movement has inherited from its antecedents *antillanité* and *negritude*, a sharply gendered identity. Like them, it is not only masculine but masculinist . . . it pushes literature written by women into the background . . . *créolité* is the latest avatar of the masculinist culture of the French West Indies."[25] Despite this resolutely masculinist stance, Condé does not reject their ideology wholesale. Formulating gendered notions of *créolité* is in fact central to her project. Going outside the paradigm of her male counterparts, Condé finds a prototypical representation of the creolized subject in Heathcliff. Brontë, very much aware that the "impure" male subject poses the most risk to family structures and inheritance of property, sets up a formula that Condé finds useful in her own revision of male nationalist ideas of francophone Caribbean subjectivity.

One of the most important contributions of *Windward Heights* is its representation of what creolization means for both men and women as gendered subjects. In her essay "Chercher nos vérités", Condé explains that mixing has always been met with suspicion and fear by societies that need to delineate strangers from citizens: "*Métissage* has always terrorized societies that wanted to protect the womb of their women against the sperm of strangers and therefore against change."[26] Her use of a specifically biological metaphor plays out in the pages of the novel. Taking the plot of *Wuthering Heights* and transferring it to Guadeloupe at the turn of the twentieth century, Condé embodies racial mixing in Cathy Gagneur, the beautiful daughter of the mixed-race creole Hubert Gagneur, who inherits a small property that places the family at the periphery of the white plantation elite. Razyé, the Heathcliff character, is also racially mixed, and his love for Cathy is fully consummated. Brontë sidesteps the issue of racial mixing and its resulting genealogy by *disembodying* the romance, relegating realization of the union between Catherine and Heathcliff to the spiritual realm. Ghosts, after all, do not produce children or make claims to material wealth. One of the important postcolonial interventions Condé makes in rewriting the novel is to insist on corporeality and materiality, refusing the lovers a transcendent union and emphasizing instead the reality of their bodies and the weight of their signification in a racialized plantation economy. She takes Brontë's innovations in Gothic characterization a step further, reading the "light" and "dark" elements of the composite Gothic hero and heroine portrayed in *Wuthering Heights* as markers of race. In doing so she offers a critique of both essentialized creole womanhood as outlined by the Créolistes and the ideologies of racial purity espoused by colonial discourse.

Condé makes important changes to Heathcliff's character in Razyé, but elements of his "Irishness" remain constant in the novel. His origins are unknown, he is the darkest character in the novel, he has a savage nature and he is likened many times over to Satan and devils. Careful not to consolidate colonial ideology, Condé uses these elements of Heathcliff's otherness in her construction of Razyé's character to reveal how white power operates in plantation societies, to reclaim blackness as beautiful and powerful, and to disrupt notions of human nature as determined by racist interpretations of physiognomy. Thus, although Razyé is not Irish, these elements of Heathcliff's "Irishness" provide Condé with the means to critique French colonialism in the Caribbean.

The child Razyé appears during a hurricane on the plains of Guadeloupe, where Hubert Gagneur finds him and decides to take him in. Hubert, an exemplary figure of creole identity who eschews French culture and speaks only Creole, is delighted by Razyé, much to the dismay of his own son, Justin. Instead of being named for a lost child, Razyé is named after the land where he was found: *razyé* is a Creole word referring to the harsh landscape where he was discovered. Like Heathcliff, he is described by Nelly (Raboteur this time, not Dean) in terms of his darkness and grime. As Nelly relates to the white woman to whom she speaks on a ferry, "I was looking at what he was clutching between his knees: a dirty, repulsive, seven- or eight-year-old boy, completely naked, with a well-developed sex, believe me; a little black boy or Indian half-caste. His skin was black, and his tangled curly hair reached down his back."[27] As with Heathcliff, no one knows where Razyé comes from, and also like Heathcliff, his racial identity remains indeterminate. In Nelly's first account of him, he could be of African origin or Indian or both. The novel refuses to give us an answer, and as an adult he is again described in terms that could link him to anywhere on three continents: "He was dressed all in black in the French fashion, from his tightly-laced leather boots to his felt hat sewn with a large hem stitch. His skin too was black, that shiny black they call Ashanti, and his hair hung in curls like those of an Indian half-caste, the Bata-Zindien."[28] Nelly does not call his speech "gibberish" and we assume that he already speaks Creole when he is adopted into the family. His masculinity and sexual prowess are hyperbolized throughout the novel; he fathers not only Cathy II with Cathy (after she marries a white plantation owner) but also many other children with his white wife, Irmine.

Razyé's darkness is emphasized throughout the novel and increases with his power. Most of the characters are in awe of his blackness, and Aymeric, Cathy's husband, is afraid of him. When Aymeric sees Razyé for the first time, he finds him "an athletic, well-formed man of towering height and upright carriage. His tight curly hair fell over his forehead; his eyes were full of black fire, his cheeks shaven and his skin so black that the cloth of his coat seemed light by comparison."[29] Aymeric claims he has no animosity towards Razyé on the basis of his racial identity, telling Cathy and Irmine: "I'm not talking about his colour. The Lord knows that in my eyes a negro is no different from a white or a mulatto. But he's an individual without a name, without an education and without any virtue whatsoever. We don't know what he does or how he earns his living."[30] Aymeric's objection to Razyé resembles Cathy's rationale for rejecting Heathcliff. They are both racialized, but race becomes secondary to the trappings of class. Yet those class markers are denied to Razyé precisely because of his racial identity, so that both categories become mutually constitutive, and although Aymeric wants to pretend that race does not exist, it is in fact what structures Guadeloupian plantation society. Razyé's darkness, like Heathcliff's, gives him power, and it is also a marker of his dignity and his appeal to women and men alike. He wears his darkness proudly; his features distinguish him rather than make him an outcast when he returns to Guadeloupe as an adult to seek his revenge. In fact, blackness is associated throughout the novel with life, beauty and reason, while the white characters – or those who choose to associate with the white creole *béké* class – are most likely to become impoverished or to die.

Most of the white *békés*, unlike Aymeric, conform closely to the colonial script. Condé subtly satirizes white terror of racial mixing in the colonies. When Cathy marries Aymeric, the whites liken the event to the apocalypse, asking themselves, "Was this the sign of the end of the world? Were families, one after the other, going to marry into mulatto families . . . ? Or worse still into black families? And who knows, one day into Indian families? Was Guadeloupe going to become one vast pig-swill where you couldn't tell one colour or origin from the next?"[31] As the characters think of this devastating possibility for the white power structure of the plantation society, they each resolve that they would rather be dead than face a world without the privilege that whiteness affords them. Razyé, Cathy and Justin all embody this threat, as mixed-race subjects marrying into the *béké* class. These marriages mark the beginning of the end for the Linsseuil family; they are both the reason for and the means of Razyé's revenge, when Cathy marries Aymeric and Razyé then marries Aymeric's sister Irmine.

Like Heathcliff, Razyé has a savage and violent temperament, but his nature is not so much an expression of his racial identity as a product of his social circumstances. It is difficult to entirely forgive his abuse and neglect of women and children, but his faults seem to come almost entirely from his need to seek revenge on Guadeloupian society for making it impossible for Cathy to choose him instead of Aymeric. When Cathy agonizes about whether she can be with Razyé or not, she tells Nelly, "If Justin hadn't done what he did to Razyé, I wouldn't even be thinking of this marriage. But the way Razyé is now, I could never marry him. It would be too degrading! It would be as if only Cathy the reprobate existed, stepping straight off the slave-ship. Living with him would be like starting over as savages from Africa. Just the same!"[32] As in Brontë's novel, Razyé overhears the exchange and flees the house, returning three years later with revenge in his heart. He joins the Socialists in their fight for equality but remains throughout the narrative motivated by a broken heart rather than overt political beliefs.

Razyé's reputation and countenance inspire many characters to compare him to Satan or to devils. To the white plantation owners he is Satan come to curse them. The newspapers "dragged Razyé in the mud, calling him the henchman of Jean-Hilaire Endomius and Monsieur Légitimus's Socialists, and likening him quite simply to the Devil himself".[33] Characters outside the white elite and on the periphery of French Catholicism liken him to a devil or spirit in the *vodoun* tradition by comparing him to the mythical three-legged horse of *la bête à Man-Ibè* or the wild *soubarou* man of the forest. Seeing him at night, villagers take him for a spirit "in search of wicked deeds and [cross] themselves".[34] Aside from the white *békés* who misread him as Satan, the majority of supernatural references linked to Razyé are drawn from a pan-Caribbean belief system that spans the region and represents a transnational creolization. In this way, Condé takes Heathcliff's "wicked" nature and transforms it into power and an articulation of his regional commonality. His blackness thus becomes a signifier of power and dignity, although it is ultimately the cause of his loveless life and tragic end.

We cannot go so far as to claim that Razyé is Irish, any more than we can determine whether Heathcliff is or is not definitively Irish. But the formulation of racialized and colonized identities has a shared history in the British Empire, and in reading these two novels together we can understand not only how the formula of race operates (it is entirely culturally constructed) but also how both Condé and to some extent Brontë critique its construction. Condé's choice to borrow the story from an English novel was not a casual one. Brontë's early attention to how racial mixing is a particularly gendered terror among colonizers establishes a framework that Condé can utilize to write back to colonial narratives of Caribbean subjects while simultaneously avoiding essentializing the subject as ideally masculine. If Heathcliff can be read as Irish, he can possibly also be read as one of the first instances of a creole character. Heathcliff's threat to the genealogical structure of the Heights and Thrushcross Grange is predicated on his mixed nature, his unclear origins and his dark countenance. It is this prototype that Condé takes up to tell the story of Guadeloupe's emergence as a postcolonial space that encompasses multiple subjects on equal terrain.

Notes

1.   I use the term *creole* here to describe Bertha's identity as a white person born in the colonies. The word has a long history of describing colonial subjects and has carried with it the notion of being mixed. While initially it described only whites born in the colonies, outside the colonial centre it quickly came to describe many things, including slaves born in the colonies, food, plants, animals, languages and culture. Because of this use, the adjective *white* is often added to *creole* when attempting to describe racial identity. While both Charlotte Brontë and Jean Rhys use the label *creole* to distinguish Bertha and Antoinette from the majority black Jamaican population, in both cases it also implies a mixed racial identity. This conception of *creole* as a way to describe mixed-race identities is found throughout colonial and postcolonial discourse and is a key term to which I will return throughout the chapter.

2.   See Césaire's 1969 play *Une Tempête* [*A Tempest*], Lamming's 1960 collection of essays *The Pleasures of Exile*, and Nunez's 2006 novel *Prospero's Daughter*.

3. Maryse Condé, *Windward Heights*, trans. Richard Philcox (London: Faber and Faber, 1998).

4. See, for example, L.P. Curtis, *Apes and Angels: The Irishman in Victorian Caricature* (Washington, DC: Smithsonian Institution, 1997).

5. See Nancy Armstrong, "Imperialist Nostalgia and *Wuthering Heights*", in *Wuthering Heights: A Case Study in Contemporary Criticism*, ed. Linda Peterson (Boston: St Martin's Press, 1991), 428–49.

6. Emily Brontë, *Wuthering Heights*, ed. Linda Peterson (Boston: St Martin's Press, 1992), 51.

7. Elise Michie, *Outside the Pale: Cultural Exclusion, Gender Difference, and the Victorian Woman Writer* (Ithaca, NY: Cornell University Press, 1993), 54.

8. Ibid., 58.

9. Ibid.

10. Ibid.

11. Elizabeth Gaskell, *The Life of Charlotte Brontë* (1857; reprint, London: Penguin, 1997), 75.

12. Terry Eagleton, *Heathcliff and the Great Hunger: Studies in Irish Culture* (London: Verso, 1996), 3.

13. Ibid.

14. Ibid., 3–9.

15. Ibid., 19.

16. Brontë, *Wuthering Heights*, 51.

17. Ibid., 54.

18. Susan Meyer, *Imperialism at Home: Race and Victorian Women's Fiction* (Ithaca, NY: Cornell University Press, 1996); Maja-Lisa von Sneidern, "*Wuthering Heights* and the Liverpool Slave Trade", *ELH: English Literary History* 62, no. 1 (1995): 171–96.

19. Brontë, *Wuthering Heights*, 62.

20. Carine M. Mardorossian, *Reclaiming Difference: Caribbean Women Rewrite Postcolonialism* (Charlottesville: University of Virginia Press, 2005), 94.

21. Northrop Frye, *The Secular Scripture: A Study of the Structure of Romance* (Cambridge, MA: Harvard University Press, 1976), 304.

22. Von Sneidern, "*Wuthering Heights*", 186.

23. Ibid., 184.

24. Jean Bernabé, Patrick Chamoiseau and Raphaël Confiant, *Éloge de la créolité* (Paris: Gallimard, 1993), 80.

25. A. James Arnold, "The Gendering of Créolité: The Erotics of Colonialism", in *Penser la créolité*, ed. Maryse Condé and Madeleine Cottenet-Hage (Paris: Karthala, 1995), 120.

26. The original French reads: "Le métissage a toujours été la terreur des sociétés constituées qui veulent protéger le ventre de leurs femmes contre le sperme des males

étrangers et par conséquent contre le changement"; Maryse Condé, "Chercher nos vérités", in *Penser la créolité*, 309.

27.   Condé, *Windward Heights*, 21.

28.   Ibid., 7.

29.   Ibid., 55.

30.   Ibid., 65.

31.   Ibid., 49.

32.   Ibid., 41.

33.   Ibid., 134.

34.   Ibid., 213.

Appendix

Timeline of Events Related to the Irish Experience in the Caribbean in the Seventeenth and Early Eighteenth Centuries*

*Records for the early period are sparse and not always reliable.

1611–12	An Irish settlement is established in the Amazon Basin.
1623–32	St Christopher, Barbados and Montserrat, among other Leeward Islands, are settled by the English.
1632	Anthony Brisket of Wexford becomes governor of Montserrat.
1641	Rebellion erupts in Ireland as Catholics attempt to reclaim control of political administration and property. The rebellion causes instability in the West Indies and several Irish seek asylum within Spanish Caribbean territories.
1643	The "sugar revolution" commences in the anglophone Caribbean.
1644	A short-lived act prohibiting arrival of the Irish in Barbados is passed.
1649	Roger Osborne, an Anglo-Irishman, is named governor of Montserrat.
1649–60	The Cromwellian policy of transplantation sends Irish prisoners of war, vagrants and the dispossessed to the New World.
1650	Irish Jesuit John Stritch arrives in St Christopher and later Montserrat, attempting to inconspicuously serve the Catholics of the islands.
1650s	The Roches, Lynches and Kirwans, Irish families from Galway, establish themselves as planters in French Martinique.

1655	Minutes of the Barbadian Council indicate that "several Irish servants and negroes [are] out in rebellion".
	Governor Searles of Barbados issues a proclamation to deter impoverished Irish from wandering the countryside, begging for assistance and stirring up trouble.
	The English invade Jamaica as part of Cromwell's "Western Design".
1656	In Barbados, Irishman Cornelius Bryan receives twenty-one lashes for saying "that if there was as much English Blood in the Tray as there was meat he would eat", while serving his master a plate of meat.
1660	Military officials and parish churchwardens in Barbados are ordered to account for the whereabouts of every Irish person on the island and to report their names and locations, as well as make special mention of those considered dangerous; they are further ordered that no Irish may be commander or part-owner of any Barbadian ship.
1665	French–English feuds begin on St Christopher, in which the Irish living within the English zones side with the French.
1666	The French invade Montserrat and many Irish on Montserrat join their cause.
1668	John and Henry Blake leave Galway for Barbados and Montserrat, respectively, to begin careers as overseas plantation owners and Atlantic World merchants, the first of many Galway families to become involved in international trade.
	Governor Willoughby of Barbados claims that the island is in ill condition in regard to its "multitudes of negroes and Irish".
	William Stapleton, an Anglo-Irishman, is named governor of Montserrat. In 1671 he is named governor of the Leeward Islands.
1675	Planters and officials in Barbados request free trade with Scotland to facilitate trade in Scottish indentured servants, as they find the Irish to be "of small value".
1686	In his will, Cornelius Bryan, the Irishman who suffered twenty-one lashes in Barbados, leaves his family his "mansion", twenty-two acres of land and eleven enslaved Africans.
1689	Small groups of Irish Catholics rise up in rebellion in St Christopher and Montserrat.
1692	A slave rebellion conspiracy in Barbados involves several Irishmen.

1713	The signing of the Treaty of Utrecht leaves the entirety of St Kitts (St Christopher) in the hands of the English. Irish merchants and planters begin returning due to diminished fears of Irish alliance with the French.
1730s	The Montserrat Assembly prohibits Sunday markets and marriage between whites and blacks, in an attempt to minimize interaction between slaves and the Irish and Irish creole working and middle classes.
1747	The Danish crown assumes control of Saint-Croix, which, because of Danish neutrality, remains open to all investors. A group of Irish merchant families invests heavily in land, slaves and sugar production.
1750	Samuel Martin, an Antiguan of Ulster Royalist roots, publishes his widely read *Essay on Plantership*, which describes the ins and outs of operating a successful sugar plantation.
1756–63	The Seven Years' War causes tumult in the Caribbean, with several islands changing imperial hands.
1759	Wealthy Irish planter Nicholas Tuite petitions for a Catholic mission on St Croix. Eight Irish priests arrive; many write letters and accounts of their time in the West Indies and some invest in plantations.
1762	According to Olaudah Equiano, he is purchased by Captain James Doran, an Irishman with family connections to Montserratian planters, and later sold to a Quaker planter in Montserrat in 1764; however, the veracity of Equiano's narrative has been questioned. Equiano's autobiography, *The Interesting Narrative of the Life of Olaudah Equiano; Or Gustavus Vassa, the African,* published in 1789, would become a famous first-hand account of the horrors of slavery and the slave trade.
1768	A rebellion plot is uncovered in Montserrat in which creole slaves (born in Montserrat rather than Africa) planned to rebel after planters became drunk during St. Patrick's Day celebrations.
1779	The Irish Brigade, under the command of General Arthur Dillon and his brother Edward, arrives in Grenada with d'Estaing as part of the French army and a Catholic alliance. They successfully take back control from the British.

1782–84	Hugh Mulligan, an Anglo-Irishman, publishes a series of early anti-slavery poems.
1791–1804	The Haitian Revolution results in establishment of the first free black state in the New World, dramatically affecting Atlantic World politics, economy, history and society.
1792	Dubliner Mary Birkett pens *The African Slave Trade, Addressed to Members of Her Own Sex*, a radical critique of slavery and the slave trade.
1798	The United Irishmen rebel against British rule in Ireland.
1807	The slave trade is abolished by the English.
1828	Daniel O'Connell is elected a member of Parliament; he remains an outspoken member of the anti-slavery movement.
1834	The Emancipation Act comes into effect on August 1. An apprenticeship period is to last until 1838, when full freedom of all enslaved people will become law in the English colonies.
1834–36	The Marquess of Sligo serves as governor of Jamaica. R.R. Madden and Dowell O'Reilly, both Irish Catholics, hold high offices under Sligo's command.
1835	More than three hundred Irish labourers are recruited in New York to construct a railroad in Cuba.
1838–39	James Kelly and Benjamin McMahon publish *Jamaica in 1831* and *Jamaica Plantership*, respectively, chronicling their experiences on the island as plantation employees, bookkeepers, overseers and middle managers.
1841	The *Robert Kerr*, one of the last ships to carry Irish people to Jamaica, leaves Limerick. Accounts vary as to whether the passengers were a few women or a large contingent of male workers.

Resources for Further Study

A Note on Archives and Collections

Few archives or available databases hold specific collections that deal with Caribbean Irish connections. Those that are available are listed below. However, aside from these few collections, significant scholarly research (including material presented in this volume) has been conducted without the benefit of such resources. Rather, much research has been undertaken through meticulous examinations of national and other public or private archival materials. Many national archives throughout the Caribbean hold extensive wills and deeds that, with careful attention, can disclose significant information about Irish individuals. Such documents can disclose information about the holdings of Irish persons at the time of their death, the buying or selling of property by individuals, or lists of the Irish as servants passed from seller to buyer. Additionally, as research throughout this volume indicates, national archives in Europe and North America hold a slew of primary materials that contain information about the Irish in and around the Caribbean. While such holdings are beyond the scope of this outline, references to specific records and sources should be consulted for those interested in pursuing such research.

The library of the Barbados Museum and Historical Society holds a small collection of materials specifically dedicated to the Irish in the Caribbean that is available upon request from staff members. The collection contains miscellaneous newspaper articles chronicling the Caribbean Irish connection, as well as various historical sources that discuss the connection in more detail. A similar small collection at the Montserrat Public Library contains a bibliography of sources that address Irish history on the island.

Resource Guides

Beyond specific collections that contain information about Caribbean Irish connections, resource guides, when available, are beneficial, as they provide specific details about where sources can be found and what information they contain. The existing guides are largely limited to the English West Indies and are listed here.

Comitas, Lambros. *The Complete Caribbeana, 1900–1975*. New York: KTO Press, 1977.

Covington, Paula Hattox. *Latin America and the Caribbean: A Critical Guide to Research Sources*. Westport, CT: Greenwood, 1992.

English, T. Savage. *Records of Montserrat* (1930). Montserrat Public Library.

Gropp, Arthur E. *Guide to Libraries and Archives in Central America and the West Indies, Panama, Bermuda, and British Guiana: Supplemented with Information on Private Libraries, Bookbinding, Bookselling and Printing*. Publication no. 10. New Orleans: Middle American Research Institute, Tulane University, 1941.

Handler, Jerome S. *A Guide to Source Materials for the Study of Barbados History, 1627–1834*. Carbondale: Southern Illinois University Press, 1971.

———. *Supplement to a Guide to Source Materials for the Study of Barbados History, 1627–1834*. Providence, RI: John Carter Brown Library and Barbados Museum and Historical Society, 1991.

Ingram, Kenneth E. *Manuscript Sources for the History of the West Indies*. Kingston: University of the West Indies Press, 2000.

———. *Sources of Jamaican History, 1655–1838: A Bibliographical Survey with Particular Reference to Manuscript Sources*. Vol. 1. Inter Documentation, 1976.

———. *Sources of Jamaican History, 1655–1838*. 2:708–16. Inter Documentation, 1976.

Irish Migration Studies in Latin America. This journal contains some articles which include a Caribbean focus.

McCusker, John J. "New Guides to Primary Sources on the History of Early British America". *William and Mary Quarterly* 41, no. 2 (1984): 277–95.

Walne, Peter. *A Guide to Manuscript Sources for the History of Latin America and the Caribbean in the British Isles*. Oxford: Oxford University Press and Institute of Latin American Studies, University of London, 1973.

Manuscript Collections

Stapleton Manuscripts

Manuscripts relating to the Stapleton family are of specific interest in pursuing Caribbean Irish connections. William Stapleton, an Anglo-Irishman, was governor of the Leeward Islands from 1671 to 1685. He and his descendants were prominent socialites, politicians and wealthy plantation owners. The Stapleton manuscripts are housed in the Ryland Libraries at the University of Manchester. They include commissions and appointments to offices, public accounts, militia lists, correspondence, grants and leases of land, plantation accounts and inventories, lists of slaves and sugar accounts.

A smaller collection of Stapleton manuscripts relating to their time in the West Indies is housed in the library at Bangor University, Wales, under the title Stapleton-Cotton.

Sligo Manuscripts

Howe Peter Browne, Lord Sligo, an Anglo-Irishman, was governor of Jamaica during the apprenticeship period. Copybooks of his correspondence are housed in the National Library of Jamaica, at the Institute of Jamaica in Kingston, and in the archives at Westport House, County Mayo, Ireland.

Irish Resources

The National Library of Ireland houses several manuscripts under the title "Irish Abroad, West Indies". The Public Record Office of Northern Ireland, in Belfast, also houses several items of interest to research on the Irish in the Caribbean.

Prendergast, John Patrick. *The Cromwellian Settlement of Ireland*. London: Trafalgar Square Publishing, 1865 (reprinted 1996).

Substantial archival material housed in the National Archives of Ireland, in Dublin, much of which contained significant resources about the Irish in the Caribbean, was lost in the fire of 1922 during the civil war. While the loss of material is lamentable, John Prendergast was able to use much of the material for his 1865 *Cromwellian Settlement*. This volume contains pertinent information, supported by primary materials that are no longer available, about the Cromwellian policy of transplantation that sent thousands of Irish to the New World.

Gwynn, Aubrey. "Documents Relating to the Irish in the West Indies". *Analecta Hibernica* 4 (1932): 139–286.

Irish Jesuit historian Father Aubrey Gwynn devoted many years to study of the Irish in the West Indies. His extensive article is one of the most comprehensive collections of primary sources that deal with Caribbean Irish connections. Additionally, several pages are devoted to description of primary sources and their state of availability. While many of these sources have been digitized or have since been moved or are no longer available, it provides a thorough introduction to the primary resources that cover the subject. The Jesuit Archives in Dublin also holds sixteen boxes under the title "Aubrey Gwynn, S.J.". These boxes contain, among other materials, the notes that informed his 1932 article. For more information on Gwynn and his scholarship, see Fergus O'Donoghue, "Aubrey Gwynn: The Jesuit", *Studies: An Irish Quarterly Review* 81, no. 324 (1992): 393–98.

Messanger, John C. "Montserrat, Article on the Irish in". May 1966. 29 pp.

The James Hardiman Library, National University of Ireland, Galway, holds a typescript copy of this article on the Irish in Montserrat from 1632 to 1900, by John C. Messanger, associate professor at the Folklore Institute of Indiana University and visiting professor at University College, Galway in 1959–60.

Index

womanhood, 298; creolization of gendered subjects, 297–98; Heathcliff as agent of decolonization, 291; postcolonial re-vision of *Wuthering Heights*, 290–91

Winston, Brian, Griersonian documentary, 178

women, colonial socioeconomic restrictions on, 266, 267

The Words upon the Window-Pane (Yeats), 285

The Wretched of the Earth (Fanon), 183

Writing the Irish West (Wall), 243–44

Wuthering Heights (Brontë): comparison to *Windward Heights*, 290–91; Heathcliff as famine migrant, 11; Heathcliff as Gothic hero/villain, 295, 296; Otherness of Heathcliff, 292–94

Yeats, Elizabeth, Dun Emer Press, 168

Yeats, Jack: *A Broad Sheet*, 168; collaboration with Colman Smith, 157; *Green Sheaf* (magazine), 163, 168–69

Yeats, John Butler, on Colman Smith, 166–67

Yeats, Lilly, Dun Emer Press, 168

Yeats, William Butler, 149; as "agricultural-poetic tourist", 243; collaboration with Colman Smith, 9, 157, 166, 167–68; cultural cosmology, 190; epiphany of "The Lake Isle of Innisfree", 190–91, 199n9; Irish folklore and mythology, 161, 191, 197, 199n16; Irish place names, 192, 200n20; pentameter, 192, 200n24

Yeats, William Butler: works: *Autobiographies*, 190–91; *The Countess Cathleen*, 166; "Down by the Salley Gardens", 197, 202n57; *Fairy and Folk Tales of the Irish Peasantry*, 191; *Grania*, 168; *The Land of Heart's Desire*, 161, 166; *Purgatory*, 285; "The Lake Isle of Innisfree", 10, 189–91; "The Tower", 78; *A Vision*, 190; *The Wanderings of Oisin and Other Poems*, 197; *When There Is Nothing*, 168; *The Words upon the Window-Pane*, 285

Zacek, Natalie, 41, 42, 45–46n26

Contributors

Editors

ALISON DONNELL is Professor of Modern Literatures in English, University of Reading, United Kingdom. Her publications include *Twentieth Century Caribbean Literature: Critical Moments in Anglophone Literary History* and a number of edite works, including *Una Marson's Selected Poems; The Routledge Companion to Anglophone Caribbean Literature* (co-edited with Michael A. Bucknor); and *The Routledge Reader in Caribbean Literature* (co-edited with Sarah Lawson Welsh).

MARIA McGARRITY is Associate Professor of English, Long Island University, Brooklyn, New York. Her publications include *Allusions in Omeros: Notes and a Guide to Derek Walcott's Masterpiece; Washed by the Gulf Stream: The Historic and Geographic Relation of Irish and Caribbean Literature;* and *Irish Modernism and the Global Primitive* (co-edited with Claire A. Culleton).

EVELYN O'CALLAGHAN is Professor of West Indian Literature, Department of Language, Linguistics and Literature, University of the West Indies, Cave Hill, Barbados. Her publications include *Woman Version: Theoretical Approaches to West Indian Fiction by Women* and *Women Writing the West Indies, 1804–1939: A Hot Place, Belonging to Us.* She edited the nineteenth-century Caribbean novel *With Silent Tread,* by Frieda Cassin and the reissue of Elma Napier's early Dominican novel *A Flying Fish Whispered.*

Other Contributors

JEAN ANTOINE-DUNNE is Senior Lecturer in Literatures in English, Department of Literary, Cultural and Communication Studies, University of the West Indies, St Augustine, Trinidad and Tobago. Her publications include *Interlocking Basins of a Globe: Essays on Derek Walcott* and *The Montage Principle: Eisenstein in New Cultural and Critical Contexts* (co-edited with Paula Quigley).

K. BRISLEY BRENNAN is a PhD student at the Centre for Comparative Literature, University of Toronto.

JEROME S. HANDLER is Senior Scholar, Virginia Foundation for the Humanities, Charlottesville, Virginia. His publications include *The Unappropriated People: Freedmen in the Slave Society of Barbados*; *Plantation Slavery in Barbados: An Archaeological and Historical Investigation* (with F.W. Lange); and *Enacting Power: The Criminalization of Obeah in the Anglophone Caribbean, 1760–2011* (with K. Bilby).

LEE M. JENKINS is Senior Lecturer in English at University College Cork, Ireland. Her publications include *The Language of Caribbean Poetry*; *The Cambridge Companion to Modernist Poetry* (co-edited with Alex Davis); and *A History of Modernist Poetry* (co-edited with Alex Davis).

LAURA McATACKNEY is an archaeologist and Irish Research Council postdoctoral research fellow, School of Social Justice, University College Dublin. Her publications include *An Archaeology of the Troubles: The Dark Heritage of Long Kesh/Maze*; *Modern Materials: The Proceedings of CHAT Oxford, 2009* (co-edited with Brent Fortenberry); *Envisioning Landscape: Perspective and Politics in Archaeology and Heritage* (co-edited with Dan Hicks and Graham Fairclough); and *Contemporary and Historical Archaeology in Theory: Papers from the 2003 and 2004 CHAT Conferences* (co-edited with Matthew Palus and Angela Piccini).

RICHARD McGUIRE is a PhD student in the Department of Literature, Film and Theatre Studies, University of Essex, Colchester, United Kingdom.

HARVEY O'BRIEN is Lecturer in Film Studies at the School of English, Drama, and Film, University College Dublin. His publications include *Action Movies: The Cinema of Striking Back*; *The Real Ireland: The Evolution of Ireland in*

Documentary Film; and *Keeping It Real: Irish Film and Television* (co-edited with Ruth Barton).

ELIZABETH F. O'CONNOR is Assistant Professor of Twentieth Century British and Post-colonial Literature, Washington College, Chestertown, Maryland.

MATTHEW C. REILLY is a postdoctoral fellow, Joukowsky Institute for Archaeology and the Ancient World at Brown University, Providence, Rhode Island.

NINI RODGERS is Honorary Senior Research Fellow, School of History and Anthropology, Queens University, Belfast. Her publications include *Ireland, Slavery and Anti-Slavery, 1612–1865* and *Equiano and Anti-slavery in Eighteenth-Century Belfast*.

KRYSTA RYZEWSKI is Assistant Professor of Anthropology, Wayne State University, Detroit, Michigan.

ELAINE SAVORY is Associate Professor of Literature, New School, New York. Her publications include *Jean Rhys*; *The Cambridge Introduction to Jean Rhys*; and *Out of the Kumbla: Caribbean Women and Literature* (co-edited with Carole Boyce Davies).

LEIF SCHENSTEAD-HARRIS is a doctoral candidate in the Department of English at the University of Western Ontario, London, Ontario.

EMILY TAYLOR is Assistant Professor of World Literature, Department of English, Presbyterian College, Clinton, South Carolina.

KARINA WILLIAMSON is Honorary Fellow at the Institute for Advanced Studies in the Humanities, Edinburgh University. She is editor of the anonymous nineteenth-century novel *Marly; or, A Planter's Life in Jamaica* and *Contrary Voices: Representations of West Indian Slavery, 1657–1834*.

KEVIN WHELAN is Director, Keough–Notre Dame Centre, Dublin. His publications include *The Tree of Liberty: Radicalism, Catholicism and the Construction of Irish Identity, 1760–1830* and *Fellowship of Freedom: The United Irishmen and the 1798 Rebellion*.

www.ingramcontent.com/pod-product-compliance
Lightning Source LLC
Chambersburg PA
CBHW021808270326
41932CB00007B/98